Site
Investigation
Practice

Site Investigation Practice

Michael D. Joyce
Consulting Geotechnical Engineer

London   New York
E. & F. N. SPON

First published 1982 by
E. & F. N. Spon Ltd
11 New Fetter Lane, London EC4P 4EE
Published in the USA by
E. & F. N. Spon
733 Third Avenue, New York NY10017

© 1982 M. D. Joyce

ISBN 0 419 12260 5

Printed in Great Britain by
J. W. Arrowsmith Ltd, Bristol

British Library Cataloguing in Publication Data

Joyce, Michael D.
  Site investigation practice.
  1. Civil engineering   2. Engineering geology
  I. Title
  624.1'51   TA705

  ISBN 0-419-12260-5

Library of Congress Cataloging in Publication Data

Joyce, Michael D.
  Site investigation practice
  Bibliography: p.
  Includes index.
  1. Building sites.   2. Soil mechanics.
I. Title.
TH375.J68   624.1'51   82-6491
ISBN 0-419-12260-5   AACR2

Contents

In most civil engineering works worthy of the name, the unexpected happens. To be prepared for such eventualities, and to forestall their effects, is the test of good constructional practice.

H. Harding, 1946

Preface

Site investigation holds two great fascinations for me. One is the process of discovery and the other is the engineering challenge. Who is not intrigued by holes in the ground? Open up a trial pit in a road and I doubt if there is a single passer-by who does not at least give it a cursory glance. Yet site investigation goes much further than that. We can now drill to vast depths, recover samples, test them and build up a picture of the ground and its properties. With this picture we can meet the engineering challenge of trying to determine how a structure will interact with the ground such that a practical, safe and economic design can be produced. I hope this book will show that the process is not just one of drilling boreholes but rather one where clues are gleaned from many sources and slowly built up to a solution.

No book can be all things to all men. Geotechnical engineers will not find that this book pushes back the frontiers of science but I hope they will find it a useful summary of their art because successful site investigation is as much an art as a science with engineers relying heavily on their experience, their creativity and their judgement. I hope it will give the non-geotechnical engineer a clear insight into the techniques available and the benefits that can be gained from using them. I hope it will be read by students because no engineering work should be contemplated without at least some site investigation. Last but not least I hope it will be read by the drillers and technicians employed in site investigation since they too can benefit if they appreciate how their work contributes to the overall process. But remember that no book can be a substitute for sound experience.

Thinking of acknowledgements the greatest thanks must go to the many engineers with whom I have discussed site investigations and who have shared their experiences

xiii

with me, either directly or through papers and conferences. Without this interaction the book would not have been possible. I should like to thank my wife, Christine, whose support and patient conversion of scrawl to type have both been invaluable. I also owe much to all involved with the County Surveyors' Society Site Investigation Course and particularly Don Richardson for discussions which got the book started; to John Herring and Phillip Brown for the illustrations and graphics work and to John Powell and Bill Anderson who offered useful criticism of the text.

Material from BS5930:1981 is reproduced by permission of the British Standards Institution, 2 Park Street, London W1A 2BS from whom complete copies can be obtained.

Finally throughout the book please read 'he or she' for 'he'. The former looks clumsy and in the true spirit of male chauvinism I elected to use 'he' even though I know there to be many excellent lady engineers.

Mike Joyce, 1982

1

Introduction

1.1 Objectives

Most civil engineering and building works are constructed on or in a relatively thin layer of the earth's crust. This thin layer comprises soils, rocks, air and water but the number of ways in which they vary and the ways in which they can combine together to produce totally different site conditions is infinite. It is doubtful if any two sites anywhere on the surface of the earth are the same. Each one will have its own peculiarities and each one will react in a different way to the works of the civil engineer. Some idea of the variations that might occur in say a river valley are shown in Fig. 1.1.

The civil engineer is entrusted with the design of all manner of works and his prime responsibilities are to ensure safety and economy. To do this he must understand how the site will respond to his design and how his works will be affected by site conditions. Site investigation can be said to be the study of the environment and the ground conditions at the location of civil engineering and building works and it is the object of this book to describe, in practical terms, the techniques and methods that can be applied to this study. It is important to recognize the difference between *site* investigation and *ground* investigation. Site investigation covers *all* the techniques and enquiries that can be used to gain information on a particular site whether this is by the study of maps or aerial photographs, site reconnaissance, boreholes or whatever and might include details on access routes, services, rainfall and so on. Ground investigation on the other hand is restricted purely to the in-depth investigation of material beneath a site.

The text should be relevant to anyone connected with civil engineering whether they be engineers, technicians, students, architects or builders. Site investigation is a

1

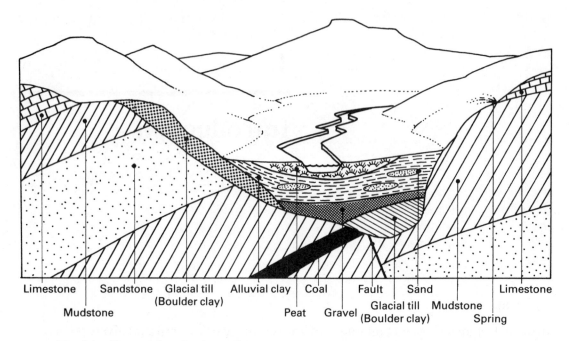

Fig. 1.1 Cross section of a river valley.

specialist branch of civil engineering but like all specializations its application and basic concepts should be understood by all who are to make use of them. Specialists in the field of site investigation will not find that the book pushes back the frontiers of science and will find that only relatively brief details have been given on some of the more specialized techniques. This is not the object of the book. Instead the most commonly used techniques are described in some detail and brief coverage is given to the more specialized techniques to keep the book to a manageable size. In general terms percentage coverage in the book has been related to percentage usage in practice.

Site investigation is often thought of in terms of boreholes but it is often not appreciated how much useful information can be gained from a brief desk study, a humble trial pit, a simple hand-augered borehole or a quick walk over the site. This is not to say that specialized techniques do not provide useful information since they most certainly do and on some occasions it is essential to use them. It is, therefore, important to know what techniques are available and when and how they can be usefully employed. Most geotechnical engineers have to work within a limited budget and it is making the most of the available money that reveals true skill and professionalism.

Some topics have been dealt with at a fairly basic level. This is because it has been the author's experience that drillers and technicians have an interest not only in their own work but also in the context in which their work is used. For this reason topics such as basic geology have been included because it is hoped that the book will not only be read by professional personnel but also by drillers and technicians. It is important that the driller has some knowledge of the engineer's work and that the engineer appreciates how the equipment is operated in the field. The technician too must understand how the samples have been obtained and how the test results are used.

The book is primarily concerned with site investigation practice in the United Kingdom but most of the techniques described are in common use throughout the world. In different countries the emphasis may be on different techniques. For instance Holland with its alluvial soils makes great use of penetrometers and America tends to use flight augering equipment instead of shell and auger. These countries have simply developed and used the equipment that has been found to be of most use to them in the investigation of their indigenous soils and rocks. This should be the approach of the geotechnical engineer wherever he finds himself since he must decide on the best means of discovering the necessary information.

The chapter sequence in the book is intended to follow the pattern of a typical site investigation, namely that of planning, boring, sampling, testing and reporting. Whilst logical it does unfortunately mean that the reader will find reference early on in the book to later chapters. For the reader who finds this irritating perhaps a study of the contents list followed by a personal choice of sequence is the answer. The dilemma is that it is no use describing what to do with something until you have described how to obtain it and it is no use describing how to obtain something if you do not know why you are obtaining it.

Some of the many different disciplines that might contribute to a successful site investigation are illustrated in Fig. 1.2 but there are doubtless others. However, this figure should not be viewed with the misconception that all are essential in every case, even though on a large scheme they may all be employed. On the smaller schemes it is the geotechnical engineer who must have at least a basic appreciation of these specializations and it is up to him to be as versatile as possible. Although this text cannot cover all the various specializations it is hoped that it will at least engender a feeling for this essential versatility and that it will encourage curiosity and further reading. To this end a bibliography has been included so that the reader with a special interest will be able to undertake further research.

1.2 Site investigation in the civil engineering process

It is important to realize how site investigation fits in with the civil engineering process from initial conception to completion and even beyond it. There are many types of civil engineering structures but all interact with the ground on or in which they stand. The civil engineer has considerable control of the materials he is to use in the structure (for a

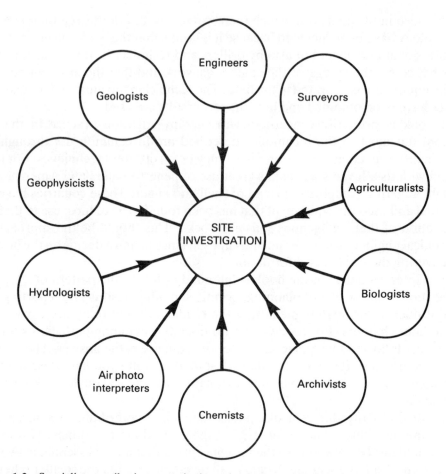

Fig. 1.2 Specialist contributions to a site investigation.

highly readable text on the strength of materials see Gordon (1968)) but little or no control over the materials upon which his structure will rest. When reference is made to Fig. 1.3 some of these interactions should be obvious. For example, the buildings apply load to the ground, some water will seep under the dam and fill materials apply pressure to the tunnel. In addition each structure must fulfill its purpose, that is a building should not collapse due either to shear failure or excessive settlement of the ground beneath it, neither should a canal leak, nor should a dam move and so on. The projects illustrated in Fig. 1.3 have varying levels of importance which to some extent determine the budget available. It is within this budget that the engineer must produce a design that has an acceptable factor of safety, is practical and which satisfies his client. These requirements are often summarized by the phrase 'a professional engineering solution'.

Fig. 1.3 The civil engineering environment.

Each of the schemes shown in Fig. 1.3 will initially be promoted as an idea by a client who will approach an engineer or an architect to investigate the feasibility of the scheme. Initially some sketches will be produced of possible practical ideas for the client's comments. At this stage an engineer will be required to make an assessment of the site and he will consider the ground affected by the scheme. Possible factors involved in four particular stuctures are illustrated in Table 1.1.

Where ground conditions are difficult the depths of investigation may be considerably greater than shown below but the figures serve to make some comparisons. Just as the table is not intended to presuppose a fixed depth of investigation neither is it intended to imply that only the ground beneath a structure is investigated since this is not true. The engineer must consider the whole environment in which his structure is to be placed and he must consider the cost of his investigations. This is illustrated in Table 1.2.

This table is only shown for comparison purposes. If for instance a whole housing estate were to be investigated the site investigation cost per house would fall as would

5

Table 1.1

Scheme	Approximate site area (m^2)	Typical depth of foundation (m)	Typical depth of investigation (m)	Approximate cost of structure at 1981 prices (£)
House	150	1.0	5	60 000
1 km of motorway at ground level	30 000	0.5	3	1 000 000
Major road bridge	1 000	3.0	30	500 000
Large factory	5 000	2.0	8	500 000

Table 1.2

Scheme	Volume of the earth's crust to be investigated (m^3)	Possible expenditure available for site investigation at 1981 prices (£)	Cost per m^3 investigated (p)	Site investigation cost as a percentage cost of completed structure (%)
House	750	300	40	0.5
1 km of motorway at ground level	90 000	5 000	5.5	0.5
Major road bridge	30 000	15 000	50	3.0
Large factory	40 000	5 000	12.5	1.0

the cost per cubic metre investigated. From the above tables it will be clear that there is a whole range of expenditure available but this is not expended all at the same time. It might for instance be split between desk study, preliminary investigations, ground investigations, interpretation and follow up studies when the subsoils are revealed during construction. On difficult sites or where subsoils are highly variable expenditure on site investigation may amount to 5% or more of the completed cost of the works. Figure 1.4 illustrates some of the features of the four structures and from this figure it will be clear that each structure interacts with the ground in different ways. The house, having strip foundations, will apply only modest loads whereas the loading due to the bridge will be much higher and in the example shown use has had to be made of piles to transmit the loads to sound strata. The motorway involves an enormous area of ground but the traffic loading will quickly be dissipated by the pavement construction. The factory is shown resting on pad foundations and the difference in affected volumes between this and the bridge will be obvious.

There are clearly different choices of foundation type available to the engineer and different site problems will lead to different solutions. In all cases the clearer the

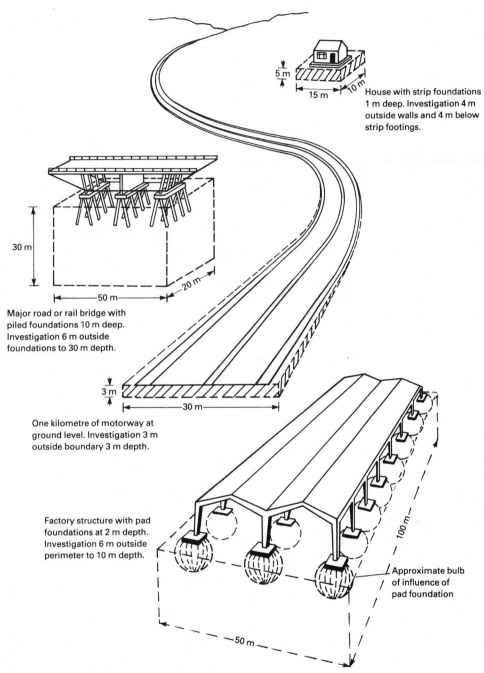

Major road or rail bridge with piled foundations 10 m deep. Investigation 6 m outside foundations to 30 m depth.

House with strip foundations 1 m deep. Investigation 4 m outside walls and 4 m below strip footings.

One kilometre of motorway at ground level. Investigation 3 m outside boundary 3 m depth.

Factory structure with pad foundations at 2 m depth. Investigation 6 m outside perimeter to 10 m depth.

Approximate bulb of influence of pad foundation

Fig. 1.4 Structures and the ground. The figure illustrates the interplay between area, depth and volume of ground affected by various structures.

statement of proposed site usage the better the investigation can be planned and the more economic it will be. No investigation can ever be said to be 'complete' since sites are so variable and our knowledge so limited. However, sufficient resources must be made available to reduce risks to an acceptable level. Experience of what is an acceptable level of risk has been built up over several hundred years but the development of new techniques and methods of analysis continue and they should lead to greater safety and greater economy.

It is interesting to speculate on the importance and value of site investigation. During 1979 a total of £15 million was spent on site investigation in Great Britain and this represents 0.75% of construction spending of about £2000 million. Also in that year about £65 million was paid in successful claims; a fair proportion of which experience shows was probably attributable to uncertainty over ground conditions. Add to this cost the cost of uneconomic foundations (e.g. unnecessarily wide strip footings) and the cost of failures and remedial works, then the potential value of sound site investigation soon becomes apparent. Cripps and Woodman (1980) show that monetary losses due to uncertainty over ground conditions can be substantially reduced by increasing the amount of site investigation. They show, however, that this does not continue indefinitely and that there is an optimum amount of site investigation when the monetary loss plus the cost of the site investigation reaches a minimum. The cost effectiveness of site investigations is of course always open to speculation but the engineer should ask himself if he is doing sufficient site investigation work for any scheme since history would tend to indicate this is often not the case. Put another way, confidence can be increased by increasing the technological input. However, this costs money and a point can be (but rarely is) reached where increased expenditure does not appreciably improve the confidence. Judgement is needed to recognize this point.

In a report published in August 1981 by the Science and Engineering Research Council and the Departments of Environment and Transport, recognition was given to the benefits that could be accrued by further investigation and research into the field of geotechnics and in particular site investigation.

Having established that site investigation is cost effective within the civil engineering process the geotechnical engineer must ensure his investigations are themselves cost effective in that as much relevant information as possible is produced for a given budget. It is hoped that this work will help in achieving this.

A new code of practice for site investigations (BS5930) was published by the British Standards Institution in 1981 and this forms an essential guide to current good practice. As a code of practice it takes the form of recommendations and it does not attempt to define rigidly the precise way in which to conduct any particular site investigation. Instead it outlines desirable procedures, their application and their limitations and it discusses those points which should be considered by any geotechnical engineer undertaking a site investigation. Since it does not attempt to lay down formal rules it must not necessarily be regarded as the only definitive guide to good practice. In fact the British Standards Institution point out in the text that compliance with it does not confer immunity from relevant statutory and legal requirements. On the other hand the geotechnical engineer might well be guilty of negligence if he did not fully consider the points of good practice that are described in the code.

The code was published to encourage good practice and some degree of consistency but it does not attempt to take away the geotechnical engineer's responsibility and initiative. It is up to him to choose the most appropriate means of investigating a site, to ensure it is carried out correctly and to interpret the results. Several important points are made in BS5930 regarding personnel involved in site investigations and states:

> In view of the importance of ground investigation as a fundamental preliminary to the proper design and efficient and economical construction of all civil engineering and building works, it is essential that personnel involved in the investigation should have appropriate specialized knowledge and experience, and be familiar with the purpose of the work.

1.3 Problem solving in site investigation

Having set the scene for the place of site investigation in the civil engineering process it is worthwhile considering how the geotechnical engineer is to tackle the problems that he will encounter. His first essential is a sound knowledge of construction methods and the design process. (Gordon (1978) gives an excellent first text on the theory of structures.) He must also understand all the techniques he has at his disposal, when to use them, their limitations and how to interpret the results they give. Geotechnical engineering in its broadest sense is as much of an art as a science with the engineer relying heavily on case histories, his own experiences and his professional judgement. It is true that knowledge of soil-mechanics theory, geology, site history and soil properties are all essential but in the end many problems still boil down to professional judgement.

Many methods of analysis assume soils to be homogeneous, isotropic and elastic but in fact they are ususally heterogeneous, anisotropic and inelastic. That is not to say that the methods are invalid but their limitations must be recognized. It is very often necessary to simplify situations since without some simplification the problem might not be capable of any solution at all. This essential simplification not only applies to theory but it also applies to the interpretation of ground conditions. The geotechnical engineer must endeavour to produce a picture of the site and its ground conditions that is simple enough to be capable of analysis and is readily understandable by other engineers. It is no good setting problems that are difficult or even impossible to solve if the accuracy of the answers that are required does not warrant it.

Pure scientists seek to understand but engineers must act. The engineer must recognize when the search for the ultimate truth has to stop and a practical solution

9

formulated. Obviously he must make every effort to avoid a failure since he would be guilty of negligence if he did not but he must provide a solution and this solution should be as economic as possible.

The engineer must keep up to date with developments in his profession, he must learn from his own and from other people's experiences, he must observe closely works under construction and he must look critically at other reports and case histories. He will no doubt make mistakes, since it is only those who do nothing who never make mistakes, but he should learn from them. Failures have occurred in the past and they will no doubt occur again, but a great deal has been learnt from them and they should help to avoid future failures.

It is not intended to end this chapter on a pessimistic note since reasonably accurate predictions can be and are made in the geotechnical field providing a professional engineering approach is taken. Where the engineer is sure of the soil conditions and properties he is justified in using lower factors of safety (or perhaps they are factors of ignorance) than where conditions are less well known. However, the predictions must be made with due regard to all the variables involved. Providing this is done the predictions can be most cost effective in that the money spent on obtaining them can be offset many times over against the savings to which they lead.

2

The nature and occurrence of soils and rocks

2.1 Introduction

In a book on site investigation the nature of the materials that are being investigated clearly cannot be ignored but to describe them in detail is way beyond the scope of this book. Geology, geomorphology, glaciology and so on are vast subjects and there are many excellent texts dealing with them. Several of these texts are aimed at the engineering application of these subjects and a number are listed in the bibliography. However, it is vitally important to have a basic understanding of the geological processes that have given rise to the ground that is to be investigated. An understanding should lead to an appreciation of the variations and potential problems that may arise on any site and how these might affect the planning of the investigation and the works that are to be constructed on or in it.

In addition to basic geology there must also be a historical understanding of the effects that man has had on the surface of our planet. The earth's surface is being changed faster now than at any time in the past and it is being changed in such a way as to present far more problems to the casual, unwary observer. No one can understand the full situation merely by looking at it. Everyone must inquire and investigate in order to understand and curiosity is invariably fruitful. We may never fully understand but the more we know of a site the greater the benefits we may reap in terms of eliminating unknowns, saving money and producing safe, efficient and economic engineering designs. It is the purpose of this chapter to present the reader with an outline of our planet's geological history so that it may stimulate curiosity which should ultimately lead to better understanding.

2.2 The form of the earth

The earth can be regarded roughly as a sphere with a radius of 6370 km and is thought to be about 4500 million years old. The inner core of this sphere, 3470 km in radius, consists mainly of molten iron and nickel. This is surrounded by a 2870 km thick mantle of plastic rocks at very high temperatures. The outer crust has a variable thickness, generally of about 30 km but less under the oceans, and tends to float on the mantle. The thickness of the crust can be compared to the thickness of the rubber on a blown up balloon. The crust is the cooled oxidized layer adjacent to the atmosphere and it consists mainly of oxygen (47%) and silicon (28%) with lesser amounts of aluminium, iron, calcium, sodium, potassium and magnesium. These major elements form a wide range of crystalline minerals which go to make up an even wider range of rock types. The crust is continually moving and it is being weathered to form new rocks which in turn are weathered and altered to form still newer ones. The form of the earth is shown in Fig. 2.1.

2.3 Movements in the earth's crust

In recent years geologists have developed the concept of a series of crustal plates, about 100 km thick, containing the oceans and the continents. These plates are slowly moving over the earth's surface at about 50 mm per year, probably due to some form of convection currents in the lower mantle and the core. Originally there was probably only one huge land mass before these movements started to occur. Some of the plates are moving towards one another, others apart and some are sliding past one another. They go to form a huge spherical jigsaw an example of which is the way that the west coast of Africa fits the east coast of South America.

Where plates are moving towards one another the colossal slow-motion collisions cause earthquakes, mountain building and occasionally volcanoes. This is shown in Fig. 2.1 whilst Fig. 2.2 shows the way that rocks can be folded by earth movements. The Himalayas and the Alps are the results of these slow motion collisions. Where plates are moving apart there is a zone of weakness produced and hot material wells up towards the surface sometimes forming volcanoes. The ocean trenches, as in the Atlantic, and the rift valleys are other results of this outward movement. Passing plates result in huge faults and associated earthquakes, one example being the San Andreas fault in California. On top of all this there is our planet's weather; its winds, rain, heat and cold.

This then sets the scene for the evolution of the planet as we know it today. The processes that are at work are by no means as simple as those outlined above but they will serve to illustrate the ways in which the many hundreds of rock types have been formed.

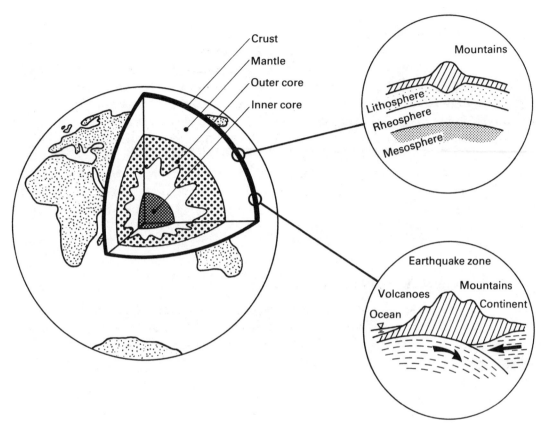

Fig. 2.1 The form of the earth. Enlarged detail of crustal structure and of two crustal plates moving towards one another is shown.

2.4 The formation of rocks

All rocks can be classified under one of three group headings; igneous, sedimentary or metamorphic. Igneous rocks are those formed by the cooling and solidification of liquid material or 'magma'. Sedimentary rocks are composed of particles which have been transported to their place of deposition or which have been formed by the aggregation of organic matter or by chemical deposition. Metamorphic rocks are existing rocks which have been altered by the effects of high temperatures and pressures. These groups will be considered in more detail in the next section. Their relationships to one another are shown in Fig.2.3.

Fig. 2.2 The folding of rocks at South Stack, Holy Isle, North Wales (photograph: Institute of Geological Sciences).

2.5 Igneous rocks

The mantle of the earth contains liquid rock at high temperatures and pressures which is sometimes forced to the surface. At other times existing rocks are forced downwards where they become liquid. When the liquid rock or 'magma' is forced to the surface it cools and the various components crystallize out. If the cooling is fast as with a volcano the crystal grains are small and if it is slow, as with plutonic rocks, they are large. This is one way of classifying igneous rocks, the other is by composition. Rocks with a high silica or quartz content are light in colour and are termed 'acid' whereas ones with a low silica content are darker and are termed 'basic'. A simple classification is given in Table 2.1.

Igneous rocks can be formed when magma flows to the surface as in volcanoes or it can be forced through existing rocks to form dykes and sills. Alternatively it can be formed deeper in the earth and subsequently be revealed by erosion where it is known as a batholith. These rocks do not contain fossils.

14

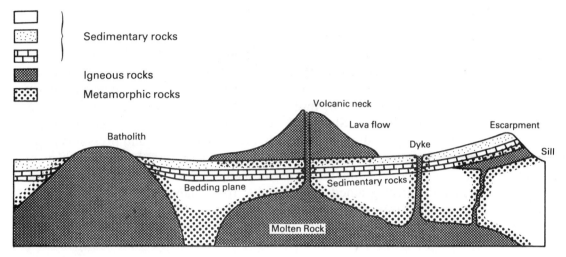

Fig. 2.3 Sedimentary, igneous and metamorphic rocks.

2.6 Sedimentary rocks

Rock on the surface of the earth is exposed to weathering by the sun, ice, frost, wind and water. These tend to break the rock into small particles which can then be moved by ice, wind or water to be deposited elsewhere. Great pressures or cementing type fluids can then turn the loose deposits into new sedimentary rocks. Rocks formed in this way are termed 'clastic'. Examples are conglomerates and breccias (coarse grained), sandstones (medium grained) and siltstones, shales and mudstones (fine grained). Alternatively rocks can be formed *in situ* by chemical deposition. Limestone and chalk are formed as an accumulation of calcium carbonate from marine organisms or seawater. Evaporites are formed as the sun's heat evaporates seawater to leave the salts behind and coals are the result of compressing dead vegetation. Oil and natural gas can become trapped in sedimentary rocks as microscopic animals and plants decay.

Table 2.1

Colour	Silica (%)	Type	Igneous rock name	
			Coarse grained	Fine grained
Light	70	Acid	Granite	Rhyolite
	60	Intermediate	Diorite	Andesite
Dark	50	Basic	Gabbro	Basalt

15

2.7 Metamorphic rocks

When existing rocks have been changed either by great pressures and/or temperatures they are termed metamorphic and occur as rocks are pushed down into the earth, are compressed or come into contact with other very hot rocks. The temperatures and pressures cause some of the constituents to alter chemically or to melt and then to recrystallize in a different form. The four major types of metamorphic rocks are slates, schists, gneisses and marbles. Slates are rocks where the fine grained constituent particles have been realigned under relatively low temperatures and pressures to give planes of weakness called 'cleavage' unrelated to their original bedding. Schists are formed when the component minerals have completely recrystallized to form new ones. Gneiss is a much coarser-grained metamorphic rock than a schist and often has a banded appearance. Marble is a recrystallized limestone. Rocks can also be affected by the circulation of very hot water which sometimes appears at the surface as geysers.

2.8 *In situ* movements of rock

As discussed earlier the earth's crust is continually moving (see Fig. 2.2). It only moves slowly but on a geological time scale it can produce dramatic effects on the rocks near the surface. It can fold them, shear them or move them upwards or downwards. The folds are similar to those produced when two parts of a tablecloth are pushed towards one another. An upward fold is termed an anticline and a downward one a syncline (see Fig. 2.4). The forces in the earth's crust can push rocks into vertical planes or can even push them completely over one another, sometimes producing thrust faults in the process. When rocks can no longer bend to accommodate the stresses imposed upon them they shear and faults can occur. Where a series of rocks have been folded, erosion can occur to level the ground surface before further rocks are deposited over them. Both series of rocks can then be affected by earth movements but whether they are or not the junction between them is known as an unconformity. Geological interpretation is a skilled operation, some of the problems of which are illustrated in Fig. 2.5 which looks at possible interpretations of the strata revealed in two boreholes.

2.9 Geology of the British Isles

The known geological history of the British Isles is a long story, going back over 600 million years, of mountain building, erosion, submergence, and deposition of sediments plus volcanic and other igneous activity. By studying the various rock types present and their structure certain ages can be recognized when particular conditions existed. These ages are shown in the geological column in Fig. 2.7 and will be discussed in more detail below. As is the wont of geologists a lot of confusing words are used but a little perseverance should overcome the problem. The various strata emphasize the way

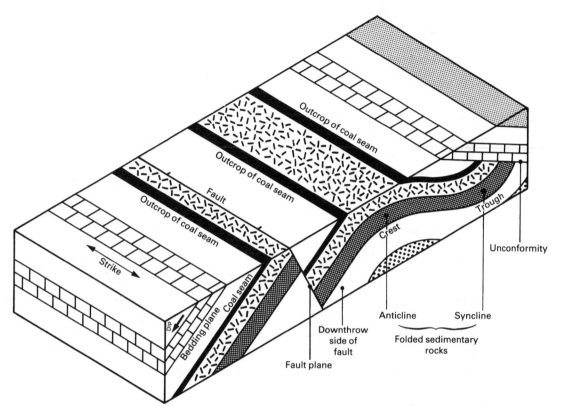

Fig. 2.4 Elements of structural geology.

in which the crustal plate containing the British Isles has drifted around the globe from near the poles to the equator. To appreciate the colossal time scale involved it is worth remembering that *Homo sapiens* has only been on the planet for about 35 000 years. (i.e. one-hundred-thousandth of the age of the earth.) A simplified geological map of the British Isles is shown in Fig. 2.6 and the stratigraphical column is shown in Fig. 2.7.

In looking at the map and the stratigraphical column it must be remembered that what is given is an extremely simplified view of geology. Within any element of the stratigraphical column there are likely to be wide variations in the rock types present and reference has only to be made to a large-scale geological map, which is in itself a simplification, to see just how complex the geology of any given area can be. More details on the geology of the British Isles are given in the eighteen regional handbooks listed in Fig. 2.8. These handbooks are produced by the Institute of Geological Sciences.

17

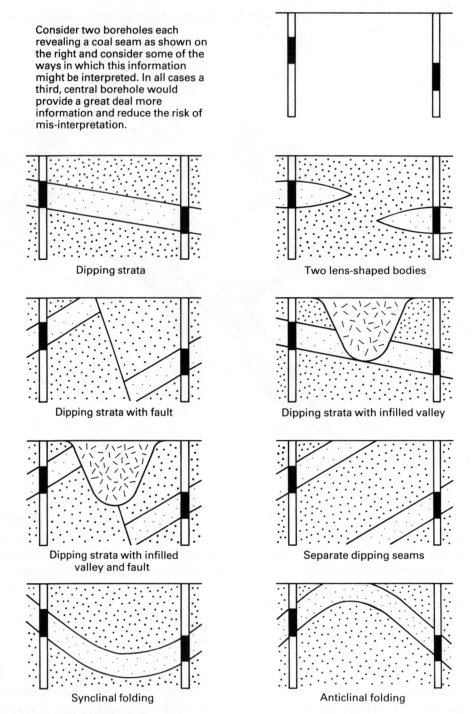

Consider two boreholes each revealing a coal seam as shown on the right and consider some of the ways in which this information might be interpreted. In all cases a third, central borehole would provide a great deal more information and reduce the risk of mis-interpretation.

Dipping strata

Two lens-shaped bodies

Dipping strata with fault

Dipping strata with infilled valley

Dipping strata with infilled valley and fault

Separate dipping seams

Synclinal folding

Anticlinal folding

Fig. 2.5 Geological interpretation.

18

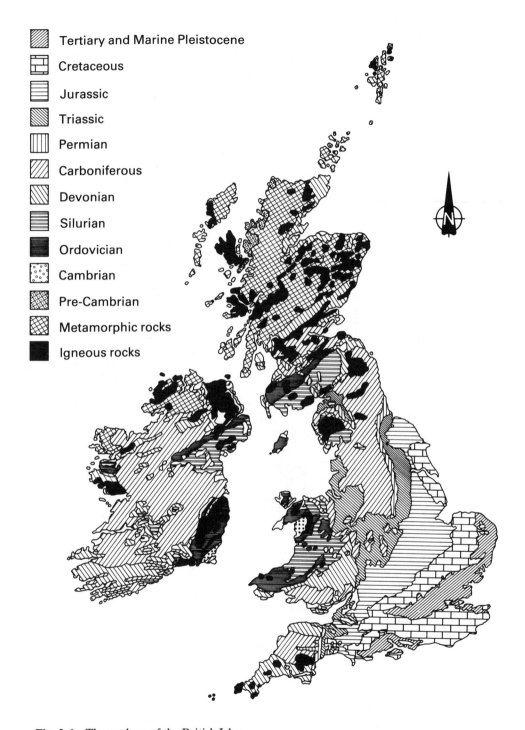

Fig. 2.6 The geology of the British Isles.

Tertiary and Marine Pleistocene
Cretaceous
Jurassic
Triassic
Permian
Carboniferous
Devonian
Silurian
Ordovician
Cambrian
Pre-Cambrian
Metamorphic rocks
Igneous rocks

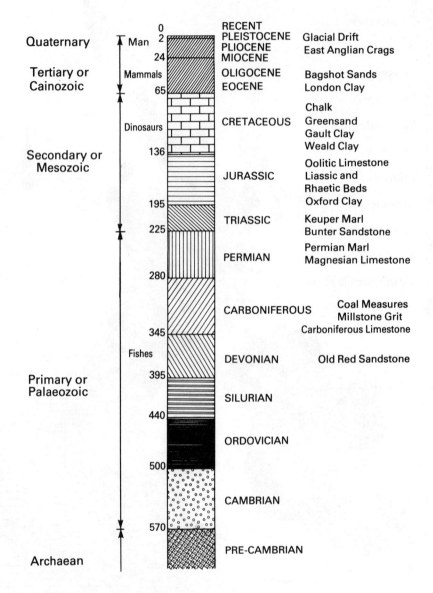

Fig. 2.7 A simplified stratigraphical column showing the geological systems and their ages in millions of years together with the better-known rocks.

Northern Highlands

Grampian Highlands
Tertiary Volcanic Districts

Midland Valley of
Scotland

South of Scotland

Northern England

East Yorkshire and
Lincolnshire

The Pennines and
adjacent areas

North Wales

Central England

East Anglia

Welsh Borders

South Wales

London and Thames Valley

Bristol and Gloucester

The Wealden District

Hampshire Basin

South-West England

Fig. 2.8   The eighteen regional *Handbooks of the Geology of Great Britain.*

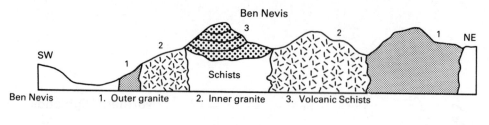

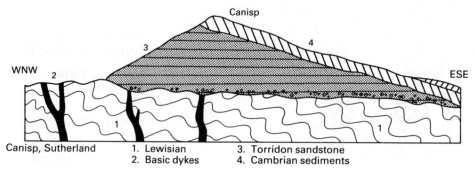

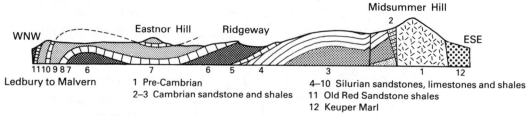

Fig. 2.9 Typical geological sections (after Blyth and de Freitas).

2.9.1 The Pre-Cambrian (over 570 million years ago)

These are the oldest recognizable rocks in the British Isles and occur at only a few localities. They range from sandstones to gneisses with many volcanic intrusions. After they were formed they were raised above sea level and many were weathered away over a period of hundreds of millions of years.

2.9.2 Cambrian, Ordovician and Silurian (570–395 million years ago)

These mainly sedimentary rocks cover large areas of Scotland, the Lake District and Wales and they contain many volcanic intrusions which have produced a variety of metamorphic rocks. The rock types associated with these ages include slates, sandstones, gritstones, shales and a few limestones. At the end of the Silurian, prolonged mountain building took place and it was the erosion products of these mountains that produced the next succession of rocks. Figure 2.9 shows a typical section through rocks of these ages.

2.9.3 Devonian (395–345 million years ago)

Two conditions existed during this period. In the north of the British Isles desert conditions prevailed and sandstones were produced whilst in the south it was the age of the fishes with sediments being laid down in seas and large lakes which eventually formed sandstones, shales and limestones (see Fig. 2.9). A number of granite intrusions and some slates also developed during this period.

2.9.4 Carboniferous (345–280 million years ago)

So named from the coal seams it contains, the Carboniferous started with a submergence of the land when limestones were produced in the seas. These were followed by the deposition of grit and sand in shallow deltaic waters. Later the Coal Measures themselves developed when estuarine and swamp conditions predominated with the dense forests producing the coal seams. These alternate with beds of mudstone, siltstone and sandstone. A few volcanic intrusions occurred during the Carboniferous and further mountain building took place at the end of the period with some granite intrusions. Figure 2.10 shows a section across the Pennines which are mainly composed of carboniferous rocks.

2.9.5 Permian (280–225 million years ago)

After the mountain building there was a dry period and desert sandstones were laid down. Marls (marine mudstones) were also deposited in shallow seas off a desert coast and some evaporites were formed. The period ended with limestones being produced in large inland lakes (see Fig. 2.10).

2.9.6 Triassic (225–195 million years ago)

This period represents a slightly more temperate time when red-coloured sandstones, marls and a few limestones were laid down in a large inland basin surrounded by mountains (see Fig. 2.10).

2.9.7 Jurassic (195–136 million years ago)

The climate continued to become more temperate and shallow seas gave rise to an alternating sequence of limestones and clays with some sands; these now dip gently to the south-east. Several of the Jurassic rocks are shown in Fig. 2.10.

2.9.8 Cretaceous (136–65 million years ago)

This, the age of the dinosaurs, started with a series of shallow lakes but the sea intruded and sands, clays and the chalk were produced. The period ended with further uplifting of the land and subsequent erosion. A typical section through Cretaceous and Tertiary rocks is shown in Fig. 2.10.

2.9.9 Tertiary (65–2 million years ago)

This period covers the eocene, oligocene, miocene and pliocene ages when mammals

23

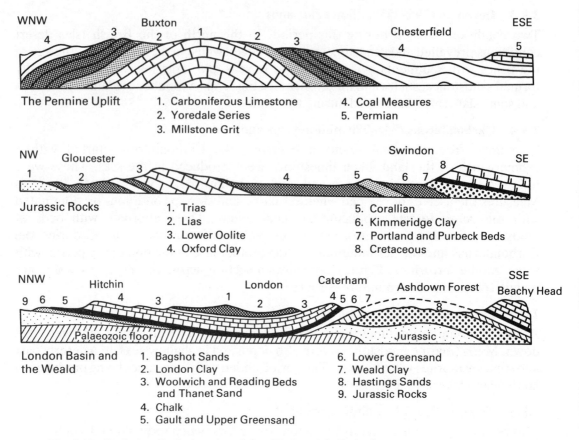

Fig. 2.10 Typical geological sections (after Blyth and de Freitas).

developed. In geological terms the deposits are young and consist of relatively unconsolidated sands and clays including the well-known London Clay (beloved of soil mechanics researchers). The deposits are today only found in the south of England. Gentle mountain building again affected the British Isles during this period (see Fig. 2.10).

2.9.10 Quaternary or Pleistocene (2 million years ago to present)

During this period the climate became colder and the Arctic Ice Cap expanded to produce an ice age in the British Isles with the north of the country covered by thousands of metres of ice. This has had a dramatic effect on our landscape and its effects will be considered in more detail below. It is during this period that many soils developed due to the weathering of existing rocks.

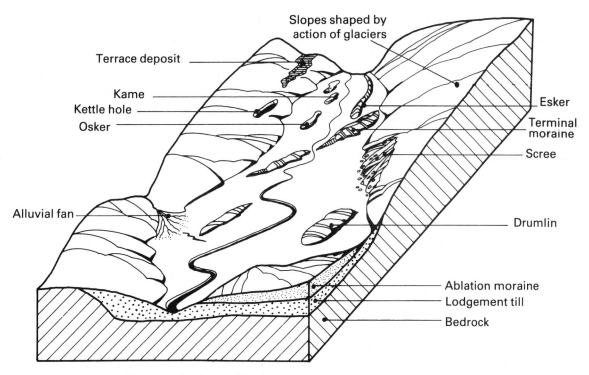

Fig. 2.11 Features of a glaciated landscape.

2.10 The Ice Age

The ice which covered the British Isles was not static; on several occasions it grew and advanced and each time it melted it retreated. This produced a wide range of conditions. As the glaciers and ice sheets moved they scoured the countryside and redeposited the material picked up elsewhere in the form of variable boulder clays or tills. When a glacier stopped it left great mounds of material known as moraines which contain a whole variety of materials. As the ice melted vast quantities of water were released which scoured out deep valleys, removed material and laid it down elsewhere in deposits which vary from clays and silts to sands and gravels. Some of the glaciers formed dams and huge lakes developed. The meltwaters flowed into these lakes carrying sediments which later settled out to give rise to laminated deposits of sand, silt and clay. Figure 2.11 illustrates a number of other features associated with glaciation. It will be clear from the above that the ice ages gave rise to a wide variety of materials and this is the most significant message that can be given to anyone investigating a site affected by glaciation. The deposits can alter rapidly both vertically and laterally from clays to silts to sands to boulders or any combination of these.

25

The cold climate also had other significant effects even where no glaciers were present. It produced deep weathering of rocks, turning sandstones back to sands, mudstones back to clays and so on. In this way the typical profiles developed that we now see in boreholes. Beneath the topsoil we might find a clay which becomes stiffer with depth; small particles of rock are found in the clay and these increase in number until the clay passes into weathered mudstone and finally into intact rock. Many large landslides developed in weathered material and material flowed down hillsides as ice in the soil melted, the latter being termed 'head'.

2.11 Recent geological activity and the formation of soils

Many of the processes that have been described in the previous sections are still active today. The sun, wind, water and frost are causing weathering of the rocks to produce the soils which are so important to the site investigator of today. These soils are being eroded by water and the rivers are depositing their sediments as unconsolidated alluvial clays, silts, sands and gravels. The sea is active too, eroding cliffs and depositing sand banks. Vegetation grows and peats form. Landslides still occur. Sand is blown from one place to another. Estuaries and lakes silt up. All these activities go to produce a complex series of 'drift' deposits overlying the solid geology which must be appreciated by the site investigator if he is to unravel the secrets beneath the topsoil.

To the engineer a 'soil' is any unconsolidated deposit that can be excavated by earth-moving plant without the need to blast it first. Many 'soils' have already been mentioned as they occur in the stratigraphical column from the Jurassic onwards. However, any of the rocks in the stratigraphical column, whether they be igneous, sedimentary or metamorphic, can weather to form residual soils and these are even more variable than the rocks from which they originated. Apart from 'residual' soils the other main types are the 'transported' soils such as the alluvial silts, clays and sands and the numerous variable glacial deposits that were discussed in Section 2.10.

With all the processes that are at work it will be clear from the above that considerable variability might be expected in the soils and rocks encountered on any site and this is most certainly found to be so. The main rock types that have been described contain numerous sub-divisions with each one often containing widely differing materials. Rocks and soils can therefore vary in type and degree of weathering and can alter very rapidly both vertically and horizontally. These are the very reasons why careful site investigation is so necessary. As more boreholes are sunk in any region they serve to illustrate an ever increasing complexity in the structure and form of the ground beneath our feet.

One major part of the site investigation process is the interpretation of the information revealed by the boreholes. Where the structural geology is complex, considerable expertise is required to piece together all the borehole information.

However, this process is outside the scope of this book and the reader is referred to one of the texts in the bibliography although Fig. 2.5 (p. 18) serves to illustrate some of the potential problems.

Appendix G of BS5930 gives a useful summary on the nature and occurrence of soils and rocks. The appendix covers soils, drift deposits and the various rock types together with some discussion on structural geology and tectonics.

2.12 Man's activities

As stated in the introduction man's activities are changing the surface of the planet faster now than at any time in the past. He is altering the shape of the land, farming it, building on it, quarrying it, mining beneath it, forming new lakes, irrigating it, dumping waste products on it and so on. Any of these activities can present real problems to a site developer and the site investigation must be aimed at determining what has happened in the recent past as well as in the geological past.

A search should be made for records of old underground workings and shafts whether they have been made for coal, metallic ores, salt, potash or other minerals. Opencast mining and quarrying has gone on for a long time and the nature of any backfill is extremely important since many old quarries have been filled with domestic or industrial wastes which may be toxic, highly compressible or combustible. A hard crust on an old slurry lagoon might conceal semi-liquid material and any previous industrial complexes might have been left with underground chambers, old foundations and waste dumps. Demolished urban areas too can be left with cellars, old sewers, wells, cesspits, tunnels and drains.

2.13 Water

In addition to all the variables of soil and rock types discussed above, water may be present and this in itself presents a whole new range of problems. It has often been stated that 'water is the enemy' and in most engineering problems it usually is. The sun evaporates water from the seas and lakes and the moisture vapour then circulates around the earth eventually to fall as rain on the land masses. Here it seeps into the ground, flows through it and emerges into springs and rivers which eventually return it to the sea. Water is therefore present to some degree in virtually all soils and rocks, and it is here the problems start. It softens and weakens soils; it erodes away material; it causes dam failures; it leads to settlement; it freezes and expands and it produces piping. The list is long and because of its obvious serious consequences no site investigation is complete without a full and careful study of groundwater in and around the site.

3

Planning and preliminary investigations

3.1 Planning

The role of site investigation in the civil engineering process was discussed in Chapter 1 and a number of important points were made.

(1)   The variability of construction sites and the need for their individual treatment.
(2)   The importance of the interaction between the structure and the ground.
(3)   The development of a safe and economic 'professional engineering solution' taking into account all the factors which might affect the proposed works.
(4)   The need for site investigation to be carried out as effectively as possible within a fixed budget.

It is important that a site investigation reveals, as far as is practically possible, all the conditions which affect the planning, design, construction and operation of any civil engineering works. There cannot be definite rules laid down concerning exactly how this should be done because the method and amount of site investigation needed will vary from site to site. More investigation will be needed on sites with highly variable subsoils and on sites where the risk of failure must be kept to an absolute minimum such as dams and bridges. In addition serviceability criteria must be considered. The important thing is to make the investigation as effective as possible within any budgetary limitations and in order to do this careful planning is needed.

It may be salutory to examine briefly two examples where poor planning and site investigation proved disastrous. The first is the Silent Valley Dam in Northern Ireland. An investigation in 1913 predicted rockhead at a depth of 20 m below the bottom of the valley (see Fig. 3.1). Contracts were signed on the basis of this information but before the geology of the site had been assessed in detail. Further investigations prior to construction in 1924 showed that the 1913 boreholes had terminated in large boulders and that the true maximum depth to rockhead was 60 m through water-bearing sand. As a consequence the dam took nine difficult years to build. This trouble could have been easily avoided if the emphasis on the geology of the area had been stressed during the preliminary investigation.

A second example of bad planning was shown where a tunnel line was decided upon purely from geometric considerations and a single phase site investigation was carried out along this line, more as an afterthought than a prime design consideration. As a result of the investigation a geological feature was discovered which caused the designers to move the line of the tunnel just a few metres to avoid it, with no further investigation being carried out. This movement drastically increased the length of tunnel to be drilled through very weak material with subsequent delays and problems (see Fig. 3.1). The fault was attributed directly to the site investigation, which if it had been planned in phases involving preliminary investigation, route location, site selection and detailed investigation, would have cost very little more and would have identified the hazards in advance.

When completed, the site investigation should provide recommendations regarding the suitability of the site for the proposed works with consideration being given to alternatives. It should also lead to a safe and economic design and should indicate the best methods of construction by foreseeing potential problems. In some cases investigation may also be required into sources and properties of naturally occurring construction materials.

The investigation should be carried out with a view to establishing the distribution and boundaries of the materials, including water, beneath the site, their structure and their engineering properties. This can be done in a series of well-defined stages and these are illustrated in Fig. 3.2. In some cases the procedure may be modified. If the job is simple and straightforward there may be no necessity for a preliminary investigation but on a complex site there may be several preliminary stages with an assessment being made after each one to establish whether any modification to the design concept is needed, and the amount and type of any further investigation. Nevertheless, whatever is done should be done with careful consideration for the requirements of the job.

Site investigations can also be carried out at the site of a failure in order to determine the cause. Investigations such as these may not follow the typical pattern described in this section but they are extremely important in terms of extending our engineering knowledge and ensuring that a similar failure does not occur in the future. The investigation itself should of course be aimed at producing recommendations for any necessary remedial works.

Another important aspect of any site investigation is the safety of existing works and

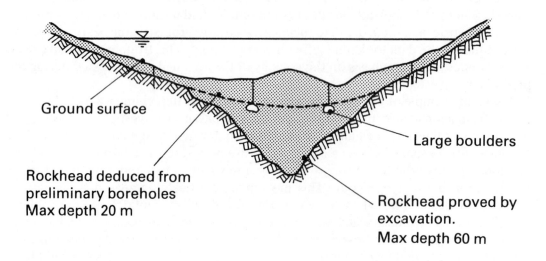

Ground surface

Rockhead deduced from
preliminary boreholes
Max depth 20 m

Large boulders

Rockhead proved by
excavation.
Max depth 60 m

Section of the Silent Valley Dam

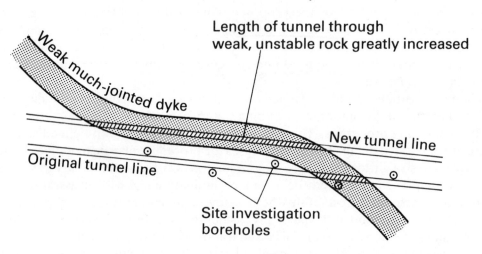

Length of tunnel through
weak, unstable rock greatly increased

Weak much-jointed dyke

New tunnel line

Original tunnel line

Site investigation
boreholes

Plan showing change of tunnel line
without further site investigation

Fig. 3.1   Examples of the consequences of poor planning.

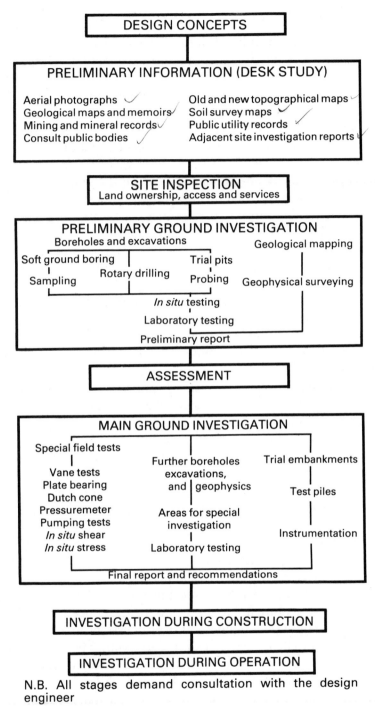

DESIGN CONCEPTS

PRELIMINARY INFORMATION (DESK STUDY)

Aerial photographs   Old and new topographical maps
Geological maps and memoirs   Soil survey maps
Mining and mineral records   Public utility records
Consult public bodies   Adjacent site investigation reports

SITE INSPECTION
Land ownership, access and services

PRELIMINARY GROUND INVESTIGATION

Boreholes and excavations   Geological mapping

Soft ground boring   Trial pits

Sampling   Rotary drilling   Probing   Geophysical surveying

In situ testing

Laboratory testing

Preliminary report

ASSESSMENT

MAIN GROUND INVESTIGATION

Special field tests
                           Further boreholes   Trial embankments
Vane tests   excavations,
Plate bearing   and geophysics   Test piles
Dutch cone
Pressuremeter   Areas for special
Pumping tests   investigation
In situ shear   Instrumentation
In situ stress   Laboratory testing

Final report and recommendations

INVESTIGATION DURING CONSTRUCTION

INVESTIGATION DURING OPERATION

N.B. All stages demand consultation with the design engineer

Fig. 3.2   Stages of a site investigation.

31

what effect any new works might have on them. Existing structures can be affected by tunnelling, excavations, demolition, groundwater lowering, vibration, shrinkage, ground freezing, additional induced stresses and interruption of established drainage patterns. All these phenomena need careful consideration if expensive claims for damages are to be avoided.

For a normal site investigation the first stage shown in Fig. 3.2 is a study of the design concepts. The importance to the geotechnical engineer of a knowledge of construction methods and design was stressed in the introduction. It is equally important that as much as possible of the client's brief and the structural engineer's design thoughts is known at an early stage. It is true that the design may be altered depending on what the investigation reveals but the more that is known the better the investigation can be planned and the more economically it can be carried out. Knowledge of the design proposals should include layout, alignments, function and probable loadings. Once these points have been established by discussion with the design engineer, the geotechnical engineer can proceed to gathering preliminary information. This has generally become known as the 'desk study' and has often been much underrated and underutilized. A great deal of useful information can be gained from the study of such things as aerial photographs, topographical and geological maps, past reports and old records and this is discussed in the remainder of this chapter. A summary of the information required for a desk study is given in Fig. 3.17 at the end of this chapter.

Having gleaned all he can from the records and maps the geotechnical engineer should then make a thorough reconnaissance of the site and its surroundings. He should follow up any anomalies he may have seen on the aerial photographs or on the maps and should examine exposures, springs and so on as discussed in Section 3.8. At the same time he should look into such matters as land ownership, entry permission, access problems, water supply and the location of underground services. The consequences of drilling through high pressure gas mains and 40 kV cables are horrific.

Planning can now begin on the preliminary ground investigation; this being a specific part of the site investigation concerned with exploratory holes and testing. Having critically examined all the available information the geotechnical engineer should be aware of its shortcomings and of those areas which are important to the design engineer. He may wish to test the feasibility of the initial design or examine alternatives, but it is at this stage that he must decide the sort of field information he requires and how he is to acquire it. He should not be too concerned with providing the detailed answers but should be looking to answer questions in a general manner. For instance, are piles likely to be needed or can spread footings be used? Is there any very soft material that will have to be removed? Can excavated materials be re-used elsewhere? Some of the methods he may call upon are listed in Fig. 3.2. They are discussed in general terms in Chapter 4 and in more detail in the remainder of the book.

Mapping in terms of engineering geology can be an extremely useful technique and

Table 3.1

	Comparative cost per metre	Metres per shift
Shell and auger boring	1.0	8
Hand augering	0.6	15
Mechanically dug trial pits to 3 m	0.5	20
Rotary percussive drilling	0.3	50
Open-hole rotary drilling	0.7	30
Diamond core drilling	2.0	8
Static cone penetrometer	0.2	30

Note   Geophysics, specialized *in situ* testing and other specialized services are normally paid for on an hourly basis.

should not be overlooked. The engineer must build up experience of the advantages and limitations of the various techniques and be able to recognize which techniques to use in specific situations. He must also consider the costs involved and Table 3.1 gives some generalized comparisons although it must be stressed that there can be wide variations under extreme conditions.

Once the preliminary ground investigation is complete the geotechnical engineer should be in a position first to make an assessment of the site and secondly to plan the main ground investigation. A preliminary report may be required at this stage and this should contain relevant plans, sections and discussion on the various materials present and their characteristics. Some generalized recommendations regarding the obvious problems, choice of alternatives and so on may also be included. The report should indicate the necessary extent of the main ground investigation; the essential elements of which are shown in Fig. 3.2. Once again regular discussions with the design engineer are essential.

The planning of the main ground investigation should be done after careful consideration of the information already available and an awareness of information that is still needed. The engineer should be able to decide where boreholes are needed, how deep they should be, what kind they should be, where the geological structure needs to be examined, where *in situ* testing should be carried out, where geophysics might be useful and what laboratory testing will be needed to enable him to answer the questions of the design engineer. The geotechnical engineer will ultimately have to produce a detailed report as discussed in Chapter 13, and he must ensure he obtains the information necessary to write it. Throughout all the above stages the geotechnical engineer should liaise closely with the design engineer to ensure that he is also obtaining all the information he needs. The whole process is one of discovery with each new

33

discovery perhaps modifying the approach. It should be obvious from the above that the full site investigation process can take some time and it is a common failing to make insufficient allowance for it.

In deciding on the spacing and location of boreholes the engineer must decide what is needed to give a clear picture of the ground conditions. He should anticipate the likely problems and plan to provide sufficient information for their solution. Obviously simple sites will need only a limited investigation. For instance a small housing site may only require a few trial pits with no necessity for any boreholes or testing at all. However, the more complex and problematical sites will require a great deal more and there should always be sufficient to provide for the essential, feasible, safe and economic design. The geotechnical engineer should be aware of the risks and should ensure that they have been reduced to an acceptable level. He should also question whether or not additional expenditure would bring real benefits.

Clearly no rules can be laid down for the spacing and depths of boreholes and rigid preconceived patterns should be avoided. However, one or two examples of typical practice can be given. These must *not*, however, be regarded as definitive. In motorway construction a borehole spacing of 100 m might be used to start with but more boreholes would probably be needed in cuttings in order to provide reliable typical cross sections. Bridges will require at least two boreholes at each pier or abutment position. Dams would have boreholes at say 30–60 m centres, large buildings 10–30 m and small, light buildings at 20–60 m. The boreholes should generally be taken to a depth of at least one-and-a-half times the width of the loaded area or to the bottom of any very soft materials. Boreholes at dam sites should extend to a depth equal to twice the depth of water or to an impermeable stratum. In many cases deep boreholes will be required to define the geology or to solve particular problems. It is often useful to start the ground investigation with one or two deep boreholes to establish the general pattern which may or may not modify the future work.

It should not be thought that the investigation ends with the main report since there is a lot that can be done during construction itself. It is at this stage that the engineer will have revealed far more of the ground than was ever seen during the ground investigations. This will enable him to check his interpretation of the distribution of the subsoils and their properties. He will also be able to check the validity of any assumptions he has made and may modify the design if this is considered necessary. Instrumentation may have been installed in order to monitor the performance of the works. This is covered in more detail in Chapter 11. A great deal can be learnt from the so called 'observational method' in civil engineering where careful examination and simple measurements can reveal new insights into the behaviour of soils and rocks. By these means an engineer really extends his experience and paves the way to improving his skill and judgement. Investigation may well continue even after the works have been constructed. Instruments may need to be read, settlements measured and ground

34

Table 3.2

Scale	Inches to the mile	Area covered by a single sheet	Colour
1:1250*	50 ins to 1 mile	500 m × 500 m	No
1:2500*	25 ins to 1 mile	2 km × 1 km	No
1:10 000	approx 6 ins to 1 mile	5 km × 5 km	No
1:10 560	6 ins to 1 mile	5 km × 5 km	No
1:25 000	$2\frac{1}{2}$ ins to 1 mile	10 km × 10 km	Yes
		or	
		20 km × 10 km	Yes
1:50 000	$1\frac{1}{4}$ ins to 1 mile	40 km × 40 km	Yes
1:63 360†	1 in to 1 mile	40 km × 40 km	Yes

Notes   * Coverage limited to urban areas
           † Now largely replaced by the 1:50 000 maps

movements monitored in order to check that the works are performing in the way they were predicted to behave.

3.2 Topographical maps

The maps of the Ordnance Survey of Great Britain give detailed information on surface features and form the major base on which other information can be recorded as the site investigation proceeds. Maps are published at different scales and the ones of use are listed in Table 3.2.

The 1:25 000 map is the largest scale map of general use in site investigations and an example is shown in Fig. 3.3. For those not using maps regularly a careful study of the conventional symbols will be necessary; the object being to build up a realistic mental picture of the site area. The symbols are shown in Fig. 3.4 and their possible significance in the desk study is described below. However, it must be remembered that in order to show certain features clearly on a map their size may have to be exaggerated and their outline simplified. The 1:50 000 and 1:10 000 maps also have their uses in site investigation and they can be interpreted in a similar way to the 1:25 000 sheets.

Road, track, footpath	ease and type of access
Railway, canal	site development, drainage
Cutting	possible exposure of strata and indication of stability
Tunnel	records may show sub-surface strata
Embankment	may cross flood plain or other soft lying ground

35

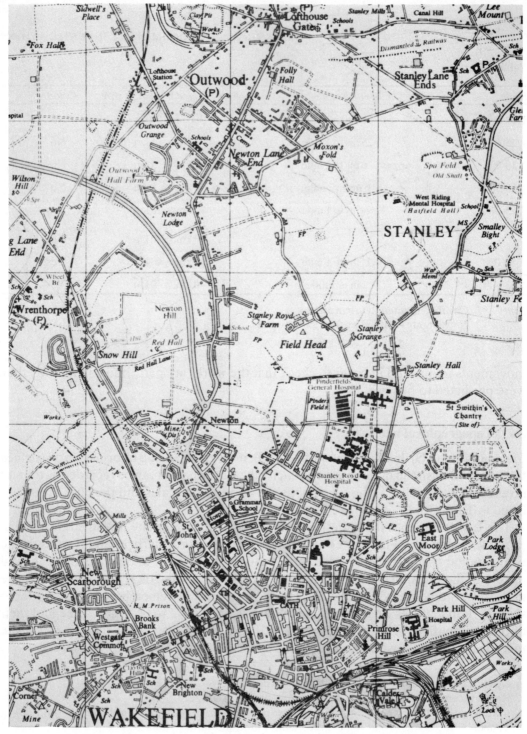

Fig. 3.3 Extract from a 1:25 000 Ordnance Survey Map of Great Britain.

36

Conventional Signs

Note :- Road fillings and numbers are shown in orange on the map.

Motorway, Trunk and Main Road (Dual Carriageway) — M 4 or A 6(M)   A 123 or A 123(T)

Trunk & Main Road — A 123 or A 123(T)

Secondary Road — *Fenced*   B 2314   *Unfenced*

Road Under Construction

Other Roads — *Good, metalled*   *Poor, or unmetalled*

Footpaths — *FP Fenced*   *FP Unfenced*

Railways, Multiple Track — Station   Road over   FB (Footbridge)   Sidings   Cutting   Tunnel

"   Single Track — Viaduct   Level Crossing   Embankment   Road under

"   Narrow Gauge

London & Glasgow Transport Underground Stations ○   Interchange Stations ⊗

Aerial Ropeway — *Aerial Ropeway*

Boundaries { County or County Borough

"   County of City (in Scotland)

"   "   "   "   with Parish

"   Parish

Pipe Line (Oil, Water) — *Pipe Line*

Electricity Transmission Lines (Pylons shown at bends and spaced conventionally)— ⊗ – – – – ⊗

Post Offices (In Villages & Rural Areas only)   P   Town Hall   TH   Public House   PH

Church or Chapel with Tower ▪ Church or Chapel with Spire ▴ Church or Chapel without either ●

Triangulation Station   △   on Church with Tower △   without Tower △

Intersected Point on Chy ○   on Church with Spire ○   without Spire ✳   on Building ▬

Guide Post GP.   Mile Post MP.   Mile Stone MS   Boundary Stone BS ○   Boundary Post BP○

Youth Hostel Y   Telephone Call Box (Public) T   (AA) A   (RAC) R   Antiquity (site of) +

Public Buildings ▬   Glasshouses ▪

Quarry & Gravel Pit   Orchard

National Trust Area — Sheen Common NT   Furze

"   "   Scotland   NTS   Rough Pasture Heath & Moor

Osier Bed   Marsh

Reeds   Well   W ○

Park, Fenced   Spring   Spr○

    Wind Pump   Wd Pp.

Wood, Coniferous, Fenced

Wood, Non-Coniferous Unfenced   Contours are at 25 feet vertical interval.

Brushwood, Fenced & Unfenced   Spot Height   123 ·

Ferries   Sand Hills

Foot   Vehicle   Flat Rock

LWMMT   Mud

Slopes   △ Beacon

HWMMT   Sand   ⚡ Lightship

Lake   Bridge   *Highest point to which Medium Tides flow*   Sand & Shingle

Canal   Lock   Weir

Towing   Aqueduct   Cliff

Path   Ford   FB (Footbridge)   Lighthouse ⚑

Dam

High & Low Water Mark of Ordinary Spring Tides, in Scotland

Note :- Sand is shown as an orange stipple on the map.
Sand and shingle are shown in orange, and mud
as a combined blue and orange stipple.

Fig. 3.4   Conventional signs used on a 1:25 000 Ordnance Survey Map.

Aerial ropeway	may be associated with mining or quarrying
Pipeline	sub-surface obstruction, records may show strata
Overhead lines	obstructions to rigs and cranes
Town Hall	source of local information
Public house	source of local information and refreshment
Churches	rural vicars often used to have an interest in geology
Major buildings	investigations may have been carried out prior to construction
Quarries and pits	possible exposures and indication of stability
Orchards, furze, rough pasture, heath and moor	general land use, vegetation may indicate subsoil type
Osier beds, marshes	low lying, poorly drained, soft subsoils
Well, spring	water table and possible sub-surface flow
Woods	type may indicate subsoils
Contour lines	these show ground shape and drainage pattern, may show geomorphology, ground slope can be calculated
Lakes and streams	natural or artificial drainage
Cliffs	possible exposure of sub-soils, indication of stability

There are also old maps available for reference in libraries and other archives. Maps of use to the geotechnical engineer date from early in the nineteenth century and these may indicate past land usage, old quarries, old ponds, adits, infilled wells, former buildings, waste tips and so on.

3.3 Aerial photographs

Photogrammetry is the technique of making accurate measurements from photographs and air-photo interpretation is the study of the ground's surface, vegetation and man-made structures as revealed by aerial photographs. Photographs may be taken either vertically or obliquely. If vertical photographs are taken such that they overlap then the ground surface may be viewed through a stereoscope to give a three dimensional image whereas oblique photographs merely give an impression of the ground shape.

Both techniques can have an important role in site investigation although probably the vertical photographs are of most use (see Fig. 3.5). The aircraft's flying height and the camera's focal length are chosen to give the required scale and Fig. 3.6 shows the area coverage at different scales although it must be remembered that the photographs are not true to scale over their whole area. The speed of the aircraft and time interval between photographs is adjusted so that each photograph overlaps the field of view of the previous one by about 60%. The pattern of overlap is shown in Fig. 3.7 and it will be seen that there is also a lateral overlap of about 25%. With such photographs a three dimensional image can be obtained by viewing adjacent ones under a stereoscope as shown in Fig. 3.8. Two photographs that can be viewed three dimensionally are termed a stereopair.

Fig. 3.5 Aerial photograph (9 in × 9 in, 1:14 000) of Coalport showing a variety of soil types and land usage.

Aerial photography is used today to provide a considerable amount of information for the preparation of contoured topographical maps but ground control is essential. Normally these maps will already be available to the geotechnical engineer although not necessarily in remote areas. Photogrammetric measurements can also be digitized and fed into a computer which can then produce perspectives, profiles, contours and even time lapse contours which indicate movements or changes in volume if

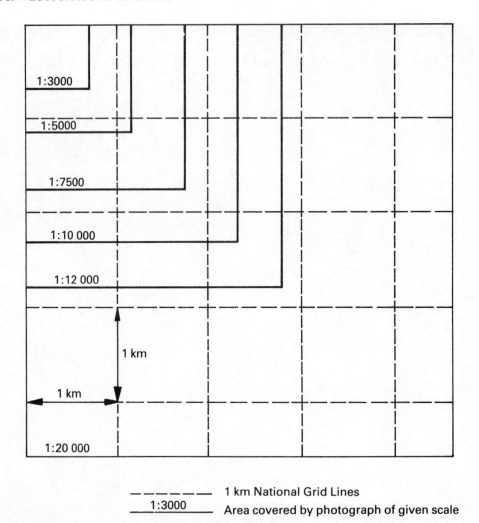

1:3000

1:5000

1:7500

1:10 000

1:12 000

1 km

1 km

1:20 000

------- 1 km National Grid Lines

1:3000 — Area covered by photograph of given scale

Fig. 3.6 Area coverage of different scale photography.

photographs are taken at appropriate time intervals. In Great Britain air photograph coverage is available for most of the country but its usefulness will depend on scale, the weather and the time and date of the photography so a search should be made for the most suitable ones. The photographs are useful on site and can be annotated with a chinagraph pencil which can be easily cleaned off. Aerial photographs can be used with varying degrees of success in many ways and these are listed below.

(1) Geological interpretation.

40

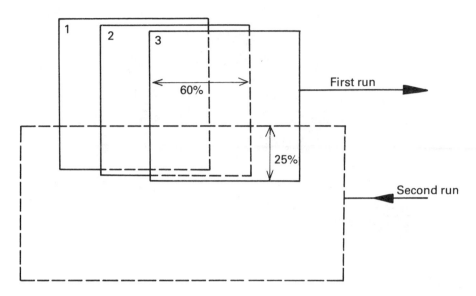

Fig. 3.7 Overlap of aerial photographs. 1 and 2 or 2 and 3 can be viewed stereoscopically over 60% of their area.

(2) Land form studies including the detection of landslides.
(3) Vegetation studies (which may reflect sub-soil type).
(4) Land use studies including mining and mineral extraction.
(5) Determination of drainage patterns.

One of the major advantages which stereoscopically viewed photographs have is that the vertical scale is exaggerated and this can help in identifying features which might not be seen on the ground, for example; changes in slope (which may indicate change in strata), darker poorly drained areas, circular patterns of old shafts and so on. Another advantage is that the photograph reveals all the detail in its true form whereas a map may leave some out and use symbols for the remainder. Some of the major features which might be observed are discussed below although many may not be obvious in heavily developed areas.

3.3.1 Rock outcrops

These indicate areas where joints and structures might be revealed and samples taken. Where there are large areas of exposed rock, dip and structure may even be obvious from the aerial photographs. Different rocks often exhibit different textures and colours on the photographs.

41

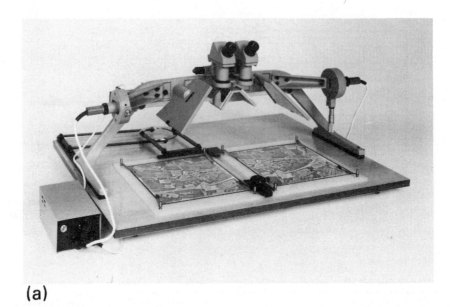

(a)

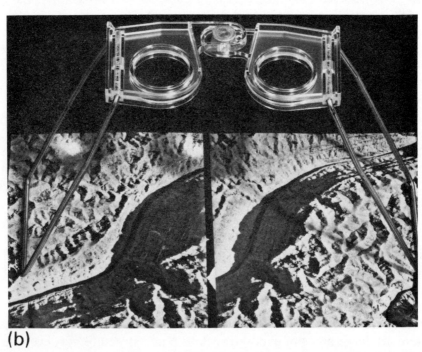

(b)

Fig. 3.8 Stereoscopes. (a) Mirror stereoscope (photograph: Cartographic Engineering Ltd). (b) Folding pocket stereoscope (photograph: C.F. Casella and Co. Ltd).

3.3.2 Faults

Faults may be visible where there is a clear difference in the nature of the ground surface either side of a given line on the ground. This difference may be in colour, vegetation or texture. Faults may also be indicated by lines of the disappearance or emergence of water.

3.3.3 Pits, quarries and spoil tips

These are indicative of ground disturbance and of locations for study and sampling. Photography from different dates may prove the extension or infilling of quarries.

3.3.4 Changes of soil type

Different soils may be indicated by different tones, colours or textures and they may support different types of vegetation or have different drainage patterns. Darker tones on a consistent soil type may indicate wet areas.

3.3.5 Unstable ground

This may be evident by the hummocky nature of the ground or by the crescent-shaped back slopes of landslides. Old mineshafts can often be seen as dark, circular areas.

3.3.6 Man-made features

Pipelines, overhead cables, access tracks, crops, agriculture and so on may all be visible.

It is not possible in this book to show examples of the interpretation of aerial photographs but the reader is strongly advised to consult Transport and Road Research Laboratory Report LR369 which comments on several interesting stereopairs. New developments in the field of aerial photography include multi-spectral, infrared, colour, false colour and radar imagery and these are becoming available taken from both aircraft and satellites. They can make interpretation much easier in some cases.

3.4 Geological maps and memoirs

Geology was discussed briefly in Chapter 2. This was not intended to do any more than explain some of the concepts and terms used by geologists and hopefully to whet the uninitiated reader's appetite for further reading. One of the important end products of the geologist's work is the geological map and this is probably the single most important source of preliminary information to the geotechnical engineer.

Complete coverage of Great Britain is available at a scale of 1 in to 1 mile (1:63 360) with some recent revisions at 1:50 000. An example of part of one of these maps is shown in Fig. 3.9 and the index, explanation and generalized vertical sections are shown

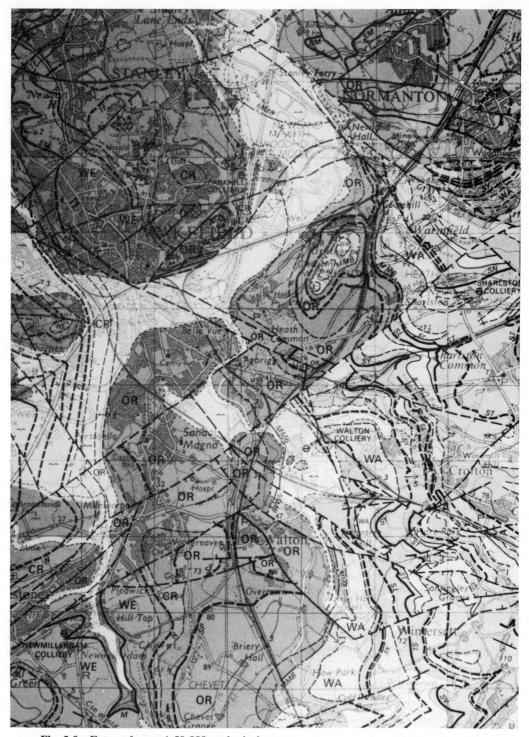

Fig. 3.9 Extract from a 1:50 000 geological map.

44

in Fig. 3.10. It can be seen that these maps give a good idea of the structure and type of materials occurring in a particular locality. 'Solid' and 'drift' editions are generally available. The 'solid' editions show the bedrock types only whereas the 'drift' maps show the nature and distribution of glacial, alluvial and other recent materials in addition to the solid geology.

The 6 in to 1 mile sheets contain much more detailed information and even include brief details of deep boreholes and wells. To accompany the maps there are the thirteen *Handbooks of British Regional Geology* for England and Wales and five for Scotland which describe the general geology of each region (see Fig. 2.8). For more detail there are memoirs available for many of the 'one inch' sheets which go into much more detail (see Fig. 3.11). In addition to the published information the Institute of Geological Sciences has a great deal of unpublished information in the form of notes, field maps and so on which may be consulted at their London, Leeds, Exeter, Edinburgh and Belfast regional offices. They also have limited mapping on such topics as geotechnical engineering, engineering geology, geophysics, environmental conditions, hydrology and industrial minerals.

The geological map shows the distribution of geological formations in an area, printed over a topographical base map. Information is given on lithology (the types of rocks present), on stratigraphy (the way in which the rocks were successively laid down) and on the structure (dips, faults and so on). Where the boundary between adjacent formations is known it is shown on the map as a continuous line. Where the boundary is uncertain it is shown as a broken line and such boundaries may be over a kilometre from their true position in certain cases. A section showing the succession of the various geological strata is provided in the margin of the map and a key is given for the structural and topographical data. The succession of rocks is divided into the geological formations on the basis of differences in age and type as discussed in Chapter 2.

Although every effort is made to make the maps accurate this can not always be guaranteed since geological mapping is a complex process and in some areas it has to be done with less than desirable amounts of field information. It must also be stressed that variability is encountered in the nature of the rocks within any geological formation and the information given on the map should be treated with some caution. For instance, the London Clay may contain sand beds or a Carboniferous Sandstone may contain mudstone bands. The memoirs or handbooks will probably contain discussion on the sort of variations that are known to occur. A typical cross section is usually provided on the smaller scale maps and it is often constructive to draw one for the 6 in to 1 mile map when it is necessary to obtain a picture of the stratigraphy and structure.

Dips are shown on the maps; the point of the arrow being at the position where the dip was recorded. The arrow points in the direction of the dip of the strata and the number adjacent to it is the angle of dip to the horizontal in degrees. Dip is important since it represents the plane on which the beds were laid down and can often be a natural

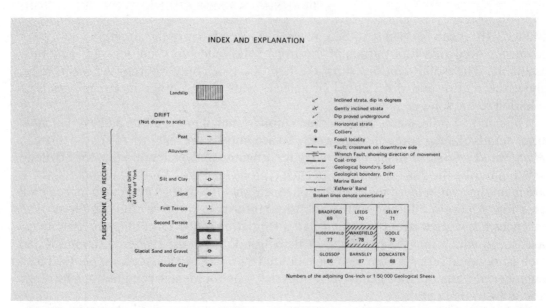

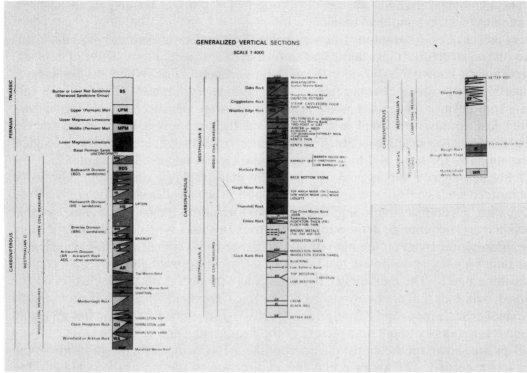

Fig. 3.10 Index, explanation and generalized vertical section for the 1:50 000 geological map.

plane of weakness. If the dip is with the slope of the ground and there are soft materials on the bedding planes then there may well be a risk of sliding especially if excavations are made into the slope. Bedding planes are often zones along which groundwater moves.

Faults are planes within the strata on which there have been differential movements (see Fig. 2.4) and are shown with ticks on the downthrow side. Where the line of a fault is uncertain it is shown by a broken line. It is normally only the relatively major faults which are shown on the maps and it must be recognized that many minor ones may exist which are not shown. It must also be recognized that major faults may exist as quite wide zones rather than planes and these zones often contain soft material, and may also be zones of groundwater flow. A fault may displace rocks with poor foundation properties against more favourable ones. This might produce problems of differential settlement in the supports for a structure. Where mining occurs across the line of or up to a fault this can cause exaggerated and unpredictable movement at the surface. In parts of the world where there is seismic activity it is very unwise to build structures across faults; for example across the San Andreas fault in California.

Glacial deposits comprise highly variable unsorted materials left behind by the melting of the ice sheets which at some stage or another have covered large areas of the earth's surface. The composition of the materials reflects the nature of the rocks over which the ice sheets moved. Where the rocks were soft the glacial materials will be clayey but where they were hard sand and boulders will predominate. The nature of the deposit also varies depending on which part of the glacier it originated from (see Fig. 2.11). Fluvioglacial deposits resulted from the deposition of materials by glacial meltwater and can comprise boulders, sands and gravels, silts or laminated clays. Head deposits represent material which has moved down slopes often as a result of periglacial freezing and thawing. This process is known as solifluction. Both the glaciers themselves and their meltwaters cut deep channels through the countryside and these may be filled with alluvial materials (see Fig. 1.1). Flows of water in some rivers were often considerably greater in the past when sand and gravel terraces were laid down at levels above the present day flood-plain level.

Other features which should be noted on the geological maps include springs and sumps, swallow holes, potholes and landslips. Springs occur where water, passing through a permeable formation, encounters an impermeable one and flows along its surface to emerge at ground level (see Fig. 1.1). Sumps are essentially the opposite effect where flows of water disappear into the ground. Potholes originated as groundwater dissolved away the rock and formed cavities, sometimes these collapsed and the depression at the ground was infilled. These are known as swallow holes and can be difficult to locate. Old landslips are extremely important since even small engineering works might produce a change in their circumstances and reactivate large-scale movement.

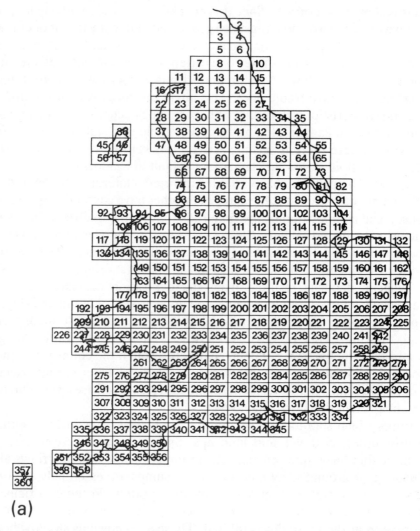

(a)

Fig. 3.11 (a) Index map to the 1:63 360 and the 1:50 000 Geological Survey Maps of England and Wales and to the 1:63 360 Maps of the Soil Survey of England and Wales. (b) Index map to the 1:63 360 and the 1:50 000 Geological Survey Maps of Scotland and Northern Ireland and to the 1:63 360 Maps of the Soil Survey of Scotland.

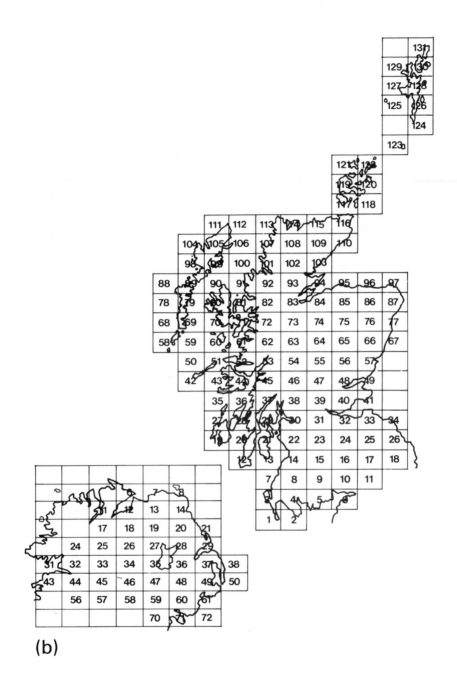

(b)

49

In areas where no geological maps are available it may be necessary to carry out full-scale geological mapping but the extent of this will depend on how much information it has been possible to obtain during the desk study.

3.5   Soil Survey of Great Britain

The Soil Survey of Great Britain deals with the agricultural classification of soils and is only really concerned with materials in the top 1.0–1.5 m which are affected by vegetation and weathering. However, these surface materials often reflect the nature of the deeper layers from which they were formed and the maps can therefore be a useful source of information to the geotechnical engineer; particularly those maps where hand augering has been used to examine the soils present. The soil groups shown on the maps reflect geology, drainage, land forms and chemical and physical properties and the maps usually contain a brief description of each group. Limited coverage is available at a scale of 1:63 360 or 1:50 000 together with special mapping areas and some memoirs. An example of a specially mapped area is shown in Fig. 3.12.

The unit used to describe soils for mapping is the soil profile, the vertical section from the surface to a depth of 1.0–1.5 m. It usually has some visible stratification, and such strata are called horizons. These are identified by colour, texture, stoniness, structure and consistence. The character of the soil can be inferred from the horizons. For instance, uniformly brown horizons mean a well-aerated soil with good internal drainage. Slight mottling usually with rusty or grey colours on an otherwise uniformly coloured background suggest imperfect drainage while dull greys indicate waterlogging and very poor drainage. Texture reflects the particle size distribution. Gley soil is the term given to indicate poor drainage, and this is usually accompanied by mottling. A loam is a well-drained soil with modest amounts of clay or silt and is favourable for agricultural purposes. Surface soils tend not to have well-defined boundaries but the maps can nevertheless be most useful in indicating the parent material and drainage.

3.6   Land use and planning maps

National land utilization survey maps for Great Britain are available at a scale of 1:25 000. These show residential settlements, industry, transport, derelict land, open spaces, grass, arable land, market gardens, orchards, woodlands, heaths, moorland, rough land, water, marshes, unvegetated land, dunes, the sites of the extractive industries and active tips. Agricultural land classification maps may give an indication of land values and engineering characteristics. In the UK these are available at a scale of 1:63 360.

Planning maps may also be useful and there are many different types available, both nationally and at local level. Some of the features shown on the maps which might be of

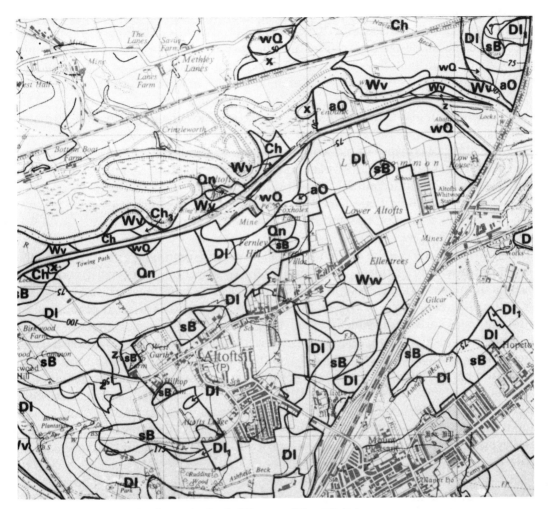

Fig. 3.12 Example of mapping by Soil Survey of Great Britain.

interest to the geotechnical engineer are power lines, pipelines, agricultural land, peat, conservation areas, green belts, uplands, steep slopes, mineral reserves, mining subsidences, flood plains and so on. Of more definite interest are the plans concerned with mineral resources such as sand and gravel, minerals, coal, building stones, ironstones, evaporites, oil, gas and water.

3.7 Other sources of information

All manner of materials have been removed from the surface of the earth either by

51

excavation or by deep mining and the geotechnical engineer must be aware of the drastic consequences these may have on proposed works. Shallow workings often necessitate special design precautions and the costs of dealing with unforeseen mining activity can be substantial. A 1:625 000 map of Great Britain is available showing areas of known mining activity. The aspects of mining which are of concern are listed below.

(1) Presence of old workings existing as cavities which might be susceptible to collapse.
(2) The effect of collapse of old workings on the strata above.
(3) The presence of old shafts which may not have been properly infilled.
(4) The effects of future mining and subsidence.
(5) The presence of infilled surface excavations and underground cavities.
(6) The presence of spoil tips and silt lagoons.

If an investigation is to be carried out in a known area of mining activity it is prudent to consult a mining engineer, a mineral agent or some other specialist about past, present or future workings. A typical plan relating to coal workings is shown in Fig. 3.13 and this illustrates some of the features of importance. It is wise to obtain mining information as early as possible in the investigation since it may well affect the type of subsequent investigation that needs to be carried out. The National Coal Board have a great many records of shafts and old workings and will supply this information to interested parties but it must be remembered that a great deal of mining activity took place before any records were kept and that some of the records that do exist may not be accurate. The Health and Safety Executive have records of workings other than for coal and these include non-metalliferous minerals such as chalk, flint, limestone, sandstone and gypsum; metallic ores such as iron, tin, lead, zinc, fluorspar and barytes; salt and potash.

The regional water authorities may be able to provide information on the hydrological or hydrogeological aspects of a site. On the hydrological side they will have records of drainage patterns, rainfall and flooding whilst on the hydrogeological side they may have results of their own investigations, details of wells, permeabilities, abstraction rates, rock structure and so on.

Where works are positioned near estuaries, harbours or other coastal areas the appropriate Admiralty chart can be invaluable. These give details of soundings, the topography and composition of the bottom, the positions of mud flats and sand banks and the high and low water levels. They also show navigation channels, navigation aids, moorings, wrecks and submarine utilities such as power cables and pipelines.

Local authority archives may be able to provide a sight of old maps, planning maps, local historical records and rating records. Local libraries usually have a considerable amount of historical material and photographs which can be useful in determining the

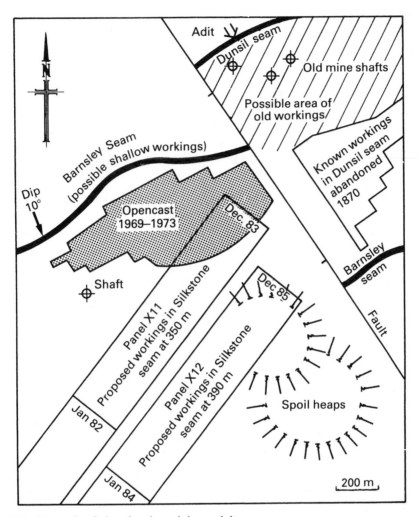

Fig. 3.13 Example of plan showing mining activity.

former use of a site. Some authorities keep libraries of site investigation reports as do the Institute of Geological Sciences. A start has been made on a National Registry of Ground Investigation Reports by the Construction Industry Research Association.

The statutory undertakers such as electricity, water, gas, telephone and sewage boards are important not merely from the point of view of ensuring that boreholes do not damage their apparatus but also from the point of view of the records they may have. They often retain details of their own site investigations and sometimes keep construction records of trenches they have dug.

3.8 Site reconnaissance and local enquiries

Having reviewed all the data obtained from the sources described in the preceding sections the engineer should then make a thorough inspection of the site and its surroundings. This should be done on foot and enquiries made of any long-term residents when he pauses for refreshment in the local public house. It is important that the inspection is made armed with topographical and geological maps, aerial photographs and so on since this will enable cross checks to be made and any peculiarities investigated. The engineer should also take with him a base map on which to record his observations, notebook, clinometer, hand lens, compass, camera, geological hammer and knife. He may also wish to take a spade, hand auger and sampling bags since even digging down to just below topsoil level can reveal a lot about the types of material present and their distribution.

Long-standing residents of an area can often recall extremely useful observations but their information must be regarded with caution since memories dim and their recollections may be highly subjective and unscientific. Residents can usually remember past uses of a site and they may know the positions of wells, shafts, springs, areas of flooding, old workings and so on. They may even be able to remember excavations they have seen or construction difficulties but local names given to materials and other features can be misleading.

In his walk across the site the engineer should look at the topography and drainage and look for evidence of the materials present, their distribution and their properties. He should record any differences or omissions from his plans and should look for springs, seepages, sink-holes, wet ground and marshy vegetation. He should examine rock or soil exposures on or near the site and record visible structure, dips and so on. He should look at excavations and stream banks and be aware of possible clues as to any former use of the site such as old foundations and spoil. He should try and delineate areas of peat whether it be hill peat or peat associated with alluvial valleys. He should look for evidence of swallow holes, effects of past subsidence such as cracked buildings, old shafts and old mineral workings. He should record slope angles and look for any sign of instability since this can have such a major influence on the proposed use of a site. Some of the features associated with landslides and unstable slopes are shown in Fig. 3.14 which include bent trees, tension cracks, scars and hummocky ground. He should also look at surrounding developments and perhaps enquire into their construction and whether or not a site investigation report is available. Finally the engineer should take photographs to illustrate the general site and any special features. Figure 3.15 from BS5930 forms a useful check list for the engineer engaged on a site reconnaissance.

With all the information so far gained the engineer should then draw up a geotechnical map to record his observations. The geotechnical map should be based on a detailed land survey showing details of access, services, drainage, existing site use,

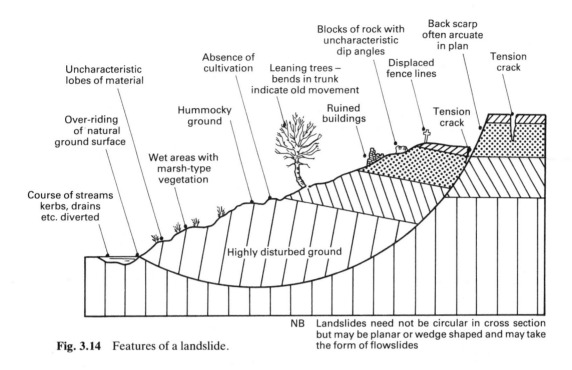

Fig. 3.14 Features of a landslide.

NB Landslides need not be circular in cross section but may be planar or wedge shaped and may take the form of flowslides

existing structures, adjoining property and the positions of survey markers. Hydrological and hydrographical information can also be included where necessary with details of catchment areas, river and stream flows, flood levels, erosion features, marine conditions, dunes, cliffs and so on as appropriate. Climatic information where required can be recorded in the margin. The geotechnical information should include details of the geology and geomorphology with details of slope angles, unstable ground, exposures, wet areas and so on. The map might also show details of materials for use in the construction process and these include topsoil, fill, aggregates, stone and water. In 1972 a working party of the Engineering Group of the Geological Society put forward proposals for the presentation of geological and geotechnical information on maps and their report was published in the *Quarterly Journal of Engineering Geology* **5** (4). Some of the more commonly used symbols recommended for use on engineering geology maps and sections are shown in Fig. 3.16 although there are many more in the report, which also contains a number of practical examples. Such maps are extremely useful and often essential. However, the working party emphasized that the availability of an engineering geological map in no way provides a substitute for detailed site investigations for important developments.

Figure 3.17 is taken from BS5930 and presents a useful checklist of the general information required from a desk study.

Notes on site reconnaissance

1 Preparatory

(a) Whenever possible, have the following available: site plan, district maps or charts, and geological maps and aerial photographs.

(b) Ensure that permission to gain access has been obtained from both owner and occupier.

(c) Where evidence is lacking at the site or some verification is needed on a particular matter, for example, flood levels or details of changes in site levels, reference should be made to sources of local information such as: Local Authority, Engineer's and Surveyor's Offices, early records and local inhabitants (see appendix B).

2 General information

(a) Traverse whole area, preferably on foot.

(b) Set-out proposed location of work on plans, where appropriate.

(c) Observe and record differences and omissions on plans and maps; for example, boundaries, buildings, roads and transmission lines.

(d) Inspect and record details of existing structures.

(e) Observe and record obstructions; for example, transmission lines, telephone lines, ancient monuments, trees subject to preservation orders, gas and water pipes, electricity cables, sewers.

(f) Check access, including the probable effects of construction traffic and heavy construction loads on existing roads, bridges and services.

(g) Check and note water levels, direction and rate of flow in rivers, streams and canals, and also flood levels and tidal and other fluctuations, where relevant.

(h) Observe and record adjacent property and the likelihood of its being affected by proposed works.

(i) Observe and record mine or quarry workings, old workings, old structures, and any other features which may be relevant.

3 Ground information

(a) Study and record surface features, on site and nearby, preferably in conjunction with geological maps and aerial photographs, noting as follows:

(1) Type and variability of surface conditions.

(2) Comparison of surface lands and topography with previous map records to check for presence of fill, erosion, or cuttings.

(3) Steps in surface which may indicate geological faults or shatter zones. In mining areas, steps in the ground are probably the results of mining subsidence. Other evidence of mining subsidence should be looked for, compression and tensile damage in brickwork, buildings and roads; structures out of plumb; interference with drainage patterns.

(4) Mounds and hummocks in more or less flat country which frequently indicate former glacial conditions; for example, till and glacial gravel.

(5) Broken and terraced ground on hill slopes which may be due to landslips; small steps and inclined tree trunks can be evidence of creep.

(6) Crater-like holes in chalk or limestone country which usually indicate swallow holes filled with soft material.

(7) Low-lying flat areas in hill country which may be sites of former lakes and may indicate presence of soft silty soils and peat.

(b) Inspect and record details of ground conditions in quarries, cuttings and escarpments, on site and nearby.

(c) Assess and record, where relevant, ground water level or levels (often different from water course and lake levels), positions of wells and springs, and occurrence of artesian flow.

(d) Study and note the nature of vegetation in relation to the soil type and to the wetness of the soil (all indications require confirmation by further investigation). Unusual green patches, reeds, rushes, willow trees and poplars usually indicate wet ground conditions.

(e) Study embankments, buildings and other structures in the vicinity having a settlement history.

4 Site inspection for ground investigation

(a) Inspect and record location and conditions of access to working sites.

(b) Observe and record obstructions, such as power cables, telephone lines, boundary fences and trenches.

(c) Locate and record areas for depot, offices, sample storage, field laboratories.

(d) Ascertain and record ownership of working sites, where appropriate.

(e) Consider liability to pay compensation for damage caused.

(f) Locate a suitable water supply where applicable and record location and estimated flow.

(g) Record particulars of lodgings and local labour, as appropriate.

(h) Record particulars of local telephone, employment, transport and other services.

Fig. 3.15 Notes on site reconnaissance (from BS5930:1981).

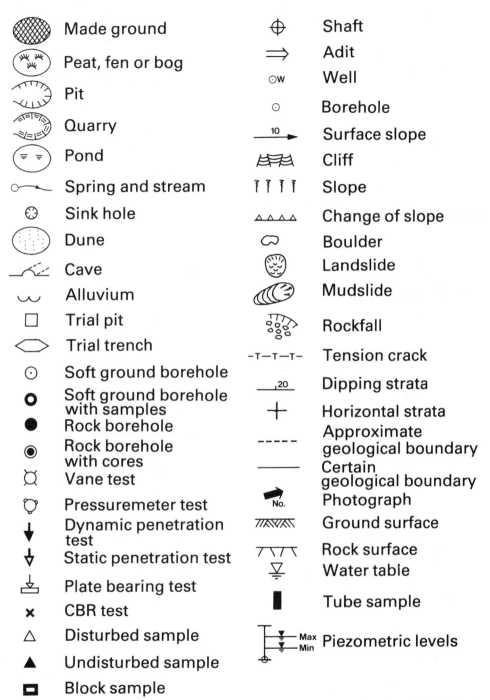

Made ground		Shaft	
Peat, fen or bog		Adit	
Pit		Well	
Quarry		Borehole	
Pond		Surface slope	
Spring and stream		Cliff	
Sink hole		Slope	
Dune		Change of slope	
Cave		Boulder	
Alluvium		Landslide	
Trial pit		Mudslide	
Trial trench		Rockfall	
Soft ground borehole		Tension crack	
Soft ground borehole with samples		Dipping strata	
Rock borehole		Horizontal strata	
Rock borehole with cores		Approximate geological boundary	
Vane test		Certain geological boundary	
Pressuremeter test		Photograph	
Dynamic penetration test		Ground surface	
Static penetration test		Rock surface	
Plate bearing test		Water table	
CBR test		Tube sample	
Disturbed sample		Piezometric levels	
Undisturbed sample			
Block sample			

Fig. 3.16 Abbreviated list of symbols used on geotechnical maps and sections. For full details see *Quarterly Journal of Engineering Geology* (1972), **5** (no. 4) which gives additional symbols to cover topography, boreholes, rock structure and geophysics together with examples of their use.

General information required for desk study

1 General land survey

(a) Location of site on published maps and charts.

(b) Air survey, where appropriate.

(c) Site boundaries, outlines of structures and building lines.

(d) Ground contours and natural drainage features.

(e) Above ground obstructions to view and flying, for example, transmission lines.

(f) Indications of obstructions below ground.

(g) Records of differences and omissions in relation to published maps.

(h) Position of survey stations and bench marks (the latter with reduced levels).

(i) Meteorological information.

2 Permitted use and restrictions

(a) Planning and statutory restrictions applying to the particular areas under the Town and Country Planning Acts administered by appropriate Planning Authorities.

(b) Local authority regulations on planning restrictions, listed buildings and building bye-laws.

(c) Board of Trade regulations governing issue of industrial development certificates.

(d) Rights of light, support and way including any easements.

(e) Tunnels; mine workings, abandoned, active and proposed; mineral rights.

(f) Ancient monuments; burial grounds, etc.

3 Approaches and access (including temporary access for construction purposes)

(a) Road (check ownership).

(b) Railway (check for closures).

(c) By water.

(d) By air.

4 Ground conditions

(a) Geological maps.

(b) Geological memoirs.

(c) Flooding, erosion, landslide and subsidence history.

(d) Data held by central and local authorities.

(e) Construction and investigation records of adjacent sites.

(f) Seismicity.

5 Sources of material for construction

(a) Natural materials.

(b) Tips and waste materials.

(c) Imported materials.

6 Drainage and sewerage

(a) Names of sewerage, land drainage and other authorities concerned and by-laws.

(b) Location and levels of existing systems (including fields, drains and ditches), showing sizes of pipes, and whether foul, storm-water or combined.

(c) Existing flow quantities and capacity for additional flow.

(d) Liability to surcharging.

(e) Charges for drainage facilities.

(f) Neighbouring streams capable of taking sewage or trade effluents provided they are purified to the required standard.

(g) Disposal of solid waste.

(h) Flood risk:
    (1) to proposed works
    (2) caused by proposed works.

7 Water supply

(a) Names of authorities concerned and bye-laws.

(b) Location, sizes and depths of mains.

(c) Pressure characteristics of mains.

(d) Water analysis.

(e) Availability of water for additional requirements.

(f) Storage requirements.

(g) Water source for fire fighting.

(h) Charges for connections and water.

(i) Possible additional sources of water.

(j) Water rights and responsibilities under the Water Resources Act 1963, which controls permissions to take water from any natural source.

8 Electricity supply

(a) Names of supply authorities concerned and regulations.

(b) Location, capacity and depth of mains.

(c) The voltage, phases and frequency.

(d) Capacity to supply additional requirements.

(e) Transformer requirements.

(f) Charges for installation and current.

9 Gas supply

(a) Names of supply authorities concerned and regulations.

(b) Location, sizes and depths of mains.

(c) Type of gas, thermal quality and pressure.

(d) Capacity to supply additional requirements.

(e) Charges for installation and gas.

10 Telephone

(a) Address of local office.

(b) Location of existing lines.

(c) GPO requirements.

(d) Charges for installation.

11 Heating

(a) Availability of fuel supplies.

(b) Planning restrictions (smokeless zone; Clean Air Act 1956 administered by local authorities).

(c) District heating.

Fig. 3.17 Information required for a desk study (from BS5930:1981).

4

Site investigation equipment and methods

4.1 Introduction

This chapter is intended as a brief guide to the most appropriate form of investigation. Once the desk study and preliminary investigations are complete there should be a clear indication of the type of information that is required and a rough idea of the likely soils, rocks and groundwater regimes that might be encountered. Armed with this information and a knowledge of the proposed works the engineer should then select the plant and equipment he is to use in the field such that he will obtain the fullest possible picture of the soils and rocks present, their distribution and their properties. The investigation should be carried out economically and with the minimum amount of disturbance.

The following points should be considered:

(1) The scope of the proposed works.
(2) The amount of existing information.
(3) The probable nature of the ground and its potential variability.
(4) The possible groundwater regimes.
(5) The type of samples required.
(6) The type of *in situ* and laboratory testing required.
(7) The availability of plant and equipment and its appropriateness to the site and the proposed works.
(8) The cost of the investigation.
(9) The capabilities of each item of equipment.

(10) The manpower requirements in terms of operation, supervision and levels of skill required.

(11) The topography of the site, access limitations, obstructions and any necessary temporary works.

(12) The need for ancillary plant e.g. compressors, water carts and excavators.

(13) Form of reinstatement and minimization of damages.

The chapter gives a brief description of the methods available, their applications and their limitations, which should enable a preliminary selection to be made. The most common methods in use (i.e. shell and auger boring and rotary coring) are considered in some depth in later chapters; the other methods will also be covered although not in as much detail since shell and auger boring and rotary core drilling are used in over 90% of all current site investigation fieldwork in the UK.

4.2 Trial pitting (Fig. 4.1)

4.2.1 Brief description

Trial pits up to 5 m deep can be quickly and cheaply dug using a hydraulic backacter. If access for personnel is required temporary supports will be necessary or use made of battered sides. The excavators can be wheel mounted or mounted on caterpillar tracks for access to difficult sites.

4.2.2 General application

Pits are useful for preliminary investigations in overburden or made ground when ten or more can be completed in a day. Trial pits permit a visual assessment of *in situ* ground conditions and reveal a greater proportion of the ground strata than a conventional borehole. They can also reveal the orientation of joints and bedding planes in weak rocks and the degree of variability. The pits can be extended into trenches to follow or cross particular features of interest such as faults. Hand-dug pits are often essential in locating services prior to drilling.

4.2.3 Sampling and *in situ* testing

Disturbed samples can be readily obtained from the bucket. Sample tubes can be hand driven in supported trial pits or they can be pushed in by the machine. *In situ* vane tests, penetrometer tests and plate bearing tests, either vertically or horizontally can be performed at various stages as the hole is dug. Simple soakaway tests can be carried out and block samples can be cut from the sides.

Fig. 4.1 Mechanical excavator. JCB 3CX wheeled backacter (photograph: JCB Ltd).

4.2.4 Limitations

Very loose materials can cave in and excavations below the water table are difficult if not impossible. Excavation is not practical in hard rocks although trial pits are useful in defining 'rock head'. Trial pits cause a considerable degree of ground disturbance and should not be left open and unprotected. It is not safe to enter deep trial pits that are not properly supported.

Further details of trial pitting are given in Chapter 5.

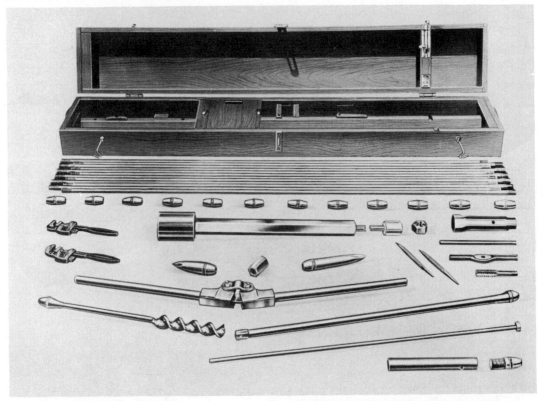

Fig. 4.2 Mackintosh probing apparatus (photograph: Engineering Laboratory Equipment Ltd).

4.3 Probing (Fig.4.2)

4.3.1 Brief description

In its simplest form a sharpened steel rod or one with a bullet shaped tip is pushed or hammered into the ground. A variety of small samplers, augers and probe heads have been developed but have only limited use. Some measure of the strength can be obtained by counting the number of blows required to drive the probe into the ground and comparing the results with known conditions.

4.3.2 General application

This is a quick and cheap method of determining the depth to a hard stratum where the overburden is not too strong or too thick. The equipment is easily portable and can be used to profile peat or soft alluvial deposits and also to locate mineshafts where probes might be required on a 1 m or 2 m grid. Petrol driven probes are available which can penetrate much stiffer overburden.

4.3.3 Sampling and *in situ* testing

No satisfactory samples can be taken although 'through flow' heads have been developed which can indicate the type of material at the base of the hole. *In situ* testing is not generally practicable. Probe holes can sometimes be used for groundwater observations and the installation of instrumentation.

4.3.4 Limitations

The apparatus is only usable in soft ground and it can give misleading results where cobbles or boulders are present which might be mistaken for bedrock. It is only really used in conjunction with boreholes or where the general ground conditions are already known.

Probing is covered in more detail in Chapter 5.

4.4 Hand augering (Fig. 4.3)

4.4.1 Brief description

In this method use is made of light, easily portable, hand-operated augers; a variety of which are available to suit differing ground conditions. They give boreholes up to a maximum of about 6 m deep with diameters from 50 mm to 200 mm in diameter.

4.4.2 General application

Hand augering is useful as a fairly quick and cheap method of boring in soft but self supporting deposits. It can be used in remote country where access is difficult or where equipment has to be manhandled. It is useful as a preliminary investigation tool and it can be used for groundwater observations and for installing instrumentation.

4.4.3 Sampling and *in situ* testing

Disturbed samples are available throughout boring and small open-drive sample tubes can be driven in the borehole. Light *in situ* testing equipment can be used down the hole, for example light vane testing apparatus and penetrometers.

4.4.4 Limitations

Casing is not normally used and hence caving ground and water can prevent penetration. Boulders, hard obstructions or very stiff clays can also prevent penetration.

Chapter 5 contains more details on hand augering.

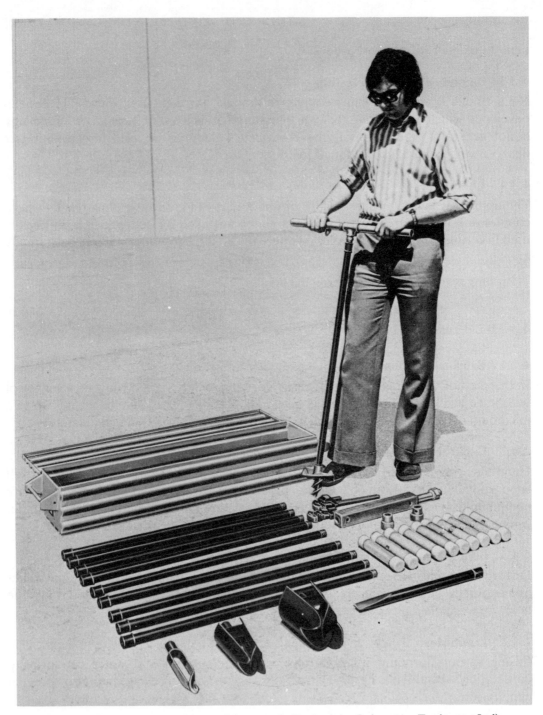

Fig. 4.3 Hand-augering equipment (photograph: Engineering Laboratory Equipment Ltd).

64

Fig. 4.4 Pilcon Wayfarer 1500 shell and auger (or cable percussion) drilling rig with boring and sampling tools (photograph: Pilcon Engineering Ltd).

4.5 Shell and auger boring (Fig. 4.4)

4.5.1 Brief description

This method uses a simple lightweight rig developed from old well boring techniques and towable by a Land Rover. It consists of a tripod fitted with a diesel powered winch with clutch and brake. The winch is used to lift and drop a variety of tools down the hole which is normally 150–200 mm in diameter. The tools used are chosen to suit the strata and groundwater conditions that are encountered. Sometimes known as 'light cable

65

percussion boring'. Casing can be installed to support caving ground or to seal off groundwater.

4.5.2 General application

This is the most commonly used method for site investigation in the UK. It is extremely versatile and can be successfully used in most soils and overburden materials above or below the water table. Depths of up to 60 m can be achieved in the right soils. Weak rocks or obstructions can be 'chiselled' and rotary coring attachments for hard rocks can be driven from a power take-off. The rig is light enough to be winched across poor ground.

4.5.3 Sampling and *in situ* testing

In addition to continuous disturbed sampling, 'undisturbed' 100 mm diameter samples can be obtained and standard penetration tests carried out using a 140 lb hammer. The borehole can be used for a wide range of *in situ* tests, instrumentation can be installed and groundwater observations made.

4.5.4 Limitations

The operation of the rig demands skill in its use and some care is needed in obtaining representative and undisturbed samples. The rig demands about 6 m of headroom and should not be erected near overhead power lines. Some fine material can be lost in boring granular deposits below the water table and piping needs to be controlled by the addition of water.

Chapter 6 is devoted to shell and auger boring.

4.6 Rotary core drilling (Fig. 4.5)

4.6.1 Brief description

In this system drill rods are mechanically rotated and the rotation is transmitted to the drilling bit (usually diamond or tungsten carbide tipped) at the bottom of the borehole. The rig also applies pressure to the bit. The rods may either pass through a rotating mechanical chuck or they may be rotated from the top by a hydraulic motor. The bit is lubricated and cuttings are brought to the surface by use of a flushing medium (mud, air, water or foam). The core of rock so cut is retained in a core barrel and is then brought to the surface for examination and testing.

4.6.2 General application

This is the normal method of rock exploration and a wide variety of rigs exist from

Fig. 4.5 Edeco stratadrill chuck type rotary coring rig, lorry, mounted and with integral high pressure drill pump (photograph: English Drilling Equipment Co. Ltd).

lightweight skid-mounted rigs to heavy rigs erected on site using a crane. There are many types of drilling bits available for different types of rock and, depending on the rig chosen, holes of several hundred metres can be drilled.

4.6.3 Sampling and *in situ* testing
With the right drilling techniques 100% core recovery is possible and the rock core can be logged and tested as required. A variety of *in situ* tests can be carried out in the hole that is formed.

4.6.4 Limitations
Casing will be needed in unstable ground to keep the hole open. Considerable experience is needed in choosing bit type, amount of flushing medium, speed of rotation, bit pressure and so on to obtain good core recovery. Where soft and hard

67

rocks alternate, the softer material (which is usually the most critical to the engineer) may be lost. Access on to difficult sites may be a problem with the larger rigs. If rotary core drilling is started too soon in weak rock valuable samples may be lost.

Rotary core drilling is covered in detail in Chapter 7.

4.7   Rotary percussive and openhole drilling (Fig. 4.6)

4.7.1   Brief description

Rotary percussive type drills are often to be seen in quarrying and blasting operations. They can be crawler, lorry or tractor mounted and use compressed air as the flushing medium. The hammering action can be applied at the top of the drill string or at the bottom using a 'down the hole' hammer. The drill bits can be button bits or shaped 'drill steels'. They are sometimes known as jack hammers or wagon drills. Non-coring rock roller bits can be used on conventional rotary coring machines to produce a straightforward open hole with either air or water flush.

4.7.2   General application

The above methods form a very quick and cheap means of sinking holes in rock and are often used in the search for old mine workings where a large number of holes on a grid spacing is required to locate cavities. A rough idea of the strata being penetrated is obtained from the rate of penetration and the nature and colour of the small chippings produced.

4.7.3   Sampling and *in situ* testing

As stated above the only samples obtained are dust and very small chippings but a variety of *in situ* tests can be performed in the hole produced.

4.7.4   Limitations

The sampling can only give a broad picture of the strata being penetrated. Noise may be a problem and dust suppression is normally required. In ground which is not self supporting casing is needed and this can add considerably to the cost. Moisture in the borehole can produce 'balling' of the ground-up rock and it may then be necessary to resort to water flushing. To obtain maximum information the full-time attendance of an engineer or geologist is necessary.

Fig. 4.6 Halcotrack 400C rotary percussive drilling rig (photograph: Halifax Tool Co. Ltd).

4.8 Mechanical augering (Fig. 4.7)

4.8.1 Brief description

In this process a mechanical rotary rig drives an auger which may have a solid or a hollow stem. The solid stem produces purely disturbed samples but the hollow stem auger can either give a continuous semi-disturbed sample or can be used to admit sampling tubes or *in situ* testing apparatus. The rig is normally lorry mounted.

69

Fig. 4.7 CME-75 rotary drilling rig showing flight augering (photograph: Christensen Diamond Products Ltd).

4.8.2   General application

The method is fast in cohesive soils and if a continuous sample is obtained this can be very ueful in detecting minor changes in soil type e.g. thin lenses of sand. Typical auger sizes are 150 mm to 250 mm in diamter and depths of 50 metres can be achieved in the right ground. In self supporting ground a short solid auger can be raised to the surface to remove the soil. If rock is encountered boring can be extended using small diameter diamond core drilling through the hollow stem.

4.8.3   Sampling and *in situ* testing

Disturbed samples are available throughout and a variety of other tests can be performed through the hollow stem, e.g. standard penetration and vane tests. In addition, sample tubes can be driven through the hollow stem.

4.8.4   Limitations

Problems occur using this rig in cohesionless soils particularly below the water table or where obstructions or boulders occur. The rig tends to be heavy because of the high power needed and access on soft ground can be difficult. Precise identification of changes in strata is difficult whilst augering is in progress. Water observations can be precluded if the ground caves in after removal of the auger since casing is not normally used.

Further discussion on mechanical augering is given in Section 7.12.

4.9   *In situ* testing (Fig. 4.8)

4.9.1   Sounding

A number of tests exist (e.g. Dutch cone test) which can assess the strength of soils. In static tests the force required to drive in a probe is measured and in dynamic tests the number of blows required to drive the probe are measured. These tests may also be termed penetration tests or probing.

4.9.2   Vane testing

The torque required to turn a cruciform vane in soft or firm clays can be used to assess the shear strength of a soil.

4.9.3   Pressuremeter testing

A probe is inserted into soils or weak rocks and the pressure required to expand it laterally is measured. The deformation characteristics of the ground are also measured.

Fig. 4.8 Pilcon 10 000 kg Dutch cone penetrometer, fully self-contained with rods, cones and ground anchors, own engine and hydraulics, powered ground anchor spanner shown in foreground (photograph: Pilcon Engineering Ltd).

4.9.4 Loading tests

These can be carried out on any soils or rocks at ground level, in pits or in boreholes. A plate or probe is loaded and its penetration into the ground measured. Plate bearing tests, *in situ* California Bearing Ratio tests and pile load tests are all examples.

4.9.5 Pore pressure probes

A probe is steadily pushed into soft or loose deposits and the water pressure in the pores of the soil is measured.

4.9.6 Permeability tests

A wide range of tests exist in which flows or head losses of water in boreholes are used to assess the ease with which water can flow through soils or rocks.

4.9.7 Field density tests

The density of soils or weak rocks can be determined by weighing the amount of soil removed from a measured volume.

4.9.8 Stress measurements

The state of stress in the ground may be measured using strain gauges, photoelastic discs, hydraulic cells or various loading techniques.

4.9.9 Shear tests

In these tests the force required to shear off a block of soil or rock is measured.

4.9.10 Other *in situ* tests

Physical properties of soils or rocks can be measured in boreholes using geophysical techniques e.g. temperature, resistivity, density, dynamic modulus and absorption of gamma rays.

Chapters 8 and 12 contain further details on the techniques described above.

4.10 Instrumentation (Fig. 4.9)

In order to understand more fully the behaviour of particular soils and rocks, instruments can be installed in boreholes or incorporated in large-scale field trials. A number of the more common ones are listed below.

4.10.1 Piezometers

Since the shear strength of a soil largely depends on the pressure of water in its pores these instruments measure these pressures *in situ* and can be used to monitor changes in

Fig. 4.9 Hydraulic piezometer read-out unit showing de-airing apparatus (photograph: Geotechnical Instruments Ltd).

pore pressure beneath embankments induced by filling operations. They can also be used to measure *in situ* permeability.

4.10.2   Earth pressure cells
Soils transmit pressures in a number of ways depending on their properties and pressure cells can be installed in the ground or in backfill to study these effects. They may also be installed beneath or adjacent to structures.

4.10.3   Inclinometers
These indicate lateral movements in the ground and can be used to monitor movements in landslides or measure the response of soils to applied loads.

4.10.4   Settlement gauges
These essentially measure the vertical deformation of soils as loads are applied to them. The deformation is linked to water being squeezed out of the soils and can be related to pore pressures.

Chapter 11 is devoted to instrumentation.

Fig. 4.10 Signal enhancement seismograph (photograph: Engineering Laboratory Equipment Ltd).

4.11 Geophysics (Fig. 4.10)

This is very much a specialized subject but given the right sort of ground conditions it can be used to give a cheap and rapid means of detecting anomalies or variations in strata across a site or between boreholes. All the methods depend on measuring variations in certain physical properties of the soils or rock and work best when there is a clear-cut contrast between them. A number of specialist techniques for overwater investigation also exist. The main types of geophysical investigation are listed below.

4.11.1 Resistivity

In this method electric current is passed into the ground through electrodes and the potential difference is measured between two other electrodes. Variations in electrical resistivity can then be measured both vertically and laterally by varying the electrode arrangement. The variations may then indicate the changes in strata.

4.11.2 Seismic

Shock waves travel through different materials at different speeds and if differences can be detected an interpretation can be made as to stratification. The technique measures the speed of travel to a number of points (geophones) from a source of shock waves which may be produced by a hammer or by explosives.

4.11.3 Gravimetric

A very precisely positioned and levelled instrument is used to measure the earth's gravitational field to a high degree of accuracy. Changes from place to place may indicate major faults or hidden mine shafts.

4.11.4 Magnetic

Different rocks exhibit different degrees of magnetism within the earth's magnetic field and in suitable circumstances these differences can be detected but it must be remembered that metal objects, pipelines and cables can also produce variations in the earth's magnetic field.

These methods are only really useful when there are strong anomalies or where no more than two or three different strata exist which have markedly different physical properties. Because of the complexity of the analysis of results and the risk of misinterpretation geophysics should be confirmed by physical borings. The geophysical contrasts on which the methods rely may not match engineering contrasts and multiple layers or transition zones can give rise to insurmountable problems.

Chapter 12 covers the use of geophysical techniques.

4.12 Other methods

4.12.1 Shafts and adits

Trial pits can be extended into shafts or adits dug into the ground. This is usually done by hand and is therefore expensive.

4.12.2 Wash boring

This is a rarely used method in which a pipe is surged into overburden whilst jetting large quantities of water down it. The water returns can indicate the general soil type being penetrated but no reliable samples can be obtained.

4.12.3 Calyx or shot drilling

This is likewise rarely used and is an inefficient rotary coring technique which cuts the rock by feeding hard steel shot to the end of a hollow, rotating cylinder.

4.12.4 Becker drill

A heavy diesel hammer is used to drive double-wall drive pipes into overburden which can then be removed using powerful jacks.

4.12.5 Field trials

To understand more fully the behaviour of the ground a large-scale field trial can be carried out which simulates the actual engineering works proposed. In order to make the most of the trial the site should be fully instrumented to measure the soil's response to the applied loads. Boreholes might be required in which to install the instruments. In this way ground movements, stresses and pore pressures can be measured. Trial embankments and excavations, pile tests, ground anchor tests, tunnel drives, grouting trials, blasting trials and so on are all examples and careful observation is the key to obtaining the maximum amount of information (see also Section 12.5).

5

Trial pitting, hand augering and probing

5.1 The use of trial pits in site investigation

Trial pits are sometimes looked upon as the poor relation in site investigation and some engineers tend to think only in terms of boreholes when in fact a great deal more can often be learnt from a trial pit. It is true that trial pits are limited in the depth they can reach and that they preclude certain types of *in situ* testing. They are also limited if the ground tends to cave in or if there are large inflows of groundwater. Nevertheless they do have a very important role to play in site investigation and many minor investigations, for say housing, can be successfully accomplished without resorting to boreholes at all. Even on large investigations they can provide information which would be difficult to obtain in any other way and it is probably true to say that there are very few investigations which cannot economically incorporate trial-pit excavations. Some of the particular uses to which trial pits can be put are listed below.

(1) The visual inspection of *in situ* soil conditions.
(2) The detailed examination of soil variability, structure and weathering profile.
(3) The observation of water seepage and its measurement.
(4) The carrying out of large-scale soakaway tests.
(5) The search for geological or archaeological features or existing foundation details.
(6) The determination of the mode of failure of cuttings, foundations or embankment slopes by locating slip planes for example.
(7) Obtaining low cost detailed coverage of a large site area.
(8) Isolation of geological faults by extending a trial pit into a trench to cross the fault.
(9) Correlation of geophysical survey data with strata horizons.

Fig. 5.1 Track-mounted backacter for the excavation of trial pits.

(10) Assessing the ease of excavation for construction cost estimation and determining rockhead levels.
(11) Carrying out large scale *in situ* tests including plate bearing tests and horizontal loading tests.
(12) Locating services prior to borehole drilling.
(13) Obtaining large bulk samples, block samples or high quality hand-cut specimens.
(14) Assessing the stability of excavations.

Trial-pit excavation by hand may be necessary where access is restricted and this can be expensive if an appreciable depth is required. However, where a wheeled or tracked excavator, such as is shown in Fig. 5.1, can be brought onto site ten or more trial pits to 3 m depth can be dug in a day. This figure would be reduced where it is necessary to carry out *in situ* tests or where undisturbed sampling is required. The cost per metre excavated in the zero to 4 m depth range is substantially less than the cost of shell and auger boring but if greater depths are required or if trench sheeting is needed to support the sides it can be considerably greater. The excavation of trial pits does require the full

79

time attendance of a geotechnical engineer to log and sample the materials present and to carry out any *in situ* testing. It should also be remembered that trial pits produce a considerable zone of disturbance and should not be located directly below say a proposed pad foundation for a column.

5.2 Field techniques for trial pitting

This section covers the equipment required for trial pitting, the recommended field procedures for measurement and logging, basic sampling and simple field testing.

Trial pitting is carried out most economically using a wheeled or tracked backacter and there are many models available for hire. The smaller machines have a depth capability of about 3.5 m whereas some of the larger machines can go down to 7 m but their hire rate is at least twice that of the smaller wheeled machines. The wheeled machines are the easiest to get to the site but where soft, steep or difficult ground is encountered the tracked machines are better even though they have to be brought to the site on a low loader. When hiring a machine for excavation to a fixed depth, 0.5 m should be deducted from the maker's stated reach so that a reasonably flat bottom to the trial pit can be achieved. In assessing the sort of ground that any machine can penetrate obviously the more powerful machines will successfully penetrate much harder materials but the size of the bucket used is also an important factor. The smaller the bucket the harder the ground that can be dug.

Before embarking on a trial-pit investigation all the necessary equipment must be collected together and a suggested check list for this is shown in Fig. 5.2. When planning a trial-pit investigation one of the first considerations is the location of the trial pits in order to obtain the required information. Where there is some tolerance in this each location should be chosen such that crop damage or disturbance by either the trial pit itself or by the access to it is kept to a minimum. Having chosen the locations the trial pits are set out with pegs and the excavator set up. The turf and topsoil should first be stripped and placed well clear of the pit for future reinstatement. The machine should then remove thin layers no more than 300 mm thick over the full length of the trial pit, one at a time until it is necessary to log, test or sample the soils. Disturbed samples can be taken at any stage but reasonably smooth undisturbed surfaces are needed for hand vane, pocket penetrometer or California Bearing Ratio tests. The exact location and depth of each sample or test should be recorded.

When access is required to the pit for sampling, logging or testing a careful assessment of stability should be made. All pits deeper than 1.5 m where access is required should either have their sides battered back or should be provided with side support such as trench sheeting. Soft peat requires close sheeting sometimes with depths even less than 1.5 m as do soft clays and silts. Firm or stiff clays should be open sheeted below 1.5 m and close sheeted below 5.0 m but sand or silt lenses can present a

Trial pit investigation – equipment check list

☐ Pencils
☐ Timber crayon
☐ Thick felt-tip pen
☐ Log sheets
☐ Scale rule
☐ Clip board
☐ Site plan
☐ Compass
☐ 3 m tape
☐ 20 m tape
☐ String line
☐ Spirit level
☐ Geological hammer
☐ Lump hammer
☐ Trowel
☐ Scoop
☐ Knife
☐ Palette knife
☐ Sampling tray
☐ Level, tripod and staff
☐ Camera
☐ Hand penetrometer
☐ Mackintosh probe
☐ Hand shear vane
☐ MEXE penetrometer
☐ Watch with second hand
☐ Water pump
☐ Hand auger equipment

☐ Special sample cutters
☐ Plate bearing test apparatus
☐ Overalls
☐ Sample bags
☐ Sample jars
☐ String
☐ Labels
☐ Masking tape
☐ Safety helmet
☐ Boots
☐ Road signs
☐ U100 tubes
☐ U38 tubes
☐ Sliding hammer (U100)
☐ Sliding hammer (U38)
☐ Drill rods
☐ Sling for lifting
☐ Block and tackle
☐ Rope
☐ Scaffold boards
☐ Trench sheeting equipment
☐ Ladder
☐ Setting out pegs
☐ Shovel
☐ Pick
☐ Spade
☐ Fencing

Not all the above equipment will be needed on every job and, on some, additional items will be required

Tick items required, cross when loaded

Fig. 5.2   Equipment check list.

serious hazard particularly if they are water bearing. Sands and gravels below the water table should always be close sheeted but open sheeting can be used for shallow pits above the water table. Fissured or heavily jointed rocks generally require open sheeting but attention should be paid to the possibility of rock falls. All sheeting should be braced with sound walings and props as shown in Fig. 5.3. An easier alternative is to use one of the easily portable proprietary trench shoring systems which are lowered into the pit and the sheets expanded by a screw action. A ladder is essential for access purposes.

When excavation of the pit has been completed two pegs should be driven and a string line set up as shown in Fig. 5.4. Measurements of strata horizons and the locations of samples and tests can then be made by measuring vertically from the line as shown. Levels should be taken and the orientation of the trial pit measured with respect to the north point. A log can then be drawn up as shown in Fig. 5.5 using the standard description method outlined in Chapter 9. Particular note should be made of water seepages together with estimates of the rate of seepage, changes in level and so on, for example; inflow 20 l in 15 min from 0.5 m depth, water encountered at 1.7 m, level in pit rose to 1.5 m after 30 min. Field test results should also be included on the log.

It is preferable to backfill the pit before the end of the shift but if it is necessary to leave it open it must be fully protected. Pits should be backfilled in no more than 200 mm layers with the bucket of the excavator being used to compact each layer. The topsoil and turf should be replaced last of all and the machine driven backwards and forwards over the area of the trial pit. Any other damage such as rutting and fence breaks should be rectified and all gates closed. It is wise to make a check for settlement some weeks after reinstatement. Finally it should be borne in mind that trial pits can always be extended into shafts or adits but that this requires specialist skills.

5.3 Field testing and sampling in trial pits

The sampling procedures adopted will depend on the requirements of the job but generally disturbed samples should be taken at 0.5 m intervals of depth and at each change of strata unless specified otherwise. Small hand samples can be cut from the pit by hand or they can be taken from the bucket. To take large bulk samples it is advisable to start with a clean, flat bottomed pit and then to take a shallow full length bite with the excavator. This can then be tipped onto a sampling tray and any contamination removed before bagging and labelling. For grading, classification and California Bearing Ratio tests about 25 kg should be taken unless the material is essentially gravel sized when 50 kg should be taken. About 100 kg is needed for compaction tests and even more for concrete mix design or for soil/cement tests.

Undisturbed samples can be taken using 38 mm or 100 mm diameter cutting tubes (U38 and U100 samples) or they can be cut by hand. California Bearing Ratio (CBR) test moulds can also be driven into the ground. The U38 samples can be hand driven

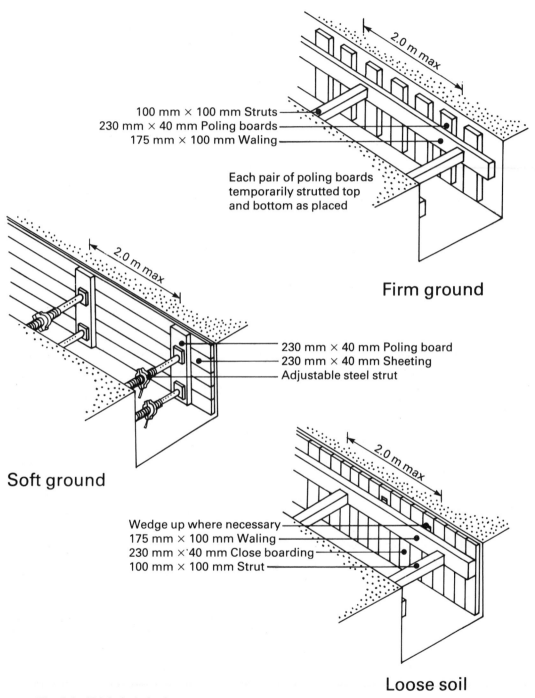

100 mm × 100 mm Struts
230 mm × 40 mm Poling boards
175 mm × 100 mm Waling

Each pair of poling boards
temporarily strutted top
and bottom as placed

2.0 m max

Firm ground

230 mm × 40 mm Poling board
230 mm × 40 mm Sheeting
Adjustable steel strut

2.0 m max

Soft ground

Wedge up where necessary
175 mm × 100 mm Waling
230 mm × 40 mm Close boarding
100 mm × 100 mm Strut

2.0 m max

Loose soil

Fig. 5.3 Trial pit timbering.

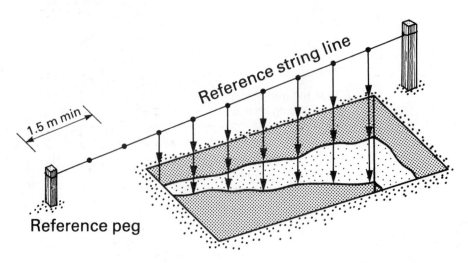

Fig. 5.4 Measurement of trial pit depths.

using a sliding hammer by standing on two planks spanning the trial pit, alternatively an arrangement can be devised whereby the tubes can be gently pushed in using the machine. U100 sample tubes can also be pushed in by machine but care is needed to prevent buckling. The sliding hammer needed to drive a U100 tube is too heavy for comfortable operation by hand and if driving is needed it is worth rigging up a block and tackle on the raised bucket of the excavator. A slip rope on a capstan winch on a Land Rover can also make life easier.

Where hand-cut block samples are required the trial pit should be fully shored and protected from rain and direct sunshine in order to prevent changes in moisture content. The block itself is cut using a box-type former as a guide. This is slid over the block and any gaps filled with wax. With the box in place a cut can be made at the base and the sample lifted out. Hand cutting of samples is a lengthy business and can be expensive. Great care should therefore be taken with the packaging, labelling and transport of the samples. Block samples can be protected from drying out by using layers of waxed cheesecloth. The exact location should be recorded as should the depth and orientation of the sample and the date of sampling. The sample itself should be packaged so that it can be reorientated in the laboratory.

There are a number of useful hand instruments that can be used in trial pits to obtain some measure of soil classification and consistency. They can also give an approximation of the soil's shear strength but it must be stressed that this is very approximate and is no real substitute for proper laboratory testing. However, having said this there are some jobs where accurate testing is not justified and a greater factor of safety than normal can be used without any loss of economy, for example with lightly

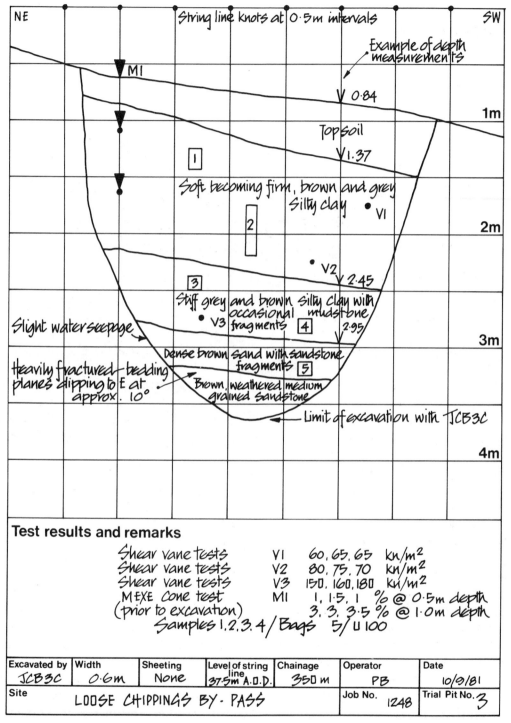

Fig. 5.5 Typical trial pit log.

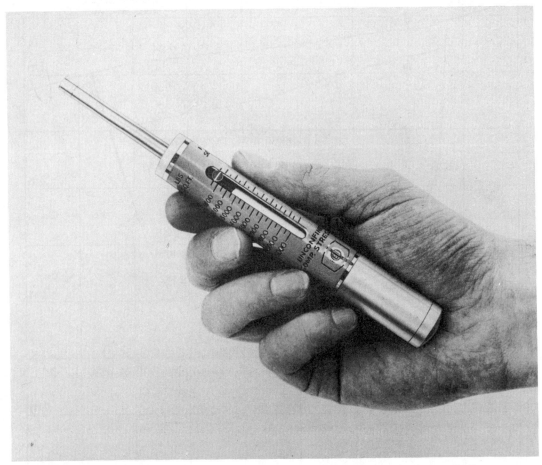

Fig. 5.6 Pocket penetrometer (photograph: Engineering Laboratory Equipment Ltd).

loaded house foundations. From the indicated shear strength the consistency of the soil can be described as discussed in Section 9.4.

Figure 5.6 shows a typical pocket penetrometer. It is used by pushing the spring loaded plunger into a cleanly cut soil surface which may be either vertical or horizontal. The plunger is gently pushed in as far as the cut graduation line and the maximum reading read off a sliding indicator on a marked scale. This may read shear strength directly or the reading may have to be converted to shear strength. The test takes only a few seconds to do once a clean, undisturbed surface has been prepared and consequently a large number of readings can be taken and averaged. Where lenses or intrusions of different soil occur they can be identified by penetration readings taken on a grid basis in the side of the excavation. Some penetrometers have a scale calibrated for

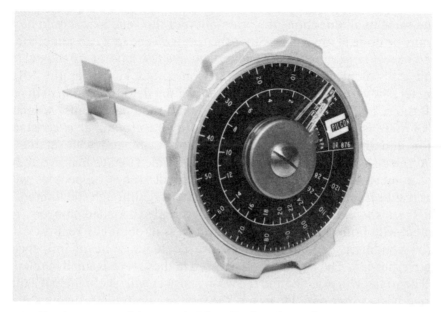

Fig. 5.7   Hand vane tester (photograph: Pilcon Engineering Ltd).

unconfined compressive strength and to obtain the approximate shear strength of purely cohesive soils this is divided by two. The penetrometer should be regarded as a simple aid to the classification of soils and for comparing different soil types and not as a precision measuring instrument. As a further sophistication the unconfined compression test apparatus can be used on site and this is described in Section 10.3 and Fig. 10.10.

One example of a hand shear vane tester is shown in Fig. 5.7 and this can be used on clay soils which contain no more than small amounts of sand or gravel. The tester measures the torque required to shear a small cylinder of soil within the soil mass. Before use the vane itself should be clean and undamaged. It is pushed gently into a prepared soil surface to at least two-and-a-half times the vane length and turned steadily at a rate of one revolution per minute. This is made easier by following the second-hand of a watch. Once the vane starts to shear the small cylinder of soil, it will be felt on the tester and the maximum reading pointer will remain stationary whilst the other needle drops back. If an estimate of residual shear strength is required the vane should be turned gently through several revolutions and the test repeated. Different vane sizes are available to suit different soil strength ranges and a calibration chart to obtain shear strength should be provided by the manufacturers. Care is needed to ensure that the capacity of the vane is not exceeded and that the rods are not bent. In the right soil this test is more accurate than the penetrometer and is again quick to do, so a number of tests can be performed and the average taken. Since soil shear strength is not usually the same in all directions the orientation of the vane axis should be recorded. The test may be done at any angle. Since the test is so cheap it can sometimes be more valuable to have a large number of vane tests than a few laboratory triaxial tests.

The soil assessment cone penetrometer, sometimes known as the MEXE cone penetrometer, shown in Fig. 5.8, is a useful tool for the field estimation of the California Bearing Ratio (CBR) which is used in the design of road pavements. A small cone on the end of rods is simply pushed steadily into the ground at a constant rate of penetration and the approximate CBR read off a moving scale at the top. The instrument can also be used to assess the ease with which plant can move about on site. However, it must be remembered that even small stones or pebbles will lead to erroneous results if the cone tip rests on one. A better, although still limited, test is the *in situ* CBR test where the penetration into the ground of a loaded plunger is measured. The problem with both this and the previous test is in obtaining realistic estimates of compaction conditions, equilibrium moisture contents, zone of influence and the effects of overburden. The depth of soil stressed in these tests is small in relation to that which will be stressed in practice and the wrong answer will be obtained if a thin layer of stiff soil overlies a softer one. However, the tests are useful in providing quick, cheap field estimates of CBR.

Plate bearing tests can be easily carried out at ground level or in trial pits as shown in Fig. 5.9. If the arrangement shown is used for testing in a trial pit the lorry will straddle the pit and a check is necessary to ensure the sides are stable and adequately supported. When properly executed and interpreted the tests can provide invaluable information on bearing capacity, settlement and modulus of subgrade reaction which can be converted to CBR. The test involves loading a plate and measuring its penetration into the ground thus giving the stress/strain relationship for the soil. Plate bearing tests are discussed further in Chapter 12.

Knowledge of the *in situ* density of soils, particularly granular ones, can be useful in obtaining empirical estimates of soil shear strength and in enabling laboratory samples to be remoulded to *in situ* conditions. *In situ* density measurement is also used as a means of checking the compaction of earthworks. There are a number of techniques available but the most common and the most versatile is the sand replacement density test, the equipment for which is shown in Fig. 5.10. A 200 mm diameter hole is dug using a sample-tray template and the soil removed is carefully collected and weighed. The hole is then filled with a standard dry sand of known density by pouring it from a special cylinder. By knowing the weight of sand in the cylinder before pouring, the weight remaining after pouring and the weight contained by the cone below the valve, a calculation can be made to determine the volume of the excavated hole. Thus the wet density can be determined by dividing weight removed by volume. If the moisture content of the excavated soil is measured then the dry density can be calculated. The

Fig. 5.8 Soil assessment cone penetrometer.

apparatus and the sand used require regular calibration and the sand must be kept dry.

An alternative way of removing a known volume is to use a core cutter of a known size and to weigh the core. This is appropriate for cohesive soils. Another means of determining the volume of the hole is to use a water-filled rubber balloon. In the case of rockfill, plastic sheeting can be used to line an excavation which can then be filled with water in order to determine its volume. If representative discrete lumps of soil are available which do not disintegrate during either handling or submersion in water these can be weighed in air and in water to obtain their volume and hence their density. For uniformly graded sands a 25 mm pin can be driven into the soil and the volume of heave measured using apparatus known as the comprimeter. Although this test is very quick it is solely restricted to uniformly graded sands. Finally there is a nuclear method which entails the measurement of back scatter from a source of radiation. This method

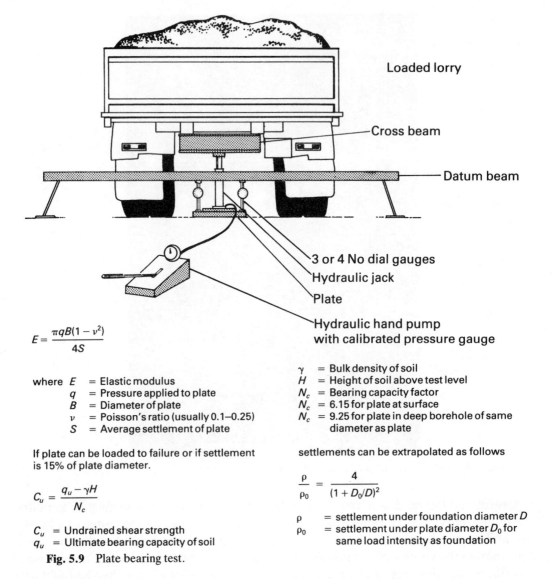

Loaded lorry

Cross beam

Datum beam

3 or 4 No dial gauges
Hydraulic jack
Plate
Hydraulic hand pump
with calibrated pressure gauge

$$E = \frac{\pi q B (1 - v^2)}{4S}$$

where E = Elastic modulus
q = Pressure applied to plate
B = Diameter of plate
v = Poisson's ratio (usually 0.1–0.25)
S = Average settlement of plate

γ = Bulk density of soil
H = Height of soil above test level
N_c = Bearing capacity factor
N_c = 6.15 for plate at surface
N_c = 9.25 for plate in deep borehole of same
  diameter as plate

If plate can be loaded to failure or if settlement
is 15% of plate diameter.

settlements can be extrapolated as follows

$$C_u = \frac{q_u - \gamma H}{N_c}$$

$$\frac{\rho}{\rho_0} = \frac{4}{(1 + D_0/D)^2}$$

C_u = Undrained shear strength
q_u = Ultimate bearing capacity of soil

ρ = settlement under foundation diameter D
ρ_0 = settlement under plate diameter D_0 for
  same load intensity as foundation

Fig. 5.9   Plate bearing test.

requires extensive calibration for each soil type and is very little used in site investigation.

5.4   Hand augering

Hand augering was discussed briefly in Section 4.4 and the equipment was illustrated in Fig. 4.3. Hand augering is limited to self supporting soft or firm ground which is above

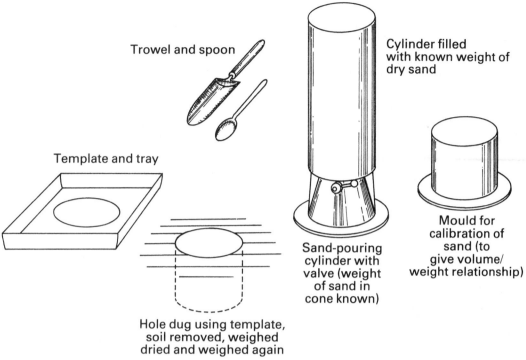

Trowel and spoon

Cylinder filled
with known weight of
dry sand

Template and tray

Mould for
calibration of
sand (to
give volume/
weight relationship)

Sand-pouring
cylinder with
valve (weight
of sand in
cone known)

Hole dug using template,
soil removed, weighed
dried and weighed again

Fig. 5.10 Sand replacement density test equipment.

the water table and which does not contain coarse gravel or boulders. This may sound restrictive but the equipment is cheap to use, can be carried by hand, causes the minimum of disturbance to the land and can locate soil horizons with a high degree of precision.

The equipment shown in Fig. 4.3 would be suitable for hand augering to a depth of about 8 m in the right soil. The kit shown contains four types of auger: a 100 mm soil auger, a 150 mm soil auger, a 50 mm Dutch auger and a 150 mm gravel auger. The latter is shown connected to the rods and handle and is also suitable for use in clays and in spite of its name is in fact probably the most versatile and widely used of the four. The 900 mm extension rods of diameter 0.75 in are threaded male at each end and there are female-threaded connectors. Stillson wrenches are required to couple and uncouple the rods and a chisel is shown for breaking through light obstructions. Also shown are two sampling adaptors and a set of 38 mm diameter sampling tubes (known as U38s). The complete set can be carried in the box shown.

The operation is self evident but one useful tip is not to take too big a bite since this makes removal of the auger very difficult. The cost of hand augering depends very much on the strata penetrated and the depth required. For instance in soft clays up to

3 m deep it would be about one-third the cost of shell and auger boring but the cost might double for boreholes to 6 m. For boreholes greater than about 5 m in firm or stiff clays it is generally cheaper to use shell and auger methods. Sampling is generally confined to disturbed samples or U38 tube samples but a hand shear vane can be used down the hole and this can give a useful strength/depth profile. Hand-held penetrometers can also be used down the hole and it can be extended using probing apparatus. Casing the hole is not really feasible but it is possible in some cases to insert plastic tubing and continue boring in a smaller diameter. The restriction with casing leads to the problems mentioned above of caving ground and ingress of water preventing further penetration.

5.5 Probing

Section 4.3 gave a brief discussion on the use of probing equipment for hand operation and the more sophisticated mechanized probes and penetrometers are discussed in Chapter 8. One version of the basic hand equipment known as the Mackintosh probe is shown in Fig. 4.2 (p. 62) and this can be used for probing and simple prospecting to a depth of 14 m in the right soil conditions. Contained in the kit shown are twelve boring rods each 1.22 m long with twelve couplings of greater diameter than the rods thus helping to reduce friction. These rods can be fitted with a variety of tools. There are two driving points, one auger, one clay sampling tube and one core tube with cleaning rod. The rods are driven using the sliding hammer shown in the centre of the picture. Although not forming a standard test it can be useful to count the number of standard blows for each 100 mm of penetration thus indicating the relative consistencies of the strata being penetrated. On some sites it may be possible to correlate this with Standard Penetration Test results. Also shown in Fig. 4.2 are a lifting tool, various items for maintenance and a carrying box which makes the equipment easily portable.

The equipment is of most use for interpolating ground conditions between boreholes and in defining the extent and profile of soft soils such as peat when a large number of probe holes can be completed in a day at very low cost. The sampling equipment provided with the Mackintosh probe is only suitable for the general identification of the materials being penetrated and there is rarely sufficient for any laboratory testing. To take some of the hard work out of probing there are petrol-driven probes available which will penetrate much stiffer ground. These can be used in a similar way to the hand-operated equipment but in this case it is worth recording the time taken for each 100 mm of penetration to give some measure of variability. The petrol-driven probes can be useful for locating old mine shafts and they can be converted to pneumatic drills for breaking out road construction and the like. Through-flow samplers are available for use with the petrol-driven probes and these will show the type of material at the bottom of the hole when the rods are lifted.

6

Shell and auger boring

6.1 Introduction

Shell and auger or strictly speaking light percussive boring is the most used and most popular method of sinking boreholes in the United Kingdom. It is an extremely versatile method and there are virtually no soils or weak rocks in which it cannot be employed successfully – providing of course that the correct techniques are used. Its early beginnings derived from the percussive method of well boring but since then the method has been developed to suit the requirements of the engineer needing a soil survey and much, though by no means all, of the manual work has been removed. Although having said this the job of drilling is still an arduous one. The equipment is heavy and difficult to handle if it is cold and wet. Most rigs offer little or no weather protection to the operators and the area around a borehole tends to become wet and muddy. Working room too may be limited. In spite of these poor working conditions a great deal of skill is required from the driller and it is vital that he realizes the importance of his work. The requirements of soil exploration are reasonably rapid penetration to the required depth with the ability to sample continuously the ground in a representative fashion, to obtain 'undisturbed' samples and to carry out *in situ* tests. In order to supplement the essential shell and auger equipment a number of 'add on' facilities have been developed for the basic rig particularly for the site where it is necessary to obtain short rock cores.

The object of this chapter is to describe the equipment and tools, how the rig is erected and how the various tools are used in differing types of ground. Basic sampling and *in situ* testing techniques are discussed and this is followed by details of the recommended practice for describing the work on the field record. Because of the importance of water in soils and in the engineering works themselves, the recording of the driller's observations in this area is covered in some detail. In fact the emphasis throughout the chapter will be on good practice, the acquisition of truly representative samples (undisturbed where necessary) and the carrying out of accurate field tests. Most people can sink a hole into the ground but whether or not the above requirements can be satisfied depends on skill and conscientiousness on the part of the driller. This may well require some determination when he is up to his knees in mud with rain pouring down his neck.

No written text can teach anyone to drill boreholes; that can only come from experience in the field but it is hoped that this chapter will enable drillers to recognize the requirements of their work and for engineers to appreciate how the work should be carried out, because unless this part of the investigation is right there can be no hope of getting the rest of it right. No amount of laboratory testing or engineering analysis can make up for mistakes in the field. Mistakes which might eventually result in catastrophic failures and the loss not only of millions of pounds but also, and more importantly, of lives.

Labourers, drillers, technicians and engineers are seen in different lights, but in the field of site investigation they must be seen as one team. The driller must know how to obtain the right samples and understand the requirements of the technician in the laboratory. The engineer must appreciate how the drilling has been carried out and all must be able to communicate with each other to ensure that all relevant facts are recorded in an unambiguous manner. The final objective of this team is to produce a concise, accurate and informative report such that the design engineer can produce a safe and economic design.

6.2 Shell and auger rigs

The shell and auger or light percussive rig is a simple, robust, lightweight, mobile unit which can be operated by two men. Figure 6.1 shows how easily transportable the basic rig is. It can be towed by a Land Rover directly to the majority of borehole positions where it can be quickly erected as shown in Fig. 6.2. If access is difficult the rig can be winched into position or craned in where necessary (its weight is around 1500 kg). However, one drawback is that it requires about 6 m of headroom and this can be a problem inside buildings, under power lines, under trees and so on.

The basic rig consists of a tubular or box section mast (sometimes known as a derrick, tripod or 'A' frame) at the top of which is a pulley or crown sheave arrangement incorporating a towing eye. The mast normally incorporates an axle and a pair of Land Rover-type road wheels. In the towing position the rig forms a trailer with its own suspension system and over-ride brakes. On some rigs the mast can be divided into two lengths for ease of transport. The rear legs of the mast normally contain rungs for access

94

Fig. 6.1 Shell auger rig on tow (photograph: Pilcon Engineering Ltd).

to the crown sheave. Once erected the mast is braced by means of two high level cross bars and a spreader bar between the two back legs. A wire rope passes over the pulley at the top of the mast and this rope carries the various drilling tools; the up and down motion of the tools being provided by a winch and power unit. A small diesel engine of around 10–20 horse power drives the winch drum via a hand operated mechanical or hydraulic heavy duty clutch. The engine may be hand, spring or electric starting.

The winch drum itself is usually in two parts, one half being used for the length of rope which is being worked at any one time, and is provided with a powerful footbrake which is sometimes combined with a handbrake. The clutch and brake combination enable the operator to get a real 'feel' for the drilling operation and enable easy and precise control at all times. In some rigs the engine is provided with a second sheave and a cathead on the winch can be used with a second rope to operate sampling or *in situ* testing equipment independently of the main tools. The engine, winch, clutch and brake unit are mounted on a 'skid' type frame which pivots to ground level as the rig is

Fig. 6.2 Wayfarer 1500 shell and auger rig with hydraulic power take-off powering pendant rotary drilling attachment (photograph: Pilcon Engineering Ltd).

erected and to which a lighting board can be attached when towing. With all rigs the road wheels are removable and in some cases they are mounted on a separate removable axle unit. Table 6.1 lists some of the shell and auger rigs available in the UK in 1981 and compares their specifications.

Another form of percussive boring rig is shown in Fig. 6.3. In this rig the percussive action has been mechanized and hydraulic rams incorporated to pull down the casing.

96

Table 6.1 Comparison of shell and auger rigs

Manufacturer	English Drilling Equipment	Duke and Ockenden			Pilcon Engineering		
	1 ton light	Dando			Wayfarer		
Model	percussion	100	150	175	750	1500	2000
Rig capacity i.e. max safe working load on shear legs (tonnes)	5	5	6	7	4	7	15
Engine type	Diesel	Diesel	Diesel	Diesel	Diesel	Diesel	Diesel
Engine horsepower	16.2	8	16	20	10	20	30
Weight including rope (kg)	1270	860	1000	1100	870	1140	2200
Winch capacity single line (tonnes)	1.00	0.75	1.50	2.00	0.75	1.50	2.00
Rope speed (m min^{-1})	37	20–40	20–40	20–40	68	52	56
Capacity of drum for 12 mm rope (m)	76	100	180	240	120	120	180
Nominal rig capacity 150 mm diameter (m)	76	40	75	90	45	90	140
Nominal rig capacity 200 mm diameter (m)	58	20	45	65	23	50	75
Nominal rig capacity 250 mm diameter (m)	40	N.S.	35	45	10	30	55
Erected height (m)	5.8	5.5	5.5	6.0	5.8	6.5	5.2
Travelling length (m)	4.6	7.0	7.5	8.5	7.0	8.15	6.3
Accessories	None	None	a b c d	a b c d	None	a b c d	a b c d

Notes   1. Information supplied by the manufacturers summer 1981.
2. Accessories: a, Pendant; b, Penetrometer; c, Ground anchor driver; d, Jacking unit.
3. N.S. = Not specified
4. This table does not include all rigs available.

The engine produces hydraulic power which drives a winch unit incorporating an automatic oscillator. The rig is heavier than the conventional shell and auger rig, requires more setting up, involving ground anchors, and is considerably more expensive. It is, however, rather more versatile since it can be used for rotary drilling and cone penetration tests.

Fig. 6.3 Mechanized percussion rig (photograph: Conrad Stork Ltd).

6.3 Shell and auger tools

In shell and auger boring the borehole is advanced using the percussive action of a variety of tools. These tools together with other necessary pieces of equipment are shown in Fig. 6.4 and the numbers in parentheses below refer to the items shown.

In order to prevent the borehole caving in and to seal off any ingress of water, seamless steel casing (1) is required and this comes in 150 mm, 200 mm, 250 mm and 300 mm diameters and is normally 1.5 m long although short lengths can be supplied. The casing is threaded male at one end and female at the other and it is important to protect the threads, particularly the male ones, during transit. The bottom of the casing is provided with a hardened steel shoe (2) so that the casing can be driven into the ground where this becomes necessary. The top of the casing is fitted with a drive head (3) which is a heavy steel collar screwed to the top of the casing to act as an anvil when driving the casing and to protect the threads. It is shown fitted with a tapping down bar to knock or surge the casing in the borehole. It can also be fitted with a clevis and cross pin (4) for lowering and raising. A casing clamp (5) is used to prevent the casing slipping down the borehole and a chainpipe wrench (6) or a pair of stillsons (7) are used to couple and uncouple casing, drill rods or other tools.

98

The actual tools used for the boring operation are shown as numbers 8–21 in Fig. 6.4. The shell (8) is an open length of tube fitted with a clack valve (9) and hardened cutting shoe (12) at one end and is used to lift granular cuttings from the borehole. It is shown with an API tapered thread connection although a Whitworth thread can be used in conjunction with the boring rods. It comes in diameters of 140 mm, 194 mm or 245 mm to suit the casing used and is also termed a 'bailer' since it can be used to remove water from the borehole. When fitted with a clack valve and auger (10) it can be used to penetrate and recover soft waterlogged ground. The auger is normally rotated manually via the drilling rods and can be a useful way of cleaning out the bottom of the borehole.

For cutting and removing cohesive soils from the borehole the claycutter (11) is used. This is an open tube with two windows cut in the sides and fitted at one end with a replaceable hardened shoe (12) or serrated shoe (13) either of which are used in conjunction with a slightly undersized tapered claycutter ring in order to retain the soil and to prevent it becoming too tightly packed in the tube. Claycutters are supplied in the same diameters as the shell. An alternative claycutter is the cruciform or cross blade type (14) which can give rapid progress in homogeneous clays and which gives only moderately disturbed columns of soil in each quadrant. A swivel (15) is fitted between the tools and the wire rope to minimize twisting. For fragmenting rocks or obstructions the impact of a California bit (16) can be used. The bit provides a chiselling action and the same effect can be produced using different shapes (17 and 18). Sinker bars (19 and 20) can be added to the drill string in order to increase weight and penetration when percussive boring. An auger cleaner (21) is used to remove material from any of the tools.

Drilling rods for use in shell and auger boring can be either square section rods with 1.5 in Whitworth threads (22) or steel tube (BW size 54 mm outside diameter) and are used in conjunction with a swivel (23). The rods are made in standard 3 m, 1.5 m and 0.75 m lengths to suit requirements. The joints between rods are made or broken using a wrench or handdog (24) and can be turned using a rod tiller (25) when augering. When coupling or uncoupling the square section drilling rods a rod fork or 'bitch' (26) is used to prevent them falling down the hole, alternatively an auger board (27) can be used. For actually grasping the boring rods when raising or lowering them in the borehole, a lifting dog (28) is used.

During shell and auger boring problems inevitably arise and a common one is that pieces of equipment are lost down the borehole. To recover them a number of tools have been developed. The bell box (29) is rather like the shell and the box end of rods can be trapped in the clack valve. The crowsfoot (30) is used in a similar fashion. The bell screw (31) can be used to latch onto male threads and the recovery tap (33) can recover tools which have a female thread uppermost. The rope spear (32) can sometimes catch onto a tangled rope which may have broken down the borehole.

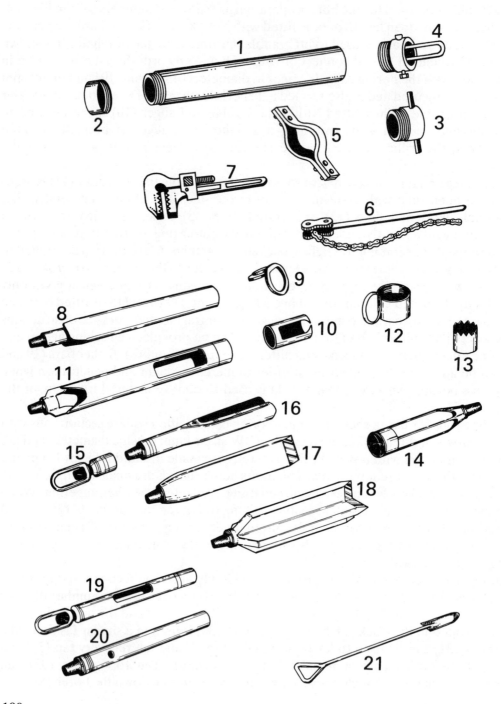

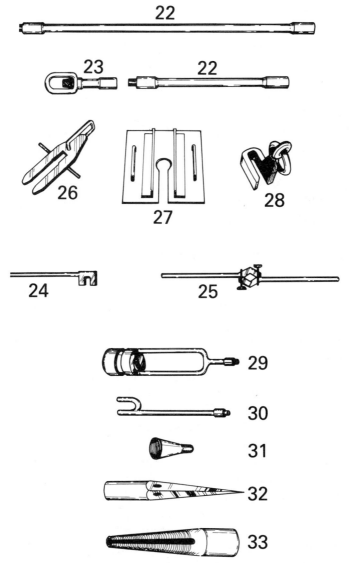

Fig. 6.4 Site investigation equipment. 1, casing; 2, casing shoe; 3, drive head with tapping down bar; 4, drive head with clevis and cross pin; 5, casing clamp; 6, chain pipe wrench; 7, stillson wrench; 8, shell; 9, clack valve; 10, auger; 11, claycutter; 12, cutting shoe; 13, serrated shoe; 14, cross blade claycutter; 15, API swivel; 16, California chisel; 17, chisel; 18, chisel; 19, sinker bar with swivel; 20, sinker bar; 21, auger cleaner; 22, boring rods; 23, rod swivel; 24, hand dog; 25, rod tiller; 26, rod fork (or bitch); 27, auger board; 28, lifting dog; 29, bell box; 30, crowsfoot; 31, bell screw; 32, rope spear; 33, recovery tap.

6.4   Erection, dismantling, basic operation and maintenance

Access of the rig onto the site should be planned to cause the minimum of damage not only in consideration of the landowner, his crops, stock and property but also in consideration of any compensation that might have to be paid.

Having checked services and overhead clearance particularly in respect of electricity cables, and having prepared a reasonably level piece of ground at the borehole position the rig is manoeuvred such that the hole to be drilled is about 1.8 m from the winch-leg pivots (see Fig. 6.5). On sites where Land Rover access is difficult the rig can be unhitched, the wire rope run out to an anchorage such as a tree or a 'deadman' and the rig winched into position using its own power. The rig can easily be craned into other difficult positions. On undulating sites it is well worth spending some time preparing the area around the borehole to give a stable, level area for the rig with adequate working space around it. This may entail excavation, build up with timbers or even scaffolding if the slopes are very steep.

For work over water a scaffold platform can be built as shown in Fig. 6.6 or work can be carried out through a well in the centre of an anchored barge or pontoon. Casing will be necessary but this should not be attached to the barge in any way so that the barge can rise and fall with changes in the water level. Further discussion on work over water is given in Section 7.11. In some cases a crane or even a helicopter may be needed to lift a rig into position and it has been known for floors of buildings to be removed so that a rig can work in the basement.

To erect the rig each of the two back legs are 'walked around' through 180° to the position shown in Fig. 6.5. As this is done the legs must be rotated on their long axis through 180°. If there is insufficient room to walk the legs round they can be unbolted and carried to the correct position. The legs are positioned equally spaced about the rig centre line and the spreader bar is bolted between them. A 6 in snatch block is then attached to the front of the chassis and the winch line is run from the underside of the winch drum up to and around the crown sheave, back around the snatch block at the chassis and finally to a wire sling on the spreader bar. The eye on the end of the rope is then secured to the sling with a shackle pin. The crown sheave is now lifted by hand to a height of about 1 m ready for winching and supporting timbers are placed under the chassis ensuring a stable level platform is produced.

The chassis is secured by driving steel pins through holes into the ground to prevent the rig moving. If this cannot be done the road wheels should be securely chocked. With personnel clear of the back and sides of the rig the legs are winched in towards the chassis, making sure nothing fouls any obstructions, until they are approximately 3.5 m from the winch-leg pivots. As the legs move in the chassis settles down onto the timbers. The brake is then applied and the legs are lifted one at a time onto suitable timbers. A check is then made that the rig is square and truly vertical and adjustments are made if

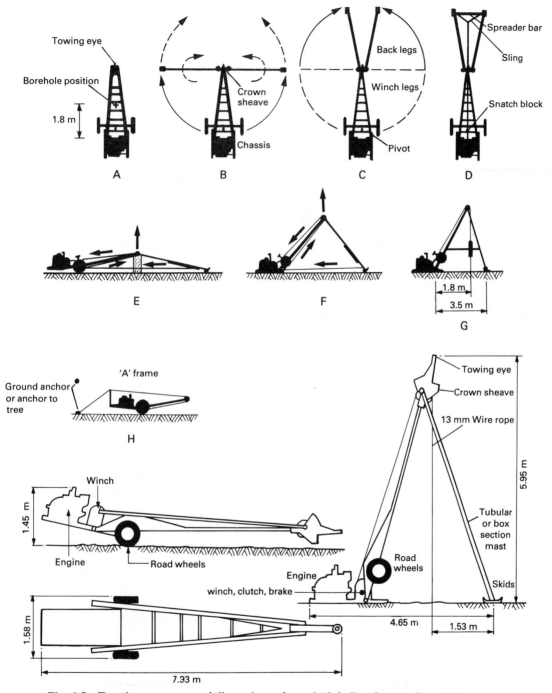

Fig. 6.5 Erection sequence and dimensions of a typical shell and auger rig.

103

Fig. 6.6 Shell and auger rig with pendant drilling attachment illustrating temporary works.

necessary with wedges or thin pieces of timber. An alternative method of erecting the rig known as 'over the back' is shown in Fig. 6.5H. It must however be stressed that this method is not recommended by the manufacturers and accidents have occurred using the method. The wire rope is attached either over an A frame or to a tree as shown, the rig is then winched up to a near vertical position and the legs allowed to swing into place. It is a hazardous operation and total collapse can occur if the crown sheave is pulled up too far.

With the rig erected the winch line should fall on the chosen borehole position which should be on the rig centreline. Once all adjustments have been made the back legs should be securely nailed to the timbers to prevent movement during boring operations. The two cross-bracing struts can then be bolted into position thus preventing the tripod from collapsing. The rope is removed from the snatch block and a length of rope wound onto the working side of the winch drum. The rig is now ready for boring to start but a careful check should be made to ensure absolute stability since serious injury can result if the rig were to move during drilling.

To dismantle the rig the above procedure is essentially reversed. The wire rope is connected as before and the side stays are removed but the chassis is left pinned to the ground. The nails are removed from the foot of the back legs and with one man on the winch another then levers the legs backwards, sliding them on timbers if this is necessary. The winch operator should keep tension on the cable at all times to make sure that the legs do not run out of control and no personnel should stand beneath or to the sides of the rig during lowering. The crown sheave is thus lowered to the ground, the cable removed and wound in, the engine stopped and the spreader bar removed. The chassis pins are then removed and the legs walked back rotating them through 180° at the half way stage.

To operate the rig the engine is started in accordance with the manufacturer's instructions making sure that the winch brake is locked on. The eye on the end of the wire rope is connected to a swivel which is either screwed onto a drilling rod or the appropriate tool; alternatively a 'D' shackle pin can be used. To hoist the tool the brake is released and the hand clutch is pulled back thus engaging the winch which winds in the rope. To allow the tool to free fall for percussive drilling the clutch lever and foot brake are both released. To stop the free fall the foot brake is applied and the tool can then be raised again by pulling back on the clutch and releasing the brake. During most of percussive drilling only relatively small up and down movements (usually less than 300 mm) of the tools are needed and some skill is required in actuating the clutch to obtain the right sort of movement without making it too great or introducing a lot of slack into the wire rope. During this rhythmic up and down motion the brake need not be used.

The brake should be regularly adjusted to allow for wear such that it is firmly on when in the locked position. The wire rope should be checked daily as should all shackles and pins since serious injury or death could result if the heavy tools were to fall on any personnel. The wire rope that is used should only be of a type approved by the manufacturer (normally a 13 mm, 19 strand, right hand ordinary lay wire rope). All shell and auger drilling rigs are subject to statutory lifting regulations and this is covered in more detail in Chapter 14. It is the responsibility of the operator to ensure that work done using the rig is carried out safely. As stated above the winch is divided into a working portion and a rope storage portion. The appropriate length of rope should always be used on the working portion; the amount is determined by having three or four turns on the drum with a tool at the bottom of the hole. Using the working portion gives the winch a sensitive and positive action, it prolongs the rope life, it gives maximum pull, it gives easier judgement of drilling depth, and it minimizes rope crushing. When the working end of the rope becomes damaged it can be cut off and the rope progressively shortened so that maximum life is obtained.

Once the rig has been set up over the required borehole position a square of turf should be removed and retained and the claycutter dropped under guidance in order to get the hole started. Once a depth of 1 m is reached a short length of casing can be added and the work continued through it. It is well worth spending some effort in maintaining a clean and tidy working area with the tools and sampling equipment neatly laid out, preferably on benches for easy lifting. Provision should be made to drain water away from the hole and waste from the hole should be kept in a tidy heap. Good housekeeping on site leads not only to more efficient boring but also makes the site safer.

The maintenance of the rig should be in accordance with the manufacturer's instructions but the following general points should be observed.

(1) Compliance with the Health and Safety at Work Act 1974 (see also Chapter 14).
(2) Compliance with the appropriate Construction Regulations particularly those relating to lifting operations.
(3) Certification of testing of lifting equipment (rig, shackles, rope, etc.)
(4) Compliance with road vehicle regulations.
(5) Checking and lubrication of winch, clutch, bearings, drive mechanism, engine, towing eye, rope, sheave, cables, wheels and power take-off if fitted.
(6) Checking of brake and clutch fluid levels and tyre pressures.
(7) Adherence to engine maintenance instructions.
(8) Checking and adjustment of brake, clutch and over-ride brake.
(9) Checking of structural integrity of all components; mast, lifting equipment, bolts etc.

6.5   Boring in clays

Having discussed the rig, its tools and its basic operation a description will be given of the procedures for boring, sampling and testing the various soil types that may be encountered.

Clays are soils which exhibit cohesiveness or stickiness and shell and auger or light percussive boring is an ideal means of creating a borehole in them. In firm or stiff clays or in weak rocks there may not be any necessity to support the hole with casing but if they are soft or waterlogged then casing will be required to prevent them from squeezing into the hole. The size of casing should be chosen in the light of required borehole depth and the likely nature of the ground to be penetrated. If made ground or gravel or cobbles are anticipated it is wise to use at least a 200 mm diameter hole and if a depth much over 15 m is to be achieved the hole should be started in a large diameter in

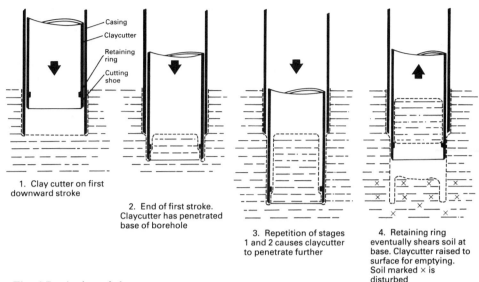

1. Clay cutter on first downward stroke

2. End of first stroke. Claycutter has penetrated base of borehole

3. Repetition of stages 1 and 2 causes claycutter to penetrate further

4. Retaining ring eventually shears soil at base. Claycutter raised to surface for emptying. Soil marked × is disturbed

Casing
Claycutter
Retaining ring
Cutting shoe

Fig. 6.7 Action of claycutter.

order that the casing size can be reduced in steps down the hole e.g. 0–10 m at 250 mm diameter, 10–20 m at 200 mm diameter and 20–30 m at 150 mm diameter since this will facilitate working the casing into the hole and withdrawing it. When a step down in casing size is used it is often desirable to seal about 1.5 m of the annulus between the casings with clay or bentonite to prevent granular material rising up and jamming them. Casing is also desirable if strata which are liable to cave in overlie the clay or if it is necessary to seal off an ingress of water from a higher level.

The tool commonly used in clay is, as the name suggests, the claycutter whose action is illustrated in Fig. 6.7. In this figure the claycutter is shown operating inside the casing. On the first downward stroke some of the clay passes into the body of the claycutter past the retaining ring and repetition of the stroke causes more clay to pass into the claycutter until it is raised to the surface for emptying. Each time the claycutter is lifted the clay is sheared off at the level of the retaining ring and obviously the material inside the claycutter is quite seriously disturbed as is the small plug of soil in the bottom of the hole. As the claycutter is lifted there is an appreciable suction effect at the bottom of the borehole and this causes further disturbance. The action of the claycutter should be one of short, repetitive, light strokes; care being taken not to overfill the claycutter since this makes changes in strata difficult to detect and makes it more difficult to empty. In general the softer the strata the gentler the blows. There is nothing to be gained from dropping the claycutter from a great height since this only causes more disturbance at the bottom of the hole and can lead to tools becoming stuck.

107

In soft or firm clays no difficulty will be experienced in recovering the clay but in very stiff or friable clays it may be necessary, although only as a last resort, to add a little water. This will obviously modify the properties of the clay and a note should be made on the log whenever any water is added. There is a tendency amongst drillers to add far too much water and this is to be avoided. Sensitive clays are ones which tend to collapse once a critical shear strength is reached and particular care is needed in boring and sampling such materials. Other types of clay may be subject to shrinkage or swelling during boring and these phenomena should be recognized and recorded wherever they occur.

The important part of drilling is not to make a hole in the ground but to know exactly what is present and in what state it is; the addition of water can only hide this. The claycutter can often be used in quite granular deposits providing there is sufficient clay present to hold the material together. Following withdrawal of the claycutter which should always be done slowly to minimize suction effects, the casing can be advanced to the bottom of the hole by surging or gentle tapping. To surge the casing down it is lifted and allowed to fall under its own weight; this has the advantage that the casing will be known to be free in the hole. If a sample is required at the bottom of the hole allowance should be made for the disturbed zone by either removing it using an auger or accepting that it is present and discarding it when it is removed.

An alternative form of claycutter, the cross-blade type, is shown in Fig. 6.8. This consists of a sharpened cutting ring into which is welded a cruciform section piece of steel with a sharpened, concave shaped end. The tool is used in exactly the same way as the conventional claycutter but when it is withdrawn from the hole a cut is made as shown and the four quadrants of soil peeled away. These quadrants of soil readily show the strata through which the claycutter has passed. No attempt should be made to remove the material inside the cutting ring since this assists recovery of the next sequence. The cross blade claycutter enables extremely rapid progress to be made in soft or firm homogeneous clays but is less suitable for very stiff clays or ones which contain gravel, cobbles or lenses of sand.

Whilst boring in clay the ingress of water is unlikely to be a problem since clay is relatively impermeable and water will only enter the borehole slowly. If water enters the borehole through thin layers of sand these can usually be sealed off by advancing the casing. However, since clay is so impermeable a considerable time must be allowed if it is required to know the natural groundwater level within it.

6.6 Boring in sands and gravels

Whilst boring in granular deposits which have no cohesiveness or natural cementing action it is essential to use casing and this should always be inserted close to the bottom of the hole to prevent overshelling (i.e. removing material to form a large cavity at the

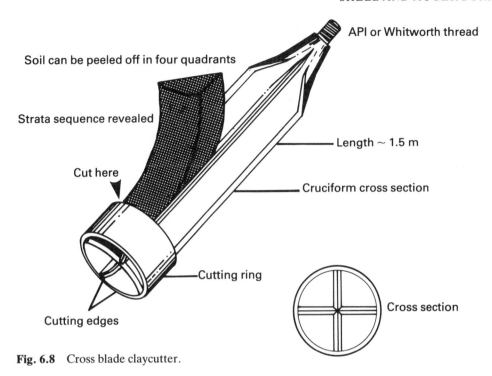

API or Whitworth thread

Soil can be peeled off in four quadrants

Strata sequence revealed

Length ~ 1.5 m

Cruciform cross section

Cut here

Cutting ring

Cutting edges

Cross section

Fig. 6.8 Cross blade claycutter.

bottom of the borehole). The size of casing used depends on the ground conditions, the maximum size of particles present and the depth of the borehole. In general the larger the particles present the larger the casing that will be required although in boulder clay which contains only occasional boulders better progress may be made using the 150 mm diameter size which tends to push the odd small boulder out of the way. Further discussion on the choice of casing size is given in Section 6.5.

Boring in granular non-cohesive deposits such as sands and gravels requires the use of the shell which is sometimes known as the pump or bailer and this was illustrated in Fig. 6.4. The basic action of the shell inside a casing is shown in Fig. 6.9. The cycle starts with the shell on the bottom of the borehole flush with the base of the casing. Free water is usually present in alluvial sands and gravels. As the shell is raised a few inches the clack valve is held closed and the whole unit acts as a piston and granular material is drawn into the base of the shell and at the same time the casing is drawn down. As the casing is lowered the clack valve opens and material passes into the shell, in suspension if water is present. On the next upstroke the clack valve closes retaining some material in the shell and the cycle is repeated until the shell contains a reasonable amount of material when it is withdrawn and emptied. The shell should never be overfilled.

As can be gathered only a short stroke of about 150–200 mm is required to effect the

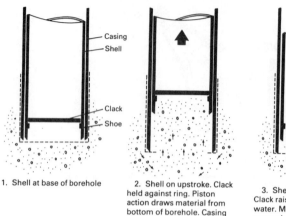

1. Shell at base of borehole

2. Shell on upstroke. Clack held against ring. Piston action draws material from bottom of borehole. Casing advanced

3. Shell on downstroke. Clack raised by resistance of water. Material in suspension passes into shell

4. Shell on upstroke. Clack closed and material held in shell

(N.B. Cycle is repeated several times before the shell is brought to the surface. Normal shelling stroke is about 150–200 mm)

Fig. 6.9 Action of shell.

sequence described. When the shell is operating effectively it will be moving up and down rhythmically and a regular clunking sound will be heard as the valve opens and closes. As the shell gradually fills the casing should follow downwards although in certain deposits considerable side friction can build up and some assistance may be required by either vibrating, rotating or tapping the casing. However, care should be taken to ensure that the bottom of the casing is not allowed to advance beyond the bottom of the hole. It is well worth regularly checking that the casing is free to move and has not become stuck at any stage since with deep boreholes it is all too easy to get the casing stuck such that it is beyond the capacity of the rig to pull it out.

The operation described above is appropriate to a borehole where water is present and indeed the shell can be used to remove water from the borehole. Ground water is often present in granular deposits since in the UK they are usually associated with alluvial flood plain conditions. There are however a number of potential problems and the main one is of piping. It is not uncommon to see an inexperienced driller removing vast quantities of sand from a borehole without actually increasing its depth. There may be a local lowering of ground level but each time the shell is emptied and lowered back down the borehole it only returns to the same level or even higher. The reason for this phenomenon is invariably that the ground water outside the casing is at a higher level than that inside it and it therefore flows from the higher pressure outside the casing to the lower pressure inside it, taking with it particles of silt, sand and even fine gravel.

Unless the ground water is under artesian pressure, piping can be prevented by maintaining a head of water inside the casing equal to or greater than that outside it. This is accomplished by allowing the water to reach an equilibrium level inside the

110

casing and then ensuring that the water level is never allowed to fall below it, remembering that every time the shell is removed from the hole water is also removed. In practice it is normal to top the borehole up to ground level thus usually giving a reasonable safety margin since the shell itself applies a small suction. It may also be beneficial to use a shell somewhat smaller than the casing. The shell, itself, will operate perfectly well below water level but large, rapid movements of it inside the casing should be avoided. In the case of water under artesian pressure (i.e. the equilibrium level is above ground level) it will be necessary to extend the casing above ground level to prevent any outflow. If piping has occurred there is no point in doing Standard Penetration Tests since the granular deposits will be loosened for some depth below the bottom of the hole.

Another common problem is of casing becoming stuck in sand and gravel deposits particularly where it has been left overnight. The important thing here is to get the casing moving again and this can be done by vibrating, rotating or surging it. Alternatively there are casing rotators driven using hydraulic power from the rig engine power take off. Sticking of the casing in the hole can be minimized by using an appropriate step down in size of the casing as discussed earlier. As a last resort heavy jacks may be required to raise a stuck casing string.

In very loose materials, particularly fills, no recovery may be achieved since material can be pushed out of the way instead of entering the shell. This is usually best avoided by using a large diameter shell and casing. If very large boulders are encountered they can sometimes be chiselled away directly or a pilot hole can be drilled through them using rotary methods and then the excess rock chiselled away. Certain types of loose sands can be liquified by vibration or shock and particular care is needed firstly in recognizing such materials and secondly in boring and sampling them. Recovery in hard, dry, granular deposits can be a considerable problem. Augering can be tried or a little water may be added but if the requirement is for representative samples then alternative means must be found. A grab device can be used in large diameter boreholes.

Whenever water is present in granular materials there is a risk of losing the finer particles through them getting washed away and great care is needed when emptying the shell to ensure that all material is recovered. This will involve filtering or the use of settling tanks. Where it is vital to observe the structure of granular materials they can be grouted and then cored with allowance being made for the grout.

6.7 Boring in silts and other materials

Silts are essentially granular materials but the particles are too small to be seen with the naked eye and they can present problems in drilling. They are normally alluvial in origin, often below the water table and extremely prone to piping. Either the claycutter or the shell can be used depending on whether or not there is any clayey material present within the silt. Where pure silt is encountered below the water table it will be necessary to keep the borehole topped up with water and use made of the shell. When the shell is used, particular care is needed to avoid any loss of fines as discussed above.

Peats are very soft organic materials and great care is needed to obtain full recovery since boring tools tend to sink into them under their own weight without becoming filled. The nature and mode of deposition of soils and rocks being what they are can obviously lead to any combination of the soil types previously described being present and the best method of dealing with them must come from experience.

Made ground is a term used to denote any material laid down by man and as such it can contain virtually anything. It may be cohesive or granular, it may contain wood, metal or any of the industrial waste products, it may even be on fire emitting toxic fumes and as such all sorts of problems can occur. In made ground or carboniferous rocks it is sometimes necessary to determine a temperature/depth profile and this can be accomplished using a remote reading thermocouple. It is the variability of made ground that usually presents the biggest problem to the engineer and it is often better to look at it on a larger scale in deep trial pits. After the trial pit has been dug and examined a length of casing can be dropped in and the pit backfilled around it thus allowing drilling to proceed to greater depths.

It is not possible to lay down hard and fast rules as to the type of equipment that should be used nor as to the way in which it should be used but a good driller must always be prepared to vary his techniques and determine which method is the most effective. He will thus build up experience of how best to tackle the range of problems he will encounter. The range is as wide as all the permutations of all the different soil and rock types combined with varying ground water conditions.

6.8 Backfilling of boreholes

Once a borehole has been successfully completed it is important not to neglect the backfilling. Some authorities may specify backfilling with lean concrete or grout to prevent settlement or with impermeable material to prevent seepage of water. It can be appreciated how important a poorly backfilled borehole containing water might be if it were to lie on the line of a proposed tunnel. It is equally important not to allow air to get at coal seams where it could lead to spontaneous combustion. Whether or not any particular method is specified the hole should always be backfilled such as to minimize settlement. Every effort must be made to compact the material put back into the hole and if necessary a paving slab can be placed over the hole 300 mm to 500 mm below ground level. Several expensive claims have had to be met by site investigators after humans or animals have broken their legs in boreholes where the backfill has settled.

Backfilling of boreholes where artesian water is present can be a problem. Dry mixes of bentonite and cement in cloth bags can be rammed down as the casing is withdrawn in an attempt to plug the borehole but if this fails it may be necessary to install a permanent control valve.

Before leaving a site as much damage as possible should be reinstated. Surplus material should be removed from the site and the borehole position re-turfed if necessary. Any gates and fences that had been removed should be replaced and wheel tracks should be filled in. Care should be taken that no tools or other pieces of metal are left in the grass where they might damage farm machinery. Even where as much damage as possible has been reinstated it may still be necessary to compensate the landowner for inconvenience, loss of crop, necessary reploughing and so on and this will obviously be subject to negotiation. Good public relations are well worth encouraging.

6.9 Basic sampling

Obtaining samples for examination and testing is an integral part of shell and auger boring but samples can be obtained in different ways and with varying degrees of disturbance. It is therefore important to decide exactly what is the object of the sampling and what the samples are to be used for. Even with such consideration it must be remembered that any sample is probably only a very small part of the ground under investigation. As such it may or may not be representative of the ground as a whole since there may be rapid changes in soil type or there may be planes of weakness such as fissures which are not seen in a small sample. There are a number of ways in which samples can be obtained. Disturbed samples can be taken from the drilling tools as the boring proceeds or tubes can be driven into the ground. Alternatively samples can be obtained by rotary coring or blocks can be cut by hand from trial pits.

It is important to recognize the quality of the sample that is being obtained in order that the value of subsequent testing can be assessed. Table 6.2 illustrates five classes of sample: Class 1 being the best and Class 5 being only suitable for identifying the type of strata that is present. The table does not imply that say strength tests cannot be carried out on Class 2 samples but if they are they must be treated with some caution. To obtain true Class 1 samples will require great care and may necessitate the cutting of large blocks in order for them to be representative of the structure of the ground. Table 6.3 shows the relationship between soil type, sampling method and sample quality. The weights of sample that should normally be taken are shown in Table 6.4 although particular job requirements may cause these to vary. Figure 6.10 shows a specimen sample label that should be securely attached to any sample that is taken. All disturbed samples should be sealed in jars or polythene bags and the labels protected from water.

In shell and auger boring the most commonly taken 'undisturbed' sample of cohesive soils is that obtained using a 100 mm diameter open drive sampler. This is known as a

Table 6.2 Classification of quality of soil samples (see Table 6.3)

Quality	Grade	Properties that can be reliably determined
Class 1	Undisturbed (cut block samples or certain driven samples)	Classification e.g. particle size and index properties Moisture content. Density Strength, deformation and consolidation characteristics
Class 2	Undisturbed (driven samples)	Classification Moisture content Density
Class 3	Disturbed (from dry excavations or boreholes sunk by claycutter or auger and certain driven samples)	Classification Moisture content
Class 4	Disturbed (from wet excavations or boreholes sunk by claycutter or auger)	Classification
Class 5	Disturbed (from non-cohesive soil in wet excavations or in boreholes sunk by shell)	None Strata sequence only

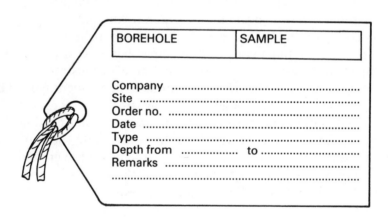

Fig. 6.10 Specimen sample label.

Table 6.3 Relationship between soil type, sampling method and sample quality

Soil type	U100 sampler	Piston sampler	Bishop sand sampler	Penetration test sample	Block samples	Disturbed sample	Rotary core sample
Sensitive clay	Class 2	Class 1	—	—	—	Class 3	—
Non sensitive clay	Class 1/2	Class 2	—	—	Class 1	Class 3	—
Stiff clay	Class 2/3	—	—	—	Class 2	Class 3	Class 2/3
Loose silt	Class 3	Class 1	Class 2	Class 3/4	—	Class 3/4	—
Dense silt	Class 2	Class 2	Class 2/3	Class 3/4	—	Class 3/4	—
Loose sand	—	—	Class 2	Class 3/4	—	Class 3/4	—
Dense sand	—	—	Class 2/3	Class 3/4	—	Class 3/4	—
Fine gravel	—	—	—	Class 3/4	—	Class 3/4	—
Medium/coarse gravel	—	—	—	Class 3/4	—	Class 3/4	—
Soft rock	Class 3	—	—	Class 3/4	Class 2	Class 4/5	Class 1/2
Hard rock	—	—	—	—	—	Class 4/5	Class 1

A dash indicates an impossible or inappropriate form of sampling
For definition of sample class see Table 6.2

Table 6.4 Weights of sample required

Purpose of sample	Soil type	Weight of sample required (kg)
Soil identification including Atterberg limits, sieve analysis, moisture content and sulphate content tests	Clay, silt, sand	1
	Fine and medium gravel	5
	Coarse gravel	30
Compaction tests	All	25–60
Comprehensive examination of construction materials including soil stabilization	Clay, silt, sand	100
	Fine and medium gravel	130
	Coarse gravel	160

U100 and, when the diameter was expressed in inches, as a U4. The sampler is shown in Fig. 6.11; it consists of a steel or alloy tube with an open cutting shoe at one end and a screw-on drive head assembly at the other. The drive head incorporates a non-return valve and connects to the drill rods. The valve allows air or water to be expelled as the sampler is driven into the ground and assists in retaining the sample as the tube is withdrawn. The tube is driven on the end of the drill rods using the sliding hammer shown in Fig. 6.11. The number of blows is normally recorded for comparing one soil type with another. The tubes themselves are 450 mm long and two are often joined together so that the top sample, which may be disturbed, can be discarded.

In loose soils of low cohesion a cutting shoe incorporating a core catcher device can be used. The screw on cutting shoe is designed with an internal diameter about 1% less than the internal diameter of the tube thus minimizing friction as the sample enters the tube which itself should be clean and as smooth as possible. Too small an internal diameter on the cutting shoe would allow the sample to expand thus increasing the disturbance. The outer diameter of the cutting shoe is slightly greater than that of the tube to aid penetration and withdrawal. The area ratio defined in Fig. 6.11 should be kept as low as possible subject to maintaining sufficient strength in the tube. In the standard U100 it is about 30% but in thin wall samplers for soft sensitive soils it is about 10%. Although the U100 sample is classed as 'undisturbed' this is inevitably not so and the effect of driving the sampler into a laminated soil is illustrated in Fig. 9.3.

The procedure to be adopted in taking U100 samples is to clean the bottom of the hole of all disturbed material, preferably using an auger. Alternatively the two-tube or even a three-tube method can be used and any disturbed material rejected. If groundwater has been encountered the hole should be kept topped up with water to prevent piping unless of course the groundwater has been sealed off by the casing. An undamaged sample tube is normally driven into the ground using repeated blows of a hammer without any jarring on the upward stroke but it can also be pushed or jacked into the ground. Care should be taken in recording levels so that the tube is not overdriven since this would cause compression and disturbance. The tube should always be removed slowly and the length recovered compared with the length driven. If the former is less than the latter the sample of soil has not fully entered the tube, has been compressed or has partially slipped out. Nil or partial recoveries should be noted. As soon as the sample has been obtained the tube should be labelled and securely sealed, preferably using multiple layers of micro-crystalline wax to prevent loss of moisture. The top and bottom of the sample must also be identified. Since a lot of time and trouble is taken in obtaining samples and since a great deal will depend on the test results obtained from them, they should be treated with care. They should be handled carefully, not allowed to dry out or get wet, protected from heat, sun, wind and frost and should be transported and stored so that they do not deteriorate and can be easily retrieved.

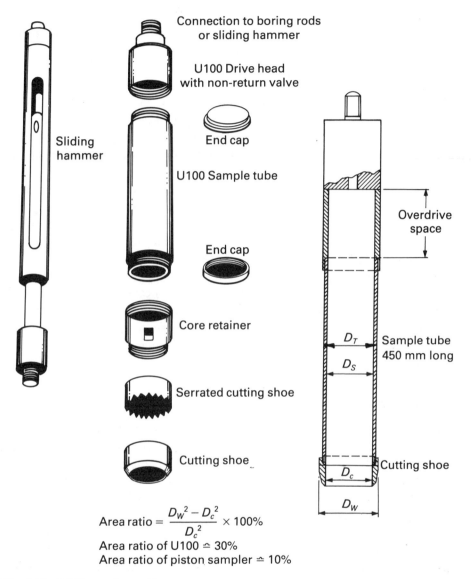

Connection to boring rods
or sliding hammer

U100 Drive head
with non-return valve

End cap

U100 Sample tube

Sliding
hammer

End cap

Core retainer

Serrated cutting shoe

Cutting shoe

Overdrive
space

D_T

D_S

Sample tube
450 mm long

D_c

Cutting shoe

D_W

$$\text{Area ratio} = \frac{D_W^2 - D_c^2}{D_c^2} \times 100\%$$

Area ratio of U100 $\simeq$ 30%

Area ratio of piston sampler $\simeq$ 10%

Fig. 6.11   U100 sampler and hammer.

The frequency with which samples are taken will depend on the requirements of the investigation but a typical investigation would demand sampling of cohesive soils using U100 tubes at each change of strata and at 1.0 m to 1.5 m centres within them and with disturbed samples between them. In non-cohesive granular soils Standard Penetration

117

Tests are normally carried out at each change of strata and at 1.0 m centres within them with additional disturbed samples from each penetration test position and from points midway between them. For special investigations it may be necessary to take continuous samples or choose a more specialized method of sampling or *in situ* testing as described in Chapters 8 and 12.

In order to eliminate the problems associated with the disturbed zones at the top and bottom of U100 samples it is common to carry out 'double-hole sampling' with the sample centre in one hole corresponding to the disturbed zone in an adjacent borehole. The second borehole should be about 1 m from the first in order to avoid its disturbed zone.

It is important that any investigation is assessed and critically reviewed as it progresses to ensure that the best methods of boring, sampling and testing are being used at all times such that the requirements of the investigation can be fulfilled. This must be done with economy in mind but it is of little use taking economy to extremes if it results in obtaining insufficient useful information.

All sampling should be aimed at determining the character and structure of all strata together with their properties. Special care and close supervision of the drilling process is required to ensure that thin layers of different material in the general soil mass are not missed. Where only thin layers of different materials are present it may be necessary to sink a number of boreholes in order to obtain sufficient samples for all testing requirements.

6.10 Standard Penetration Tests

The Standard Penetration Test is the most commonly employed *in situ* test that is carried out during shell and auger boring. It gives an N value of the soil which indicates its relative density. The N value is used in many empirical methods of foundation design and a great deal of work has been carried out in order to relate the test results to other soil properties and to the way in which structures perform in the field. The test is ideally applicable to granular deposits above or below the water table. It can also be used in weak rocks or cohesive materials although with the latter it is usually preferable to obtain 'undisturbed' U100 samples.

The test itself is a dynamic penetration test in which a 50 mm diameter sampling tube with either a solid 60° cone or an open cutting shoe at the end is driven into the ground using a standard weight (65 kg) freely dropping a standard distance (760 mm). The open sampler is used for sands, silts and clays and the solid cone for coarse gravels and weak rocks, but this does not produce a sample. The number of blows needed to drive the sampler a distance of 300 mm is recorded as the N value. In practice the blows needed for each 75 mm are recorded separately to check for consistency and it is convenient to mark the rods off in these increments. The tube is normally driven 450 mm and the

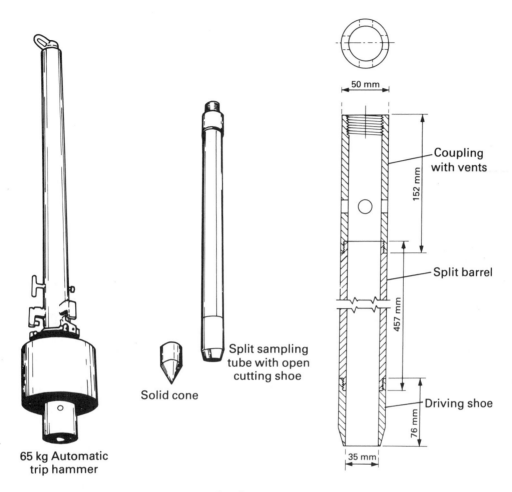

Fig. 6.12 Standard Penetration Test (SPT) equipment.

blows required for the first 150 mm excluded from the calculation to allow for possible disturbance. An automatic trip hammer as shown in Fig. 6.12 is preferred in the test to ensure a consistent height of drop. With such a hammer the weight is picked up as the drilling rope is slackened off then raised to the correct height above an anvil where it automatically releases and falls. If the blow count exceeds 100 it is common practice to stop the test and extrapolate the N value. For example if it has taken 100 blows to drive the sampler 150 mm after the potentially disturbed initial 150 mm the N value is extrapolated as 200. A term descriptive of the density of granular soils is used depending on the blow count as shown below.

119

N	0–4	Very loose
N	4–10	Loose
N	10–30	Compact
N	30–50	Dense
N	over 50	Very dense

The precise procedure to be adopted in carrying out the test is given in British Standard 1377, 1975, *Testing of Soils for Civil Engineering Purposes*, Test 19, 'The determination of penetration resistance using the split-barrel sampler'. The first requirement is to clean out the bottom of the borehole and to ensure that no piping has occurred by keeping the borehole topped up with water when boring below the water table. It is sometimes worth driving the solid cone sampler more than 450 mm through any disturbed soils but a total drive of over 1.5 m should be avoided since friction on the sides will become significant. The sampler should always be used on the end of straight, tightly screwed boring rods which should be prevented from whipping about in the borehole. The trip hammer should also be checked for weight and a truly free drop. If the test is performed by hand, great care is needed to ensure a completely free drop from the correct height. When the sampler is removed from the borehole the cutting shoe and head can be removed and the two longitudinal halves of the tube separated; hopefully to reveal a relatively undisturbed sample. The test is cheap and simple and gives useful information on the *in situ* soil properties but it is not fool proof and if any doubt exists as to its correctness it is adviseable to check by using say plate loading tests or Dutch Cone Tests (see Chapters 8 and 12). Chapter 8 also gives further discussion on the interpretation of penetration tests.

There are many factors which can lead to errors in the determination of the N value in the Standard Penetration Test. These are listed below and care should be taken to eliminate them.

(1) Inadequate cleaning of the bottom of the borehole.
(2) Sampling spoon not seated on undisturbed material.
(3) Part of test not carried out below the casing.
(4) Failure to maintain sufficient head of water to prevent piping.
(5) Not using standard weight or standard drop.
(6) Weight not falling freely.
(7) Weight not striking drive cap squarely.
(8) Guide rod not used.
(9) Damaged sampling spoons.
(10) Use of non-standard drill rods.
(11) Extreme length of drill rods (over 15 m).
(12) Inaccurate count of blows given.

(13) Use in large-diameter boreholes.
(14) Inadequate supervision.
(15) Incorrect sample description which affects interpretation.
(16) Ground disturbance due to boring technique.

6.11 Shell and auger accessories

The shell and auger rig is in itself an extremely versatile piece of equipment being able to cope adequately with most soils and weak rocks but the manufacturers have produced a variety of add-on accessories. The engine is used to drive a hydraulic pump and it is the hydraulic power so generated which drives these accessories.

Since the shell and auger rig uses a percussive action no coring or augering can be carried out and it is for this reason that attachments are available to perform these functions. A framework is erected within the mast or fastened to the casing and it is up and down this framework that a rotary coring head can be moved. The head incorporates a swivel and a hydraulic motor which can turn the drill rods at varying speeds. The drill rods can then be fitted with either a core barrel or an auger. The techniques of using these items are described in Chapter 7. Hydraulic power can be used to apply additional downward pressure on say a core barrel and it can also be used to extrude samples from the core barrel or from a claycutter. Generally speaking these attachments are not as effective as purpose made rotary coring units but they can be useful in proving bedrock or penetrating boulders.

Where considerable depths of granular deposits exist a casing rotator can be used to overcome the problem of casing sticking in such materials. This is again driven hydraulically. When it comes to removing casing the rotator will help considerably or use can be made of hydraulically powered heavy duty jacking units.

6.12 Groundwater observations

The importance of groundwater to the engineer cannot be overemphasized. It has a great deal of significance in all manner of engineering problems whether it be directly (e.g. flowing into excavations and tunnels) or indirectly (e.g. altering soil properties). It is present in virtually all civil-engineering problems since it falls as rain, seeps into the ground and flows through it. The engineer must know how the groundwater will affect his final design, his temporary works and what affect his works will have on the groundwater regime of the surrounding area. The contractual consequences of unknown or misleading information on groundwater conditions can also result in substantial claims from contractors. Groundwater level should not be regarded as a single surface at a certain depth below ground level but rather as a potential variable in some or all of the strata present.

121

Groundwater can exist in different strata at different pressures and its level can vary laterally but even if water is not present in its free state, moisture exists to some extent in all soils and rocks. If there is a sequence such as sand–clay–sand then there may be a water table revealed in the upper layer of sand but not in the clay. This is known as a perched water table. As the casing is driven down into the clay the water from this layer will be sealed off but water will probably again be encountered in the deeper layer of sand and this may be another perched water table or the true equilibrium groundwater level. If this water were under pressure it would tend to rise up inside the casing in which case it would be known as artesian water. The water levels encountered in the two sand layers may vary quite independently of one another. They will vary depending on the time of year, the weather conditions, possibly with the tides and with pumping from nearby wells.

Groundwater is also variable in the ease with which it can flow through soils and rocks and this has a profound effect on the way it is observed. Obviously the water level in a permeable gravel will reveal itself in a borehole within seconds but in an impermeable clay it may take several years to reach an equilibrium level. For this reason it may be necessary to install some form of tube or instrument to monitor the groundwater and its pressure. Such monitoring would also be required where it is necessary to determine seasonal variations. Water can rise up above the actual water table by capillary action, this being much greater in clays than in gravels, and can result in soils being fully saturated above the water table.

In terms of soil properties it is obvious that the more water there is in a soil then the lower will be its strength and the more it will settle when load is applied to it and the water squeezed out. It is less obvious that increasing the pressure of the water in the pores of the soil will reduce its strength. This is the case and if a water table at the surface were undetected it would be possible to overestimate the shear strength of soil at depth by as much as 100%. This would obviously be of critical importance if an embankment were to be designed on the basis of a certain soil strength.

The observation and detailed recording of groundwater is therefore of extreme importance. Any change whatsoever in the water conditions within a borehole must be accurately recorded and this applies equally to water encountered in the ground and to water added to assist boring or prevent piping. The depth at which water is first encountered must be recorded and boring suspended in order that any change can be observed. Some contracts specify waiting 20 min to see if the level rises or falls but it is more sensible to record the level say at 5 or 10 min intervals and see if and when an equilibrium level is reached or if the readings are tending towards one. If seepage is only very slow it is usually acceptable to record this fact and continue boring but again the requirements of the investigation must be considered. If water is encountered which is subsequently sealed off and then more water is encountered this too should be recorded. The water level in the borehole is always recorded at the beginning and end of each shift and every observation should be accompanied by details of borehole depth and casing depth. It is sometimes desirable to leave boreholes open for some time in order to observe changes.

The true picture of groundwater conditions may be difficult to obtain from the borehole since the water may not have had time to reach equilibrium or water may have been added to prevent piping. In these cases it may be necessary to monitor groundwater levels over a period of time and for this purpose a standpipe or piezometer is required. Before deciding exactly where or how to install them, consideration must be given to exactly which water table needs to be measured and in which stratum. In the example quoted above two possible groundwater levels could be monitored and they would require different instrument installations.

The simplest problem will be considered first and that is of a simple standpipe monitoring a single groundwater level. The installation is shown in Fig. 6.13(a) and consists of a porous element on the end of a 20 mm diameter plastic pipe and surrounded by a filter medium which is sealed at the top to prevent ingress of surface water. This therefore monitors the average groundwater level over the whole length of the filter section. If it is desired to monitor groundwater at the base of a borehole the arrangement shown in Fig. 6.13(b) is used and if it is desired to monitor groundwater in a particular stratum Fig. 6.13(c) is followed. The latter two installations are known as piezometers as distinct from standpipes. It is possible to install more than one piezometer in each borehole but this is undesirable and it is generally better to drill separate boreholes since seepage can occur between two porous elements in a single hole. Various types of porous element are available to suit different conditions but the important factor in making a choice is that the permeability of the element should be greater than the permeability of the soil in which the groundwater level is to be monitored. With any piezometer there is a time lag before a true water level or pressure is recorded. This may only be a matter of minutes with sands and gravels but could be several weeks or even months with a clay. Using either standpipes or piezometers it is possible to carry out field permeability tests and these are discussed in Chapter 8.

Because of the previously discussed importance of groundwater the borehole must be drilled with care to prevent disturbance of the soil structure and the piezometer must be installed with equal care. Assuming, as will probably be the case, that casing has been used this is slowly withdrawn as uncontaminated layers of backfill, sealant, sand or filter medium are built up. This procedure should be carried out slowly to cause the minimum of disturbance particularly where water is already present in the hole. Any material placed must be thoroughly compacted using some form of rammer to prevent future settlement which might destroy the installation.

The porous element should be fully saturated and filled with water before it is placed in the hole and it should be surrounded by clean, well-graded sand which may be fed in as a sand–water mixture. The seals normally employed are those using bentonite clay in

123

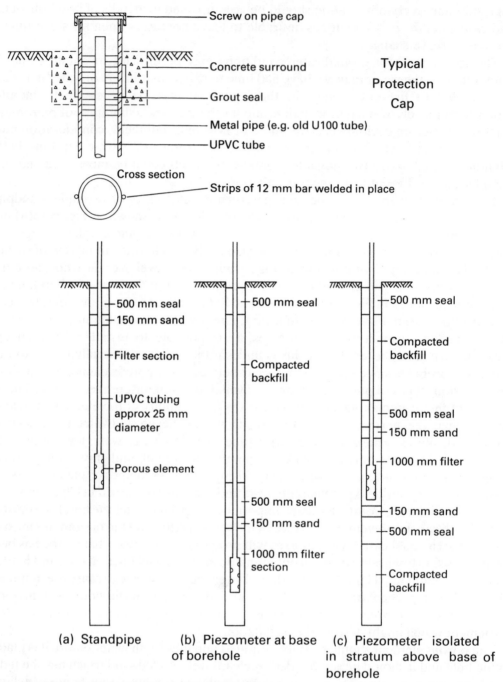

- Screw on pipe cap
- Concrete surround
- Grout seal
- Metal pipe (e.g. old U100 tube)
- UPVC tube

Typical
Protection
Cap

Cross section
- Strips of 12 mm bar welded in place

(a) Standpipe
- 500 mm seal
- 150 mm sand
- Filter section
- UPVC tubing approx 25 mm diameter
- Porous element

(b) Piezometer at base of borehole
- 500 mm seal
- Compacted backfill
- 500 mm seal
- 150 mm sand
- 1000 mm filter section

(c) Piezometer isolated in stratum above base of borehole
- 500 mm seal
- Compacted backfill
- 500 mm seal
- 150 mm sand
- 1000 mm filter
- 150 mm sand
- 500 mm seal
- Compacted backfill

Fig. 6.13 Standpipe and piezometer installations.

124

the form of hand prepared balls, filled open-weave sacks or pellets and are all virtually impermeable following compaction with a horseshoe shaped punning tool. If pumped grout it used to fill or seal boreholes a suitable mix would be 4 parts bentonite, 1 part cement and 10 parts water. Care must be taken to ensure that each layer is kept separate from its neighbour; over compaction for instance can cause mixing.

Once the piezometer or standpipe is installed its operation should be checked by adding or taking out water and checking that the level returns to the original. The actual reading of water level is normally done with a simple electronic dip meter in which a circuit is completed when a probe touches the water surface. This may give a meter reading, a light or an audio signal and should be related to a fixed datum.

Figure 6.13 shows a typical arrangement for securing the instrument at ground level. Half a U100 sample tube is embedded in concrete and the cap may be drilled to allow for a bar and padlock. Many other possible arrangements exist but they should all be water tight but not air tight and should not allow surface water to get into the UPVC riser pipe. The ground around the instrument should be shaped to shed water rather than allow it to pond. Once the piezometer is installed it may be used to carry out permeability tests as discussed in Chapter 8.

Assessing the probable action of chemically or bacteriologically contaminated groundwater on steel and concrete is an important feature of any site investigation and care must be taken that any groundwater sample recovered is truly representative. For instance concrete can deteriorate in soils possessing high concentrations of soluble sulphates. The sample taken must not be contaminated by surface water, rainfall or drilling fluids and should be placed in a clean jar. More stringent requirements using sophisticated samplers may be required in investigation into possible groundwater pollution. Geophysical techniques, particularly resistivity, can also be used to assess the aggressive potential of groundwater.

6.13 Field records

The basic objectives of site investigation have been discussed earlier but it is worth repeating them. They are to ensure that the site is suitable for the proposed works, that the investigation leads to a safe and economic design, that it leads to an effective and feasible method of construction and that it indicates what changes the works will produce on the local area. Recommendations concerning these objectives are passed on to the client in the form of a report and this report must present all the information on which the recommendations are based. Communication of everything revealed by the boreholes is therefore a paramount importance. The major cost of a site investigation lies in the fieldwork and as much as possible must be obtained from it. Remember that in the end the only tangible result is the report; it is no use drilling a borehole unless exactly what is found is described in this document in an unambiguous manner.

125

The field records must therefore be completed conscientiously as the work proceeds. They should be clear and should contain all field data and test results that are obtained. The actual form used for recording the data should be simple and easy to use so that the driller is encouraged to provide all the information needed. An example of such a form taken from the British Standard code of practice on site investigation is shown in Fig. 6.14 but individual requirements may vary and this should not be regarded as definitive. The driller should be encouraged to record any observations he may make on the back of the form since at the drilling stage it will not be known just what is relevant and what is not. The location of the hole must of course be defined and a sketch plan is often helpful. Unnecessary observations can always be deleted but events and measurements made on site are soon forgotten if they are not recorded. Too much information is infinitely preferable to too little. Some drillers have a rough book and transfer the information to the daily report when they have clean hands.

The essential information required is discussed below.

(1) Site, Job, Number, Date, Sheet Number, Ground Level, Names of Driller and Crew, and Weather are self explanatory.

(2) The type of rig used should be described since different machines perform in different ways.

(3) The type of tool used may vary throughout the day as differing strata are encountered.

(4) In the strata record two factors are important. First the strata encountered must be described in accordance with the standard procedure described in Chapter 9 and secondly the depths at which changes occur must be recorded. Before making a sample description the driller must be satisfied that his samples are representative of the strata he is in. Depth measurements are usually made with a weighted water resistant tape. The measurement is made to the top of the drive head on the casing and the height of this above a fixed point at ground level is then subtracted to give depths below ground level. Allowance must be made for the size of the sinker weight used on the end of the tape. Measurements should be made to an accuracy of at least ± 50 mm, preferably less. An experienced driller will know at any time what total length of casing he is using and will also know the total length of tools and rods in use and measurements can be made relative to these. The total length of casing must be known to ensure that the casing is not allowed to penetrate beyond the bottom of the hole and thus cause disturbance. In clays it should be kept four diameters above the bottom. The importance of recording all changes of strata cannot be over-emphasized since even very thin layers may be extremely important. An example would be a thin layer of loose, water-bearing sand

Daily report of cable percussion boring						Site:		Location:	
Casing record						Job No:		Borehole No:	
		250 mm	200 mm	150 mm	125 mm	Date:		Sheet: of:	
	From, m					Ground level: m (Ordnance datum)		Crew/operator:	
	To, m					Weather:			
Type of rig:						Tool used:			

Strata record — Depth at start

Sample and test record

Disturbed samples (bulk; small jar; water)

Depth, m					
Type					

Disturbed samples (continued)

Depth, m					
Type					

Undisturbed samples

Sample depth (top), m					
No. of blows					
Length of sample, m					
Dia., mm					
Casing depth, m					

Penetration tests

Starting depth, m					
Blows per 75 mm 1 2 / 3 4 / 5 6					
Casing depth, m					
Cone or spoon					
Depth of water in borehole, m					
Is hole "blowing"?					

Depth at finish

Water record

Time record, h

Water levels, m				on pulling casing	24 h after pulling casing	Total (this sheet)		Boring	
Time of day						Moving (including pulling casing) from borehole		To borehole	
Depth to water						Chiselling between	m and	m	
Depth cased						Chiselling between	m and	m	
Depth of hole						Chiselling between	m and	m	
At what levels was water encountered?						Standing times (details in remarks)	(i)	(ii)	(iii)
Did the level rise?									
If so, how much and how fast?									

Water added to assist boring?	Remarks
If so, at what depths?	
At what depths was water cut off by casing?	
If standpipe inserted, to what depth?	
NOTE. If more than one water level is encountered give details of them all.	

Fig. 6.14 Typical daily report form of cable percussion boring (from BS5930:1981).

127

within a clay stratum which would be highly significant in assessing the stability of excavations or the time of consolidation.

(5) Samples should be taken as discussed in Section 6.9 and details recorded on the form. It should be noted that casing depth is recorded with the details of undisturbed samples and penetration tests since this can affect the results obtained. Details should be given of undisturbed sampling even if, as occasionally happens, no sample is recovered. In the penetration test great care must be taken to ensure that no piping has occurred since if it has the results are meaningless.

(6) All parts of the section headed 'Water Record' should be completed with care; the importance of this has already been discussed. All readings should be taken using a dip meter. Water rising in a borehole can be described as a seepage if it rises 300 mm in 10 min and fast if it rises 600 mm or more in 10 min. The depths of any slight seepages which do not give rise to an actual water level should also be recorded. Water added to assist boring in stiff clays should be kept to an absolute minimum and all additions should be recorded. Water levels should be recorded at the start and finish of each shift. If no water is encountered nil should be entered in the appropriate box.

(7) The time record gives a useful indication of the ease of boring and may be required for payment purposes. Details of chiselling in rock give a useful guide when assessing depths of piling or rippability. If progress is slow using the chisel it is probably better to start rotary coring.

(8) The remarks section is the column for all observations not covered elsewhere and as such it may extend to the back of the sheet. Comments can be given on lost time, breakdowns, weather, site visits by engineers, access problems and particular difficulties encountered during boring. Anything at all relating to the site investigation should be recorded, perhaps even a piece of relevant local knowledge gleaned from a passer by. The end of shift should be clearly differentiated from the end of borehole. The daily report so far described has been for straightforward shell and auger or cable percussion boring and it should be freely adapted to meet specific needs. Separate sheets will probably be required for special testing, piezometer observations and the like and the driller should not forget that a simple sketch may say more than several dozen words. The daily report is the end product of the driller's work and as such it should be treated with due regard to its importance.

The information on the driller's daily report will contribute a great deal to the final borehole log, an example of which is shown in Fig. 6.15. It is logs such as these that form the bulk of any site investigation report and they must be accurate and unambiguous. It

128

Name of company: A N Other Ltd.								Borehole No. 1 Sheet 1 of 1		

Equipment & methods: Light cable tool percussion rig. 200 mm dia. hole to 7.00 m. Casing 200 mm dia. to 6.00 m.		Location No: 6155								

Carried out for: Smith, Jones & Brown		Ground level: 9.90 m (Ordnance datum)		Coordinates: E 350 N 901				Date: 17–18 June 1974		

Description	Reduced level	Legend	Depth & thickness	Samples/tests				Field records
				Depth	Sample Type	No.	Test	
Made Ground (sand, gravel, ash, brick and pottery)	9.40		(0.50) 0.50	0.20	D	1		
Made Ground (red and brown clay with gravel)	9.10		(0.30) 0.80	0.70 – 1.15	U D	2 3		24 blows
Firm mottled brown silty CLAY (Brickearth)			(1.20)	1.15				
	7.90		2.0					
Stiff brown sandy CLAY with some gravel (Flood Plain Gravel)			(1.65)	2.10 – 2.55 2.55	U D	4 5		50 blows
	6.25		3.65	3.60 – 4.05 3.65	D U	6	S N27	No recovery
Medium dense brown sandy fine to coarse GRAVEL (Flood Plain Gravel)			(1.65)	4.00 – 4.30 4.00 – 5.00	B	7		
	4.60		5.30	5.00 – 5.30 5.30	D	8	S N15	Standpipe inserted 5.30 m below ground level
Firm becoming stiff to very stiff fissured grey silty CLAY with partings of silt (London Clay)			(2.15)	6.00 – 6.45	U	9		35 blows
	2.45		7.45	7.00 – 7.45	U	10		44 blows
End of borehole								

Water level observations during boring

Date	Time	Depth of hole, m	Depth of casing, m	Depth to water, m	Remarks
18 Jun	1615	7.00	0.00	3.65	casing withdrawn
24 Jun	1200	0.00	0.00	2.37	standpipe readings
27 Jun	0915	0.00	0.00	2.33	
27 Jun	1420	0.00	0.00	2.11	
28 Jun	1000	0.00	0.00	2.46	
1 Jul	1015	0.00	0.00	2.46	

SPT: Where full 0.3 m penetration has not been achieved, the number of blows for the quoted penetration is given (not *N*-value). Depths: All depths and reduced levels in metres. Thicknesses given in brackets in depth column. Water: Water level observations during boring are given on last sheet of log.	Sample/test key D Disturbed sample B Bulk sample W Water sample I Piston (P), tube (U) or core sample; length to scale S Standard penetration test V Vane test C Core recovery (%) r Rock Quality Designation (RQD %)	Remarks Water added to facilitate boring from 0.50 m to 7.00 m. Borehole back filled with natural spoil from 7.00 m to 5.30 m, gravel to 0.80 m, clay to 0.50 m, a concreted cock box to ground level.	Logged by: Scale:

Fig. 6.15 Typical log of data from a light cable percussion borehole (from BS5930:1981).

1. General

The comments given in this report and the opinions expressed are based on the ground conditions encountered during the site work and on the results of tests made in the field and in the laboratory. There may, however, be special conditions prevailing at the site which have not been disclosed by the investigation and which have not been taken into account in the report.

The comments on ground water conditions are based on observations made at the time the site work was carried out. It should be noted, however, that ground water levels vary owing to seasonal or other effects.

2. Borehole records: symbols and abbreviations

Soil samples

U   General purpose: 100 mm diameter sample.
U+   Sample not obtained.
U*   Full penetration of sampler not obtained.
U↓   Full penetration obtained but limited sample recovered.
U̲   Open sample: 40 mm diameter; 300 mm in length.
$\bar{P}_a$ Piston sample: 100 mm diameter; 600 mm in length.
P_b Piston sample: 250 mm diameter; 300 mm in length.
D   Disturbed sample.
BD   Bulk disturbed sample.
W   Water sample.
*   Ground water first observed.

NOTE. Depths are given to the tops of samples.

Rock core descriptions

TCR   Total core recovery. The length of the total amount of core sample recovered expressed as a percentage of the length of core run.

SCR   Solid core recovery. The length of core recovered as solid cylinders, expressed as a percentage of the length of core run.

RQD   Rock quality designation. The sum length of all core pieces that are 10 cm or longer, measured along the centre line of the core, expressed as a percentage of the core drilled.

Rock strength test, standpipe and piezometer installations

I_s Point load index. This test, carried out on rock cores following their extraction, gives a measure of the strength of the rock material. Values are given in the in situ test columns on the borehole record in MN/m^2.

    Base of standpipe (shown in legend column).

    Centre of piezometer (shown in legend column).

In situ tests

S   Standard penetration test (SPT). A 50 mm diameter split spoon sampler is driven 450 mm into the soil using a 65 kg hammer with a 760 mm drop, and the penetration resistance is expressed as the number of blows required to obtain 300 mm penetration below an initial penetration of 150 mm through any disturbed ground at the bottom of the borehole.

In the borehole record, the depth of the test is that at the start of the normal 450 mm penetration. The number of blows to achieve the standard penetration of 300 mm (the 'N' value) is shown after the test index letter, but the seating blows through the initial 150 mm penetration are not reported unless the full penetration of 450 mm is not achieved. In the latter case, the symbols below are added to the test index letter:

S^+ Seating blows only.
$S^‡$ Blow count includes seating blows.
S^* No penetration.
S +   Split spoon sampler sank under its own weight.

The test is usually completed when the number of blows reaches 50. For tests achieving the full penetration of 450 mm, the depth at which the test procedure is commenced is given in the depth column on the borehole record, whilst for those tests not achieving full penetration, the depths of both the top and the bottom of the test drive are shown. If a sample is not recovered in the split spoon sampler, a disturbed sample is taken on completion of the test drive. Both are given the same depth as the top of the SP test drive.

C   Dynamic Cone Penetration Test (CPT). A test conducted usually in coarse granular soils using the same procedure as for the SPT but with a 50 mm diameter, $60°$ apex solid cone fitted to the split spoon sampler. Variations in test results are indicated by the same symbols as for the SPT. The bulk disturbed sample taken, is given the same depth as the top of the CP test drive.

V   Vane test.
J   Borehole jack test. See text of report for full description.
K   Permeability test. See text of report for full description.

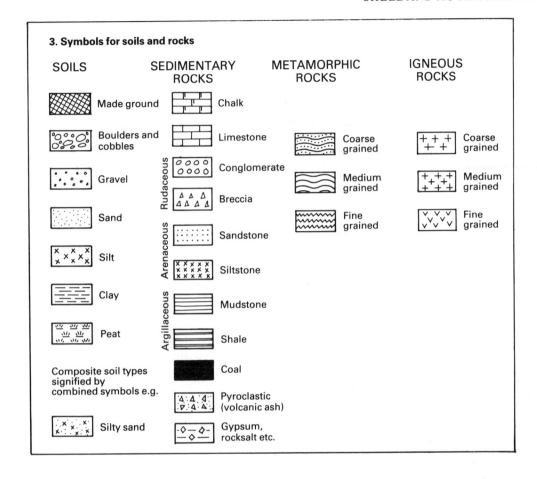

Fig. 6.16 Key to borehole logs (after BS5930:1981).

will be seen from Fig. 6.15 that the final borehole log forms an interpretation in its own right since all boreholes will have been correlated and strata described consistently. The samples that were taken will have been examined by an engineer and tests carried out on them and hence the sample description will be more accurate. Simple test results such as moisture content and Standard Penetration Test can also be included on these forms. Like the daily report the final borehole log may vary from one organization to another but the aim should be to produce a clear, easily understood and easily read log. A standard method of sample description should be used and the legend should use the standard symbols but otherwise the format can be varied. A key of some sort is normally necessary as an explanatory preface to the borehole logs themselves, see Fig. 6.16.

131

7
Rotary drilling

7.1 Introduction

This chapter covers those methods of boring which utilize a rotary action as distinct from the percussive method which was covered in the previous chapter. As such it will mainly be concerned with the rotary coring of rock but will also cover flight augering in soft ground. Rock is usually defined in civil engineering terms as 'hard strata found in ledges or masses in its original position and which in normal excavation would have to be loosened by blasting or pneumatic tools; or if by hand, by wedges and sledge hammers; or strata in drilling which requires the use of diamond or tungsten carbide bits; or boulders exceeding 0.3 m in thickness measured parallel to the axis of boring.'

When·rock is encountered during shell and auger boring progress can be made, albeit slowly, by chiselling but this only produces rock chippings which are lifted to the surface using the shell after water has been added. As such only a Class 5 sample is obtained and the engineer has at best only a knowledge of the general rock type and a rough idea of its overall strength from the rate of penetration. He will have no information whatsoever on the rock structure. Clearly when this situation arises and it is necessary to know the rock structure another method of recovering samples must be used. This is done by rotating a tube-type diamond or tungsten carbide tipped drilling bit which cuts a core of rock. The core is then protected and brought to the surface inside a core barrel. To do this a flushing medium is required which will cool the bit and lift the cuttings to the surface.

In a great many civil engineering works it is the rock structure which is of major importance. For the engineer to study this he requires full core recovery in order to observe the precise nature of the rock, its pattern of jointing, fissuring and bedding, its degree of weathering and the presence of any thin layers of softer materials either as distinct strata or as infilling to open joints. He will also require full core recovery so that samples can be taken for laboratory testing.

If a rock mass in say a quarry face is considered it should be obvious that it is not the rock itself that is of prime importance to stability but rather the degree of fracturing and jointing. If the rock mass had no planes of weakness it would be much the same as a solid block of concrete but if the rock mass were very heavily jointed or fractured it would behave more like a granular deposit or a pile of aggregate. Obviously there are many different cases between these two extremes where interlocking of blocks will aid stability. In order to make a true assessment of slope stability the degree of fracturing and jointing must be known together with the direction of these features in relation to the quarry face. It would also be extremely important if a thin layer of soft material were dipping into the quarry face and on which the harder rock mass could slide. Similar problems arise in many other engineering works such as tunnels, dams and foundations. Another example where the extent of fracturing might be important is in assessing how easily water could flow through a rock mass and here the nature of any infilling to the joints would also be important.

For the features described above to be studied, 100% core recovery is essential since if only 90% is recovered then the engineer or geologist is left with a problem, particularly since the missing 10% is likely to be softer material and therefore of more importance. The engineer or geologist will not know whether the missing 10% represents a single layer or many thin layers of infilling to the joints nor at what levels it has been lost from.

The prime objective of rotary coring is, therefore, to produce 100% uncontaminated and undisturbed core recovery. The achievement of this objective is not without complications. The driller will probably have a choice of drilling rigs, core bits, core barrels, bit pressures, rotation speeds, flushing volumes and so on and in certain rocks it may not be by any means easy to find the right combination of these. A further complication is that the driller may not know he has a problem until he has gone past it; in other words he will only know he has core missing when he brings the core barrel to the surface and compares the depth drilled with the thickness of the strata recovered. If 100% recovery is not achieved the driller must be prepared to learn from his mistakes and try different equipment and methods. If the core recovery in any borehole is unacceptably poor it will be necessary to drill another one.

The object of this chapter is to outline the common types of equipment available and offer some guidance on how to use it. The word common is stressed here since there are innumerable types of equipment available and to cover them all would be beyond the scope of this book. It is not possible to teach anyone to drill using a text book; this can only come from experience. There is not a driller anywhere who will not be learning something new each time he drills a borehole since circumstances, strata and method will be varying each time.

133

7.2 Rotary rigs

There are a large number of different units available for core drilling ranging from lightweight hand-held machines to the massive rigs used in offshore oil exploration. Some of these will be discussed later but first let us consider the requirements of a normal site investigation rotary drilling rig capable of coring to a depth of 100 m. The first requirement is for a source of power and this would be between 20 and 40 horse power. The engine power is required first to rotate the core bit and secondly to provide a means of feeding the bit into the ground under pressure and pulling it up again. There are two ways of producing the required rotation; it can be done directly through a gearbox and clutch to a chuck which grips the drilling rods or it can be done by converting the engine power to hydraulic power and driving a hydraulic motor at the top of the drill string when it is known as a 'top drive' rig. This has the advantage of a longer stroke and makes for a more versatile rig which could be used, for instance, with a 'down the hole' hammer. On the other hand top drive rigs tend to have less torque, less speed range and are generally more suited to the drilling of softer rocks.

The rotation speed of the bit should be variable up to about 1000 rpm although 500 rpm would be a typical speed for rotary coring. The torque and downward load requirements will depend on the size of bit used but typically would be up to 20 kg m and 800 kg respectively although substantial additional torque may be necessary to overcome problems of turning the core barrel in rocks which tend to swell as they are cored. In addition to the engine and transmission a mast and winch unit is needed so that drilling rods, barrels and casing can be quickly lifted in and out of the hole. The rig ideally should combine the above features in a self-contained, easily transportable unit which is rugged, simple to operate and easy to maintain. It must also be capable of providing a stable platform with no tendency to move or vibrate during coring. The rig itself may be skid mounted, trailer mounted or mounted on a four wheel-drive truck or tractor.

Figure 7.1 shows a conventional rig with a chuck and hydraulic rams to provide the pull down. On older rigs a screw feed was incorporated instead of the hydraulic pull down. Figure 7.2 shows a top drive rig where the hydraulic motor is pulled up and down the mast. Table 7.1 compares a number of currently available rigs suitable for site investigation work. In making a choice of rig, consideration must be given to the depth and diameter of the hole to be drilled, the ease of access and the method of mounting.

The description given above was for a typical mid-range type of site investigation rig but depending on the job requirements there are a number of alternatives. Small lightweight hand-held petrol-driven drills are available but these are only capable of drilling 30 mm diameter holes with about 20 mm diameter cores. The penetration rate is controlled by the operator and they are only really suitable for preliminary investigations in remote areas where shallow holes are all that is required. Casing cannot be used to support the sides of the borehole in caving ground.

Fig. 7.1 Boyles BBS 37 chuck-type rotary drilling rig mounted on county tractor with integral air compressor (photograph: Boyles Bros Ltd).

135

Fig. 7.2 Craelius B31L top-drive rotary drilling rig mounted on four-wheel-drive truck and shown using hollow stem flight augers (photograph: Craelius Co. Ltd).

Slightly larger, but still lightweight, frame-mounted drills are available and these are often used for concrete coring mounted on the back of a Land Rover or trailer for greater stability. They usually have 5–10 horse power petrol engines, but air or hydraulic motors can also be used. Small diameter rock coring is possible with these units to depths of 30 m and to about 15 m with 75 mm diameter flight-augering equipment in suitable ground. Rods, barrels and augers must be lifted by hand. These rigs are again only really suitable for preliminary investigations.

In Chapter 6 a description was given of the hydraulic units which can be attached to shell and auger rigs. Cores up to 76 mm in diameter can be obtained but 54 mm is the normal size when depths of around 30 m are possible. These 'pendant' attachments have a range of rotation speeds and pull down units are available to vary the downward pressure; rod handling is of course done with the percussion winch unit. They are not as stable as purpose-built rotary rigs and they do not have the weight available for really efficient drilling nor can the feed rate be altered but they are extremely useful for proving bedrock or drilling through obstructions. For drilling over water where a percussive rig would be moving up and down a similar unit is available which clamps to the shell and auger casing. It has a chuck which clamps and turns the drill rods and hydraulic rams which provide the pull down. It has a similar capability to any standard pendant type unit and rod handling is again using the shell and auger rig itself.

The conventional small- to medium-sized rigs for site investigation work have already been described and these are capable of achieving depths of over 200 m which is as much as is normally required. There are, however, many larger rigs available for water-well drilling and mineral exploration and of course these too can be used in a site investigation for say tunnelling where greater depths of coring are necessary.

7.3 Basic techniques

Figure 7.3 illustrates the plant and equipment necessary on site for the drilling of a typical site investigation borehole. The main elements are:

Drilling rig
This may be mounted in a number of ways and should be chosen to suit the access conditions and the requirements of the borehole.

Site transport
Normally a four-wheel-drive vehicle possibly with a trailer for moving equipment.

Living van or site hut
To afford protection to the drillers during inclement weather.

Flushing equipment
Either, (a) a high-pressure water pump supplied from a hydrant, stream, lake or water cart. If water is in short supply a recirculation system can be added, or (b) a compressor for air flushing possibly with provision for injecting chemical foams.

Table 7.1 Comparison of rotary rigs

Manufacturer		Christiansen/ Central Mine Equipment			English Drilling Equipment		Castle Drilling Rigs	Wirth Gmbh
Model		55/550	75/750	45	Stratadrill 20	40	Casdril 6000	80
Type	C = Chuck T = Top drive	C	C	C	C	C	T	T
Engine	P = Petrol; A = Air D = Diesel; E = Electric	P/D	P/D	P/D	P/D E/A	P/D E/A	D	D
Engine horsepower (US = United States measure)		124 (US)	151 (US)	68 (US)	20	40	150	30
Speed range of rods (rpm)		0–650	0–700	0–745	70–1660	60–1220	0–300	8–870
Maximum torque (kgm)		965	1170	525	207	414	830	125
Maximum pulldown (kg)		7250	9070	4080	4235	4235	15 000	2200
Feed stroke (m)		1.83	1.83	1.73	0.76	0.76	6.86	1.15–3.35
Maximum feed speed Up/down (m min^{-1})		11.2/17.5	27.4/17.5	16.7/24.1	NS	NS	36.5	27.6
Rated capacity NW rod (m)		300	485	150	213	439	1500	750
Rated capacity HW rod (m)		NS	NS	NS	152	320	1000	450
Rated capacity (m) 150 mm flight auger		NS	NS	NS	NS	NS	⎧ 20000 kg	30
Rated capacity (m) 250 mm flight auger		75	90	45	NS	NS	⎩ wt	25

Notes   Information as supplied by manufacturers or their agents summer 1981
NS = Not specified or not suitable
This table does not include all rigs available

138

Craelius					Duke and Ockenden	Boyles Bros			Pilcon Engineering	
Diamec 251	Diamec D900	Mobile B31L	Mobile B40L	Mobile B80	250	BBS15	BBS25	BBS37	Traveller 50	Traveller 30
C	C	T or C	T or C	T or C	T	C	C	C	T	T
D/E	D/E	D/P	D/P	D/P	External power source	D/P	D/P	D/P	D	D
54	40	45	65	65	100 required	26–37	43–64	58–84	66	30
20–2200	140–1120	10–418	27–716	0–716	0–800	0–1460	0–1724	0–1316	47–687	0–500
NS	157	453	824	824	600	310	520	520	313	207
4130	4400	2880	4270	5000	7500	9530	9890	9890	3290	2730
0.85 or 1.60	0.50	3.60	3.7 or 6.7	4.27	6.0	0.76	0.76	0.76	3.40	3.80
NS	NS	30.0	23.4	48.0	40.0	NS	NS	NS	26	33.7
170	500	140	305	300	350	275	425	640	350	385
110	325	105	230	230	350	185	275	410	200	220
NS	NS	41	46	75	40	NS	NS	NS	40	25–30
NS	NS	26	20	45	25	NS	NS	NS	30	20–25

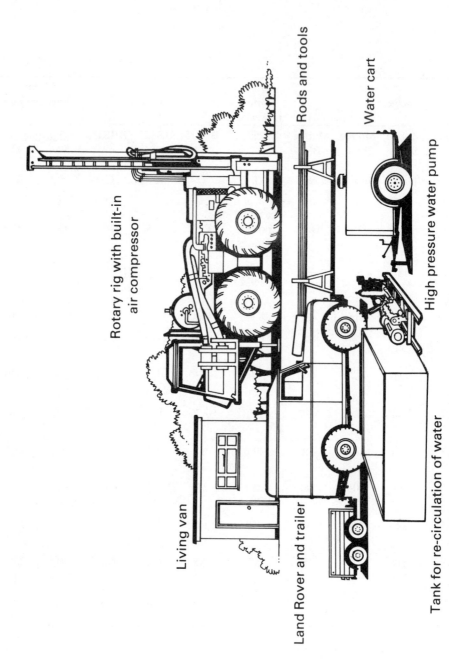

Rotary rig with built-in air compressor

Rods and tools

Water cart

High pressure water pump

Living van

Land Rover and trailer

Tank for re-circulation of water

Fig. 7.3 Site organization.

Down the hole equipment and tools
Comprising drilling rods, core barrels, core bits, casing, swivels and the tools necessary for coupling/uncoupling the above and for basic maintenance.

When planning the fieldwork for any ground investigation consideration must be given to ease of access, underground services, overhead cables and so on and the equipment chosen to suit the circumstances. It may be necessary to carry out temporary works before the rig is moved onto site and in some cases these may have to be quite extensive. Staging, scaffolding or earth moving might be involved but in all cases the important thing is to produce a safe, stable rig position with adequate working space around it. The choice of flushing medium may depend on the requirements of the investigation or it may depend on the availability of water on site. The choice of the 'down the hole' equipment will again depend on the requirements of the investigation and of the flushing medium to be used. It will also depend on the type of strata to be penetrated and this will be covered later in the chapter but the essential thing is that it should be chosen to give as near as possible to 100% core recovery.

Having established the drilling rig on site care should be taken to ensure that it is absolutely stable. It is no use expecting to get 100% core recovery if the rig is moving about or if the rods are vibrating and chattering in the hole since not only will this action break up the core but it will also cause an undersize, possibly non-circular, core to be cut which might slip out of the core barrel. With certain lightweight rigs it is advantageous to tie the rig to the ground using ground anchors so that the necessary reaction can be obtained and sufficient pressure applied to the bit.

The size and type of 'down the hole' equipment that is used will depend on what size core is required and this is where a good deal of confusion arises over nomenclature. There is obviously a wide range of different sizes of core barrels, core bits, casing and drilling rods which can be used to obtain cores of from 19 mm to 165 mm in diameter. There are for instance NW and HWY rods, BWM and NWX core barrels, NX and HW casing and NWF and HWG core bits and many other combinations of letters which relate to British and American standards (see Table 7.2).

The British Standard for rotary core-drilling equipment is BS4019 which defines sizes, designs, threads, tolerances, metal quality and so on. There is an equally wide range of types and sizes which form a separate metric system. The basic principle of both systems is that each piece of casing rests inside the next size up and that the corresponding core bit passes down inside the casing. It is also designed so that a hole drilled with a certain size of core bit will admit the next size down of casing. In this way a deep borehole can progressively reduce in diameter and casing can be added at all times to support the sides and to keep the annular area between the drill rod and the casing such that sufficient uphole velocities of the flushing medium are obtained at all times. (This will be further discussed in later sections). The principle of reducing sizes is

Table 7.2 Dimensions of rotary drilling equipment

Drill rods				Casing flush coupled				Casing flush jointed			
Size	OD (mm)	coupling ID (mm)	weight kg/3m	size	OD (mm)	coupling ID (mm)	weight kg/3m	size	OD (mm)	coupling ID (mm)	weight kg/3m
BW	54.0	19.0	22.3	BX	73.0	60.3	27.7	BW	73.0	60.3	31.3
NW	66.8	34.9	24.6	NX	88.9	76.2	35.7	NW	88.9	76.2	38.8
HW	89.0	60.5	42.8	HX	114.3	100.0	41.1	HW	114.3	101.6	50.9
				PX	139.7	122.3	55.8	PW	139.7	123.8	68.3
				SX	168.3	147.7	74.6	SW	168.3	150.8	87.1
				UX	193.7	176.2	87.9	UW	193.7	176.2	104.9

HQ   88.9   77.8
Unless stated rods and casing as detailed above

42.0	42.0	22.0	12.9								
50.0	50.0	22.0	20.5					56	54.2	47.2	13.1
60.0	60.0	25.0	24.4					66	64.3	57.2	15.7
								76	74.3	67.2	18.3
								86	84.3	77.2	20.9
								101	98.0	88.3	31.1
								116	113.0	103.3	36.1
								131	128.0	118.3	41.1
								146	143.0	133.3	46.1

Table 7.2 Dimensions of rotary drilling equipment

Core barrel design	Core bit OD (mm)	Core bit ID (mm)	Reaming shell OD (mm)	Remarks	Hole diam. (mm) approx.	Core diam. (mm) approx.	Size
BWG BWF BWM	59.6	42.0	59.9		60	42	B
BWT	59.6	44.5	59.9	*British, American*	60	45	B
NWG NWF NWM	75.3	54.7	75.7	*and Canadian*	76	55	N
NWT	75.3	58.8	75.7	*Standard*	76	59	N
HWF HWG	98.8	76.2	99.2	*Designs*	99	76	H
HWT	98.8	81.0	99.2	*(see BS4019)*	99	81	H
PWF	120.0	92.1	120.6		121	92	P
SWF	145.4	112.8	146.0		146	113	S
UWF	173.7	139.8	174.5		175	140	U
TNX	75.3	60.8	75.7	Thin wall design	76	61	TNX
HQ	95.6	61.1	96.1	Wireline	96	61	HQ
HWAF	99.5	70.9	99.6	Air flush	100	71	HWAF
HMLC	99.0	63.5	99.6	Triple tube barrel	100	64	HMLC
412	105.2	75.0	107.6	Non standard design	108	75	412
T2	56.0	42.0	56.3	*Metric standards*	56	42	56
TT	56.0	45.5	56.3	Extra thin wall	56	45	56
T6	66.0	47.0	66.3		66	47	66
T2	66.0	52.0	66.3	T2 is water barrel	66	52	66
T6	76.0	57.0	76.3	T6 is mud/water	76	57	76
T2	76.0	62.0	76.3	SK6 is wireline	76	62	76
T6	86.0	67.0	86.3		86	67	86
T2	86.0	72.0	86.3		86	72	86
T6	101.0	79.0	101.3		101	79	101
T2	101.0	84.0	101.3	(other types include	101	84	101
T6	116.0	93.0	116.3	B, K3 and T65)	116	93	116
T6	131.0	108.0	131.3		131	108	131
SK6	146.0	102.0	146.3	Wireline	146	102	146
T6	146.0	123.0	146.3		146	123	146

illustrated in Fig. 7.4 which also illustrates the relative sizes of a number of commonly used pieces of equipment.

The significance of the letters is as follows:

R E A B N H P S U Z are identification symbols relating to size and normally, but not always, are the first letter in any designation. R is the smallest size and Z the largest. N and H are common sizes of equipment used in site investigation. Each item in a compatible string of drilling rods, core barrel, bit and casing would all start with the same letter. Each size of casing nests inside the next size up. For example, an N-size core barrel and bit will pass through NX or NW casing and will drill a hole which will take BX or BW casing and so on.

W denotes a particular design of drill rod and core barrel head. Where it is used in the designation of casing it means it is flush jointed. It was originally introduced to indicate a 'worldwide' standard.

Y is used to identify a non-standard tapered thread drill rod.

X is used to identify flush coupled casing only and is lighter than the W casing although not as strong.

G denotes a universal or general-purpose double tube core barrel and core bit design.

M denotes a modified G-type design.

F applies to double tube core barrels and core bits with face discharge of the flushing medium.

T denotes a range of core barrels using thin kerf core bits which cut slightly larger diameter cores. The kerf of a bit is the cutting edge which is inset with diamonds or tungsten carbide.

L denotes a non-standard design associated with wireline drilling.

The three letters used to define a core barrel can be interpreted as follows. The first letter represents the hole size although not necessarily the core size. The second letter shows the design of rod thread in the core barrel head and the third letter defines the particular design.

All core barrels specified by BS4019 are fully dimensioned with the exception of the head where different manufacturers produce different designs, and this enables all parts of every core barrel of the same designation theoretically to be fully

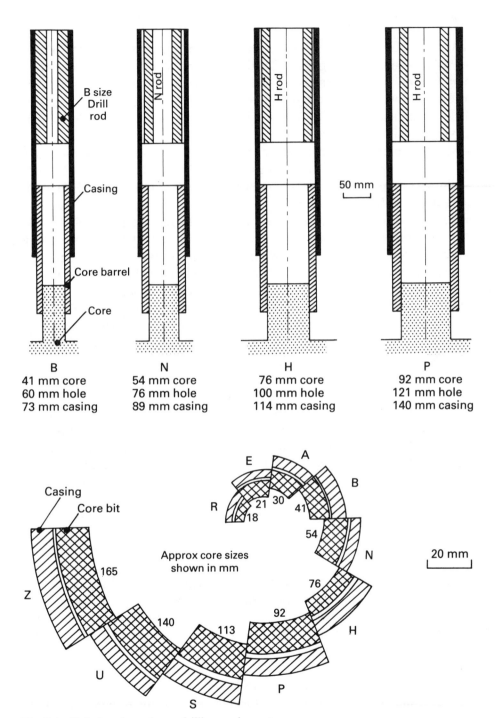

Fig. 7.4 Relative sizes of core drilling equipment.

145

interchangeable. Core bits too have specified sizes but there is a lot of scope for different designs in the cutting face. BS4019 covers a standard range of core drilling equipment but there are numerous one-off designs and items of specialist equipment in use. An example would be the triple tube core barrel used for coring soils or weak rocks. Equipment specified in BS4019 may also be modified in order that plastic liners can be inserted inside the inner barrel.

In the standard metric system equipment is generally specified by its nominal outside diameter with additional letters signifying core barrel types, for example T2 and K3; T2 being a thin-wall design. Table 7.2 lists the dimensions of common equipment in use in both the British and Metric Standards.

A typical drill string arrangement for a site investigation borehole is shown in Fig. 7.5. In this example a shell and auger borehole has been drilled through the overburden until weathered bedrock was reached when it was impossible to make further progress without resorting to chiselling. This part of the borehole is shown cased with 150 mm diameter shell and auger casing. Once bedrock has been reached a length of HX casing was drilled into the bedrock as shown. This not only supports any strata that might cave in but maintains a constant annular area between the drill rods and the casing right up to ground level. If this had not been used the upward velocity of the flushing medium inside the 150 mm diameter casing might not have been sufficient to lift the cuttings to the surface.

Looking now at the drill string in use and starting at the top there is the swivel which incorporates bearings and admits flushing medium to the drilling rods without itself turning. This is shown connected to the winch unit for lifting the drill string out of the borehole. The drilling rods shown are NW drill rods which are connected to an HWF core barrel. These rods are turned by the chuck of the drilling rig and pulled down by hydraulics. Typical speeds and pressures are shown but are only examples and will be discussed in more detail later. In the case of a top drive rig the air/water swivel is incorporated in the hydraulic drive head assembly at the top of the rods.

7.4 Core bits

If 100% core recovery is to be obtained the correct choice of borehole size and core bit , type is absolutely vital. There are innumerable designs of core bits; they come in all shapes and sizes, with different cutting edge profiles, different sizes, quantities and patterns of diamond or tungsten carbide, with different material compositions and with different provisions for discharging the flushing medium. The various designs have evolved in response to three basic demands. First, as stated, that they will lead to 100% core recovery in the particular rock being drilled, secondly that they will achieve this as rapidly as possible without becoming blocked and thirdly that they will do it as economically as possible. A diamond-tipped core bit might cost £500 and it is important

146

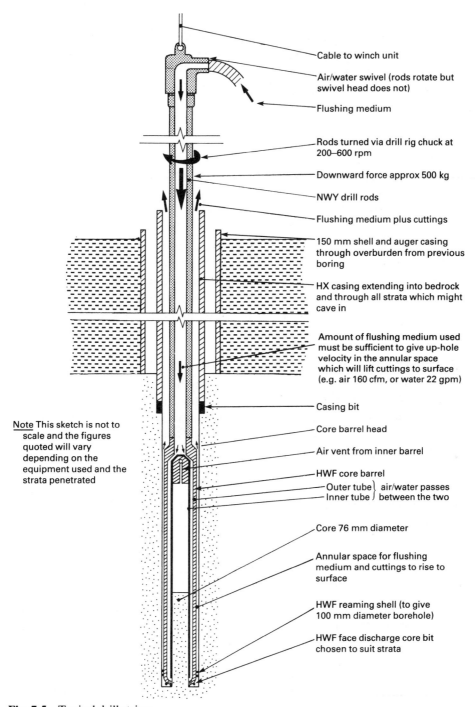

Cable to winch unit

Air/water swivel (rods rotate but swivel head does not)

Flushing medium

Rods turned via drill rig chuck at 200–600 rpm

Downward force approx 500 kg

NWY drill rods

Flushing medium plus cuttings

150 mm shell and auger casing through overburden from previous boring

HX casing extending into bedrock and through all strata which might cave in

Amount of flushing medium used must be sufficient to give up-hole velocity in the annular space which will lift cuttings to surface (e.g. air 160 cfm, or water 22 gpm)

Casing bit

Core barrel head

Air vent from inner barrel

HWF core barrel

Outer tube ⎫ air/water passes
Inner tube ⎬ between the two

Core 76 mm diameter

Annular space for flushing medium and cuttings to rise to surface

HWF reaming shell (to give 100 mm diameter borehole)

HWF face discharge core bit chosen to suit strata

Note This sketch is not to scale and the figures quoted will vary depending on the equipment used and the strata penetrated

Fig. 7.5 Typical drill string.

147

that as many metres of rock as possible can be drilled before renewal. Most operators will keep a check on their drilling costs by assessing the productivity of the rig in terms of metres per hour and by assessing bit costs on the basis of a simple formula such as is shown by the following equation.

$$x = \frac{a - b}{c}$$

where a = original cost of bit
  b = salvage value of bit (see below)
  c = total metres drilled
  x = bit cost per metre

It would be impossible to describe all the different designs of core bit but some of the factors which affect core recovery and drilling costs can be described and illustrated by reference to particular designs (Fig. 7.6). When ordering diamond core bits it is necessary to specify each of the factors listed below. Reputable manufacturers will be able to advise on the best type of bit for the equipment in use and the rock type being drilled.

7.4.1 Length and diameter
Depending on the core barrel being used bits may be short or long shank. Generally speaking the harder and more intact the rock is then the smaller the diameter of core that can be recovered successfully. In weak, weathered or heavily fractured rocks it is inadvisable to consider anything less than N or H size if 100% recovery is to be achieved. Air flush should not be used with less than H size.

7.4.2 Kerf width
The greater the kerf width, i.e. the width of the cutting edge, the greater the amount of rock that must be cut and lifted up the borehole.

7.4.3 Profile of cutting edge
Different profiles of the cutting edge are shown in Fig. 7.6. The round profile is best suited to hard rocks and the semi-round to medium and hard rocks. The semi-flat profile is again suitable for hard rocks but where lightweight machines are used. The square profile is used on impregnated types of bits and on casing shoes. The quadrant bit is best suited to soft or friable rocks where the rock can be quickly cut and then protected inside the core bit. The single or multi-step bits give increased rates of penetration where the kerf is wide.

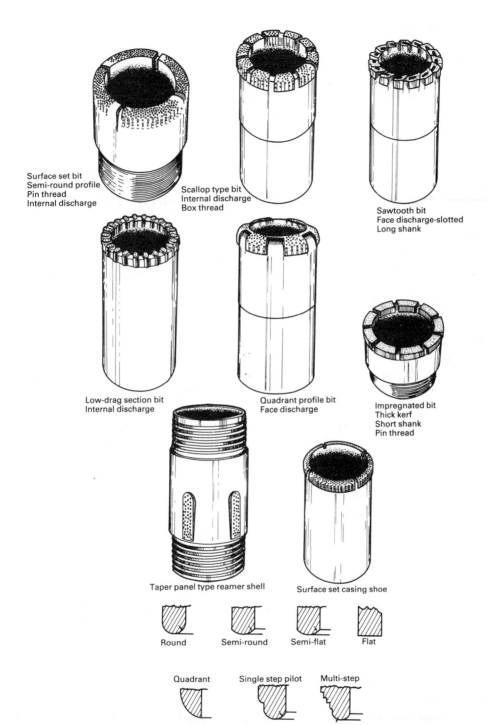

Surface set bit
Semi-round profile
Pin thread
Internal discharge

Scallop type bit
Internal discharge
Box thread

Sawtooth bit
Face discharge-slotted
Long shank

Low-drag section bit
Internal discharge

Quadrant profile bit
Face discharge

Impregnated bit
Thick kerf
Short shank
Pin thread

Taper panel type reamer shell

Surface set casing shoe

Round   Semi-round   Semi-flat   Flat

Quadrant   Single step pilot   Multi-step

Fig. 7.6   Core bits, reamer, casing shoe and cutting edge profiles.

149

7.4.4 Discharge of flushing medium

Bits can be designed for air flush or water flush or both but air flush is not normally used with the smaller sizes. The flushing medium can pass through waterways from inside the core bit to the outside as with the internal discharge, surface-set core bit shown in Fig. 7.6 or it can emerge on the face of the bit as with the sawtooth bit or the quadrant profile, face-discharge bit. The advantage of face discharge is that much less of the core is exposed to erosion by the flushing medium, a feature which is very important when drilling soft rocks which are susceptible to softening by water or rocks which are broken and friable. The disadvantage of face-discharge bits is that the ports tend to weaken the bit and in hard, broken rocks cracking can occur round the holes.

7.4.5 Basic designs

There are a number of basic designs of core bit and these are illustrated in Fig. 7.6. The normal surface-set core bit can be used to drill a wide variety of formations by varying the size and profile and the quality, number and pattern of the diamonds and their matrix but are not suitable for broken or heavily fractured rocks. A modification of this bit, the scallop type, with more waterways is better suited to broken formations. Impregnated core bits with fine diamond dust in the matrix are better suited to hard, abrasive rocks and can be used even where they are fractured or where rapid variations in hardness occur. They rely on the wearing away of the matrix in order to expose fresh diamonds.

The sawtooth type of core bit has evolved for cutting soft sedimentary rocks where rapid penetration can be achieved but it should not be used for broken strata. If rapid penetration is achieved an increase in the flow of flushing medium will be required in order to lift the cuttings to the surface and less downward pressure will be needed since the contact area is less. The low drag section bit has been developed for soft, sticky formations such as stiff clay, marl or soft shale but it is not suitable for broken strata.

7.4.6 Diamond size

With surface set and sawtooth bits the diamond size is important. It is expressed in stones per carat. A carat is 0.2 grams and the higher the stone per carat (spc) value the smaller are the diamonds. Generally speaking the harder the rock the smaller the diamond that is used. Quite large diamonds can be used in soft rocks. The diamonds in an impregnated bit have a very high spc value.

7.4.7 Diamond quality

Industrial diamonds come in a range of different qualities and there are different types available such as 'congos' and 'carbonados'. The quality of the standard 'bortz' type is based on shape, crystal structure and surface texture. The 'congo' is a rounded alluvial diamond and is used where a large size is required and the 'carbonado' has no regular crystalline structure, is more resistant to fracture by impact and is used on sawtooth and low-drag section bits or in broken ground of variable hardness. Synthetic man-made diamonds are available in the very fine sizes. The harder the rock the better the quality of diamond that is required.

7.4.8 Matrix

The diamonds in a core bit are held in place by a metal matrix which starts life as a powder, usually of tungsten and tungsten carbide. This matrix is heated and bonded to the steel blank. It not only holds the diamonds in place but must wear away only slightly faster than the diamond itself so that the diamond protrudes and can achieve its cutting action. When the matrix has worn away to the extent that there is a danger of losing the diamonds, the bits should be returned to the manufacturers for salvage of the diamonds which can then be re-used and the customer is credited with their value. This does not, however, apply to impregnated bits. In general terms, the harder the rock formation that is being drilled then the harder the matrix that is required. A simple chart to assist in selecting the correct type of diamond bit is shown in Table 7.3.

To get the most out of a core bit it is essential that it is used correctly. No matter how good the design and quality, 100% core recovery will not be obtained unless the bit is rotated at the correct speed, with the correct pressure applied to it, with the right amount of flushing medium and without vibration. Since core bits are an expensive item they should be treated with care; diamonds can be knocked out or broken by impact loading and can also be irreparably damaged by excessive heat if say the flushing medium fails. Diamonds can also be rendered ineffective if they are allowed to become polished by running on hard rock with insufficient load for instance.

Much of the above discussion has been related to diamond core bits but similar principles apply to tungsten carbide which can form an economic alternative for the softer rocks. Tungsten carbide bits may either have shaped pieces of metal set into the cutting face or they may consist of small random fragments bonded together in which case they are termed 'fragmented carbide bits'. They are much cheaper than diamond but are only suitable for the softer rocks and the fragmented types are difficult to manufacture to the close tolerances of the conventional types.

Shown in Fig. 7.6 are a reamer shell and a casing shoe. The former is used behind the core bit when using water flush in order to maintain the gauge of the borehole, to improve the stability of the core barrel and to protect the lower part of the core barrel from excessive abrasion and wear. There are many different designs but generally a simple arrangement as shown with either diamonds or tungsten carbide inserts set on a slight taper will achieve the objectives. The taper will ensure more even wear, a smoother action, improved penetration and it reduces vibration.

Casing is used to protect against caving strata or in strata which might squeeze in or

151

Table 7.3 Core-bit selection chart

Rock type		Core bit type						Diamond quality			Matrix		
		Surface set 5–20 spc	Surface set 20–50 spc	Surface set 50–100 spc	Sawtooth or low drag section	Impregnated	Tungsten carbide	Top	Medium	Low	Soft	Medium	Hard
Soft	Soft shale	*			*		*			*	*		
	Chalk (no flints)	*			*		*			*	*		
	Soft marl	*			*		*			*	*		
	Volcanic tuff	*			*		*			*	*		
Medium	Shale	*			*		*			*	*	*	
	Marl	*			*		*			*	*	*	
	Sandstone	*	*		*		*			*	*		*
	Limestone	*	*		*		*			*	*	*	*
	Siltstone		*		*				*	*	*		
Medium Hard	Schist	*			*				*		*		
	Marble	*							*		*		
	Serpentine	*							*		*		
	Slate	*						*	*		*		
	Hard limestone	*				*			*	*	*		
	Dolomitic limestone	*				*			*	*	*		
	Haematite	*	*			*			*		*		
	Syenite	*	*			*		*	*		*		
	Gneiss	*	*			*		*	*		*		
Hard	Amphibolite			*		*			*		*		
	Diorite			*		*		*	*		*		
	Gabbro			*		*		*	*		*		
	Porphyry			*		*		*	*		*		
	Andesite			*		*		*	*		*		
	Dolerite			*		*		*	*		*		
Very Hard	Gritstone			*		*			*			*	*
	Quartzite			*		*		*	*			*	*
	Rhyolite			*		*		*	*			*	*
	Granite			*		*		*	*			*	*
	Basalt			*		*		*	*			*	*
	Conglomerate					*						*	*
	Breccia					*						*	*
	Pyrite/Silicon ores					*						*	*

(The table represents typical rocks but all can vary in hardness, weathering and degree of abrasiveness)

swell. If there is any suspicion that these phenomena might occur it is prudent to install casing since a cave-in behind the barrel can result in the loss of a lot of expensive equipment and can cause long delays. A casing shoe has no diamonds on the inside face and is used to ream out a hole that has already been drilled. A casing bit has diamonds on the inside edge and can be used when no previous hole has been drilled. There are many types of casing shoes and bits; impregnated types do not cut as fast as surface-set ones but will last longer.

7.5 Core barrels

The essentials of core barrel design and nomenclature were discussed in Section 7.1 but will now be considered in more detail. Wireline core barrels where the inner tube containing the core can be lifted to the surface without withdrawing the whole core barrel and drill string are available but have not been considered here since they only really come into their own in very deep boreholes where a great deal of time can be lost lifting and uncoupling drill rods.

The essential requirements of a core barrel are that it will cut a core of rock with the minimum of disturbance and be able to carry this core up to the surface. The prime objective is 100% core recovery and various standard designs of core barrel exist which are common to Great Britain, America and Canada. Each of these designs are suited to different ground conditions. The common designs are described below and all come in different lengths and diameters. The designs of most practical use have one thing in common which is a tapered sprung steel core spring or core lifter which grips the core when it tries to fall out of the core barrel (see Fig. 7.7). Core barrels can be WT, WG, WF, or WM in design and may have a single or a double tube with or without swivel.

7.5.1 Starting and single tube (WT design)

These are the simplest type and only have a single tube with a core bit on the end. The flushing medium washes over the full length of the core inside the barrel and this would erode soft rocks and disturb fragmented ones. These designs are, therefore, only suitable for hard, relatively unfractured formations and are rarely used in practice.

7.5.2 Double tube rigid (WT design)

In this design there is an inner and an outer tube between which the flushing medium passes for most of the core length and therefore there is less erosion. The water itself emerges through holes at the end of the inner tube. However, the two tubes are fixed and rotate together and since the inner tube is rotating all the time this can cause damage to the core as it enters the inner tube and the design is only suited to hard unfractured formations. The advantage of the design is that narrow kerf bits are used and these have less diamonds, require less power, penetrate faster and give an

153

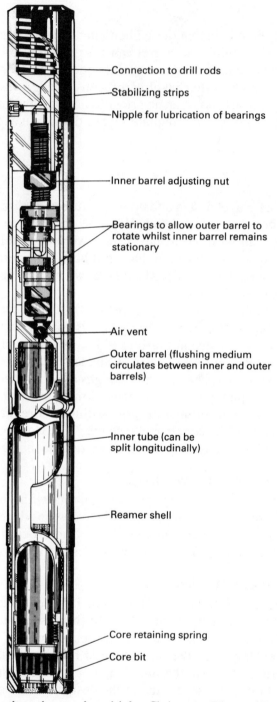

Connection to drill rods

Stabilizing strips

Nipple for lubrication of bearings

Inner barrel adjusting nut

Bearings to allow outer barrel to rotate whilst inner barrel remains stationary

Air vent

Outer barrel (flushing medium circulates between inner and outer barrels)

Inner tube (can be split longitudinally)

Reamer shell

Core retaining spring

Core bit

Fig. 7.7 Cross section through a core barrel (after Christensen Diamond Products Ltd).

increased core size over the WG, WF and WM designs. They are also less likely to jam than the single tube designs but they are still not as efficient as the double tube swivel designs described below.

7.5.3   Double tube rigid (WG design)
This is basically the same as the WT design but a thicker kerf width is employed. This gives extra strength but obviously does not have the advantages of a thin kerf.

7.5.4   Double tube swivel (WT design)
This is similar to the WT double tube rigid design but the inner tube is mounted on a swivel in the corebarrel head and does not, therefore, rotate with the outer barrel and there is less disturbance to the core.

7.5.5   Double tube swivel (WG design)
This is similar to the WT double tube swivel design but has a thicker kerf.

7.5.6   Double tube swivel (WM design)
This is similar to the WG double tube swivel design but it incorporates a core spring (or core lifter) case which further reduces the length of core exposed to the flushing medium to that inside the bit only and minimizes the length of core subject to a twisting action. It is, therefore, a suitable design for shattered, soft or weathered formations.

7.5.7   Double tube swivel (WMS design)
This is a variation of the WM design and incorporates a face discharge bit which all but eliminates erosion of the core by the flushing medium.

7.5.8   Double tube swivel (WF design)
This design is similar to the WMS design and is a face-discharge type which virtually eliminates core washing and rotation effects. It is, therefore, a good design to use in soft, weak, fractured or weathered rocks. The design can be used with mud or water flush and in the larger sizes with air flush. The parts of a typical double tube swivel core barrel are shown in Fig. 7.7.

There are also triple tube core barrels available where the extra inner tube in which the core is retained projects beyond the face of the bit and has a sharper edge. This can then be used to recover cores of soil or very soft rock and in some cases the inner tube retracts a little when hard rock is encountered. The pitcher sampler has a spring loaded inner barrel which is pushed into soils or very soft rocks in advance of the outer cutting barrel. A number of other non-standard designs exist some of which have been developed specifically for air flush.

One fairly recent development is the introduction of plastic liners which are placed inside the inner barrel. The core and liner are slid out of the barrel and the liner taped up to seal the core. The liner protects the core, aids removal, keeps the core in the correct sequence and minimizes disturbance during transit. The disadvantages, however, are that a thicker kerf bit is required, a slightly smaller core is cut and the plastic can crumple up inside the inner tube.

Removing the core, particularly one that tends to swell, from the inner barrel can be a problem. Cores should be removed with the barrel horizontal. A hydraulic core pusher is the preferred method of removal and plastic liners certainly help, but another method is to use a split tube inner barrel which when dismantled splits longitudinally to reveal the core. There are also variations in the design of the core spring or core lifter and basket-type core springs are available which have fingerlike springs instead of the tapered arrangement shown in Fig. 7.7.

A well-maintained core barrel is essential for good core recovery. In most site investigation work a double tube swivel design will be used since minimization of core damage is of prime importance. With such core barrels it is important that both tubes are never damaged during handling since if they are bent or have projections on them the inner tube will touch and rotate with the outer tube and the benefits of the swivel action will be lost. A check should be made, with the core barrel hanging vertically, that the inner tube assembly does not touch the back of the bit and that it is free to move since if it did touch, the swivel action would again be lost. The position of the inner tube is adjustable with shims or nuts in the head assembly and there should be a gap of about 3 mm between it and the back of the core bit. If the gap is any greater the flushing medium will tend to erode the core. The swivel itself must also be properly maintained to give free movement. Core barrels are subject to a lot of wear and regular checks as to their fitness for use are necessary.

7.6 Drill rods and swivels

Drilling rods serve a number of purposes. First they must transmit the necessary torque and pressure to the core barrel without whipping or vibrating. Secondly they must have a sufficient internal diameter for the required flow of flushing medium and thirdly they must produce an annular area between either the hole or the casing to give sufficient upward velocity to the flushing medium for it to lift the cuttings to the surface. Obviously for a given flow the smaller the annular area then the greater the upward velocity. In the British, American and Canadian standards there is only a W design specified but a Y series design is also in common use.

The W design shown in Fig. 7.8 was chosen to be rigid with the required inside and outside diameters. The rods are made of seamless steel tubing and are flush coupled using heat-treated steel alloy couplings although HW rods can also be obtained flush

W series drill rod and coupling

Y series drill rod, coupling and box threaded tool joint

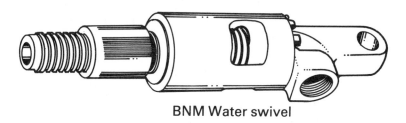

BNM Water swivel

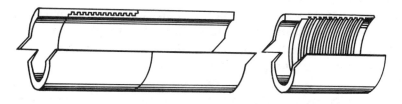

W series flush jointed casing

Fig. 7.8 Drill rods, swivel and casing.

jointed. Flush coupled drilling equipment has a box thread at one end and a pin thread at the other and in many items the threaded portion is removable so that any damaged part may be easily replaced. The Y series drilling rods have a stronger, tapered thread arrangement which is quicker to couple and uncouple and may have removable ends. Tool joints can be added at either end to suit the equipment in use.

For lifting rods in and out of the hole a swivelling hoist plug can be attached and the drilling rig winch used. As rods are lifted out of the hole some form of clamp is required to prevent them falling back down when the top one is removed. Various tools are available for coupling or uncoupling rods and on some rigs an automatic break out device is incorporated for doing this. In any event it is much easier to do if the threads are treated with anti-locking grease. On deep boreholes stabilizers can be incorporated in the drill string to minimize whipping of the rods. It is important that drilling rods are kept straight since even a slightly bent one in the drilling string can cause a great deal of vibration and hence loss of core and damage to other items of equipment.

During drilling the flushing medium, be it mud, air, water or foam, is fed into the rotating drill rods via a water swivel such as shown in Fig. 7.8. The design of swivel itself may vary to suit the flushing medium in use but all follow a similar pattern. They incorporate a lifting lug, an inlet port and bearings between the moving and stationary parts which in some designs must be greased regularly but in others are water lubricated. In choosing a swivel consideration must be given to the weight of rods and corebarrel that will hang from it and to the volume of flushing medium that can pass through it without excessive pressure being needed. The swivel in a top drive rig is incorporated in the drive head assembly.

7.7 Casing

Casing is used in loose, weak or fractured rocks to prevent caving in of the strata, in porous fissured rocks to prevent loss of the flushing medium and in soft rocks to prevent them from swelling and squeezing into the hole. It is made of seamless steel tube and may be driven or drilled into the ground and either diamond or tungsten carbide tipped shoes or bits can be used (see Section 7.4). The casing is designed so that each size nests inside the next size up. For instance HX or HW casing will admit an H-size barrel (see Table 7.2 and Fig. 7.4). In addition the hole drilled by the H-size barrel will admit NX or NW casing. Various lengths are available and all boreholes should have at least a short length of casing drilled into the rock to prevent surface material from falling down the hole and to facilitate collection of the flushing water.

Two basic designs are available, X series and W series. The X series is flush coupled with a box thread at each end and a pin to pin coupling. In this case the internal diameter of the coupling is less than that of the casing but still large enough to admit the appropriate core barrel. The W series (see Fig. 7.8) is a heavier design with thicker

158

walls. It is flush jointed with an integral pin at one end and a box at the other and its inside and outside diameters are flush throughout even at the joints and no separate couplings are needed. Casing can be lifted in and out of the hole in much the same way as the rods and casing clamps are available to prevent it falling down the hole.

Since there are both box and pin threads of different sizes and of different patterns a range of subs are available so that various items of equipment may be joined one to the other.

7.8 Torque, pressure and rotation speeds

The torque requirement during rotary drilling will depend on a number of factors including the diameter of the core bit, the weight applied to it and the strata being cored. Tests have been carried out to determine the torque required to turn a free-running diamond core bit at its optimum pressure and this is about 20 kg m for a 150 mm diameter bit but in practice this figure could increase enormously if say the rock was prone to swelling and gripped the core barrel or if the feed rate was too high or if the cuttings were not being removed efficiently. The important thing, however, is that the drill rig itself is capable of always providing sufficient power to turn the bit at the optimum speed and at the same time providing the required downward pressure.

Diamonds cut at their best at certain speeds and since they are mounted on a circular core bit it is the peripheral linear speed which is important. For a given rotation speed the peripheral speed will be higher the larger the diameter and these are related using the following formula where v is the peripheral speed, d the diameter of the bit and r the rotation speed.

$$v = \pi dr$$

Different types of bits have different ranges of optimum peripheral speeds and these are listed below.

Surface set bits	50–170 m min^{-1}
Impregnated bits	120–200 m min^{-1}
Saw tooth and low drag section bits (water flush)	75–120 m min^{-1}
Saw tooth and low drag section bits (air flush) and Tungsten bits	30–45 m min^{-1}

(The slower speeds should be used in more broken materials)

Table 7.4 relates peripheral speed, bit diameter and speed of rotation for different bit types but it must be stressed that these should only be used as a general guide and the driller must be prepared to try different speeds in any given borehole in order to find the

Table 7.4 Rotation speeds to give generally recommended peripheral speeds

Core size	Outside diameter of bit (mm)	Rotation speeds (rpm)			
		Surface set	Impregnated	Sawtooth and low drag section (water flush)	Sawtooth and low drag section (air flush) and tungsten
S	146	100–400	300–500	200–300	100–140
H	100	200–600	400–800	300–500	140–200
N	76	300–900	600–1000	400–600	180–260
B	60	300–1100	700–1300	500–800	220–340
A	49	400–1300	900–1500	600–1000	260–420

optimum. Generally speaking the softer the rock then the slower the speed that should be used and the bigger the diamonds the slower the speed. If vibration occurs it can sometimes be solved by reducing the speed.

The pressure that is applied to the face of a bit is extremely important. Too low and the bit will polish and will not be cutting as fast as it might. Too high and the bit will overheat, wear rapidly and it will tend to cut too deeply thus producing oversize cuttings which might not be flushed away easily enough. With the hydraulic pull down on modern rigs it is easy to use the wrong pressure and reference to a pressure gauge is essential.

However, the pressure gauge is not the whole answer since the submerged weight of the drill string has to be taken into account and if there is any tendency for the core to jam in the inner barrel this will take load off the face of the core bit. In addition the pressure of the flushing medium will be exerting an upward force on the bit and different rocks will need different pressures for optimum penetration rates. The pressure that is used should be adjusted in order to achieve the optimum rate of penetration without any adverse effects. In very general terms the softer the rock then the lower the pressure and the smaller the diamonds then the higher the bit load. Higher pressures might be required with higher rotation speeds but sometimes vibration is caused by too high a bit pressure. Once again the driller must be prepared to experiment with different pressures and build up experience in different rock types. In terms of the vertical load that is applied to the drill rods, and hence to the bit, obviously the larger the diameter of the core bit the greater the downward weight needed. Figure 7.9 shows the approximate relationship between downward load, bit diameter, and core bit type but it must be stressed that in the light of the factors described above these can only be taken as a very general guide.

The maximum pressure that should be applied during drilling can be looked at in a

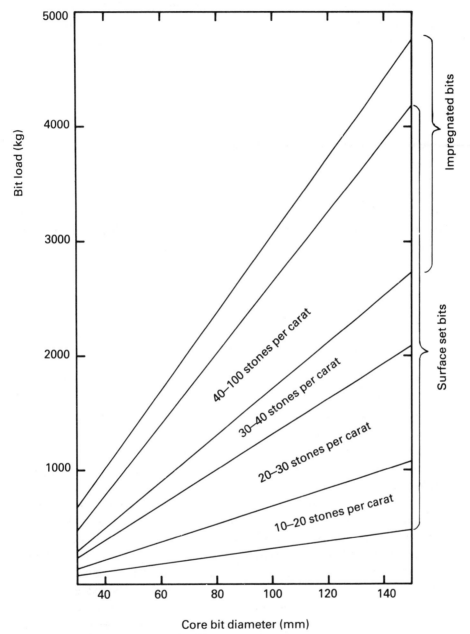

Fig. 7.9 Bit load/diameter relationship.

more theoretical way although again it must be remembered that the pressure applied at the top is not necessarily that which reaches the face of the core bit. It is known from experimental work that the loads on certain types of diamond and bit should not exceed the figures listed below.

Bortz	3.2 kg on each working diamond
Congo	2.3 kg on each working diamond
Carbonado	6.8 kg on each working diamond
Impregnated	91 kg on each square centimetre of kerf area

To determine the number of working diamonds in a bit take two-thirds of the total carat weight and multiply it by the average stones per carat value.

The approximate maximum weights that should be applied to a number of core bits are listed in Table 7.5. It must be stressed that these are not the loads at which optimum penetration will occur but loads which should not be exceeded.

Table 7.5

Core bit size	Approx OD (mm)	Approx ID (mm)	Approx kerf area (cm²)	Maximum load (kg)
A	48	30	11	1000
B	60	42	14	1300
N	75	55	21	1900
H	99	76	32	2700

The maximum load versus diameter relationship is shown in Fig. 7.9

If the rate of penetration of the drill string suddenly decreases or stops then this probably indicates a blockage and drilling must be stopped and the barrel brought to the surface to determine the reason. There are four main causes. The first is that parts of a fractured core may have distorted and jammed in the core barrel and all the downward load is acting on the column of core and not on the face of the bit. The second is that a soft rock has swollen inside the core barrel causing a similar effect. Thirdly the holes in the face of the bit for the discharge of the flushing medium may have been blocked by soft material and fourthly there may have been a failure in the system supplying the flushing medium. The latter two causes may be detected by the disappearance of air or water returns but this may also be due to loss of fluid in cavities or open fissures. If drilling is continued after blocking off all that will happen is that the rock will be ground away, no core will be recovered and the bit may be damaged.

When withdrawing a drill string and core the total weight must be considered

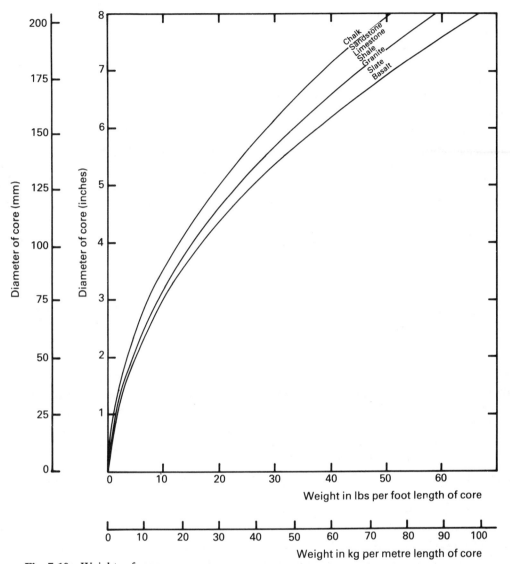

Fig. 7.10 Weights of core.

together with any loads exerted on the core barrel through swelling or trapped cuttings. The weights per metre of different diameter cores of different rocks are shown in Fig. 7.10. There must also be a force applied to break off the stick of core at the face of the core bit. This used to be done by a process known as dry blocking where the flow of flushing medium to the bit was cut off before rotation and pressure were ceased. This

163

caused a high stress build up at the face of the bit and hence fracture of the core. There is, however, a risk of damage to the core bit since diamond will start to oxidize at 500 °C and with modern core lifters or core springs there is rarely any need to resort to it.

7.9 Drilling practice and flushing mediums

The reasons for using a flushing medium during rotary drilling operations are threefold. First it is to cool the core bit, secondly to remove the cuttings and thirdly to some extent to lubricate the core bit. If the first requirement is not adequately satisfied there can be serious damage to the bit through overheating and if the cuttings are not removed efficiently the core barrel and rods will tend to jam due to a build up of waste material. In these circumstances the bit will certainly not be cutting as cleanly and effectively as it might be.

There are a number of flushing mediums available plus a wide range of additives to increase their effectiveness. The three main types are water, mud and air and these are considered below. The prime movers for these materials are pumps and compressors. A typical high pressure drill pump and an air compressor both suitable for site investigation use are shown in Fig. 7.11. The pump incorporates an engine and gearbox so that the flow can be varied over a wide range.

7.9.1 Water

Normal practice is to pump clean, sediment-free water from lakes, streams or water hydrants to a storage tank or water bowser and from there via the high-pressure drill pump to the drill string. On some sites it will be necessary to bring water to the site in water bowsers. It is preferable if the high-pressure pumping arrangement includes a flow meter so that the driller has a continual visual display of the amount of water he is using. This will ensure the correct uphole velocity is achieved such that the cuttings are lifted up the borehole, (i.e. the upward velocity is greater than the particle settling velocity).

In order to calculate the amount of water needed it is first necessary to calculate the annular area between the drill rod and the side of the borehole or casing. This is made easier by reference to Fig. 7.12. The drill rod in use is chosen from the horizontal lines and the point where this line intersects the hole size is noted. A line is then dropped vertically to the bottom horizontal scale and the annular area read off. For example NW drilling rod in an H-size borehole gives an annular area of 6.6 in². Reference can now be made to Fig. 7.13(a). The annular area of 6.6 in² is transferred to the vertical scale and a line drawn horizontally to meet the line of optimum uphole velocity of water of 90 ft min⁻¹. This gives an optimum flow from the bottom scale of 26 gal min⁻¹. If HX casing had been used this would give rise to a slightly greater annular area and the necessary flow would be greater at 30 gal min⁻¹.

(a)

Fig. 7.11(a) Boyles BBP-40 high pressure water flush pump (photograph: Boyles Bros Ltd).

These charts are given in order to make a preliminary assessment only and, as in most aspects of rotary drilling, the driller must be prepared to try different flows. For instance a reduced flow and slower rotation speeds should be used in softer rocks. If large cuttings are being obtained an increased flow might be necessary. Various oils and polymers can be added to the water in percentages of about 2% to reduce torque requirements and to increase rates of penetration and bit life when drilling hard rocks. In some cases the polymers can help to support the sides of the hole. At all times the pressure used should be such that the desired flow rate is achieved.

165

Fig. 7.11(b) Compair rotary-screw compressor shown powering a Holman Voltrack down-the-hole hammer percussion rig (photograph: Compair Ltd).

7.9.2 Air

Air can be effectively used in some soft rocks to improve core recovery and a compressor may be an easier proposition than carting water in by bowser. However, not all drilling equipment is designed for the use of air flush and the driller should ensure that all bits, barrels, rods, swivels and supply hoses are suitable for air flush before he uses it. Airflush should not be used with anything less than N-sized rods and H-sized core barrels. Face discharge or sawtooth bits are the most suitable and Y-series rods should be used. To calculate the amount of air flush needed, reference can be made to Figs 7.12 and 7.13(b) in a similar way to that for water only this time using an optimum uphole velocity of 4000 ft min^{-1}. For N rods and H-sized hole the necessary flow would be 185 ft^3 min^{-1} (cfm) and for HX casing 220 ft^3 min^{-1} but these are again only a guide. In practice it is wise to have a compressor with rather more capacity than the minimum but if too much air is used this can disturb fractured rocks and can also cause erosion on the core barrel. It can also lift the barrel off the bottom of the hole.

166

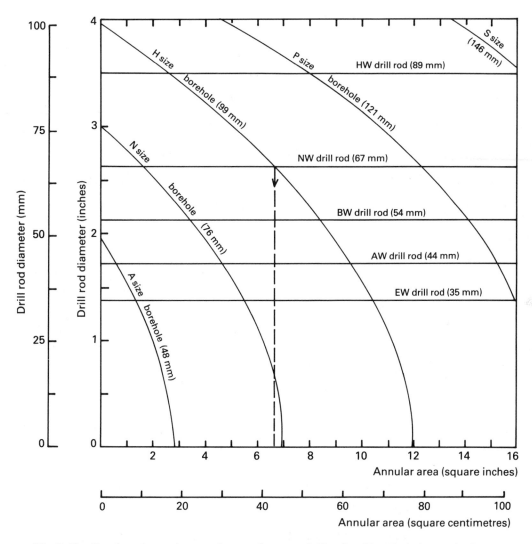

Fig. 7.12 Graph to determine annular area between drill rod and borehole (example shown NW rod in H size borehole gives 6.6 in² annular area).

During air flush drilling problems can arise if there are seepages of water into the borehole when there is a tendency for the cuttings to 'ball up' which makes them difficult to remove. This can be overcome to some extent by the use of foam drilling where a chemical foaming agent is injected into the air supply. This can also be successfully used in coring soft, loose or unstable formations and even unconsolidated sand has been cored using foam since the foam helps to support the sides of the

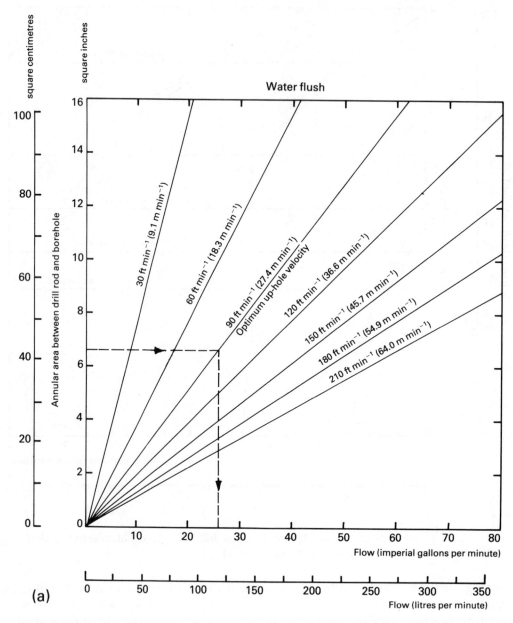

Fig. 7.13 (a) Water flow to give stated up-hole velocity (e.g. annular area 6.6 in² requires flow of 26 gallons per minute to give optimum up-hole velocity). (b) Air flow to give stated up-hole velocity (e.g. annular area 6.6 in² requires flow of 185 cubic feet per minute to give optimum up-hole velocity).

168

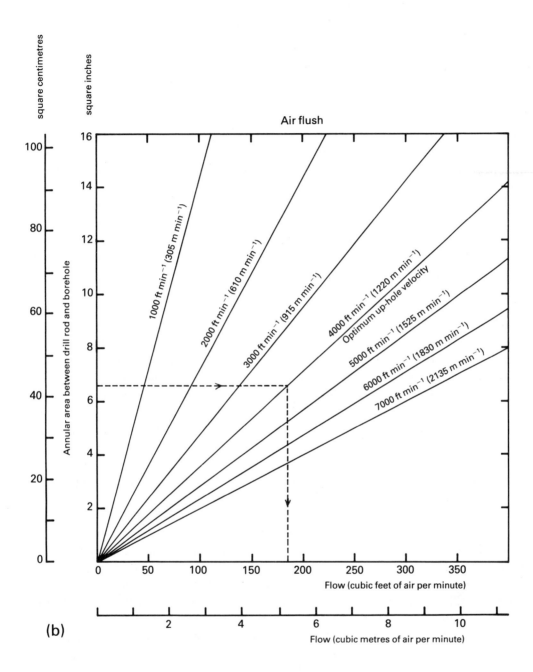

(b)

169

borehole. One disadvantage is the envelopment of the rig and driller by a white mass but it can be controlled, is bio-degradable and soon dissipates. The use of foam can also substantially reduce the flow of air needed since it is so much more effective in lifting the cuttings and it is usually possible to use a much smaller compressor.

7.9.3 Mud

Two basic types of mud flush are available. The first is a mixture of Bentonite Clay and water which, since it is denser, lifts the cuttings at a much reduced velocity and the amount of water needed is considerably reduced. The mud tends to plaster the side of the borehole hence stabilizing it and minimizing cave in. It also reduces friction and aids core recovery. However, additional plant is necessary to mix, pump and recover the mud and this is rarely cost effective on shallow boreholes. The second type of mud flush is the polymeric type which has the appearance of wallpaper paste and gives advantages similar to the conventional mud. Although it tends to be expensive it is cleaner, easier to mix and easier to recover.

Before concluding the sections on drilling practice it is worth looking at one or two miscellaneous problems. One very common problem during rotary drilling is vibration which results in poor core recovery, damage to the diamonds, increased wear and tear and low rates of penetration. There are many possible causes such as an unstable rig set up, an off-centre chuck, weak or bent rods, loose couplings, a crooked hole or the incorrect amount of flushing medium. If all these features are checked and found not to be the cause then it will be necessary to reduce the speed and the feed rate or bit pressure. Greasing the rods may also help a little. In some formations particularly those of variable hardness or ones where there are hard pebbles in a softer matrix it may be almost impossible to avoid vibration but every effort must be made to eliminate it since in a great many cases it is responsible for loss of core.

To start a borehole the rig is set up, ensuring it is stable and aligned correctly. This may not be in a vertical position since in certain circumstances it may be necessary to drill angled boreholes which can produce a lot of additional information by intercepting vertical or near vertical features within the rock mass. To do this the mast and chuck or top drive of most rigs can be rotated but directional stability is limited.

When drilling through overburden in which no sample recovery is required there are a number of alternatives and some were briefly discussed in Sections 4.6, 4.7 and 4.8. If a diamond bit is used it should be the impregnated type but it is probably cheaper to use a rock driller bit such as is shown in Fig. 7.14. Clays can sometimes be recovered by 'dry coring' using an open-ended tube with a hard cutting edge and no flushing medium. Casing should be drilled into rock head and even if it is not strictly speaking necessary it is worth installing at least one length of casing. This aids stability and control of

170

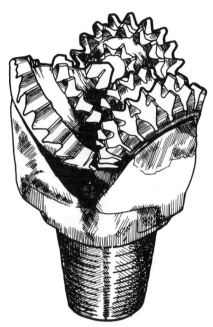

Fig. 7.14 Rock roller bit.

borehole direction and assists in the removal of water.

Before starting diamond coring the hole should be cleaned out. The flow of flushing medium should be started prior to actual drilling to ensure the flush is reaching the bit face. A light pressure and slow rotation is advisable until the bit is bedded into the rock. However, as soon as this is done the optimum speed, pressure and flushing medium should be established to prevent the bit polishing. The depth to the start of the core run should be checked and progress noted in order that overdrilling does not occur. Continual observation of the rate of penetration in mm min^{-1} is a useful means of checking the effectiveness of the techniques being used. Drilling rigs have also been instrumented in order to study the effects of torque, thrust, flow of flushing medium and speed on penetration rates and recoveries and it is work such as this which should lead to improved performance in the future.

If the blockage occurs the barrel should be withdrawn and emptied immediately. The bit should always be returned for salvage when the diamonds are badly worn or are in danger of dropping out. When screwing/unscrewing equipment the correct tools should be used so that circular sections do not become distorted and so they do not become burred or scarred. When drilling is not taking place the borehole should be covered to prevent any foreign objects dropping down the hole.

171

There are techniques of rotary drilling which utilize reverse circulation of the flushing medium and which therefore bring the cuttings up the inside of the drilling rods instead of outside them. There is a similar, although non-coring, system known as 'air lift' in which the cuttings can be collected and used to interpret the strata that have been penetrated. Yet another non-coring system utilizes two concentric pipes. The flushing medium passes down the outer annulus and up the inside pipe. The outer pipe serves as the casing and once again the cuttings can be collected and examined.

It should be noted that gases can be liberated during drilling in certain types of rock, mainly those containing oil or coal, and precautions against smoking may be necessary in such circumstances. If the flow of gas is excessive specialist advice should be sought.

One problem that arises from time to time is of losing equipment, which has either become unthreaded or broken, down the hole. A variety of recovery techniques can be used depending on what exactly has been lost and some of these techniques were described at the end of Section 6.3. Wax impressions can be taken to discover the orientation of the equipment and magnets, spears and taps can be tried. A non-coring bit can be used to grind away small items before coring commences. When simple recovery attempts have been made a conscious decision should be taken as to whether it is cheaper to spend more time or to accept the loss of the equipment and drill a new hole. When equipment becomes stuck the amount of flushing medium can be increased in an attempt to remove the cause. If this fails jarring or jacking can be tried.

Remember, research is only systemized experimentation and every driller must be prepared to experiment to see which combination of equipment and methods gives the best results in any particular situation.

7.10   Core handling and borehole surveys

Once the core has been recovered it should be carefully removed from the core barrel, preferably using a hydraulic core pusher and placed in a core box. The core should be laid out in book fashion as shown in Fig. 7.15, ensuring that every piece is placed in the correct sequence with wooden blocks inserted between core runs. Blocks should also be used to indicate where any core has been lost. The core should not be free to move around in the box. Each core run should be carefully labelled in a permanent fashion and the lid securely fastened. Core boxes can be made of wood or aluminium and can contain half sections of plastic pipe in order to hold the core more securely.

It is no use spending a lot of time and money obtaining the core if it is to arrive at the laboratories as a jumbled mass of rock fragments. Sometimes core is required to be wrapped and sealed before transporting it to the laboratories and this is made easier if the plastic lining described earlier is used. Short lengths of core can be sealed in successive layers of wax to preserve them in their *in situ* condition.

Once a borehole has been completed this is not necessarily the end of the useful work

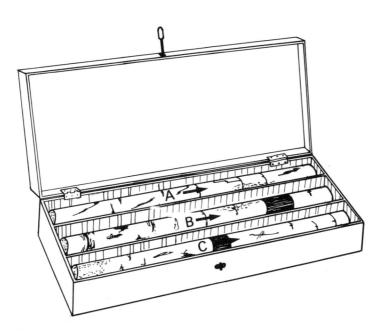

Fig. 7.15 Core-box arrangement (labels should indicate top and bottom of each core run and blocks inserted in known zones of nil recovery).

that can be done. A variety of *in situ* tests can be carried out to determine such things as the state of *in situ* stress in the rock and its permeability. Television cameras, ordinary cameras or periscopes can be lowered down to inspect such things as joints, cavities and the rock structure. Other devices are available which take a permanent impression of the sides of the borehole and again show up patterns of joints and fissures. Borehole calipers which measure the exact diameter of the borehole all the way down can indicate the presence, dip and direction of bedding planes and joints.

It is often necessary to define the orientation of the core with respect to true north in order that dip directions can be determined and there are a number of ways that this can be done. Marks can be made on the rock surface in a known direction at the bottom of the borehole or impressions taken of it so that when the core is recovered its position in the ground can be established. In the Rocha technique a small hole is drilled at the bottom of the borehole and a steel bar grouted into place with a known orientation. This is then over-cored and recovered in the main core.

With deep boreholes it may be necessary to determine the exact profile of the hole in the ground and to do this the borehole inclination and direction must be measured at intervals. This can either be done by photographing a compass and a clinometer or plumb bob at various points down the borehole or it can be done by an acid-dip survey. In this survey a special tube containing a dilute solution of hydrofluoric acid is lowered on drill rods down the borehole and left for about an hour whilst the acid etches the glass to reveal the horizontal. After withdrawal the dip of the borehole and its direction can be measured.

The borehole can also be used for a variety of geophysical logging techniques. Seismic measurements can give an indication of the stratigraphy, structure and physical properties of the various rocks. Electrical methods can also give an indication of the stratigraphy and radiation techiques can measure rock density. Temperature can also be measured. Multiparameter probes are available which combine some or all of these techniques in a single instrument. However, all these methods are subject to misinterpretation and must be treated with caution.

7.11 Drilling over water

One particular drilling situation that deserves special mention is that of work over water. This covers a range from simply erecting a platform over a shallow river to drilling through many fathoms of tidal water. This latter work is expensive and time consuming and it presents particular problems. The engineer must consider the setting out of borehole positions, levelling relative to Ordnance Datum, the effects of waves, tides and currents, the type of drilling rig and its means of support. None of these are as straightforward as for a land-based operation and experience is vital.

Drilling rigs can be supported on staging, jack up platforms on the sea bed, barges, pontoons or ships and the choice will depend on location and conditions; it may even be possible to work between tides as for a normal land-based operation. In all cases, however, consideration must be given to stability, anchorages, effects of fluctuating water levels, maintenance of position, navigational hazards, costs and last but not least safety. Drilling or boring is difficult when the platform is moving up and down relative to the ground that is being drilled. Ingenious solutions have been devised for this problem but probably the most common method is to install casing, anchored down where necessary and to drill using this as the reaction for the drilling tools whilst letting the boat or pontoon move relative to it. An alternative is to use the weight of the drill string and to apply the rotational torque via a Kelly bar arrangement which utilizes a hexagonal drive head that is free to move up and down. Another technique is to use a pendant type arrangement and tension wires to resist the torque. Hydraulically operated ballasted underwater rigs have also been used. Various specialist samplers have been developed for offshore work and these include hydraulic types, vibracoring, water jetting and air lift techniques. Inflatable packers inside the borehole can be used to give the necessary reaction for cone penetration testing.

Positioning of the drilling unit can be accomplished by triangulation or by the use of accurate marine navigation systems. Once established the position of the boat can be maintained by four or six point moorings or by computer controlled manoeuvring

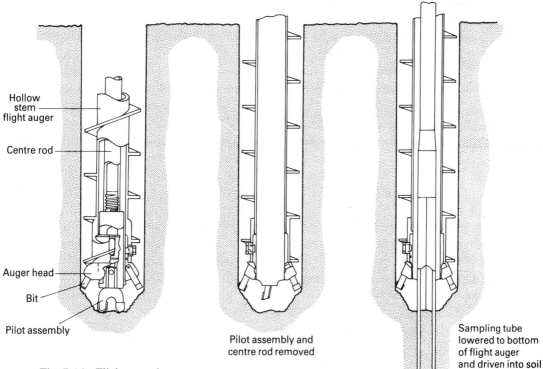

Hollow stem flight auger

Centre rod

Auger head

Bit

Pilot assembly

Pilot assembly and centre rod removed

Sampling tube lowered to bottom of flight auger and driven into soil

Fig. 7.16 Flight augering.

devices. Since the water level may well be varying the actual depth must be recorded at regular intervals and related to a nearby tide gauge in order to establish levels relative to Ordnance Datum.

Since drilling and sampling is more difficult in tidal conditions it is worth considering alternative means of investigation such as penetrometer testing and geophysics but even so some borehole information is usually essential. In all cases the necessary amount and type of ground investigation must be carefully assessed. It may be expensive but to try to economize at the investigation stage can lead to increased costs later on.

7.12 Flight augering

This technique is not for hard-rock coring but is included in this section since a rotary drilling action as distinct from a percussive one is employed. The method utilizes continuous flight augers to penetrate soft ground as shown in Fig. 4.7. A heavy drilling

175

rig is used since a large amount of torque is required to turn the flight augers and this can be a disadvantage on sites where access is difficult.

The principle of operation is also shown in Fig. 7.16. The auger is screwed into the ground complete with a centre rod and drill bit. Extra sections can be added as required. During this process soil is churned up and spirals up to the surface. This therefore produces completely disturbed samples and it is difficult to tell from what depth they have come. It is also difficult for the auger to penetrate hard or granular materials especially below the water table since no casing can be installed. Boulders too can prevent progress. However, in suitable soils progress can be extremely rapid. Flight augers are normally 150–250 mm in diameter with internal diameters of 75–125 mm and in the right conditions can reach depths of 30–50 m.

When any required depth has been reached the centre rod and drill bit can be withdrawn and a variety of devices lowered down the hole inside the auger itself. Sampling tubes can be driven or pushed into the soil and standard penetration tests can be carried out providing no piping is occurring. Alternatively cone penetration tests can be performed. If rock has been reached progress can be continued using a small diameter core barrel or rock roller bit. Even small diameter 'down the hole' hammers can be used for rotary percussive boring. The method is, therefore, an extremely versatile one but it does have its limitations.

7.13 Field records

The importance of good quality field records was discussed in Section 6.13 and many of the comments made there about shell and auger boring also apply to rotary drilling. However, somewhat different information is required. The field record sheet should be designed to be as easy to fill in as the shell and auger sheet so that the driller is encouraged to give as much information as possible. Normally the driller would enter his observations in a notebook and complete a form such as is shown in Fig. 7.17 at the end of the shift. This form is not intended to be definitive and different operators may prefer different formats but the general principles should be followed in all cases.

The form will contain spaces for the usual basic information such as site, borehole, job number, date, crew etc. After that a format appropriate to rotary drilling is adopted. The equipment that has been used should be described and should include the rig type, the flushing medium used, the size type and condition of corebits used and the types and lengths of casing used. Under the section headed core runs and strata record, details should be given on the start and finish of each core run, no matter how short, together with an estimate of the pecentage core recovery, the casing used and the time taken. This latter figure gives an indication of the ease of drilling. Obviously the strata changes will not coincide with the core runs and these should be detailed separately.

An attempt should be made by the driller to describe the various rock types

Daily report of rotary drilling	Site:	Location:
Equipment record	Job No:	Borehole No:
Type of rig:	Date:	Sheet: of:
Circulation fluid: water / air / mud	Ground level: m (Ordnance datum)	Crew/operator:
Bit and casing record	Weather:	

Bit / **Casing**

Size	Type	Condition	From	To	From	To

Strata Record

Run	From	To	Recovery	Casing depth during coring	Time taken to drill	Description of strata

Water record / **Time record, h**

Water levels, m	on pulling casing	24 h after pulling casing
Time of day		
Depth to water		
Depth cased		
Depth of hole		

At what levels was water encountered?

Did the level rise? If so, how much and how fast?

At what depths was water cut off by casing?

If standpipe/piezometer inserted, to what depth?

At what depths was full circulation not maintained and state percentage return at these depths:

NOTE. If more than one water level or circulation loss is encountered give details of them all.

Colour of water return.

Total (this sheet) ☐

Coring ☐   Open hole ☐   Casing ☐

Moving (including pulling casing)   From borehole ☐   To borehole ☐   ☐

Standing time   (i) ☐   (ii) ☐   (iii) ☐

Remarks (including explanation of all standing time, possible reasons for core loss, details of in situ tests and instrumentation, backfilling and grouting)

Fig. 7.17 Typical daily report form of rotary drilling (from BS5930:1981).

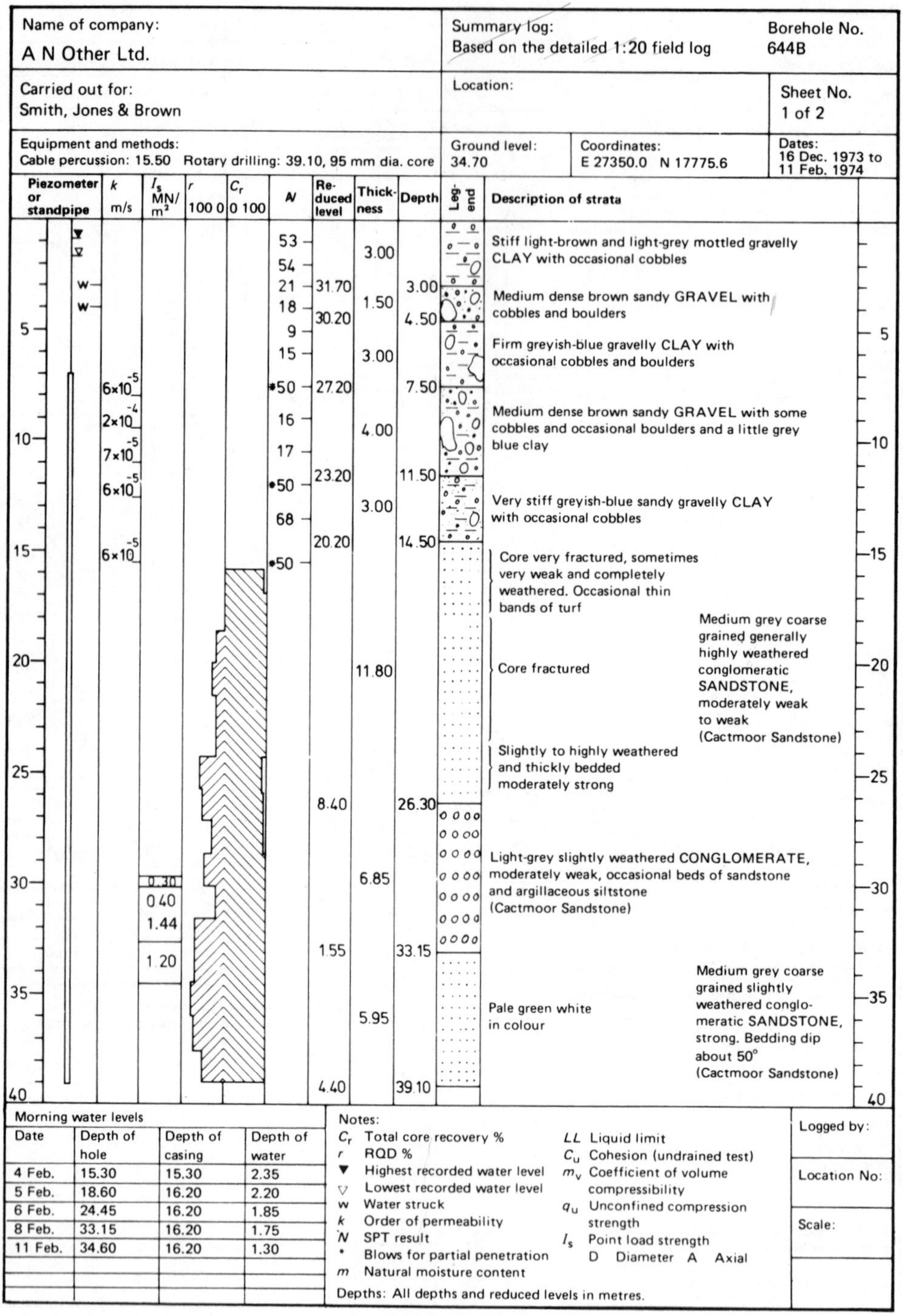

Name of company: A N Other Ltd.	Summary log: Based on the detailed 1:20 field log	Borehole No. 644B
Carried out for: Smith, Jones & Brown	Location:	Sheet No. 1 of 2
Equipment and methods: Cable percussion: 15.50 Rotary drilling: 39.10, 95 mm dia. core	Ground level: 34.70	Coordinates: E 27350.0 N 17775.6	Dates: 16 Dec. 1973 to 11 Feb. 1974

Description of strata (top to bottom):

- Stiff light-brown and light-grey mottled gravelly CLAY with occasional cobbles — 3.00 / 3.00
- Medium dense brown sandy GRAVEL with cobbles and boulders — 1.50 / 4.50
- Firm greyish-blue gravelly CLAY with occasional cobbles and boulders — 3.00 / 7.50
- Medium dense brown sandy GRAVEL with some cobbles and occasional boulders and a little grey blue clay — 4.00 / 11.50
- Very stiff greyish-blue sandy gravelly CLAY with occasional cobbles — 3.00 / 14.50
- Core very fractured, sometimes very weak and completely weathered. Occasional thin bands of turf — Medium grey coarse grained generally highly weathered conglomeratic SANDSTONE, moderately weak to weak (Cactmoor Sandstone). Core fractured — 11.80 / 26.30
- Slightly to highly weathered and thickly bedded moderately strong
- Light-grey slightly weathered CONGLOMERATE, moderately weak, occasional beds of sandstone and argillaceous siltstone (Cactmoor Sandstone) — 6.85 / 33.15
- Pale green white in colour — Medium grey coarse grained slightly weathered conglomeratic SANDSTONE, strong. Bedding dip about 50° (Cactmoor Sandstone) — 5.95 / 39.10

Column data (k, I_s MN/m², N, Reduced level, Thickness, Depth):

k values: 6×10^{-5}, 2×10^{-4}, 7×10^{-5}, 6×10^{-5}, 6×10^{-5}

N/SPT results: 53, 54, 21, 18, 9, 15, •50, 16, 17, •50, 68, •50, and lower: 8.40, 6.85, 1.55, 5.95, 4.40

I_s values near 30–35 m: 0.30, 0.40, 1.44, 1.20

Reduced levels: 31.70, 30.20, 27.20, 23.20, 20.20

Morning water levels				Notes:		Logged by:
Date	Depth of hole	Depth of casing	Depth of water			
4 Feb.	15.30	15.30	2.35			Location No:
5 Feb.	18.60	16.20	2.20			
6 Feb.	24.45	16.20	1.85			Scale:
8 Feb.	33.15	16.20	1.75			
11 Feb.	34.60	16.20	1.30			

Notes:
C_r Total core recovery %
r RQD %
▼ Highest recorded water level
▽ Lowest recorded water level
w Water struck
k Order of permeability
N SPT result
• Blows for partial penetration
m Natural moisture content

LL Liquid limit
C_u Cohesion (undrained test)
m_v Coefficient of volume compressibility
q_u Unconfined compression strength
I_s Point load strength
D Diameter A Axial

Depths: All depths and reduced levels in metres.

Fig. 7.18 Typical condensed log (from BS5930:1981).

encountered in accordance with the principles described in Chapter 9, even though the cores will doubtless be described later by an experienced geologist. The driller should also make observations on any particular problems he has had such as lost circulation, voids, blocking off, swelling and so on and he should make a note of where he thinks core has been lost from and the reasons for it. The water record may appear a little irrelevant when water has been used as the flushing medium but nevertheless useful conclusions can be drawn from careful observations since as soon as the flow of water ceases the groundwater will be trending towards equilibrium conditions. The observations required are largely self explanatory but in the section of water/air returns comments should be given on the colour of the cuttings and any losses that occurred.

The time record is again self explanatory. The driller should make full use of the remarks column, noting details of any instrumentation, *in situ* testing, backfilling or grouting that has taken place. The backfilling of a borehole should be carried out carefully with due regard to the circumstances especially if the borehole were part of a tunnelling investigation or a dam foundation. This was discussed in the previous chapter as was the installation of standpipes for the monitoring of groundwater levels. The driller should make a note of any peculiarities that he has observed and should remember that at this stage too much information is far better than too little.

Once the core has been examined by a geologist a final borehole log can be drawn up such as is shown in Fig. 7.18. This log is of the form that should be included in the final report and a key will be necessary to fully explain it. The same format can be used for both shell and auger boring and rotary drilling or separate formats can be used. Figure 6.15 showed the same type of log completed as an example of shell and auger boring and Fig. 6.16 shows the key to both this figure and Fig. 7.18. Neither the format of the log nor the key are intended to be definitive and operators may have their own preferences. The important thing is to present all the necessary information in as clear a way as possible.

8

Sampling and *in situ* testing

8.1 Introduction

Coverage was given to basic sampling and *in situ* testing in Chapters 5 and 6 but this was restricted to those techniques commonly used in a routine ground investigation. The basic 'undisturbed' sample is the U100 sample and the basic *in situ* test is the Standard Penetration Test and both are regularly carried out during shell and auger boring. U100 samples can be used for laboratory testing as described in Chapter 10 but there are many more sophisticated techniques available which give rise to less disturbed samples. There are also many different techniques of *in situ* testing which can be used in the field. However, before these techniques are described it is important to consider the reasons for·their use.

As has been stated, every effort should be made during shell and auger drilling to obtain samples which are disturbed as little as possible but with the best will in the world some disturbance is inevitable. The softer, looser and more sensitive the soil the more significant will be the effects and the more it becomes necessary to use special methods which reduce the disturbance. Employing these methods can, in some cases, be more expensive. The engineer must, therefore, decide how critical the soil conditions are and whether or not the increased expenditure will lead to real benefits in terms of safety and economy of design. In making this decision the engineer should recognize that without good samples there is little chance of obtaining accurate test results. With very soft clays for instance normal U100 sampling will produce unacceptable degrees of disturbance and will lead to erroneous test results.

Soils often contain structural features such as laminations and fissures and sometimes these occur with quite wide spacings. Thus even with high quality sampling there are

180

still problems concerning the extent to which a small sample is representative of the soil mass as a whole. There will also inevitably be some slight disturbance even if only due to the changes that occur as soon as a sample is removed from the ground. In addition the very nature of the soil itself may encourage sample disturbance, one example being the presence of gravel or cobbles in boulder clays and these may even prevent driving of a tube sampler. For these reasons there are definite advantages in testing soils in their *in situ* conditions since there will be less disturbance and a greater, and therefore more representative, volume of soil will be tested. Once again most of these *in situ* tests tend to be expensive and time consuming but they can lead to real cost savings by enabling more accurate recommendations to be made. *In situ* testing can also be used to check available design methods since the results are more representative of real ground conditions and are usually available immediately on completion of the test.

The techniques available are many and varied, some have come into common use and some have not got beyond the research stage. They do however fall into a number of different categories and these will be considered in the following sections. No attempt has been made to cover all the techniques; there are simply too many for a book of this size. Instead some of the more common and generally accepted techniques are described and from these descriptions the reader should be able to recognize the general principles and hence make an assessment of other techniques that are not mentioned but which he may come across. New and more sophisticated techniques are being developed all the time and these and the established techniques are providing a great deal of useful information for the geotechnical engineer on the way soils behave in their *in situ* conditions.

The results of *in situ* testing and their relationship to the actual performance of structures is providing definite benefits in terms of improved predictions of geotechnical behaviour. The future increased use and development of *in situ* testing techniques probably hold the greatest promise for the accurate assessment of soil/ structure interaction. Knowledge such as this will surely lead to safer and more economic designs providing of course the tests are carried out as an integral part of a carefully executed site investigation which recognizes all the potential problems. *In situ* testing gives a more representative picture of the real ground conditions and if it is necessary to have this, the penalties of cost and inconvenience must be overcome.

8.2 Special sampling techniques

The main problems with conventional U100 sampling are as follows. First the cross sectional area of the tube is fairly high compared with the cross sectional area of the sample and this causes disturbance. Secondly, disturbance is caused by the hammer blows used to drive in the sampler and thirdly there is a tendency for soft or loose soils to fall out of the tube although this can be partly cured by using a core catcher. Finally

181

there is no control over shrinkage and swelling. For these reasons many different sampling techniques have been developed to try and overcome some or all of these problems.

Hvorslev 1949 presents a detailed study of sampling techniques and it is not the intention of this book to repeat it. Instead some of the more popular well-tried methods will be described. However, the reader is strongly advised to consult Hvorslev's book even if only to see just how much disturbance can occur during sampling. The book may be over 30 years old but it contains a great deal of useful information.

Perhaps the most commonly used technique for the sampling of soft, sensitive clays and silts is piston sampling. This is illustrated in Fig. 8.1. Thin-wall sampling tubes of different diameters up to 250 mm and lengths of up to 1 m are available but the basic principle remains the same. There is another less satisfactory type not illustrated which utilizes a floating piston connected to a wire line instead of a piston fixed to rods.

In the fixed-piston type there is a piston connected to rods and a sampling tube connected to a sleeve. The rod and sleeve can be clamped together when required. The procedure is as follows. The tube and piston are clamped together with the piston at the bottom of the tube. The combination can then be pushed into soft soils or pushed through a disturbed zone until the required level is reached; a procedure which cannot be done with the floating piston type. At the required depth the rods are fixed to hold the piston stationary and the tube is forced down, using a steady pressure on the sleeve, to take the sample. The rods and sleeve are marked to prevent overdriving which would compress the sample.

To withdraw the sample the rods and sleeve are clamped together thus preventing the sample from falling out by generating a partial suction above it. However, withdrawal must be done slowly to prevent an equal suction from forming beneath the sample.

The area ratio of the thin-wall tubes is much lower than that of the normal U100 and the sample is pushed in rather than driven. There is, therefore, considerably less disturbance. When sampling below the water table, water must be added to the borehole to maintain a pressure balance and thus prevent piping. After sampling the tubes should be waxed, sealed and handled carefully to prevent disturbance. The tubes are relatively thin and will not stand up to driving in stiff soils nor those containing gravel. The technique will not recover sands unless there is some cohesive material present although some samplers have been modified with a spring finger retaining arrangement in the cutting shoe which assists recovery. There are a great number of different designs of piston sampler but all operate on similar principles.

For sampling in sand there is an apparatus available known as the Bishop sand sampler or the Bishop compressed air sampler. This is illustrated in Fig. 8.2. The sampler comprises a 60 mm diameter inner sample tube housed within an outer tube or bell. The equipment is used for sands below the water table and the borehole must be kept topped up with water during both boring and sampling.

182

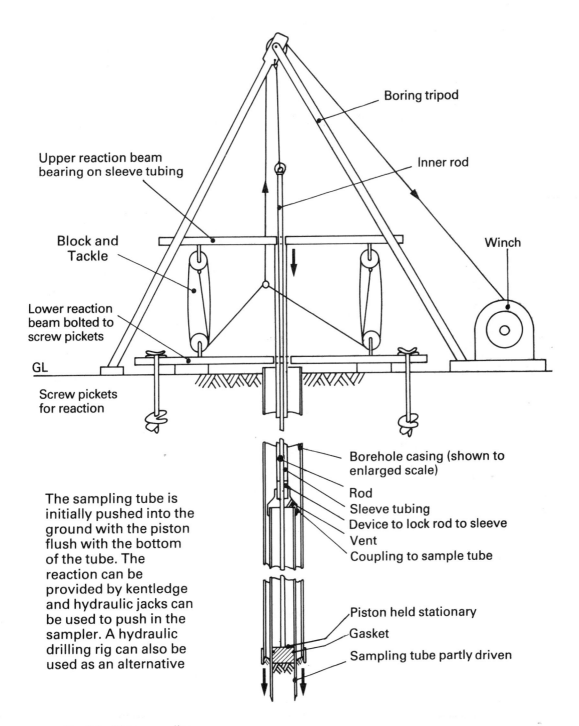

Boring tripod

Upper reaction beam
bearing on sleeve tubing

Inner rod

Block and
Tackle

Winch

Lower reaction
beam bolted to
screw pickets

GL

Screw pickets
for reaction

Borehole casing (shown to
enlarged scale)

Rod
Sleeve tubing
Device to lock rod to sleeve
Vent
Coupling to sample tube

The sampling tube is
initially pushed into the
ground with the piston
flush with the bottom
of the tube. The
reaction can be
provided by kentledge
and hydraulic jacks can
be used to push in the
sampler. A hydraulic
drilling rig can also be
used as an alternative

Piston held stationary

Gasket

Sampling tube partly driven

Fig. 8.1 Piston sampling.

183

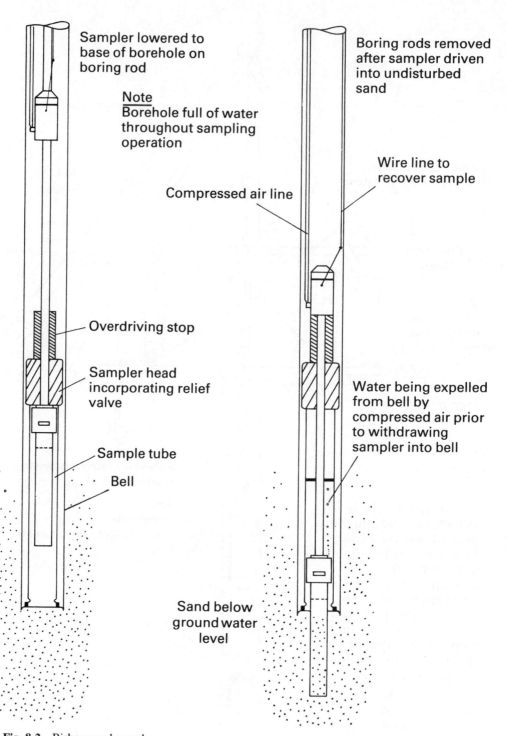

Sampler lowered to
base of borehole on
boring rod

Note
Borehole full of water
throughout sampling
operation

Boring rods removed
after sampler driven
into undisturbed
sand

Wire line to
recover sample

Compressed air line

Overdriving stop

Sampler head
incorporating relief
valve

Water being expelled
from bell by
compressed air prior
to withdrawing
sampler into bell

Sample tube

Bell

Sand below
ground water
level

Fig. 8.2 Bishop sand sampler.

The sampler is lowered to the bottom of the borehole on rods which are used to push the inner tube into the ground and a stop is incorporated to prevent overdriving. When the sample tube is full the rods are removed and compressed air is injected into the bell thus forcing the water out. The tube is then slowly retracted into the bell using a wire line recovery system and the whole sampler lifted to the surface. The compressed air which is then surrounding the sample holds it in place. In a modified version compressed air is injected at the bottom of the sampling tube.

The laboratory triaxial testing of sand samples is difficult but they can be used for detailed examination. The sampler cannot be used in very dense sands nor in very gravelly sands and there is inevitably some disturbance due to boring and to sampling. For these reasons it is generally better to rely on *in situ* testing in non-cohesive materials.

The above methods can be used to obtain discrete samples but if truly continuous sampling of soft or loose alluvial soils is required the Delft sampler can be used to obtain samples up to 15 m long. Continuous sampling is important when thin layers of sand might be present within a layer of clay which greatly affect times of consolidation or where thin layers of clay in sand might affect groundwater flow or in fact in any situation where a detailed examination of the strata is necessary and where missed layers might be of critical importance.

The Delft sampler can produce samples 29 mm or 66 mm in diameter and is normally pushed into the ground hydraulically. Just behind the cutting edge of the twin tube sampler there is a magazine containing a rolled tube of stockinet and a vulcanizing fluid. The sampler is first filled with Bentonite of about the same density as the soil being sampled and as it is pushed into the ground the stockinet impregnated with vulcanizing fluid is pulled off the magazine and surrounds the sample. When the vulcanizing fluid comes into contact with the Bentonite it cures to form a flexible waterproof membrane. At the same time the whole sample is supported by the Bentonite.

As the sampler is pushed in, extension tubes can be added until the required depth is reached when the sample can be locked into the tubes by a mechanism behind the magazine and the whole assembly withdrawn. As each extension tube is withdrawn it is uncoupled and a metre or so length of sample cut off and laid in prepared trays. The samples can then be inspected, logged and photographed by cutting into the stockinet and splitting the core in half. One half can be used for laboratory classification testing whilst the other half can be allowed to partially dry out. This often better reveals the soil structure particularly where the soil is laminated and it often enables a better log to be produced.

The Delft sampler produces little sample disturbance but some compression of the samples can occur. Where it is necessary to obtain samples for triaxial and consolidation testing a conventional borehole can be sunk adjacent to the Delft hole and, for example, piston samples can be obtained from the depths required. The Swedish foil

185

sampler is similar in principle to the Delft sampler but a thin sheet of foil is used to encase the sample.

Out of the dozen or more different samplers that have been developed it is worth briefly mentioning one or two other types that the reader may come across.

The shrew sampler is a miniature piston sampler that can be used down a Dutch deep sounding hole but it produces small disturbed samples that are only really suitable for identification purposes. The retractable plug sampler is a similar device.

The Moss sampler is a thin-wall Shelby tube used inside a hollow-stem flight auger. The cutting edge projects beyond the end of the auger but does not rotate with it. It is therefore pushed in ahead of the borehole during augering and it can be lifted to the surface without raising the auger. Shelby tubes are simply thin-wall steel tubes with cutting edges and are available in different diameters but usually 75 mm.

The Denison sampler is essentially a 600 mm long × 150 mm diameter double tube core barrel with a core catcher and uses mud flush. It can be used to core stiff clays and soft shales and even cohesive sands but it cannot be used for clean sand or anything containing gravel. There are also other double tube core barrel type samplers available.

The ribbon sampler contains flexible sprung steel cutters which are actuated from the surface to cut through the soil at the bottom of the tube and seal off the bottom thus preventing the sample from falling out. These, however, tend to have a high area ratio and cause considerable disturbance.

The Raymond sampler is the split-tube arrangement used in a Standard Penetration Test and described in Chapter 6. There are also other types and sizes of split-tube samplers and some have flap type retaining valves at the bottom.

For sea or river bed sampling various drop samplers are available. These are simply heavily weighted tubes with stabilizing fins which are dropped to the sea bed and recovered. Explosive techniques have also been used for driving sample tubes underwater.

Another sampling technique is to freeze the ground before taking the sample but in many materials the freezing process itself will cause frost heave and disturbance.

It should be appreciated that poor sampling can lead to a 50% or more reduction in the shear strength of a sensitive soil when measured in the laboratory as compared with the true *in situ* value. In other cases, where the sample is compressed, over-optimistic results can be obtained. The engineer must, therefore, critically examine the need for sampling, the type of sample needed and the quality achieved before blindly proceeding with laboratory testing, the results of which may be totally misleading. It is true that the consequences of optimistic results might well be allowed for by using a high factor of safety but if low shear strengths and high factors of safety are used an uneconomic design will be produced. In some situations this may not be very significant but in others it will and the engineer should recognize those situations where the soil properties are critical to the design process and take appropriate action.

8.3 Vane testing

Vane testing is aimed at determining the *in situ* shear strength of very soft to firm cohesive materials by determining the torque necessary to turn a cruciform shaped vane which has been pushed into undisturbed soil. From the torque required to turn the vane the soil shear strength can be calculated. The principle of the test is shown in Fig. 8.3. A brief description of the hand vane tester was given in Section 5.3 but the procedure for the larger tests is somewhat different. The technique was developed since it was found that the laboratory determination of shear strength on even slightly disturbed samples gave results which the analysis of soil slips proved unrepresentatively low.

The vanes come in a variety of shapes and sizes, but are normally cruciform in shape and commonly have a length to diameter ratio of 2. The size of vane should be chosen to suit the soil shear strength and torque available. The bottom edges of the four blades are sharpened to make for easier penetration. The shear surface produced by the vane is in the form of a cylinder and the top and bottom of the cylinder must be taken into account in calculations.

The test can be carried out below the bottom of a borehole (as shown in Fig. 8.3) or it can be carried out by pushing the vane in to successive test positions. The vane is relatively delicate and during penetration it is protected by a shoe, the extensions to which prevent friction building up on the rods connected to the vane. Before a test the vane should be pushed about 0.5 m beyond the protecting shoe which itself should be about 0.5 m beyond the bottom of a borehole if it is a borehole test that is being carried out.

The test procedure is defined by Test 18 of BS1377 which specifies a rate of rotation of the vane of 0.1 to $0.2°\ s^{-1}$ (6 to $12°\ min^{-1}$) until a peak reading indicating failure is obtained. This gives a test time of 3–15 min depending on the strain at failure. The friction on the rods can be measured using the same torque measuring device and deducted from the peak reading to give the true shear strength. Having determined the peak shear strength the remoulded shear strength can be assessed by turning the vane through six to twelve revolutions, waiting 5 min and then measuring the torque in the normal manner. The soil sensitivity is defined as the ratio of peak to remoulded shear strengths. Pages 81 and 82 of BS1377 show typical report forms for vane tests.

Since the test is carried out fairly rapidly it is essentially an undrained one unless the soils are sandy or laminated. The engineer should, therefore, consider how the test results are to be used in relation to the problem under consideration. In other words he should assess whether or not the load is to be applied slowly or quickly since if it is applied slowly there will be some drainage and the soil will increase in strength. However, in these circumstances the vane results will give a worst-case analysis.

The engineer should also consider whether or not there is likely to be any difference in soil shear strength between the vertical and horizontal planes as often happens with

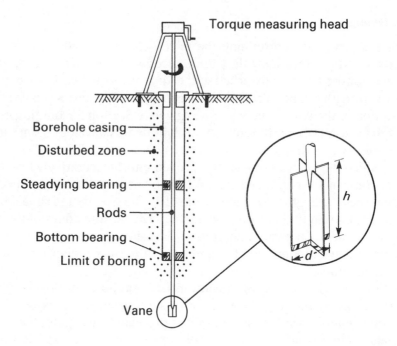

1. The vanes are pushed into the soil ahead of the boring and through the disturbed zone. The vane is then twisted to cause the soil to shear

2. The torque necessary to turn the vane is recorded and calibration charts used to assess the undrained shear strength of the soil

$$\text{Shear strength} = \frac{T}{3.67d^3}$$

for a vane where $h/d = 2$ and where T is the torque at failure and where the shear strength is the same in all directions

Fig. 8.3   Shear-vane test.

alluvial materials. Since a slip circle in say a river bank involves shearing the soil in vertical, diagonal, and horizontal directions the relevance of the normal vane test, which shears the soil mainly on a vertical plane, should be questioned. The engineer

188

may consider it desirable to check the shear strength by using the vane in different directions.

The torque measuring heads of vane testers should be periodically calibrated and it is convenient to draw up a calibration chart so that the soil shear strength can be read off once the torque has been measured. Different charts will be needed for different sized or shaped vanes.

In conclusion vane testing is relatively cheap and simple and is highly desirable, if not essential, in soft or loose cohesive soils if accurate shear strengths are to be obtained.

8.4 Penetrometers

Like soil samplers, penetrometers come in all shapes and sizes but all have one thing in common and that is they make an assessment of soil strength by measuring the load required to cause the penetration into the ground of a cone or occasionally a tube. The loads can be applied statically, that is by steady pressure, or dynamically by hammering or dropping weights or by a combination of the two methods. The most commonly used dynamic test, the Standard Penetration Test (SPT), which gives N values, was described in Section 6.10 and a simple hand-held static penetrometer was described in Section 5.3. Before describing one or two other common penetrometers in use it is worth considering how the results are used in practice but it must be appreciated that the presence of cobbles or boulders can lead to totally erroneous results.

The SPT was developed in the 1920s as the first cheap means of comparing the densities of granular deposits although the results have since been extended to anything from soft clays to weak rocks, albeit rather dubiously. As experience built up on the results of the tests various empirical relationships were established to give relative densities, Young's Moduli, safe bearing pressures and settlements. It must be stressed that these empirical relationships are by no means always accurate but since the tests are cheap and simple and since there is not always any easy alternative they do form an important part of foundation design providing a large enough number of tests have been performed. To illustrate this there are a dozen or more procedures for relating settlement to N values and a dozen different results will be obtained so engineering judgement must be used in selecting the most appropriate method.

Before an N value is used in foundation design it should be corrected for depth of overburden, position of the water table, soil type, particle size and grading (see Tomlinson, 1975). The results of other penetration tests have been correlated with the SPT test in order that their results can also be used in foundation design although the Dutch cone test can be considered as a miniature pile test. The correlations described above depend on the soil type and grading and again it must be stressed that the correlations are by no means precise. The International Society for Soil Mechanics and Foundation Engineering has issued a code for the standardization of penetration testing in Europe.

A static penetrometer, the Dutch Cone Penetrometer is shown in Fig. 8.4. It simply provides a hydraulic means of applying load and a means of measuring this load. In early machines the load was applied mechanically by screws and gears. There are various designs of cone point which can be attached to the inner rods which are isolated from friction of the ground by a sleeve. The cone and the sleeve can be driven together but pressure gauges or load cells record the loads on each. On some machines this facility is not available and the cone must first be advanced, the load recorded, the sleeve advanced and the load on the sleeve recorded. The cone should be advanced at a constant rate of penetration, normally 2 cm s^{-1}. A typical report form for the Dutch cone penetrometer is shown on page 87 of BS5930.

Measuring the friction on the sleeve can give useful information on total friction but it is even more useful if the actual friction adjacent to the cone can be recorded since, if the strata are layered, knowledge of the friction can help in identifying the soil type. For this reason the mantle cone was developed so that the friction on a short length just behind the cone could be measured. The normal procedure with the mantle cone is to measure the end resistance to the cone only over a distance of 4 cm. After this initial penetration the cone engages with the mantle and both friction and cone resistance are measured over the next 4 cm. The process is then repeated. By deduction the local frictional element can be calculated and this is then expressed as a percentage of the cone resistance to give the friction ratio. In very soft soils a correction should be made for the weight of the rods.

The most sophisticated form of cone test is the electric friction cone penetrometer shown in Fig. 8.5. In this piece of equipment the frictional force and the cone force are measured independently by strain gauges. The cone is pushed into the ground at a rate of about 2 cm s^{-1} and the cone resistance and frictional resistance are continuously recorded. The friction ratio is then calculated electronically and both end resistance and friction ratio are plotted on a chart recorder as shown in Fig. 8.6. The chart speed is linked to the rate of penetration and therefore the vertical axis becomes one of depth.

Also shown on Fig. 8.6 are the interpreted ground conditions which are arrived at using Fig. 8.7 which is appropriate to the Fugro electric cone. An alternative chart for interpretation purposes developed by Searle (1979) is also shown in Fig. 8.7 and this is appropriate to the Begemann friction jacket cone. The denser or stiffer the material being penetrated the higher will be its cone resistance. Clays have high friction ratios whereas sands and gravels have low ones.

Penetrometers such as these are often mounted in a heavy lorry to provide the necessary reaction during penetration; although they can be mounted in a variety of ways with reaction provided by kentlege or screw pickets. Different sensitivities of cone are available for different soil strengths and 10–15 tests to a depth of 15 m can be completed in a day. Cones have also been developed which can simultaneously measure pore pressures and inclination to the vertical during penetration (see also Section 8.7).

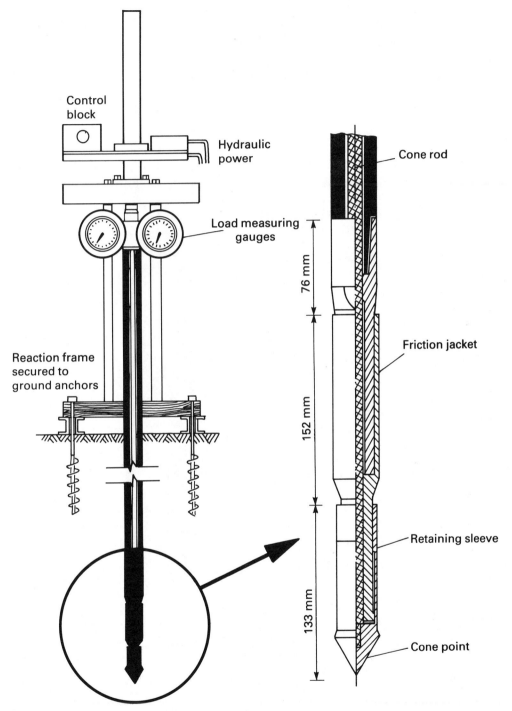

Fig. 8.4 Dutch cone penetrometer.

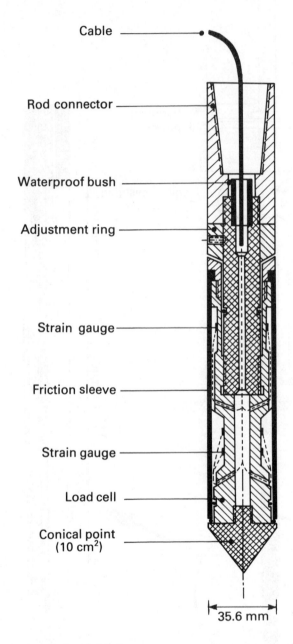

Cable

Rod connector

Waterproof bush

Adjustment ring

Strain gauge

Friction sleeve

Strain gauge

Load cell

Conical point
(10 cm^2)

35.6 mm

Fig. 8.5 Cross section of electric friction cone penetrometer.

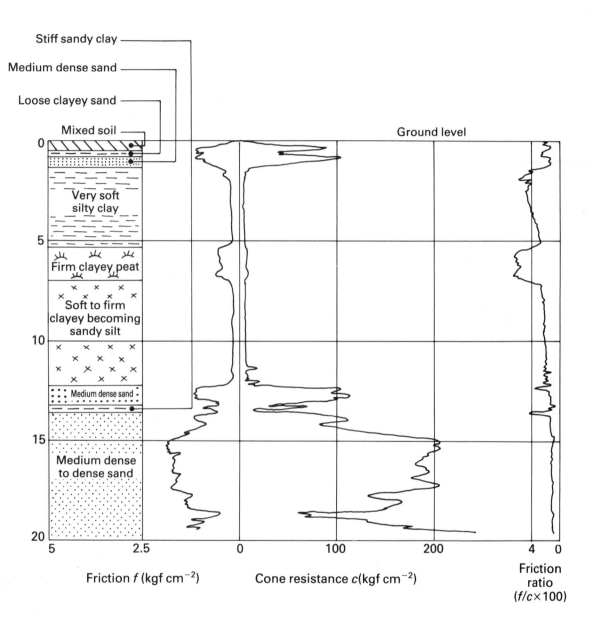

Fig. 8.6 Typical electric cone test results (after Fugro Ltd).

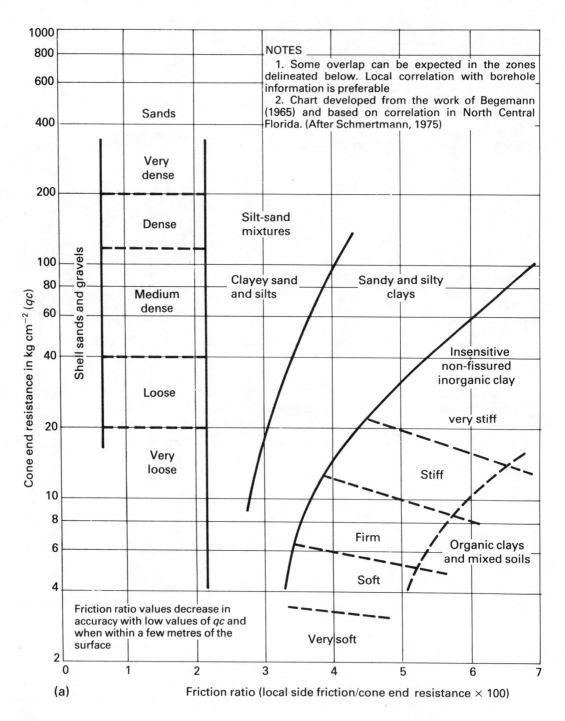

(a)

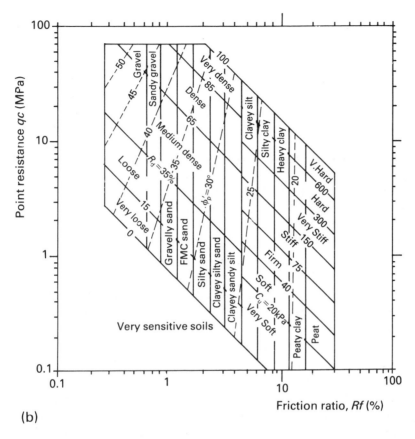

(b)

Fig. 8.7 (a) Interpretation of electric cone test results. (b) Interpretation chart for cone penetration tests (after Searle).

The maximum depth that can be reached depends on the soil conditions but can be up to 40 or 50 m. However, the cone cannot penetrate very stiff clays or very dense granular deposits with N values over about 50.

The electric cone offers a cheap, quick method of soil exploration but the strata log produced is not precise and it should be used in conjunction with control boreholes although the total number of boreholes needed can often be substantially reduced if sufficient cone penetration tests are carried out. On the other hand it has the advantage that it is testing *in situ* conditions without the problems of sample disturbance.

For foundation design the cone resistance qc can be converted to the N value using the factors below (Schmertmann, 1970).

195

	qc/N
Silts, sandy silts and slightly cohesive silt–sand mixtures.	2
Clean, fine to medium sands and slightly silty sands	3–4
Coarse sands and sands with a little gravel	5–6
Sandy gravels and gravel	8–10

For cohesive materials it is preferable to establish the relationship between cone resistance and shear strength for each clay type that is penetrated.

Since electric cone testing is relatively cheap it can play an important part at all stages of a site investigation and it has been combined with a conventional drilling rig to give a useful all-round investigation tool. It could for instance be used at a very early stage to give a rough idea of the sort of materials present and their depths. This information could then be used to help plan the main ground investigation and would help in choosing the optimum positions for boreholes. It can also be used in the foundation design process as described previously. Other applications include before and after studies of the effects of compaction, delineation of bedrock surfaces, location of cavities and pile design.

It is not intended to describe all the different penetrometers that are available but two other types will be mentioned to help illustrate the general principles. The Swedish Weight Penetrometer is a static type which uses a small screw-shaped point. This enables greater depths of penetration to be achieved by combining weight with rotation. Measurements of penetration are taken and turns of rotation counted as large weights are placed on a platform on the rods, the results are expressed as numbers of half turns needed for 200 mm penetration with a given weight.

The Ram Sounding Method is a dynamic method very similar to the SPT and uses a 45 mm diameter point with rods of a lesser diameter and a standard dropping weight. The point is normally driven as far as possible with the blows being counted for each 200 mm of penetration. At the end of the test the rods are extracted using hydraulic jacks. As with the other penetrometers the results of these tests can be used empirically in various methods of foundation design.

8.5 Pressuremeters

Pressuremeters or dilatometers are names given to a family of easily portable *in situ* testing instruments which are lowered into the ground to the required depth and expanded laterally to load the soil or weak rock radially. Measurements are made of lateral pressure (which can be converted to stress) and volume (which can be converted to radial displacement or strain) and these measurements can be used to calculate the pressuremeter modulus of deformation E_p, the undrained cohesion of cohesive soils c_u, and the angle of shearing resistance ϕ of granular soils. These values can then be used in the foundation design process but it must be remembered that the test is investigating soil conditions in the vertical plane.

The instruments have the advantages that a fairly large volume of soil is stressed and there are not the same problems of sample disturbance although there is inevitably some disturbance during the boring of the hole in which the test is carried out. Tests can be carried out at various depths and a strength/depth profile plotted. The test can also be used in soils such as boulder clays which are difficult or impossible to sample in an undisturbed manner.

One commonly used instrument, the Menard pressuremeter, is shown in Fig. 8.8 and this can be supplied in different diameters. Carbon dioxide gas is used to pressurize water which expands three flexible cells, two of the cells are guard cells which are inflated under the same pressure as the central measuring cell in order to ensure the measuring cell can only expand radially without any end effects. The volume of water entering the measuring cell is monitored, as is its pressure, and a volume or diameter/ pressure curve is plotted as shown in Fig. 8.9 and this can be used to calculate the pressuremeter modulus.

The above curve may be divided into three phases. Initially a certain pressure P_{ar} will be required to restore the *in situ* earth pressure at rest. As the pressure increases the soil deforms in a pseudo-elastic fashion until a pressure P_f is reached when the soil starts to deform plastically. A stage may be reached in some soils where the borehole expands laterally without any increase in pressure; this is known as the limit pressure. Each increment of pressure is applied for 1 min. The deformation or volume change in the period from 0.5 min to 1 min after each increment of pressure has been applied is known as the creep and this can also be plotted against pressure as shown in Fig. 8.9. This curve helps define the beginning and end of the pseudo-plastic phase. If necessary the load can be released and a re-loading curve plotted. Care is needed to ensure there is no air in the central cell or connecting tubes and corrections are needed to allow for the strength of the membrane and hydrostatic pressures due to head differences.

Tests can be carried out in soil or rock but ultimate strengths will not be reached in tests on rock and only the modulus of deformation will be obtained. In very soft soils the pressuremeter can be pushed into the ground but in other soils and rocks the apparatus must be lowered down an appropriately sized borehole. In some boreholes Bentonite will be needed to support the sides of the hole. Many different methods can be used to sink the borehole but consideration should be given to the amount of disturbance. Menard pressuremeters come in various sizes up to about 75 mm in diameter but other pressuremeters are available with larger diameters and different instruments are available with different sensitivities.

In rocks a higher capacity dilatometer known as a borehole jack can be used. This

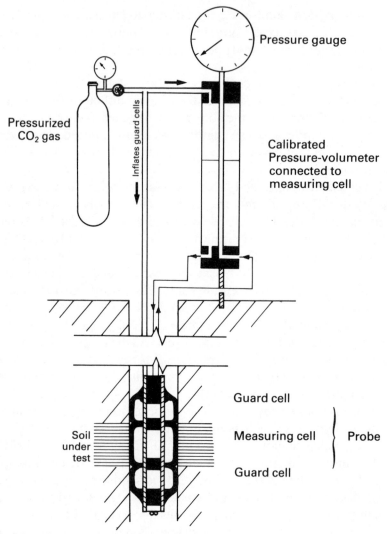

Fig. 8.8   Menard pressuremeter.

consists of a split metal cylinder which is expanded by hydraulic pressure and the expansion is monitored using electrical transducers.

To help overcome the problem of disturbance during boring a self-boring pressuremeter, the Camkometer, was developed (see Wroth and Hughes 1973). This is shown in Fig. 8.10. Penetration is affected by pushing in a rotating cutter and circulating flushing water. Expansion is achieved using gas pressure and is monitored electrically by three spring feelers to give a constant rate of expansion. A load cell and pore pressure measuring cell are also incorporated.

198

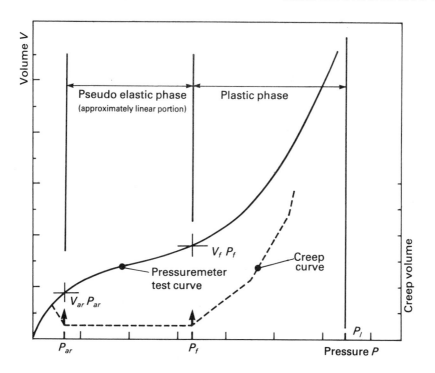

P_{ar} = initial *in situ* horizontal stress
P_f = yield pressure
P_l = limit pressure (usually taken when volume of cavity is doubled)
E_p = pressuremeter modulus
V_c = volume of central cell
$\Delta P/\Delta V$ = slope of curve at $V_m P_m$ where $P_m = (P_{ar} + P_f)/2$ and V_m is
corresponding volume
ν = Poisson's ratio (usually taken as 0.33)
E_p = $2(1 + \nu)(V_c + C_m)\Delta p/\Delta v$

If log $(\Delta V/V)$ is plotted against pressure the curved part of the graph represents the elastic region and the straight part the plastic region. The slope of the straight part can be used to determine the undrained cohesion of the soils (s' = $1/c_u$).

Fig. 8.9   Results of pressuremeter test.

Two types of Camkometer are available. The expansion type loads the soil in a similar manner to the Menard pressuremeter. This provides a plot of radial strain against applied pressure from which the shear stress/shear strain diagram for the soil can be determined by a simple graphical transformation as shown in Fig. 8.11. The load cell Camkometer senses the horizontal component of the *in situ* ground stress by balancing the external load acting on the instrument from the soil against the internal

199

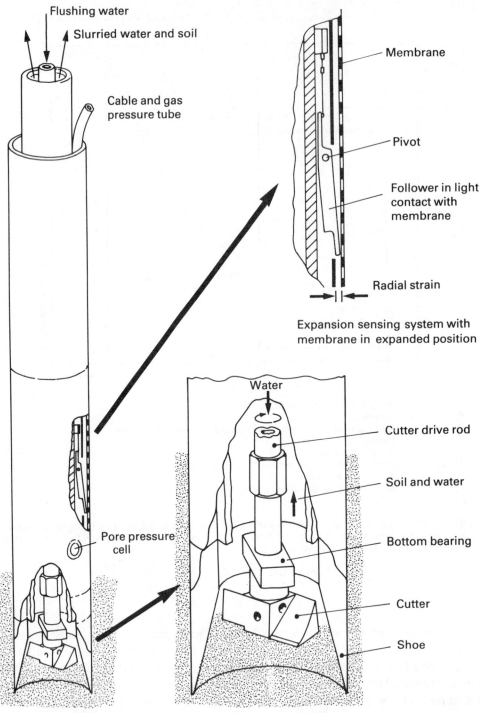

Flushing water

Slurried water and soil

Cable and gas
pressure tube

Membrane

Pivot

Follower in light
contact with
membrane

Radial strain

Expansion sensing system with
membrane in expanded position

Water

Cutter drive rod

Soil and water

Bottom bearing

Cutter

Shoe

Pore pressure
cell

Cutting arrangement

Fig. 8.10 Camkometer.

200

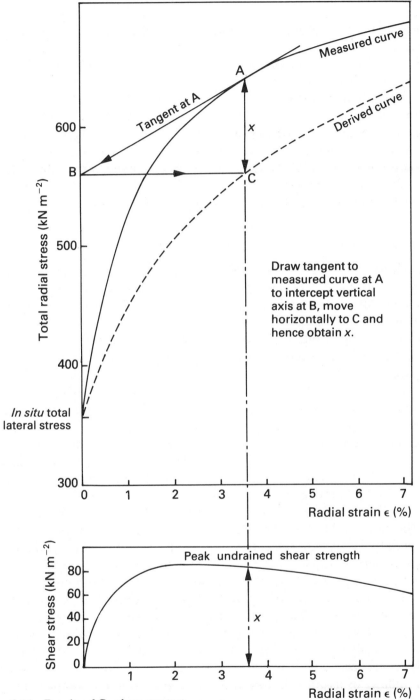

Fig. 8.11   Results of Camkometer test.

gas pressure so as to null the output of a load cell fitted flush with the external surface of the instrument.

The advantages of the Camkometer are that tests are carried out on a fairly large mass of virtually undisturbed soil which has not been allowed any stress relief. Testing is quite rapid in the right ground but the instruments will not penetrate gravels or boulder clays and they are only testing the soil in the vertical plane. One other disadvantage is the amount of complex electronics contained in the instruments which have to penetrate a hostile water-bearing environment but developments should continue which will overcome this problem. One particular advantage of the Camkometer over the Menard Pressuremeter is that the instrument can penetrate soft clays or loose sands below the water table without the risk of caving in that is associated with a borehole.

8.6 Permeability tests

The permeability of a soil is a measure of the rate at which water can flow through it. Laboratory tests for the determination of permeability are described in Chapter 10 but there are many problems in arriving at the right answers. The first problem is that tests are only carried out on small samples which in view of possible fissures and laminations may or may not be representative. The sampling process itself can cause compression, smearing or other disturbance to the sample which can greatly affect its permeability. Finally laboratory tests normally only measure the permeability in one direction. In practice there may well be considerable differences in horizontal and vertical permeabilities, particularly in alluvial soils. For these reasons permeabilities measured in the laboratory may be a factor of ten or more out from the true *in situ* conditions.

There is therefore a very real need to measure permeabilities in the field since they can have a highly significant effect on calculations involving times of settlement, dissipation of pore pressures and development of soil shear strength. Five types of field test can be carried out, rising or falling head tests, constant head tests, packer tests or pumping tests. The falling head test is the simplest and is suitable for the finer grained soils. The constant head test is more accurate but can be time consuming except in the coarser materials. The packer test can give more information and is often used in rocks where it is necessary to measure permeability at high pressures over only a short length of borehole. Pumping tests are appropriate to soils or rocks with high permeabilities and are used for the evaluation of aquifers for water supply. Tests can also be carried out using piezometers (see Chapter 11) and these can give greater control over the test conditions and more accurate results but are more time consuming unless the piezometer is already installed for the long-term monitoring of ground water levels.

Boring holes for permeability tests demands care to avoid the effects of smearing clay layers and infilling of fissures. Before tests are carried out in boreholes the borehole must be cleaned out and careful measurements made of the length of casing, length of open hole if any and the nature of any filter used. The joints in the casing must not leak and this can be achieved using fibre rings at the joints. The next stage is to determine the level of the true groundwater table and this was discussed in Chapter 6. Sufficient time must be allowed for the groundwater to reach its equilibrium level.

In the rising head test the borehole is bailed or pumped out and the rate at which water flows back into the hole determined by taking level observations at fixed time intervals. In the falling head test water is added to the hole and the rate at which it drains away is recorded but there is a danger that fine particles suspended in the water will settle out and reduce the apparent permeability. In the constant head test the rate of inflow of water is adjusted until a constant head is achieved; this may take some time. Once an equilibrium flow of water in, and therefore out, of the hole has been established it is recorded. If friction losses or high flows are expected two standpipes can be used, one to supply the water and the other to measure the true head of water at the piezometer tip. At the end of any test the borehole must be checked to ensure there has been no caving in of strata or piping. If either condition arises the results may not be of any use. Constant head permeability tests can also be performed using hydraulic piezometers. A form suitable for all these tests is shown in Fig. 8.12. There are numerous methods of calculating permeabilities from the results of these tests and the reader is advised to consult Hvorslev. A simplified summary is shown in Fig. 8.13.

Pumping tests are generally carried out by pumping water out of a borehole at a known constant rate and observing the drawdown of the water table in a series of other boreholes set out radially from the pumped hole. From these observations the drawdown curve can be plotted and the permeability calculated. These tests are particularly useful where it is necessary to establish the potential yield of water bearing rocks.

The packer or Lugeon test is normally used in N-sized boreholes to establish the permeability of rock under high water pressures and was developed to investigate the flow of water through rocks beneath dams and to investigate grout take prior to forming impermeable barriers. Two alternative methods of test are shown in Fig. 8.14. In the single packer test the bottom 3–6 m of the borehole is isolated from the rest of the hole by a flexible expanding packer which is lowered into position and inflated from the surface. The packers can be expanded mechanically, hydraulically or, more commonly, pneumatically using high-pressure nitrogen. Water is then pumped into the borehole below the packer at different pressures and the flow recorded in each case. A graph is then plotted of pressure against flow and this can be used to calculate permeabilities. The shape of the curve can also be used to give an indication of certain rock characteristics as shown in Fig. 8.15. In the double packer test a short section of borehole is isolated from the remainder of the hole using two packers as shown in Fig. 8.14. The packers must not be over-inflated so as to cause distortion of the borehole but must be inflated sufficiently to withstand the applied water pressures without leaking.

203

Job ....

Borehole No. ....   Reduced level .... (m) N.D.

Date of test ....   Operator ....

Depth of borehole during test .... (m)

Depth of borehole after test .... (m)

Depth of casing below ground level .... (m)

Depth of casing above ground level (H_1) .... (m)

Diameter of casing .... (mm)

Diameter of boring tool .... (mm)

Depth of ground water (H_4) .... (m)

Notes: 1. A piezometer may be required to establish true ground water level

         2. During test measure the depth to water from top of casing

         3. Head $(H) = H_4 - H_3$ (Falling Head Test) $H_3 - H_4$ (Rising Head Test)

         4. At time $t = 0$. Head $= H$

         5. Check for piping, caving in etc. by measuring depth before and after test

Elapsed Time Min. Sec.	Depth of Water from top of casing H_2 (m)	Depth of Water from ground level H_3 $(H_3 = H_2 - H_1)$ (m)	Head H (See Note 3) (m)	$\dfrac{H}{H_0}$ (See Note 4)
$0.0 = t_0$	0.0	+0.50	$6.00 = H_0$	1.0
0.0	0.0	+0.50	6.00	1.0
0.30	0.10	+0.40	5.90	0.98
1.00	0.25	+0.25	5.75	0.96
1.30	0.35	+0.15	5.65	0.94
2.00	0.45	+0.05	5.55	0.93
2.30	0.55	0.05	5.45	0.91
3.00	0.65	0.15	5.35	0.80
3.30	0.75	0.25	5.25	0.88
4.00	0.85	0.35	5.15	0.86
4.30	0.92	0.42	5.08	0.85
5.00	1.00	0.50	5.00	0.83
6.00	1.20	0.70	4.80	0.80
7.00	1.40	0.90	4.60	0.77
8.00	1.55	1.05	4.45	0.74
9.00	1.75	1.25	4.25	0.71
10.00	1.95	1.45	4.05	0.68
15.00	2.65	2.15	3.35	0.56
20.00	3.25	2.75	2.75	0.46

Fig. 8.12   Field permeability test.

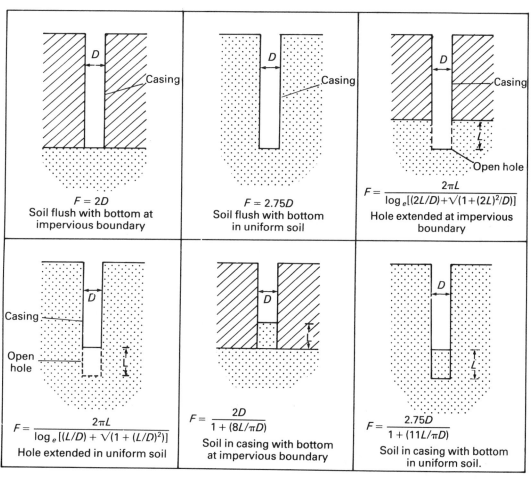

Constant head test $\quad k = \dfrac{q}{FH_c}$

Variable head test $\quad k = \dfrac{A}{F(t_2 - t_1)} \log_e \dfrac{H_1}{H_2}$

k = permeability
q = rate of flow
F = intake factor (see above)
H_c = constant head
H_1 = variable head at time t_1
H_2 = variable head at time t_2
A = cross sectional area of borehole, casing or standpipe

Fig. 8.13 Calculation of permeabilities.

205

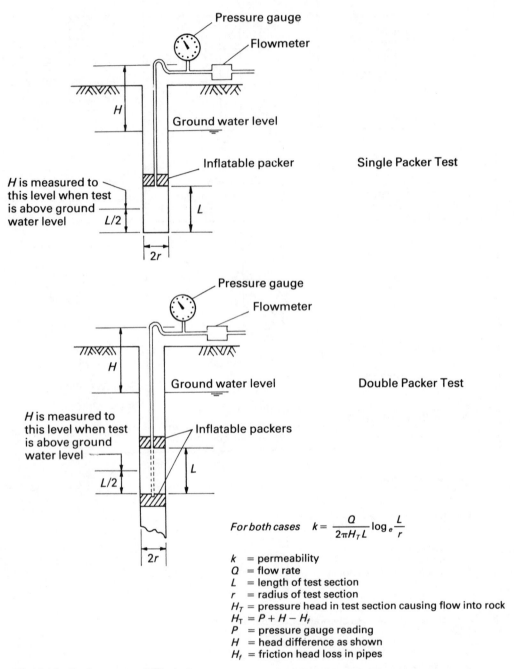

Fig. 8.14 Packer permeability tests.

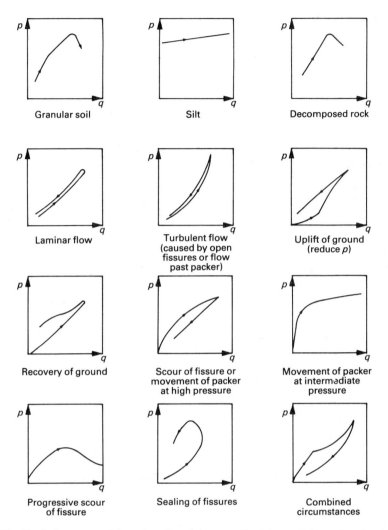

Fig. 8.15 Typical pressure (*p*) against flow (*q*) curves for interpretation of packer tests.

In addition the applied pressures must not be such as to cause uplift at the ground surface, as a guide the pressure in kN/m² is normally 12–17 times the depth in metres.

Further details on permeability testing are given in BS5930 (pages 34–40) and on pumping tests (pages 47–55). BS5930 also gives examples of typical report forms for use during field permeability testing.

8.7 Pore pressure probe

Pore pressure transducers are incorporated in the Camkometer described in Section 8.5 but there is an alternative means of sounding soil strata known as the pore pressure probe. In this test a stainless steel probe with a porous ceramic filter behind it is pushed into the ground at a constant rate of penetration and a fast response electrical transducer measures the pore pressure inside the filter section.

The penetration of the probe causes a local build up in pore water pressure. This pore pressure will dissipate rapidly in a sand but will decay only slowly in a clay (i.e. it is a function of soil permeability). Thus if the generated pore pressures are compared with the steady-state pore pressures (U_0) an indication of soil type can be obtained. The results of a typical pore pressure probe test are shown in Fig. 8.16 and as can be seen it is quite sensitive to only thin layers of sand, silt or clay. The plot shown in Fig. 8.16 is normally obtained directly on site using the electrical output from the transducer and a chart recorder.

The probe can be used to study the rate of dissipation of generated excess pore pressures and this can give an indication of soil permeability and coefficient of consolidation. It can also be used to study pore water pressures in different layers since in a complex series of strata there may be perched water tables and groundwater under artesian pressure. Finally it has been used to study the liquefaction potential of saturated sands by identifying sands which dilate during penetration (i.e. there is a pore pressure decrease) or those which collapse (i.e. there is a pore pressure increase).

8.8 *In situ* stress measurements in rock

It is important in rock mechanics problems to know the state of stress existing in the rock mass and some of the methods of determining this are described in Section 11.3 of the chapter on instrumentation. There are other methods that can be used during a site investigation and some of these will be described below. However, the much more important questions of rock type, quality and jointing must not be overlooked. The direction and frequency of joints in a rock mass usually play a major part in the solution of many engineering problems. The state of stress in soils can often be predicted from the thickness of overburden and the position of the water table. In the case of rocks it is not possible to do this because stresses can be locked into rocks by earth movements and they can be relieved or partly relieved by erosion and excavations.

It is difficult to measure stresses in rocks directly and most methods involve determining strains and interpreting stresses from a knowledge of the rock's modulus of elasticity. One simple method uses a strain gauge rosette bonded to the rock at the bottom of a borehole. Readings are taken on this rosette and it is then overcored, removed from the hole and a new set of readings taken. The change in strain is a

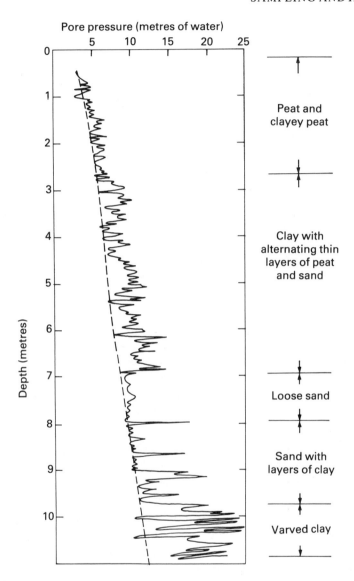

Fig. 8.16 Pore pressure probe results.

reflection of the change in stress and since there should be negligible stress on the rock once it is removed from the ground the change should correspond to the stress in the ground.

The above technique only gives stress on a horizontal plane and a more sophisticated technique must be used to establish all the principal stresses. The most widely used one

209

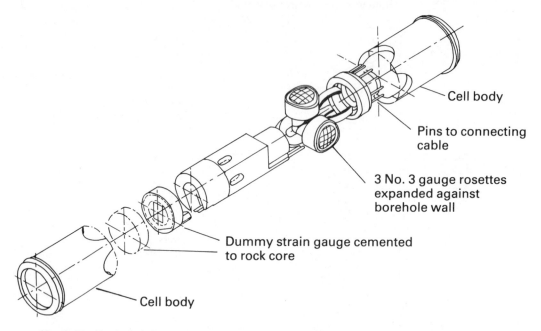

Cell body

Pins to connecting cable

3 No. 3 gauge rosettes expanded against borehole wall

Dummy strain gauge cemented to rock core

Cell body

Fig. 8.17 Exploded view of Leeman strain cell for measurement of *in situ* stress in rock.

is the Leeman cell shown in Fig. 8.17 which expands and glues three rosettes each comprising three strain gauges on to the sides of a small diameter borehole. The cell is removed leaving the strain gauges in position and the instrumented portion of rock is overcored and brought to the surface. All the principal stresses can then be calculated in much the same way as for the simpler technique.

Photoelastic discs can also be cemented onto rock surfaces as can vibrating-wire strain gauges (see Chapter 11). These are also overcored to obtain the *in situ* stress.

Another technique is to measure accurately the distance between two pins on a rock surface and then cut a slot in the rock between them. A flat hydraulic jack is then placed in the slot and pressurized until the initial distance between the points is restored. The pressure in the jack then equals the initial stress in the rock.

Hydrofracturing is occasionally used to make an assessment of rock tensile strength and *in situ* stress. Here a packer-type arrangement is used and the water pressure increased until there is a sudden drop. This indicates the point at which fracturing has been induced and fissures opened up.

The dilatometer or borehole jacks have already been described but on a larger scale jacks can be set up across a tunnel, or the inside of a tunnel can be loaded radially by a series of jacks and load/displacement graphs plotted.

9

The description and classification of soils and rocks

9.1 Introduction

This chapter describes why it is important to establish a comprehensive and universally understood method of sample description and classification and the relevance of this sample description to site-investigation problems. Reasons are given why it is important that the system adopted should be fully understood and used by everyone involved in site investigation from the driller to the engineer. Various description and classification systems exist but detailed consideration is given to the methods recommended for use in the UK. Methods of identifying the main soil types are followed by a recommended procedure for describing soils, with examples. Notes are also given on rock description.

Site investigation is concerned with determining the nature and engineering properties of the soils beneath a site and the information that is produced must be communicated to the readers of the site investigation report in an unambiguous manner. The investigation and the report are not cheap to produce and it is vital that they give the maximum amount of information possible. The former *UK Code of Practice for Site Investigations* stated: 'The purpose of classifying soils and rocks is to provide an accepted, concise and reasonably systematic method of designating the various types of material in order to enable useful conclusions to be drawn from a knowledge of the type of material'. The properties of different soils vary in many ways. The strength of a peat is obviously lower than that of a boulder clay. A building founded on sand will settle less than a similar building on soft clay. Gravel is far more permeable than silt which is in turn more permeable than clay. The suitability of a soil for founding a road on depends to a large extent on the soil type. Excavations in silt tend to collapse but in clay they may be far more stable. Sand and gravel is a much better material for construction of an embankment than a clay. Hence a good sample description tells much about the way in which a soil will behave. However, any description given to a soil must be the same as another driller or engineer would give to it, so that everyone involved with a site investigation understands one another. It can be very misleading to have different descriptions for the same material on the same site.

A standard method of sample description is absolutely vital because when such a method is adopted then experience of a soil's behaviour on one site can be extended to similar soils on another site. Research into a soil's properties always includes a full sample description so that the results of the work can be applied to other similar soils. The correlations of soil types between boreholes would be impossible without accurate descriptions.

When a driller is asked to produce a detailed description he is forced to watch closely the soil being taken out from the borehole in order that any changes are noted instantly. It is he who sees more of the subsoils than anyone else and his knowledge of the soil types can help him in making decisions on sampling and testing. The driller's description is also important since it enables him to communicate with the engineer and also serves as a useful check. The presence of only very thin bands of sand in a bed of clay can alter drastically the time taken for a building or an embankment to complete its settlement. A thin layer of soft clay in a rock slope could cause a major landslide. The cost of motorway construction and the method of construction is dependent on a correct classification of all the materials encountered during excavation. The precise nature and depths of the different soil strata dictates the choice of foundation type and depth. The strength and permeability of various soil and rock types affect the stability and water-retaining properties of dams. Obviously many other examples of the need for clear, concise sample description could be given. Examples could also be given where failures, sometimes at the cost of human life can be directly attributable to inadequate site investigation and poor sample description. Site investigation is carried out to enable a safe and economic design to be produced and it must not only be carried out with great care but the results of it must be communicated clearly to the design engineer.

The driller may be given some preliminary information on the site by the engineer from other surveys or from geological maps but on site he must expect literally anything and then accurately describe whatever he finds. He must ensure that the description he gives truly represents the *in situ* material. For instance, could material have fallen to the base of the hole from above due to inadequate casing? Has the soil been softened by the addition of water used to assist boring? Have fines been washed out of a granular deposit? Are there any fragments of brick or pottery which might indicate that a material is fill? Are there any peculiarities such as fossils, odours, cavities, roots etc? All these features can be spotted by the driller and should be communicated to the engineer.

9.2 Systems of soil description and classification

There are many different systems of soil classification some of which are intended for a specific purpose. For instance an investigation may be required for geological, agricultural or engineering purposes and the form of classification most suited to each type varies. Even in engineering terms a number of classification systems exist and their suitability depends on the type of engineering project being undertaken. Soils have been deen described since at least Roman times but methods have become progressively more sophisticated particularly in the last 30 years, as engineers became increasingly aware of the importance of the ground on which they were to build their structures. The most up to date method of sample description in the UK is described in the *Code of Practice for Site Investigations* (BS5930). This method will, therefore, be described in some detail in this chapter. The basis of the method was originally put forward by the Engineering Group of the Geological Society and is described in the *Quarterly Journal of Engineering Geology*, **5**, 4 (1972).

Classification of soils into specific categories is a sophistication of basic sample description and requires laboratory testing for full implementation. The present recommended system in the UK is the 'British Soil Classification System' (BSCS) which is also described in the code of practice and which uses a code letter system to signify soil type and basic soil properties. On site, however, laboratory test results will not be available and hence full classification cannot be made. Good, precise, orderly, sample description must, therefore, be the aim of all personnel involved in site investigation.

Other methods of sample description and classification do exist, such as the Casagrande system and the Unified Soil Classification. However, the methods described in this chapter are the ones which are recommended for use in the UK. A summary of the method of sample description is given in Table 9.1 and of the classification system in Table 9.2.

9.3 Composition of soils

Before the method of sample description is described it is important to understand what a soil is composed of and how to identify the main components. A soil, in the sense of the word as used by engineers, is a naturally occurring loose or soft deposit forming part of the earth's crust. Soils consist of rock particles, mineral grains and sometimes organic matter, together with variable amounts of water and air and may be cemented or uncemented. The rock particles and mineral grains are split into groups depending on size. Usually the particle sizes are mixed up and the way these particles may be assembled together to form certain types is illustrated in Fig. 9.1. The main size groups are shown in Table 9.3. The groups can be identified in the field by a number of methods and these are summarized in the left hand side of Table 9.1. As stated earlier the groups are often mixed up and terms such as sandy clay or gravelly sand have to be used.

Table 9.1 Field identification and description of soils (From BS5930).

Soil group	Basic soil type	Particle size, mm	Visual identification	Particle nature and plasticity	Composite soil types (mixtures of basic soil types)	Compactness/strength — Term	Compactness/strength — Field test
Very coarse soils	BOULDERS	200	Only seen complete in pits or exposures.				
	COBBLES	60	Often difficult to recover from boreholes.				
Coarse soils (over 65% sand and gravel sizes)	GRAVELS	coarse 20, medium 6, fine 2	Easily visible to naked eye; particle shape can be described; grading can be described. Well graded: wide range of grain sizes, well distributed. Poorly graded: not well graded. (May be uniform: size of most particles lies between narrow limits; or gap graded: an intermediate size of particle is markedly under-represented.)	Particle shape: Angular, Subangular, Subrounded, Rounded, Flat, Elongate	**Scale of secondary constituents with coarse soils** — Term / % of clay or silt: slightly clayey / slightly silty GRAVEL or SAND (under 5); clayey / silty GRAVEL or SAND (5 to 15); very clayey / very silty GRAVEL or SAND (15 to 35). Term / % of sand or gravel: Sandy GRAVEL / Gravelly SAND (35 to 65) — Sand or gravel an important second constituent of the coarse fraction. (See 41.3.2.2) For composite types described as: clayey — fines are plastic, cohesive; silty — fines non-plastic or of low plasticity.	Loose / Dense	By inspection of voids and particle packing.
	SANDS	coarse 0.6, medium 0.2, fine 0.06	Visible to naked eye; very little or no cohesion when dry; grading can be described. Well graded: wide range of grain sizes, well distributed. Poorly graded: not well graded. (May be uniform: size of most particles lies between narrow limits; or gap graded: an intermediate size of particle is markedly under-represented.)	Texture: Rough, Smooth, Polished		Loose	Can be excavated with a spade; 50 mm wooden peg can be easily driven.
						Dense	Requires pick for excavation; 50 mm wooden peg hard to drive.
						Slightly cemented	Visual examination; pick removes soil in lumps which can be abraded.
Fine soils (over 35% silt and clay sizes)	SILTS	coarse 0.06, medium 0.02, fine 0.006, 0.002	Only coarse silt barely visible to naked eye; exhibits little plasticity and marked dilatancy; slightly granular or silky to the touch. Disintegrates in water; lumps dry quickly; possess cohesion but can be powdered easily between fingers.	Non-plastic or low plasticity	**Scale of secondary constituents with fine soils** — Term / % of sand or gravel: sandy / gravelly CLAY or SILT (35 to 65); CLAY:SILT (under 35). Examples of composite types (indicating preferred order for description): Loose, brown, subangular very sandy, fine to coarse GRAVEL with small pockets of soft grey clay; Medium dense, light brown, clayey, fine and medium SAND; Stiff, orange brown, fissured sandy CLAY; Firm, brown, thinly laminated SILT and CLAY; Plastic, brown, amorphous PEAT.	Soft or loose	Easily moulded or crushed in the fingers.
						Firm or dense	Can be moulded or crushed by strong pressure in the fingers.
	CLAYS		Dry lumps can be broken but not powdered between the fingers; they also disintegrate under water but more slowly than silt; smooth to the touch; exhibits plasticity but no dilatancy; sticks to the fingers and dries slowly; shrinks appreciably on drying usually showing cracks. Intermediate and high plasticity clays show these properties to a moderate and high degree, respectively.	Intermediate plasticity (Lean clay) / High plasticity (Fat clay)		Very soft	Exudes between fingers when squeezed in hand.
						Soft	Moulded by light finger pressure.
						Firm	Can be moulded by strong finger pressure.
						Stiff	Cannot be moulded by fingers. Can be indented by thumb.
						Very stiff	Can be indented by thumb nail.
Organic soils	ORGANIC CLAY, SILT or SAND	Varies	Contains substantial amounts of organic vegetable matter.			Firm	Fibres already compressed together.
	PEATS	Varies	Predominantly plant remains usually dark brown or black in colour, often with distinctive smell; low bulk density.			Spongy	Very compressible and open structure.
						Plastic	Can be moulded in hand, and smears fingers.

Structure

Term	Field identification
Homogeneous	Deposit consists essentially of one type.
Inter-stratified	Alternating layers of varying types or with bands or lenses of other materials. Interval scale for bedding spacing may be used.
Heterogeneous	A mixture of types.
Weathered	Particles may be weakened and may show concentric layering.
Fissured	Break into polyhedral fragments along fissures. Interval scale for spacing of discontinuities may be used.
Intact	No fissures.
Homogeneous	Deposit consists essentially of one type.
Inter-stratified	Alternating layers of varying types. Interval scale for thickness of layers may be used.
Weathered	Usually has crumb or columnar structure.
Fibrous	Plant remains recognizable and retain some strength.
Amorphous	Recognizable plant remains absent.

Interval scales

Scale of bedding spacing:

Term	Mean spacing, mm
Very thickly bedded	over 2000
Thickly bedded	2000 to 600
Medium bedded	600 to 200
Thinly bedded	200 to 60
Very thinly bedded	60 to 20
Thickly laminated	20 to 6
Thinly laminated	under 6

Scale of spacing of other discontinuities:

Term	Mean spacing, mm
Very widely spaced	over 2000
Widely spaced	2000 to 600
Medium spaced	600 to 200
Closely spaced	200 to 60
Very closely spaced	60 to 20
Extremely closely spaced	under 20

Colour

Red, Pink, Yellow, Brown, Olive, Green, Blue, White, Grey, Black, etc.

Supplemented as necessary with: Light, Dark, Mottled etc. and Pinkish, Reddish, Yellowish, Brownish etc.

Table 9.2 British soil classification system for engineeering purposes (from BS5930).

Soil groups (see note 1)			Subgroups and laboratory identification				
GRAVEL and SAND may be qualified Sandy GRAVEL and Gravelly SAND, etc. where appropriate (See 41.3.2.2)			Group symbol (see notes 2 & 3)	Subgroup symbol (see note 2)	Fines (% less than 0.06 mm)	Liquid limit %	Name
COARSE SOILS less than 35 % of the material is finer than 0.06 mm	GRAVELS More than 50 % of coarse material is of gravel size (coarser than 2 mm)	Slightly silty or clayey GRAVEL	G — GW, GP	GW	0 to 5		Well graded GRAVEL
				GPu GPg			Poorly graded/Uniform/Gap graded GRAVEL
		Silty GRAVEL	G-F — G-M	GWM GPM	5 to 15		Well graded/Poorly graded silty GRAVEL
		Clayey GRAVEL	G-C	GWC GPC			Well graded/Poorly graded clayey GRAVEL
		Very silty GRAVEL	GF — GM	GML, etc	15 to 35		Very silty GRAVEL; subdivide as for GC
		Very clayey GRAVEL	GC	GCL GCI GCH GCV GCE			Very clayey GRAVEL (clay of low, intermediate, high, very high, extremely high plasticity)
	SANDS More than 50 % of coarse material is of sand size (finer than 2 mm)	Slightly silty or clayey SAND	S — SW, SP	SW	0 to 5		Well graded SAND
				SPu SPg			Poorly graded/Uniform/Gap graded SAND
		Silty SAND	S-F — S-M	SWM SPM	5 to 15		Well graded/Poorly graded silty SAND
		Clayey SAND	S-C	SWC SPC			Well graded/Poorly graded clayey SAND
		Very silty SAND	SF — SM	SML, etc	15 to 35		Very silty SAND; subdivided as for SC
		Very clayey SAND	SC	SCL SCI SCH SCV SCE			Very clayey SAND (clay of low, intermediate, high, very high, extremely high plasticity)
FINE SOILS more than 35 % of the material is finer than 0.06 mm	SILTS and CLAYS 35 % to 65 % fines	Gravelly or sandy SILTS and CLAYS	Gravelly SILT	FG — MG	MLG, etc			Gravelly SILT; subdivide as for CG
		Gravelly CLAY (see note 4)	CG	CLG CIG CHG CVG CEG		< 35, 35 to 50, 50 to 70, 70 to 90, > 90	Gravelly CLAY of low plasticity, of intermediate plasticity, of high plasticity, of very high plasticity, of extremely high plasticity
	SILTS and CLAYS 65 % to 100 % fines	Sandy SILT (see note 4)	FS — MS	MLS, etc			Sandy SILT; subdivide as for CG
		Sandy CLAY	CS	CLS, etc			Sandy CLAY; subdivide as for CG
		SILT (M-SOIL)	F — M	ML, etc			SILT; subdivide as for C
		CLAY (see notes 5 & 6)	C	CL CI CH CV CE		< 35, 35 to 50, 50 to 70, 70 to 90, > 90	CLAY of low plasticity, of intermediate plasticity, of high plasticity, of very high plasticity, of extremely high plasticity
ORGANIC SOILS		Descriptive letter 'O' suffixed to any group or sub-group symbol.			Organic matter suspected to be a significant constituent. Example MHO: Organic SILT of high plasticity.		
PEAT		Pt		Peat soils consist predominantly of plant remains which may be fibrous or amorphous.			

NOTE 1. The name of the soil group should always be given when describing soils, supplemented, if required, by the group symbol, although for some additional applications (e.g. longitudinal sections) it may be convenient to use the group symbol alone.

NOTE 2. The group symbol or sub-group symbol should be placed in brackets if laboratory methods have not been used for identification, e.g. (GC).

NOTE 3. The designation FINE SOIL or FINES, F, may be used in place of SILT, M, or CLAY, C, when it is not possible or not required to distinguish between them.

NOTE 4. GRAVELLY if more than 50 % of coarse material is of gravel size. SANDY if more than 50 % of coarse material is of sand size.

NOTE 5. SILT (M-SOIL), M, is material plotting below the A-line, and has a restricted plastic range in relation to its liquid limit, and relatively low cohesion. Fine soils of this type include clean silt-sized materials and rock flour, micaceous and diatomaceous soils, pumice, and volcanic soils, and soils containing halloysite. The alternative term 'M-soil' avoids confusion with materials of predominantly silt size, which form only a part of the group.

Organic soils also usually plot below the A-line on the plasticity chart, when they are designated ORGANIC SILT, MO.

NOTE 6. CLAY, C, is material plotting above the A-line, and is fully plastic in relation to its liquid limit.

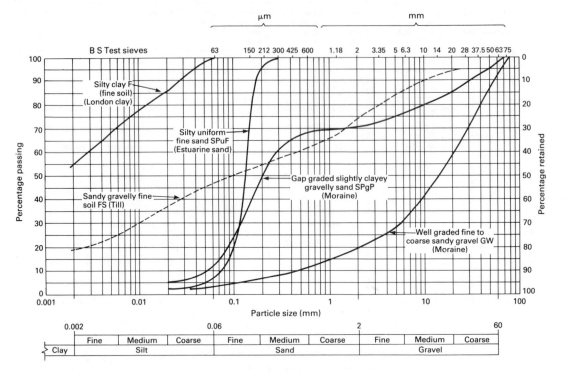

Fig. 9.1 Grading chart for soils with grading curves of selected soil types together with their classification symbols (after BS5930:1981).

Gravel, cobbles and boulders are all particles greater than 2 mm in diameter which is about the size of a large pin head. The relative proportions of the different sizes should be given in the sample description. The matrix should also be described, as should the shape and texture of the particles. The shape should be described as rounded, subangular or angular.

Sand consists of particles which cannot be broken in the hand and which are visible to the naked eye. Sand is described as well graded if there are particles of every size or uniform if all the particles are nearly the same size. Soft sand has rounded grains and sharp sand angular ones. Dry sand is not cohesive and cannot be moulded into lumps.

Silts consist of particles which are very difficult or impossible to distinguish with the naked eye but they have a slightly gritty feel, particularly on the teeth, and when dry can be dusted off the fingers. When wet silty material is patted or shaken, water appears on the surface; when squeezed the water disappears.

Clays consist of particles invisible to the naked eye. When moist they have a smooth, sticky, greasy feel and exhibit plastic properties. Dry lumps are very hard and clays crack and shrink during drying. Dry clay cannot easily be brushed off the fingers.

216

Table 9.3

Description	Particle size
Boulders	Over 200 mm
Cobbles	60 – 200 mm
Coarse gravel	20 – 60 mm
Medium gravel	6 – 20 mm
Fine gravel	2 – 6 mm
Coarse sand	0.6 – 2 mm
Medium sand	0.2 – 0.6 mm
Fine sand	0.06 – 0.2 mm
Silt	0.002 – 0.06 mm
Clay	Less than 0.002 mm
Organic material	Variable particle size
Peat	

Peat is a fibrous material composed of decayed or decaying vegetable matter. Organic clays are dark in colour and again contain decaying matter. They generally give off a characteristic odour.

When soils consist of a mixture of the above soil types it is important to decide which material its behaviour is most characteristic of. Does it behave more like a clay than a silt? If so, it should be called a CLAY or silty CLAY. If there is more silt than sand then it should be called a sandy SILT. If there is more sand than gravel it should be called a gravelly SAND and so on.

9.4 Soil sample description

It requires some experience to give an orderly and precise sample description but it can be made easier by systematically working through a set procedure. Such a procedure is described below. First of all the field strength is defined and this is followed by a description of structure and degree of weathering. The soil's colour and its particle shape and composition is then given. In the description of composition any minor constituents are described. The soil's name, which describes either the major constituent of the soil mass or its behavioural type is then given in capital letters and this is followed by the name of the geological formation from which the soil originates and

Table 9.4

Soil types	Strength		
	Term	Field test	SPT N value or shear strength
Boulders and cobbles	Loose/dense	By inspection of voids and particle packing	Variable
Sands and gravels (Coarse grained soils)	Indurated *	Broken only with sharp pick blow even when soaked. Makes hammer ring	
	Strongly cemented *	Cannot be abraded with thumb or broken with hands	
	Slightly cemented Very dense Dense	Pick removes soil in lumps, which can be abraded with thumb and broken with hands	Very dense if N over 50. Dense if $N = 30–50$
	Compact	Requires pick for excavation; 50 mm peg hard to drive more than 50–100 mm	$N = 10–30$
	Loose	Can be excavated with spade; 50 mm wooden peg easily driven	$N < 10$ (Very loose if < 4)
Silts (Fine grained soils)	Firm or dense	Can be moulded or crushed by strong pressure in the fingers	$N > 10$
	Soft or loose	Easily moulded or crushed in the fingers	$N < 10$
Clays, Silty Clays Sandy clays (Fine grained soils)	Very stiff or hard	Can be indented with thumb nail. Brittle or very tough	N over 20 Shear strength over 150 kN/m^2
	Stiff	Cannot be moulded with fingers but can be indented with thumb	$N = 10–20$ Shear strength 75–150 kN/m^2
	Firm	Moulded only by strong pressure of fingers	$N = 4–10$ Shear strength 40–75 kN/m^2
	Soft	Easily moulded with fingers	$N = 2–4$ Shear strength 20–40 kN/m^2

Soil types	Strength		
	Term	Field test	SPT N value or shear strength
	Very soft	Exudes between fingers when squeezed	$N < 2$ Shear strength $<20\,\text{kN/m}^2$
	Friable	Non-plastic, crumbles in fingers	Variable shear strength
Peat	Firm	Fibres compressed together	
	Spongy	Very compressible and open structure	Variable shear strength but usually very low
	Plastic	Can be moulded in hands and smeared between fingers	

Note   * These are essentially rocks

its classification symbols if these are known. Any minor observations on the soil can then be added to complete the description. It is important to follow the set sequence and the notes below can be used as a check list to arrive at the full engineering description, examples of which are given at the end of this section. It should be realized that undisturbed samples are required if descriptions of structure and degree of weathering are to be given. Undisturbed samples may also be essential if field strengths are to be estimated.

9.4.1   Strength
Depending on the general soil type. A term should be chosen from Table 9.4.

9.4.2   Structure
If possible a term should be chosen from Table 9.5.

9.4.3   State of weathering
This is often difficult to identify but an attempt can be made using the descriptions and scale recommended for rocks in Section 9.7.

9.4.4   Colour
Standard colour descriptions (see Table 9.6) should be used and 'Munsell Soil Colour Charts' can be used for comparison purposes. For most soils a colour should be chosen

Table 9.5

Soil types	Structure	
	Term	Field identification
Sands and gravels (Coarse soils)	Weathered	Particles are weakened and may show concentric layering
	Homogeneous	Material essentially of one type
	Inter-stratified	Alternating layers of various types (use scale of bedding in Table 9.1)
	Heterogeneous	A mixture of types
Clays, silty clays, and sandy clays (Fine soils)	Weathered	Usually exhibits crumb or columnar structure
	Fissured	Breaks into polyhedral fragments
	Intact	Not fissured
	Homogeneous	Material essentially of one type
	Inter-stratified	Alternating layers of varying types (use scale of bedding in Table 9.1)
Peat	Fibrous, fine and coarse	Plant-remains easily recognizable, retains structure and some of original strength; fine, diameter less than 1 mm; coarse, diameter greater than 1 mm
	Amorphous-granular	Recognizable plant-remains absent

Other terms may be used:
Partings of silt in clay; sand with *interbedded* clay; *cross bedded* sand; Sand *intermixed* with clay; *lenses* of sand; *disturbed bedding* of silt.
Examples of discontinuities in the soil structure are given below and these should be described whenever possible using the spacing scales given in Table 9.1: *bedding planes; joints; fissures; faults; shear planes.*

from column 3 and possibly adjectives from columns 1 and 2. Certain soils may be mottled or spotted with different colours.

9.4.5 Particle shape and composition

This term includes the particles angularity, form and surface texture (see Table 9.7). In the field, only the coarser particles can be described. If the composition of the particles is known it should be stated, for example, sandstone, limestone, flint, quartz, gypsum, shell, mica etc.

9.4.6 Soil name

The soil name should always be given in capital letters and is based on the particle sizes present and thus reflects the engineering characteristics. If a soil contains 35% or more

Table 9.6

1	2	3
Light	pinkish	pink
Dark	reddish	red
	yellowish	yellow
	brownish	brown
	olive	olive
	bluish	green
		white
	greyish	grey
		black

Table 9.7

Angularity	angular
	subangular
	subrounded
	rounded
Form	equidimensional
	flat
	elongated
	flat and elongated
	irregular
Surface texture	rough
	smooth

of fine material it is described as a silt or clay since it will tend to behave like one. If there is less than 35% fine material it is described as a sand or gravel. Problems arise when more than one soil type is present and examples are given below. The basic soil types can be also used as adjectives, for example, *silty CLAY, sandy CLAY, silty clayey SAND.* In a full description the plasticity of the material is indicated but this requires laboratory testing. Where coarse material is involved an attempt should be made to assess the relative proportions as indicated in Table 9.8.

9.4.7 Geological formation

A guide to the name of a geological formation is given on the maps of the Institute of Geological Sciences, and it should be written with capital initial letters, e.g. London Clay, Bagshot Beds, Lower Lias. The geological formation should be named only

221

Table 9.8

Term	Description (percentages are of the whole material less boulders and cobbles, and are approximate estimates in a field description)
Slightly sandy GRAVEL	Up to 5% sand
Sandy GRAVEL	5–20% sand
Very sandy GRAVEL	Over 20% sand
GRAVEL/SAND	About equal proportions of gravel and sand
Very gravelly SAND	Over 20% gravel
Gravelly SAND	20–5% gravel
Slightly gravelly SAND	Up to 5% gravel

The gravel and sand size ranges can each be subdivided into coarse, medium and fine divisions. The grading of gravels and sands may be qualified as well graded or poorly graded.

Very coarse deposits where over half the material is over 60 mm in size can usually only be described in excavations or exposures. They are classified as follows

BOULDERS or BOULDER GRAVEL — over half of the very coarse material is of boulder size (over 200 mm)

COBBLES or COBBLE GRAVEL — over half of the very coarse material is of cobble size (200 mm – 60 mm)

BOULDERS may be qualified as *cobbly* and COBBLES as *bouldery*.

Mixtures of very coarse and finer materials may be described by combining the terms for the very coarse constituent and the finer constituents as follows

Term	Description (percentages are estimates in a field description)
BOULDERS (or COBBLES) with a little finer material	up to 5% finer material[*]
BOULDERS (or COBBLES) with some finer material	5–20% finer material[*]
BOULDERS (or COBBLES) with much finer material	20–50% finer material[*]
FINER MATERIAL[*] with many BOULDERS (or COBBLES)	50–20% boulders (or cobbles)
FINER MATERIAL[*] with some BOULDERS (or COBBLES)	5–20% boulders (or cobbles)
FINER MATERIAL[*] with occasional BOULDERS (or COBBLES)	up to 5% boulders (or cobbles)

Note [*] The name of the finer material should also be included, e.g. Sandy GRAVEL with occasional boulders. Cobbly BOULDERS with some finer material (sand with some fines).

222

where this can be done with confidence since it may not be easy to tell to which formation a sample belongs, or to locate formation boundaries in a borehole or exposure. Conjecture should be avoided. The origin and nature of made ground should be described. Particular note should also be made of the presence of large objects including concrete or masonry, of cavities or collapsible hollow objects, chemical or domestic wastes, organic matter and dangerous or poisonous substances. The degree of decomposition of organic matter should be noted.

9.4.8 Classification

The group symbol for the full classification of the soil, if known, should be added at the end of the description but as this requires laboratory testing it is not included in a field description. The use of a classification symbol is discretionary but it can be extremely useful particularly in projects involving major earthworks.

Some typical descriptions are given below but it is worth remembering that any additional notes on particular observations can always be added at the end since it is invariably better to have too much information than too little.

(1) Compact, reddish brown, sub-angular, well graded sandy GRAVEL with a little finer material. Recent Alluvium.
(2) Stiff, dark grey and brown mottled, fissured, silty CLAY with occasional fragments of mudstone. Residual soil of Middle Coal Measures.
(3) Soft, light brown, inter stratified clayey SILT with some amorphous peat. Recent Alluvium.
(4) Dense, yellow, fine SAND with thin lenses of soft grey silty CLAY. Glacial drift.

9.5 Sample description in the laboratory

Obviously under the right conditions a far better sample description can be given in the laboratory than on site. All samples should be described in detail in the laboratory as soon as possible after sampling. Ideally an area should be set aside and provided with a few simple pieces of equipment. A good source of light is essential, as is a solid bench, a knife, hammer, sampling trays, an extruder, a magnifying lens and one or two sieves. Sets of standard samples and a colour chart for comparison purposes are helpful and can improve standardization. For more accurate strength descriptions pocket penetrometers or hand vane testers can be used. A low-power stereo microscope with a magnification of ×30 is another item which can often be useful and can be used to examine silt particles. Some of these pieces of equipment are shown in Fig. 9.2. In the research field scanning electron microscopes can be used for the very detailed examination of soils. With such instruments individual clay particles and soil structure can be resolved.

223

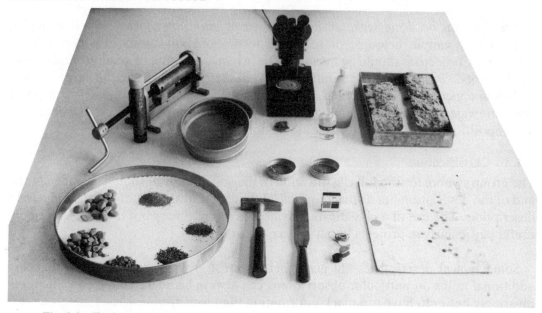

Fig. 9.2 Equipment for the laboratory description of soils.

Some samples reveal their character better if they are either wetted or dried and the description of coarse materials is easier if selected sub-samples are washed so that the nature of the individual particles can be more clearly seen. Large pieces can of course be broken open if necessary. Quick wet sieving can also assist in assessing sand and gravel percentages.

A rapid assessment of moisture content in relation to plastic limit can be made by rolling out threads of cohesive material. If these can be rolled out to less than 3 mm in diameter without crumbling the moisture content is above the plastic limit.

Where made ground is suspected the whole sample should be spread out and carefully scrutinized for any tell-tale clues such as pieces of brick or pottery. Colour changes and odour should not be overlooked.

To determine soil structure requires the careful examination of undisturbed samples. The most common type is the U100 and this should be extruded and a 25 mm deep knife cut made longitudinally down the sample. It should then be possible to split the sample open to reveal its precise lithology and structure. Lenses, laminations, fissures and any colour changes may then be described. A short period of drying out can help reveal the structure of laminated soils. It is often helpful if the final report contains photographs, preferably in colour, of these split samples in a form as shown in Fig. 9.3. After description samples should be carefully re-waxed to preserve their natural moisture content. Some organizations use sample description sheets to assist in the orderly description of soils and an example is shown in Fig. 9.4. Once a sample description has

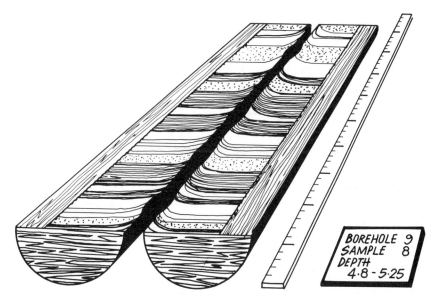

BOREHOLE 9
SAMPLE 8
DEPTH 4·8 - 5·25

Fig. 9.3 Split U100 sample of laminated clay.

been made it is convenient immediately to take a small subsample for moisture content testing if this has not already been done.

9.6 Soil classification

The British Soil Classification System (BSCS) uses laboratory-determined grading and plasticity in order to place a soil in a particular group or sub-group where it is given identifying letters (Table 9.9). In many ways it gives less information on the soil than a full description but it does give a more accurate indication of a soil's engineering behaviour under a variety of conditions.

9.7 Rock sample description

The first stage of a rock description should be to determine the basic name. This need not be the full geological name, which may be very complex, but should be a generic name indicating the basic rock type, its origin and its grain size. Table 9.10, taken from the Code of Practice, gives some guidance on the identification of rocks. The table gives rock names which are generally adequate for engineering purposes although for more sophisticated investigations it will be necessary for the rock cores to be examined and described by a geologist.

In using Table 9.10 it must first be decided whether the rock is sedimentary,

225

	SCHEME									BOREHOLE			
	LOGGED BY									DATE			

		SAMPLE NUMBER											
		DEPTH TO TOP OF SAMPLE m.											
STRENGTH	VERY DENSE	HARD											
	DENSE	STIFF											
	MEDIUM DENSE	FIRM											
	LOOSE	SOFT											
	VERY LOOSE	VERY SOFT											
	SLIGHTLY CEMENTED												
COLOUR	HUE												
	VALUE												
	CHROMA												
STRUCTURE	HOMOGENEOUS												
	HETEROGENEOUS												
	LAMINATED												
	INTER STRATIFIED												
	FISSURED												
	INTACT												
	WEATHERED (FSMHCR) SOIL												
PARTICLE SHAPE AND TEXTURE	ANGULAR	SUB ANGULAR											
	SUB ROUNDED	ROUNDED											
	FLAT	ELONGATED											
	ROUGH	SMOOTH											
	EQUIDMENSIONAL												
	IRREGULAR												
GRADING	WELL	GAP											
	UNIFORM	POORLY											
	CLEAN												
SUBSIDIARY FEATURES	SLIGHTLY	VERY											
	CLAYEY	SILTY											
	SANDY	GRAVELLY											
	COBBLY	BOULDERY											
SOIL NAME	CLAY	SILT											
	SAND	GRAVEL											
	COBBLES	BOULDERS											
MINOR CONSTITUENTS	WITH A LITTLE	< 5%											
	WITH SOME	5 - 20%											
	WITH MUCH	20 - 50%											
	WITH MANY	20 - 50%											
	WITH OCCASIONAL	< 5%											
PLASTICITY	NON PLASTIC	LOW											
	INTERMEDIATE	HIGH											
	VERY HIGH	EXTREMELY HIGH											
PEATS	FIRM												
	SPONGY												
	PLASTIC												
	FIBROUS												
	AMORPHOUS												
	CLASSIFICATION												
	WEATHERED ROCK (FSMHCR)												
	GEOLOGICAL FORMATION												
REMARKS													

Fig. 9.4 Sample description sheet.

226

Table 9.9

Coarse components	Main terms:	Gravel	G
		Sand	S
	Qualifying terms:	Well graded	W
		Poorly graded	P
		Uniform	Pu
		Gap graded	Pg
Fine components	Main terms:	Fine soil, fines – may be differentiated into M or C	F
		Silt	M
		Clay	C
	Qualifying terms:	Of low plasticity	L
		Of intermediate plasticity	I
		Of high plasticity	H
		Of very high plasticity	V
		Of extremely high plasticity	E
		Of upper plasticity range – incorporating groups I, H, V and E	U
Organic components	Main terms:	Peat	Pt
	Qualifying terms:	Organic – may be suffixed to any group	O

metamorphic or igneous (see Chapter 2). Bedded rocks are mostly sedimentary, strongly foliated rocks are mostly metamorphic and rocks with a massive structure and visible crystals are mostly igneous. Igneous rocks do not contain fossils.

If the rock is sedimentary a decision must be made as to whether it is siliceous, calcareous or carbonaceous. Siliceous rocks are formed of hard grains, mostly of quartz and will scratch glass. Calcareous rocks have grains which are softer and which are composed of the remains of shells and marine organisms and unless they contain sand they will not normally scratch glass. They also react with an acid and some limestones can be crystalline. Carbonaceous rocks are rocks such as coal or lignite. Having decided on the main sub-group, the given grain size can be estimated with the aid of a lens and the appropriate name read off from the table.

Metamorphic rocks can be difficult to identify but they are generally strong and foliated, that is they show a layered or banded arrangement of the minerals. They are also crystalline and generally contain a large proportion of quartz. Once again the name given is at least partly dependent on the grain size. Marble is a metamorphic limestone.

Igneous rocks are composed of closely interlocking mineral grains and crystals and are strong when unweathered. With igneous rocks it is usually the grain size and colour

Grain size, mm (left scale) / **Grain size (mm)** (right scale)

Bedded rocks (mostly sedimentary)

Grain size description			At least 50% of grains are of carbonate	At least 50% of grains are of fine-grained volcanic rock		
RUDACEOUS	Coarse	**CONGLOMERATE** Rounded boulders, cobbles and gravel cemented in a finer matrix. Breccia Irregular rock fragments in a finer matrix	Calcirudite*	Fragments of volcanic ejecta in a finer matrix **AGGLOMERATE** Rounded grains **VOLCANIC BRECCIA** Angular grains		SALINE ROCKS
ARENACEOUS	Medium	**SANDSTONE** Angular or rounded grains, commonly cemented by clay, calcitic or iron minerals. Quartzite Quartz grains and siliceous cement. Arkose Many feldspar grains. Greywacke Many rock chips	Calcarenite	Cemented volcanic ash **TUFF**		Halite Anhydrite
	Fine			Very fine-grained **TUFF**	Calcisiltite / Calcilutite	Gypsum
ARGILLACEOUS		**MUDSTONE** · **SILTSTONE** Mostly silt · **CLAYSTONE** Mostly clay · **SHALE** Fissile · Calcareous mudstone	LIMESTONE and DOLOMITE (undifferentiated)	Fine-grained **TUFF**	CHALK	
	Less than 0.002					COAL / LIGNITE
	Amorphous or crypto-crystalline	Granular cemented—except amorphous rocks	Flint: occurs as bands of nodules in the Chalk. Chert: occurs as nodules and beds in limestone and calcareous sandstone			

SEDIMENTARY ROCKS
Granular cemented rocks vary greatly in strength, some sandstones are stronger than many igneous rocks. Bedding may not show in hand specimens and is best seen in outcrop. Only sedimentary rocks, and some metamorphic rocks derived from them, contain fossils.
Calcareous rocks contain calcite (calcium carbonate) which effervesces with dilute hydrochloric acid.

Classification row: SILICEOUS | CALCAREOUS | SILICEOUS | CARBON-ACEOUS

Obviously foliated rocks (mostly metamorphic)

Grain size description		
COARSE	**GNEISS** Well developed but often widely spaced foliation sometimes with schistose bands. Migmatite Irregularly foliated; mixed schists and gneisses	**MARBLE** · **QUARTZITE** · Granulite · **HORNFELS** · Amphibolite · Serpentine
MEDIUM	**SCHIST** Well developed undulose foliation; generally much mica	
FINE	**PHYLLITE** Slightly undulose foliation; sometimes 'spotted'. **SLATE** Well developed plane cleavage (foliation)	
	Mylonite Found in fault zones, mainly in igneous and metamorphic areas	

CRYSTALLINE — SILICEOUS | mainly SILICEOUS

METAMORPHIC ROCKS
Most metamorphic rocks are distinguished by foliation which may impart fissility. Foliation in gneisses is best observed in outcrop. Non-foliated metamorphics are difficult to recognize except by association. Any rock baked by contact metamorphism is described as a 'hornfels' and is generally somewhat stronger than the parent rock.
Most fresh metamorphic rocks are strong although perhaps fissile.

Rocks with massive structure and crystalline texture (mostly igneous)

Grain size description				
COARSE	**GRANITE**[1]	Diorite[1,2]	**GABBRO**[3]	Pyroxenite / Peridotite
	Pegmatite — These rocks are sometimes porphyritic and are then described, for example, as porphyritic granite			
MEDIUM	Microgranite[1,2]	Microdiorite[1,2]	Dolerite[3,4]	
	These rocks are sometimes porphyritic and are then described as porphyries			
FINE	**RHYOLITE**[4,5]	**ANDESITE**[4,5]	**BASALT**[4,5]	
	These rocks are sometimes porphyritic and are then described as porphyries			
glass	Obsidian[5]	Volcanic glass		

colour: Pale ←——→ Dark

ACID Much quartz	INTERMEDIATE Some quartz	BASIC Little or no quartz	ULTRA BASIC

IGNEOUS ROCKS
Composed of closely interlocking mineral grains. Strong when fresh; not porous.
Mode of occurrence: 1. Batholiths; 2. Laccoliths; 3. Sills; 4. Dykes; 5. Lava flows; 6. Veins.

Grain size scale (mm): More than 20 — 20 — 6 — 2 — 0.6 — 0.2 — 0.06 — 0.002 — Less than 0.002 — Amorphous or crypto-crystalline

---

*A more detailed classification is given in Clark, A.R. and Walker, B.F. *Geotechnique*, 1977, 27(1), 93–99.

NOTE 1. Principal rock types (generally common) are shown in bold type in capitals, e.g. **GRANITE**. Less common rock types are shown in medium type, e.g. Greywacke.

NOTE 2. Granular rocks may be distinguished from crystalline rocks by scratching with a knife which should remove whole grains from cement matrix in the granular rocks.
The separate grains may also sometimes be distinguished using a hand lens.
Siliceous rocks are generally harder and more resistant to scratching than calcareous rocks.

NOTE 3. In the table the boundaries of the heavy lined box describe the conditions to which the rock name applies.

that determine the name; for example a light-coloured, fine-grained igneous rock is termed a rhyolite and a dark-coloured, coarse-grained rock a gabbro. In Table 9.10 the terms amorphous and cryptocrystalline refer to rocks without any or hardly any crystalline structure.

Having established the rock name the full description should be built up in much the same way as that described for soils and the sequence is described below.

9.7.1 Colour

This should be described according to the principles laid down for soils in Section 9.4.

9.7.2 Grain size

This can be estimated visually with or without the use of a lens and comparison with standard samples can help. The limit of unaided vision is 0.06 mm. Table 9.10 shows the size groups.

9.7.3 Texture and fabric

Texture refers to the physical appearance or character of the rock and its constituent crystals or grains and terms such as porphyritic, crystalline, cryptocrystalline, granular, amorphous or glassy can be used. These terms are explained in Table 9.10. Fabric refers to the arrangement and orientation of the constituent crystals or grains and to any cementing material between the grains.

9.7.4 Weathered state

The degree of weathering is more important in rock than in soils and obviously the ultimate weathering of a rock mass is in fact a soil. Weathering of rock can take two forms, either mechanical disintegration or chemical decomposition, and the two forms usually exist together. Mechanical weathering includes fracturing and cleavage whilst chemical weathering leads to the eventual conversion of silicate minerals to clay minerals. Table 9.11 gives a descriptive scheme comprising six grades of weathering. It must be realized that the degree of weathering shown in rock exposures may not be typical of the rock mass as a whole since it will have been exposed to the elements. A suggested classification of weak rocks based on N values is shown in Table 9.12.

Table 9.10 *(Opposite)* Aid to identification of rocks for engineering purposes (from BS5930). This table follows general geological practice, but is intended as a guide only; geological training is required for the satisfactory identification of rocks. Engineering properties cannot be inferred from rock names in the table

Table 9.11 Scale of weathering grades of rock mass

Term	Description	Grade
Fresh	No visible sign of rock material weathering; perhaps slight discolouration on major discontinuity surfaces	I
Slightly weathered	Discolouration indicates weathering of rock material on discontinuity surfaces. All the rock material may be discoloured by weathering	II
Moderately weathered	Less than half of the rock material is decomposed and/or disintegrated to a soil. Fresh or discoloured rock is present either as a continuous framework or as corestones	III
Highly weathered	More than half of the rock material is decomposed and/or disintegrated to a soil. Fresh or discoloured rock is present either as a discontinuous framework or as corestones	IV
Completely weathered	All rock material is decomposed and/or disintegrated to soil. The original mass structure is still largely intact	V
Residual soil	All rock material is converted to soil. The mass structure and material fabric are destroyed. There is a large change in volume but the soil has not been significantly transported	VI

Note   Other terms used to describe weathering include 'discoloured', 'decomposed', 'disintegrated' etc.

Table 9.12 Suggested classification of weak rocks

Weak rock material	Classification					
	Completely or highly weathered	Range of SPT N values	Moderately weathered	Range of SPT N values	Fresh	Range of SPT N values
Bunter Sandstone	Weakly cemented and breaks or crumbles easily in the fingers	0–50	Weakly cemented and breaks between finger and thumb with a little pressure	50–150	Cemented such that it breaks with difficulty and thumb or requires a hammer blow to break it	Over 150
Keuper Marl Coal Measures Mudstone	Shaly appearance, well fissured, some cohesion but able to be deformed by heavy pressure with the fingers, virtually a stiff or very stiff clay	0–100	Fairly massive, irregular fissuring, can be deeply scored with a knife blade and broken but not deformed by hand	100–250	Massive beds with well-defined joints, can be scratched with a knife but can only be broken with a hammer or similar means	Over 250
Chalk	Pieces of hard chalk 25–50 mm diameter in a matrix of putty like chalk with a soft to firm clay consistency	0–15	Similar to weak chalk but pieces of hard chalk 150–300 mm and matrix firm to stiff	15–35	Breaks with difficulty between finger and thumb or requires a hammer blow to break it	Over 35

This chart is intended as a tentative guide only

9.7.5 Rock name

The determination of the rock name has already been covered. The rock name should be put in capital letters. If there is any doubt as to name the general characteristics should be described and the actual naming left to a geologist.

9.7.6 Strength

A scale of strength based on uniaxial compressive strengths is given in Table 9.13. The point load test apparatus as shown in Fig. 9.5 can be used in the field to give an estimate of strength or use can be made of the field guide quoted. It must be remembered that the strength refers to the solid parts of the rock mass and that the overall strength will be affected by the joints, fractures and bedding planes.

Fig. 9.5   Point load test apparatus (photograph: Engineering Laboratory Equipment Ltd).

9.7.7 Characteristics and properties

This can include descriptions of rock structure, dip and frequency of discontinuities. Terms describing the structure include 'bedded', 'laminated', 'foliated', 'banded', 'cleaved' and 'massive'. Terms describing bedding and the frequency of discontinuities are given in Table 9.14.

Where discontinuities occur in three dimensions the rock mass can be described as blocky if the blocks are roughly equidimensional, tabular if they are flatish or columnar if their height is much greater than their cross section. Last but not least any other observations or peculiarities should be recorded such as the presence of obvious minerals or the infilling of joints. Once again it is better to have too much information than too little.

When describing rocks it is useful to have a number of pieces of equipment available. These are a geological hammer, ×10 lens, sheet of glass, knife, bottle of dilute hydrochloric acid and a steel rule. Other more sophisticated items include point load test apparatus and a microscope. Where a detailed geological and mineralogical description is required very thin slices of the rock must be examined under a polarizing microscope. Two examples of typical basic rock descriptions are given below.

Dark grey, fine grained, fresh SHALE, weak and brittle, thinly bedded with closely spaced joints (Lower Coal Measures).

Light, pinkish grey coarse grained, slightly weathered, porphyritic GRANITE, very strong and massive with widely spaced joints.

Table 9.13

Term	Compressive strength (MN/m^2)	Field indications
Very weak	<1.25	Specimens can be broken or crumbled by hand
Weak	1.25–5	Specimens crumble under gentle hammer blows. Thin slabs broken by hand
Moderately weak	5–12.5	Only thin slabs can be broken by heavy hand pressure
Moderately strong	12.5–50	Hammer edge can make indentation in specimen or light blow can break it
Strong	50–100	One hammer blow can break a hand specimen
Very strong	100–200	Several hammer blows needed to break or chip specimens. Dull ringing sound
Extremely strong	>200	Hammer blow causes sample ring, sparks fly

Table 9.14

Spacing	Bedding spacing terms	Discontinuity spacing terms e.g. joints and fissures
>2 m	Very thick	Very widely spaced
600 mm – 2 m	Thick	Widely spaced
200 mm – 600 mm	Medium	Medium spaced
60 mm – 200 mm	Thin	Closely spaced
20 mm – 60 mm	Very thin	Very closely spaced
6 mm – 20 mm	Thickly laminated or narrow	Extremely closely spaced
<6 mm	Thinly laminated or very narrow	

10

Samples and laboratory testing

10.1 Introduction

Throughout this book the emphasis has so far been on careful observation whether it be during the desk study or the drilling. This is necessary because of the extreme variability of sites and the variability in the soil types that might be present. The soils on any site may vary in age, composition, weathering and moisture content and just as these factors vary so do the engineering properties. There is, therefore, an essential need for tests which will reveal and quantify these properties so that the engineer can use this knowledge in conjunction with his theoretical knowledge, his knowledge of the past behaviour of structures in the ground, his knowledge of geology and site history and his knowledge of the proposed function of the works to produce a solution. This solution must include an engineering appreciation of the difficulties that might be encountered and possible methods for their solution within a reasonable budget.

The engineer will be expected to predict such things as whether or not the ground can safely support the structure, how much it will settle and how long it will take. To do this he must invariably test the soils in the laboratory since the number of possible soils types and therefore the number of combinations of different properties is infinite.

As the fieldwork progresses the engineer must decide the sort of information he requires from the laboratory whether it be on strength, permeability, classification or whatever in order for him to solve the engineering problems set by the works themselves. He must bear in mind the quality of the samples to be used, how many he has of each soil type, how much the soil varies and the size of the samples. He can then plan a laboratory test programme but should be prepared continually to modify it in the light of any new information he might obtain either from the field or from the

Table 10.1

Property	Sand	Clay
Particle size	Large, 0.06 mm – 2 mm Seen by naked eye	Minute, 0.002 mm. Not visible to the naked eye
Particle shape	Generally spherical or cubical	Platy
Texture	Coarse	Fine
Friction	High	Very low
Size of pores	Large	Very small
Volume of pores	Up to 50% of total volume	Up to 90% of total volume
Surface area of particles	Small	Large
Plasticity	Non-plastic	Plastic
Cohesion	Negligible	Marked
Shrinking	Negligible	Marked
Swelling	None	Considerable
Compressibility	Slight	Considerable
Response to load	Settlement occurs quickly	Settlement occurs very slowly
Permeability	Drains quickly	Drains slowly
Moisture susceptibility	Low	High

laboratory. At this stage the geotechnical engineer should be liaising with the design engineer and the discussions may result in design modifications which in turn might affect the information needed from the fieldwork or the laboratory work. The emphasis must always be on getting the right sort of information as economically as possible such that the two over-riding requirements of the proposed works, namely safety and economy, are achieved. Before discussing some of the basic tests it is worth looking at the ways in which the engineering behaviour of a sand differs from that of a clay; this is shown by Table 10.1.

We can now look at the relative way in which these two materials might behave in a number of engineering situations (Table 10.2). The table assumes a clean medium dense sand and a moderately well compacted clay of medium plasticity and a moisture content between the plastic and liquid limits and is very much a simplification of what may be complex problems. Dry clays of low plasticity will have improved strength.

Having reviewed the major differences between a sand and a clay it must be stressed that many soils are not simple types such as these but are often mixtures of clay, silt,

236

Table 10.2

Application	Sand	Clay
Bearing capacity when compacted	Good	Poor
Settlement of structures	Low	High
Time taken for settlement	Quick	Slow
Workability as a construction material	Good	Poor
Use in embankment construction	Good	Poor
Use in dam core to prevent seepage	Poor	Good
Quality as road subgrade	Good	Poor
Suitability for soakaways	Fair	Very poor
Stability of excavations	Poor	Fair
Flow of water into excavations	Rapid	Negligible

sand and gravel and the relative proportions present obviously affect the properties.

The first essential prerequisite for valid laboratory testing is conscientious field work. It is no use expecting to produce an accurate report if the recommendations are based on inaccurate laboratory test results and it is no use expecting accurate results if the samples have not been taken properly or if they are not representative. The transmission of accurate data from the field to the laboratory and from the laboratory to the engineer writing the report is vital. Consistent descriptions must be used as discussed in Chapter 9 and the personnel in the field must note carefully the materials that are present and where they change. Even small changes in soil type or thin layers can have a significant effect on the performance of the engineering work. Within any single soil type changes in the soil fabric and structure can also have a major effect on the soil properties and unless the sample tested in the laboratory is representative of conditions in the field the wrong answer will be obtained.

Site investigation field work is difficult, heavy work and on a wet day with men surrounded by a sea of mud it does not give the appearance of being a very scientific operation. However, despite its crude first impressions it is a job that must be done with care if vital information is not to be missed. There must be equal care in the selection of the sampling technique and in the sampling itself. Much of this has been covered in previous chapters when the importance of minimizing sample disturbance was stressed. The point was made that the softer and more sensitive the soil the greater the care needed in sampling with use being made of thin-wall tubes where necessary.

It is impossible to obtain a truly 'undisturbed' sample since as soon as the sample leaves the ground its *in situ* stress conditions have been changed, air gets to work on it and it starts to dry out even if the sampling process itself has not compressed, sheared, smeared or otherwise disturbed the sample. However, the personnel involved must make every effort to keep the disturbance to a minimum.

Another point made in the chapter on shell and auger drilling was the importance of sampling that was truly representative and some of the questions that should be asked were whether or not the sample had been softened by the addition of water; whether or not material had fallen in from above; whether or not water pressures had caused piping and so on.

The above questions are obviously important but one other question that is very difficult to answer is whether or not the soil structure in the sample is representative of the structure as a whole. For example if a clay contains fissures at 300 mm centres one sample might contain a fissure and another may not and obviously the strength will vary from one to the other. The strength will also vary depending on the orientation of any fissures or bedding planes in relation to the direction of loading. One means of arriving at a conservative (perhaps over conservative) solution to the problems of fissuring is to remould the sample. In all site investigations the proportion of samples tested to the soil mass as a whole is miniscule and this is the reason why the question is so important. Obviously the bigger the sample the more likely it is to be representative and much has been written on this topic (see Rowe, 1972, who gives a table of minimum sizes of sample for different soil types). Although large samples are desirable the cost of obtaining and testing them can become very expensive and as with many aspects of site investigation a compromise has to be reached. However, this compromise must be reached after carefully considering the nature of any structural discontinuities, the affect these might have on the works and how critical they might be. On large projects with many samples and test results it is advisable to study the results statistically in order to arrive at realistic design parameters.

Soils tend not only to be variable but they also tend to have different properties in different directions and this too must be considered when testing them. Laminated clay has alternate horizontal layers of clay and silt or sand and it is easier for water to pass through it horizontally than vertically. If the same clay is loaded it would make a big difference whether the lines of the laminations were in line with the line of the load, at right angles to it or diagonally to it. Much of soil testing is involved with trying to simulate, in the laboratory, conditions that exist or will exist in the field and all the factors relevant to this must be considered before a sample is taken and tested. It is no use obtaining accurate answers to the wrong problem. The prediction of soil properties that will develop in the future is difficult but allowances must be made. For instance it is known that the shear strength of fissured clays in cuttings reduces with time.

It is important that it is not only the engineer who appreciates the problems that have been described above but also the driller in the field. It is not necessary for him to understand matters in as much detail but he should have a general appreciation of the importance of careful sampling and its relevance to the solution of engineering problems. If he is aware of the way his samples are to be used it should help him produce the type of samples needed by the technician in the laboratory.

The next sections will describe the basic tests and the way the results are used by the engineer but it must be remembered that good results can only be obtained from good samples. The basic tests are only described briefly and the reader should refer to the bibliography for further details particularly BS1377 (1975) and BS5930 (1981). He should also be prepared to develop his own methods of test for the solution of particular problems. As stated above, testing is very much a simulation process and it can often be fruitful to experiment with different types of simulation.

10.2 Classification of soils

Broadly speaking the laboratory testing of soils falls into two categories. One category comprises tests which try and simulate conditions that exist or will exist in the field such as loading and drainage. The other category comprises tests which try and classify soils into certain groups. This section deals with the classification of soils and the rest of the chapter, with the exception of Section 10.7, deals with simulation-type testing.

The ways in which different soils behave was discussed in Section 10.1 and if a particular soil can be placed in a certain group then that will tell us something of the way in which we can expect that soil to behave. Much of the existing fund of knowledge on differing soil behaviour is based on experience and it is only by classifying a soil that we can apply the right sort of experience to it. It is in effect a shorthand description; we can say this soil is this particular type and can therefore be expected to behave in a particular manner. Research carried out into soil behaviour always includes classification testing in order that the results of the research can be applied to similar soils elsewhere. Classification is also used in specifications; for instance, different soil types may require differing types and amounts of compaction when they are used in earthworks. The principal classification tests are moisture content, liquid and plastic limit tests and particle size analysis and these will be briefly described in the following paragraphs.

The determination of the moisture content of a soil is probably the cheapest and most frequently carried out of all laboratory soil tests and it can tell the experienced engineer a great deal about the way in which a soil is likely to behave. It is obvious that if the moisture content of a clay is increased it will become weaker until eventually a slurry will be formed.

The moisture content is defined as the weight of water contained in the pore space of a soil expressed as a percentage of the dry weight and the normal method of test is outlined in Fig. 10.1. Moisture content can also be determined by distillation of the water, collecting it and weighing it. There are various rough and ready means of drying a soil such as heating it over a primus stove or mixing it with methylated spirits and setting light to it but the principle remains the same. Another method is to mix the soil

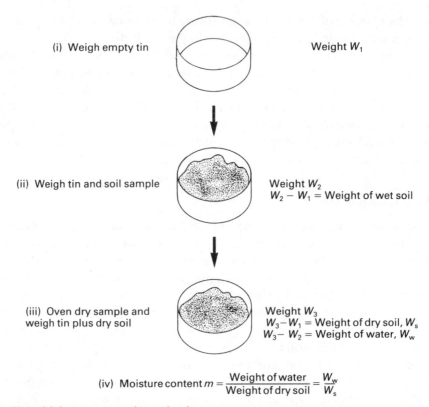

(i) Weigh empty tin   Weight W_1

(ii) Weigh tin and soil sample   Weight W_2
$W_2 - W_1$ = Weight of wet soil

(iii) Oven dry sample and weigh tin plus dry soil   Weight W_3
$W_3 - W_1$ = Weight of dry soil, W_s
$W_3 - W_2$ = Weight of water, W_w

(iv) Moisture content $m = \dfrac{\text{Weight of water}}{\text{Weight of dry soil}} = \dfrac{W_w}{W_s}$

Fig. 10.1 Moisture content determination.

with carbide in a sealed container. The carbide reacts with the water in the sample to produce gas and the pressure of the gas is proportional to the moisture content of the soil.

The normal oven determination of moisture content requires only small samples and since the test is so cheap it is worth doing one or two on different parts of say a U100 sample to check for variability. It is a good idea to measure the moisture content of all samples as soon as they are delivered to the laboratory. This again not only illustrates variability but also serves as a useful check against drying out if say a consolidation test were carried out some weeks after delivery of the sample to the laboratory. It is of course, better to do all the laboratory tests as soon as possible since the samples can change with time but often it is necessary to postpone the testing.

Atterberg proposed the concept that a soil could exist in four states; solid, semi-solid, liquid or plastic. The three boundaries between these four states were defined as the shrinkage, plastic and liquid limits and empirical tests were established to determine them.

240

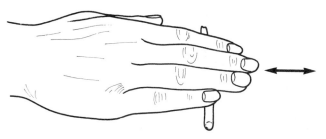

(i)   Oven dry soil sample and sieve through 425 μm sieve

(ii)   Add distilled water and mix sample such that it can be rolled into a ball

(iii) Roll ball out between the hand and a glass plate to form a thread

(iv) Continue process, thus causing sample to dry out, until the thread just begins to crumble with a diameter of 1/8 in

(v)   Determine moisture content of this sample, repeat procedure. Average moisture content represents the plastic limit

Fig. 10.2   Plastic limit test.

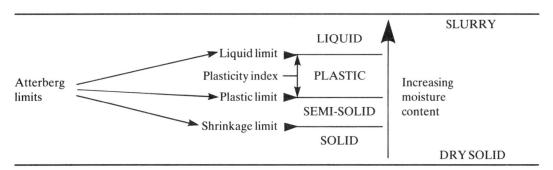

The plastic limit is an arbitrarily chosen moisture content at which soils can be said to pass from a semi-solid to a plastic state and the liquid limit is where it passes from a plastic to an essentially liquid state.

The shrinkage limit is defined as the moisture content below which there is no further reduction in volume on drying and is not as much use as the liquid and plastic limits. The method of determining the plastic limit is shown in Fig. 10.2 and Fig. 10.3 shows two alternative means of determining the liquid limit; the preferred alternative being the cone penetration test since this gives more consistent results.

Casagrande produced a plasticity chart as shown in Fig. 10.4 from which it can be seen that if the plasticity index (that is the liquid limit minus the plastic limit) is plotted against the liquid limit certain indications will be obtained with regard to the soil's plasticity and compressibility. This is even more useful if the liquid and plastic limits are viewed together with the *in situ* moisture content of the soil. For instance if the natural

241

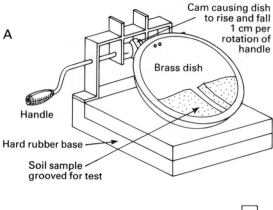

A

Cam causing dish to rise and fall 1 cm per rotation of handle

Brass dish

Handle

Hard rubber base

Soil sample grooved for test

1. Oven dry soil and sieve through 425 μm sieve
2. Add distilled water to soil sample and mix thoroughly
3. Half fill brass dish with soil and cut groove using grooving tool
4. Turn handle and count the number of blows needed to close groove over a length of 1 cm
5. Determine moisture content of sample
6. Repeat steps 2–5 to determine the number of blows needed to close the groove over a length of 1 cm for a range of moisture contents. Plot graph of moisture content against number of blows
7. Moisture content which requires 25 blows to close groove 1 cm is the liquid limit

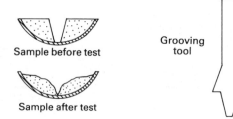

Sample before test

Sample after test

Grooving tool

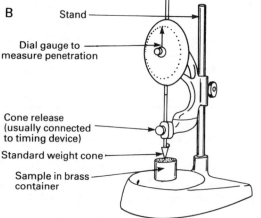

B

Stand

Dial gauge to measure penetration

Cone release (usually connected to timing device)

Standard weight cone

Sample in brass container

1. Oven dry soil and sieve through 425 μm sieve
2. Add distilled water to soil sample and mix thoroughly
3. Fill sample container and strike off excess material
4. Allow cone to penetrate sample for 5 s (usually done with automatic timing device) and measure penetration using dial gauge
5. Determine moisture content of sample
6. Repeat steps 2–5, measuring the penetration for a range of moisture contents
7. Moisture content which gives 20 mm penetration is the liquid limit

Fig. 10.3 Liquid limit determination.

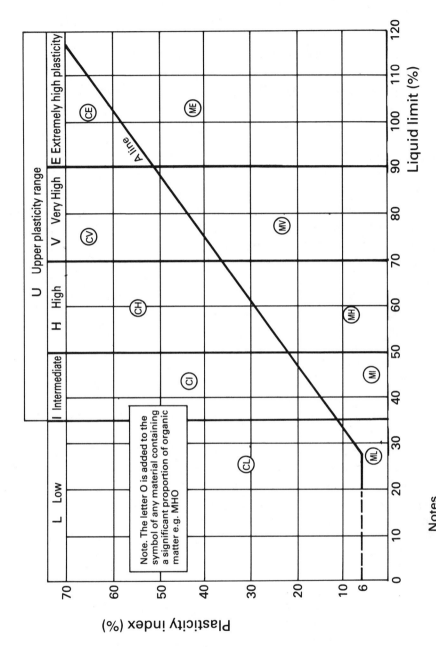

Fig. 10.4 Plasticity chart (from BS5930:1981).

Notes

Silt (M Soil) plots below A line, clay C plots above it. M and C may be combined as fine soil, F. Chart is for the classification of fine soils and the finer part of coarse soils and measurements are made on material passing a 425 µm BS sieve.

Note. The letter O is added to the symbol of any material containing a significant proportion of organic matter e.g. MHO

moisture content is above the plastic limit the soil can be expected to behave in a plastic manner whereas if it is above the liquid limit the soil can be expected to flow almost like a thick liquid. Tests can also be carried out to determine the swelling potential of a soil in the presence of water.

The determination of specific gravity, that is the weight per unit volume of the solid particles, can be said to be a classification test but the results are not particularly useful and the test is open to many errors. However, a knowledge of specific gravity is necessary in determining void ratios and in interpreting the results of particle size distribution tests on silts and clays.

Knowledge of a soil's dry density is essential in many engineering problems in order to calculate weights of soil. The dry density is the dry weight of soil per unit volume which is of course less than specific gravity since there are inevitably voids between the soil particles. Wet density or bulk density is the weight of soil plus moisture per unit volume and is therefore higher than the corresponding dry density since in the wet state some of the voids are filled with water. The wet density is, however, still less than the specific gravity.

In Chapter 9 a description was given on the basic particle sizes which go to make up any soil; namely clays, silts, sands, gravels, cobbles and boulders. Obviously these particles have differing properties and therefore a knowledge of their relative proportions in any sample can tell the engineer a lot about the way the soil is likely to behave. For coarse materials a sieve analysis can be carried out as shown in Fig. 10.5. To determine the relative proportions of fine-grained soils such as silts and clays it is necessary to measure the rate at which different proportions settle out in water since the coarser particles will settle out much faster than the finer ones. Test procedures for this method are defined in BS1377.

The chart used for illustrating the results of particle size tests, a grading chart, was shown in Fig. 9.1 which also showed the curves produced for a number of different soils. It is particularly important with these tests that the samples used are truly representative. It is very easy when sampling coarse materials to wash away the fine material. Grading tests are relevant on many materials, particularly granular ones, but they are not applicable to materials like peat, chalk or other soft rocks which would break down during sample preparation.

10.3 Shear strength of soils

Before discussing the tests used to determine a soil's shear strength it is worth looking at the way soils are loaded and stressed in the field. Figure 10.6 shows three foundation types; a pad, a raft and a piled foundation. Also shown is the pressure bulb produced when a load is applied to the contact area of the foundations. In each case the line of the pressure bulb has been plotted where the contact pressure resulting from the load has

(i) Sample is normally oven dried and then weighed

(ii) Sieves are slotted together and sample is placed in top sieve

(iii) Sample is shaken, either manually or using a vibrating table

(iv) The weight of material retained on each sieve and in the base pan is weighed

(v) The grading is now complete and the grading curve can be plotted using the percentages passing each sieve

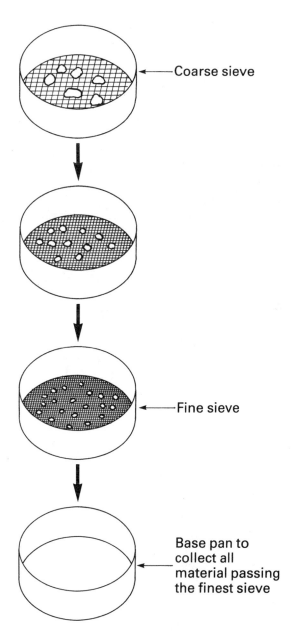

Coarse sieve

Fine sieve

Base pan to collect all material passing the finest sieve

Fig. 10.5 Sieve analysis.

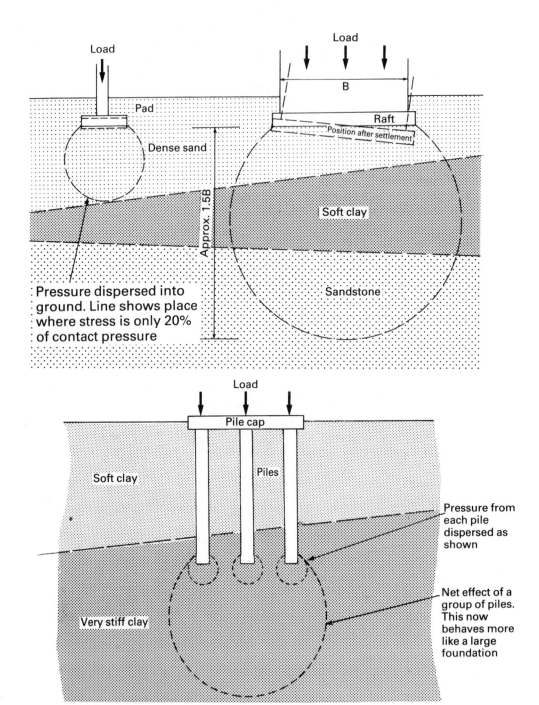

Fig. 10.6 The loading of soils.

been dispersed into the ground such that the vertical stress in the soil is about 20% of the contact pressure. The depth of this pressure bulb is roughly one-and-a-half times the width of the foundation.

The loads applied to the soil can do two things. First they can cause a bearing capacity failure as shown in Fig. 10.7 and this is essentially a shear failure along the line shown. Shear failure can also occur in a slope due to the weight of soil on a slip circle as is also shown in Fig. 10.7. Secondly they can cause settlement. In the case of the pad foundation in Fig. 10.6 it is only the dense sand which is being stressed to any extent and settlement will be small and will take place rapidly. In the case of the raft foundation a layer of soft clay is being stressed. The loads applied to this clay will cause water to be squeezed out of it and there will be movement of the particles closer to one another, thus producing settlement. Since there is a greater thickness of clay under the right hand side of the raft more settlement will occur on this side than on the other. This is termed differential settlement and would result in a tilt of the structure as shown. In the case of the piles each pile will produce a relatively small bulb of pressure and some of the load will be carried by friction on the sides of the pile. However, the net result of a group of piles would be as shown and if there were a layer of soft clay within the resulting pressure bulb settlement would occur.

The way in which soils behave under load is complex since when loaded their behaviour is partly elastic (that is the stress is directly proportional to strain or deformation), partly plastic (that is the stress produces irreversible deformations), and partly viscous (that is they tend to flow). This is illustrated in Fig. 10.8 where a graph is plotted of stress against strain. If a number of tests are carried out to determine the failure stress under different confining pressures a line can be plotted as shown in Fig. 10.8 which defines the shear strength of the soil for different stresses acting at right angles to the failure plane. However, it is not quite as simple as this since different answers will be obtained depending on whether or not water is allowed to drain out of the soil. If an undrained test is carried out quickly we obtain the undrained strength parameters c_u and ϕ_u and the shear strength $\tau = c_u + \sigma \tan \phi_u$ but if drainage is allowed and the test carried out slowly we obtain the effective strength parameters c' and ϕ' and shear strength equals $c' + (\sigma - u) \tan \phi'$ where u is the water pressure in the pores of the soil. The different results that will be obtained are illustrated below.

Undrained test on clay	c_u high	ϕ_u low or zero
Undrained test on sand	c_u low	ϕ_u moderate or high
Drained test on clay	c' low	ϕ' moderate
Drained test on sand	c' very low or zero	ϕ' high

Since strength testing is essentially trying to simulate what will happen in the field, it is important to recognize what boundary conditions exist, what drainage will occur and at

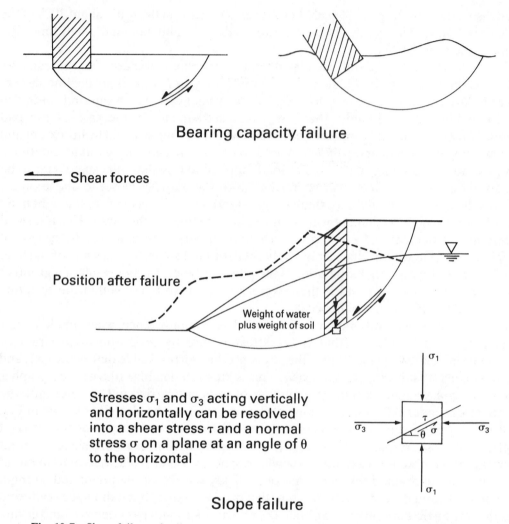

Bearing capacity failure

Shear forces

Position after failure

Weight of water
plus weight of soil

Stresses σ_1 and σ_3 acting vertically
and horizontally can be resolved
into a shear stress τ and a normal
stress σ on a plane at an angle of θ
to the horizontal

Slope failure

Fig. 10.7 Shear failure of soils.

what rate the load will be applied. It is also necessary to appreciate the problems associated with the history of the soil, the sample size and the degree to which the soil is saturated with water since all these factors will affect the results obtained. This is why it is so important to understand the environment in which the soil exists and to sample and prepare it carefully.

There are three principal laboratory tests to determine shear strength and these are shown in Figs 10.9, 10.10 and 10.11. There is also the vane shear test which was

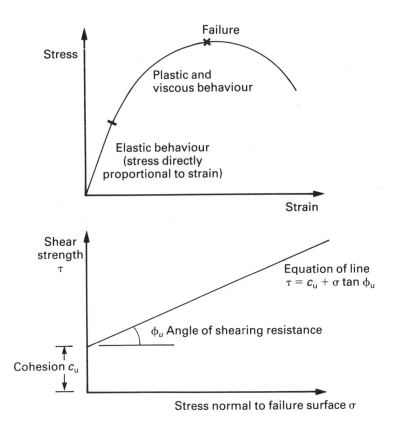

In the effective stress condition $\tau' = c' + (\sigma - u) \tan \phi'$
where u is the pore water pressure, σ is the total stress
and σ' is the effective stress i.e. $\sigma' = (\sigma - u)$

Fig. 10.8   Shear strength of soils.

described in Chapter 8. In the shear-box test (Fig. 10.9) the soil is forced to shear along
a pre-defined shear plane and there is little control of drainage. Although if the sample
is sheared slowly thereby allowing drainage the effective strength parameters c' and ϕ'
will be obtained. This test is most applicable to granular soils and either undisturbed
hand-cut samples or remoulded samples can be used. The unconfined compression test
(Fig. 10.10) can be carried out on site and used on saturated cohesive clayey soils but it
cannot simulate the confined state of soils. This can, however, be done in the triaxial
test shown in Fig. 10.11 which also has provision for allowing drainage if required and

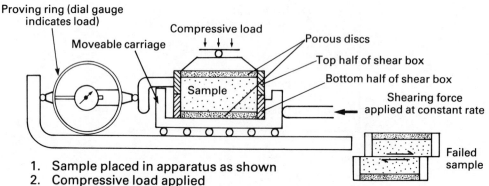

1. Sample placed in apparatus as shown
2. Compressive load applied
3. Shearing force applied to sample at a constant rate by an electric motor
4. Shearing resistance of the sample is measured using the proving ring and the maximum shear stress at failure is recorded
5. The process is repeated using different compressive loads enabling a graph of shearing resistance/compressive stress to be drawn. This is usually a straight line as shown below

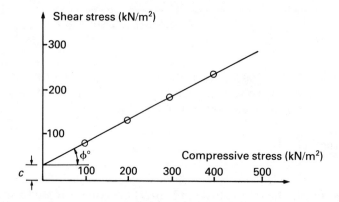

6. The cohesion (c) and the angle of shearing resistance ($\phi°$) are determined from the graph as shown

Fig. 10.9 Shear-box test.

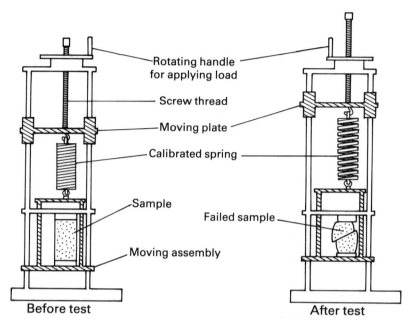

| Before test | After test |

1. Undisturbed sample is placed in test apparatus
2. Compressive load is applied to sample by manually operated screwjack
3. Graph of load against deformation is automatically plotted by a recording arm (not shown above)
4. The resulting graph is of a form as shown below

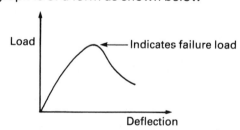

5. The failure load is used to calculate the unconfined compressive strength which equals twice the shear strength

Fig. 10.10 The unconfined compression test.

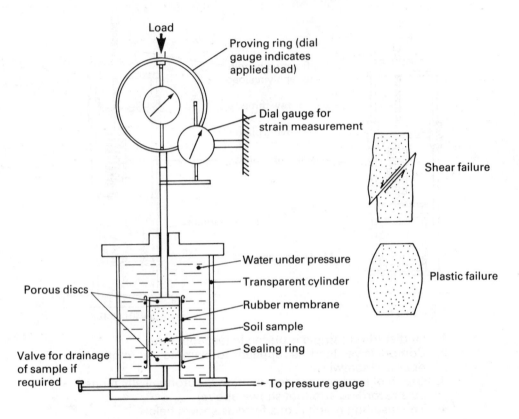

1. Soil sample is covered with a rubber membrane to prevent loss or ingress of water
2. Porous plates are placed above and below the sample allowing drainage through the valve if required. Pore water pressures within the sample can also be measured
3. The water in the cell is pressurized and this gives lateral support to the sample thus simulating the condition of a soil element in the ground
4. A vertical load is applied at a constant rate of strain until the sample fails. The vertical applied pressure at failure is measured using the proving ring
5. The test is repeated using different water pressures. A plot similar to that for the shear box is obtained from which the shear strength of the soil can be determined

Fig. 10.11 Triaxial test.

this is the test most commonly used in practice to determine shear strength or modulus of elasticity. The samples can be tested under many different conditions, the object being to simulate what will happen in practice.

One particular point to consider is in what direction the maximum shear stress will occur since soils tend to have different shear strengths in different directions. It goes without saying that undisturbed samples are necessary if the true *in situ* strength is to be obtained and care is needed to ensure the sample is representative. This may involve testing large-diameter samples if fissures are present. Another problem is of determining the shear strength at very large strains, as might occur in a landslide, and tests at such strains will give residual shear strengths often considerably lower than peak strengths. To obtain the large strains necessary, several cycles of strain can be performed with the shear box or a ring shear apparatus can be used.

10.4 Consolidation

As already discussed the two important factors in the design of foundations are bearing capacity and settlement. Bearing capacity is controlled by shear strength whilst settlement is controlled by the amount of water squeezed out of the soil and the rate at which this occurs. The two factors are interrelated since if water is forced out of a soil the particles will move closer together and the shear strength will increase.

At the instant a load is applied to a saturated soil all the load is carried by the water in the pores of the soil. This pore pressure then dissipates as water drains out of the pores. The rate of dissipation depends on the permeability of the soil. With a sand it occurs very rapidly but a clay in the field can take many years to consolidate under load.

In the consolidation test shown in Fig. 10·12 the change in volume of the soil is measured as a static load causes drainage of water out of the sample. The test is not without its problems when it comes to predicting what will happen in the field. There is the stress history of the sample to take into account, the simplifying assumptions necessary for the analysis, the representativeness of the sample and so on. One very important consideration is that of the orientation of the sample. In the test, drainage occurs upwards and downwards and this is all right if the sample is homogeneous but many clays are laminated with thin horizontal layers of sand. Such soils are therefore much more permeable horizontally than they are vertically. In the field, drainage of such clays would tend to occur horizontally but in the consolidation test it cannot because of the retaining ring. This problem can be partly solved by testing samples such that the laminations run vertically. Alternatively there is a consolidation cell, known as the Rowe cell, which accepts much larger samples and allows drainage in all directions. Consolidation tests can also be carried out in the triaxial cell. It should be noted that each increment of load produces less and less settlement since it is becoming progressively harder for the soil particles to get any closer together.

253

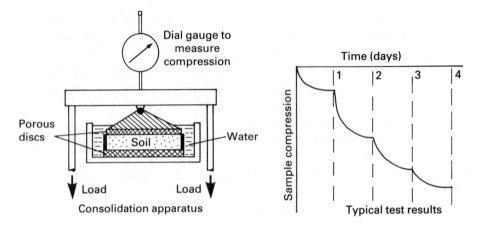

1. The soil sample is encased in a steel or brass cutting ring and filter papers and porous discs are placed above and below it. The sample is then saturated
2. A vertical load is applied which causes the sample to consolidate (i.e. reduce in thickness) by squeezing water out of the pore spaces
3. The sample compression is measured by means of a dial gauge at set time intervals.
4. The last dial-gauge reading is usually taken after 24 h since the sample will by then have achieved full consolidation under the applied load
5. A further load increment is then applied which causes further compression (consolidation) of the sample. The compression is again measured at set intervals of time over a 24 h period
6. The process is continued until the full pressure range expected on site has been covered
7. The time/compression curve may then be drawn and the co-efficient of compressibility (m_v) and the coefficient of consolidation (c_v) calculated. m_v indicates the amount of settlement that will occur and c_v indicates the time it will take

Fig. 10.12 Consolidation test.

10.5 Permeability

Permeability can be defined as the ease with which water can flow through a soil and is not to be confused with porosity which is the ratio of voids to total volume. The void ratio of a clay is high but its permeability is low. A sand may have a lower porosity and void ratio than a clay but its permeability will be many times higher. However, the higher the porosity of a sand then the higher will be its permeability. The permeability

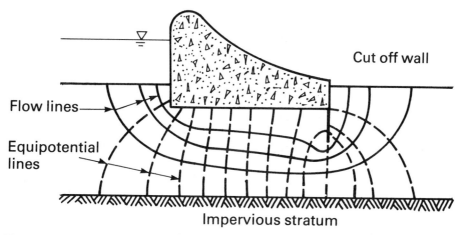

Fig. 10.13 Seepage beneath a dam.

of a soil is affected by many factors such as the degree of stratification, the nature of the minerals present, their shape and arrangement, the temperature of the water, the void ratio and the degree of saturation, so once again careful sampling is needed.

Permeability is important in many civil engineering problems, one of them being dam design as shown in Fig. 10.13. It is obviously vitally important to know how much and at what rate water will flow under the dam. Permeability is also important in determining the yield of water-bearing aquifers, in establishing potential flows of water into excavations and cofferdams and in problems involving groundwater lowering. It is also important since, as discussed in the previous sections, it affects the consolidation of soils and the rate at which shear strength is increased due to drainage.

The two principal tests for determining permeability are the constant and falling head permeability tests shown in Figs 10.14 and 10.15. The falling head test is appropriate for soils of low permeability and the constant head test for those with high permeability.

10.6 Compaction tests

When soil is used as a construction material in road embankments or dams it is important to compact the soil as much as possible since this will improve its shear strength and it will mean that less settlement will occur when it is loaded. A completely dry soil is not easy to compact and voids tend to remain in the soil mass which permit the ingress of water and possible future softening. However, if a small amount of water is present in the soil there is some lubrication between the soil particles thus allowing them to move closer together and a much denser state will be achieved. If on the other hand too much water is added the strength will be reduced because the water prevents

255

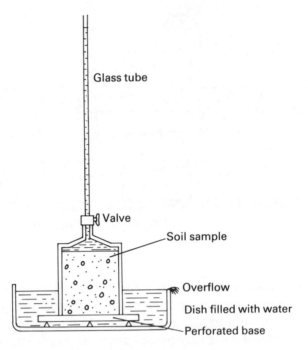

Glass tube

Valve

Soil sample

Overflow

Dish filled with water

Perforated base

1. Sample is placed in container as shown
2. Glass tube is filled with water and the soil sample saturated. The valve is then closed, the tube topped up and the level noted
3. When valve is opened water level in glass tube begins to fall as water passes through sample
4. Water passing through the sample escapes through the perforated base and causes the dish to overflow
5. The valve is now closed and the final level of the water in the tube is noted
6. Since the diameter of the tube is known and the drop in water level is known the volume of water that has passed through the sample can be calculated
7. By noting the time between opening and closing the valve it is possible to determine the rate at which the water passes through the sample

Fig. 10.14   Falling head permeability test.

the particles moving closer together. For a given amount of compactive effort there is, therefore, a certain optimum moisture content which will produce the maximum dry density.

The object of laboratory compaction tests is to determine what the optimum

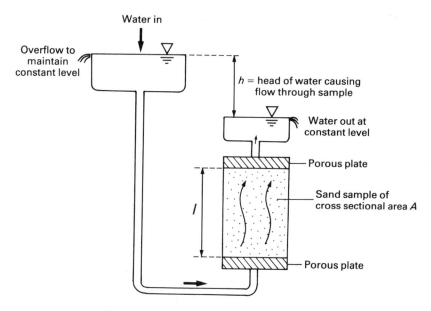

Water in

Overflow to
maintain
constant level

h = head of water causing
flow through sample

Water out at
constant level

Porous plate

Sand sample of
cross sectional area A

l

Porous plate

1. Sample placed in container as shown
2. Flow of water established into top tank, through sample
   and out of lower tank
3. Volume V flowing out measured over fixed time interval t
4. Permeability k calculated from

$$k = \frac{V}{A \times h/l \times t}$$

h/l is termed the hydraulic gradient

Fig. 10.15   Constant head permeability test.

moisture content is and what maximum dry density will be achieved so that materials can be used to their best advantage in the field. The tests consist of applying a constant amount of compaction, by either standard rammer blows or by a vibrating hammer, to a number of samples of soil in a steel mould at different moisture contents. After compaction, which is done on a fixed number of layers, the dry density is measured and a graph plotted of moisture content against dry density. The optimum moisture content and maximum dry density can then be read off the peak of the graph. It is important that the compactive effort given in the laboratory is similar to that given in the field since different amounts of compaction will give different results. *In situ* density tests can then be carried out in the field to check that the soil is at the right moisture content and that it is being sufficiently well compacted.

A form of modified compaction test known as the moisture condition test measures the volume change of a soil sample under an increasing number of standard hammer blows. The results are used to determine the moisture condition value (MCV) which can be used in the control of earthworks. Tests might also be carried out on either compacted or natural soils to determine how much heave will occur due to the effect of frost action. The heave being due to the formation of ice lenses within the sample.

10.7 Chemical tests

Although there are a great number of chemical tests that could be carried out on soils to determine their exact composition there are only a few which are necessary for the majority of engineering works. These tests are the acidity/alkalinity (pH) test, a sulphate content test and the determination of the amount of organic matter present.

The determination of the sulphate content of soil or groundwater is particularly important since sulphates attack concrete and can cause it to deteriorate to a white paste. If sulphates are present precautions have to be taken in the design of concrete in contact with the soil or water or the concrete has to be covered with a protective coating. The usual test method is to get the sulphates into solution and then to add barium chloride which precipitates the sulphates out as barium sulphate, the amount of which can be measured. Acid soils or groundwaters can attack concrete or steel and there is a simple instrument available to measure the degree of acidity or alkalinity or indicator papers can be used. It is also sometimes necessary to determine the chloride and carbonate contents of a soil or its bacteriological properties.

10.8 Miscellaneous laboratory techniques

One empirical test that has not been described in the preceding sections is the California Bearing Ratio (CBR) test which is shown in Fig. 10.16. This test was developed in America for the design of highway pavements and is now in regular use in the UK for the same purpose. In the test the load required to push a plunger into a soil sample at a controlled rate is measured and the load on the plunger at a certain depth is recorded as a percentage of a standard load. The standard loads were established as a result of tests on crushed stone samples, for instance 20 kN for a penetration of 5 mm. Thus if an actual test gave 20 kN at 5 mm the CBR would be 100% but if it only took 1 kN to produce 5 mm penetration the CBR would be 5%. There are problems in ensuring that the soil sample is in a representative state of compaction, at an equilibrium moisture content and with a surcharge equivalent to the eventual weight of highway pavement construction. Tests can be carried out on undisturbed or remoulded samples to assess the effect of soaking the sample but it is difficult to simulate the effects of long-term weathering and softening.

So far the tests that have been described are the standard ones specified in BS1377

258

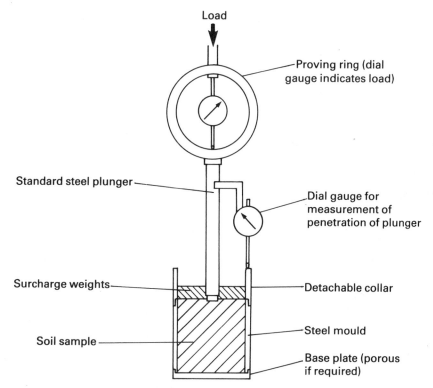

Load

Proving ring (dial gauge indicates load)

Standard steel plunger

Dial gauge for measurement of penetration of plunger

Surcharge weights

Detachable collar

Soil sample

Steel mould

Base plate (porous if required)

1. Soil sample obtained by driving steel mould into soil using cutting edge on bottom of mould. Alternatively the soil can be compacted into the mould
2. Surcharge weights can be added if required to simulate overburden pressures
3. The penetration into the sample of a standardized steel plunger is measured under increasing loads
4. The loads required to cause 0.1 in and 0.2 in of penetration are determined and expressed as a percentage of two standard loads to give the California Bearing Ratio
5. The test is repeated on the bottom of the sample

Fig. 10.16 California Bearing Ratio test.

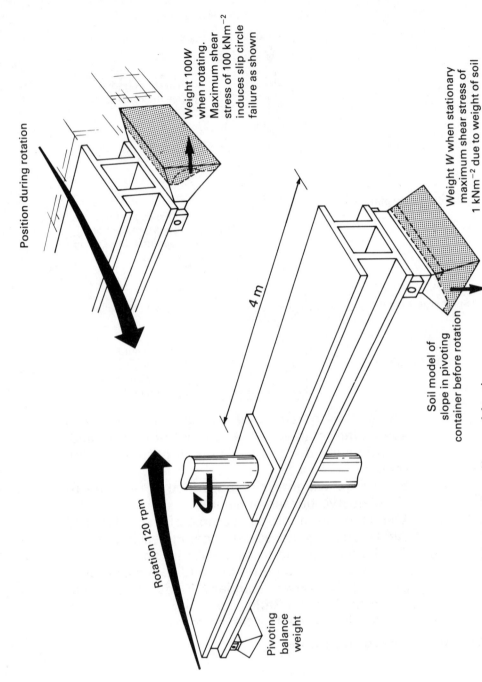

Position during rotation

Weight 100W when rotating. Maximum shear stress of 100 kNm^{-2} induces slip circle failure as shown

Rotation 120 rpm

4 m

Pivoting balance weight

Soil model of slope in pivoting container before rotation

Weight W when stationary maximum shear stress of 1 kNm^{-2} due to weight of soil

Fig. 10.17 The principles of centrifuge model testing.

(1975) but a number of others exist and these are listed with references in BS5930. However, an ingenious engineer can devise many other tests to help solve particular problems. One method is to use modelling techniques and there are an infinite number of ways in which this can be done. Model piles can be driven into bins of sand and loaded. Small footings on a bed of clay can be loaded until failure occurs. Dyes can be added to water flowing under a model dam to determine the flow lines. Model retaining walls can be loaded until movement occurs and so on. In all cases miniature instrumentation can be installed to measure deformations and pressures in much the same way as is described in Chapter 11 for the full-scale works. The engineer must ensure that stress levels are considered and scale effects taken into account. One problem is in achieving the right loading and this can be solved using a large centrifuge as shown in Fig. 10.17. In the example shown the weight of soil in an ordinary model slope is insufficient to cause failure. The effect of spinning the soil model in a centrifuge is to increase the apparent weight of the soil until failure occurs. Careful instrumentation is essential if useful information is to be obtained and television cameras mounted on the rotating arm can be used to observe the actual failure. Other models such as tunnels can be set up in the centrifuge and much valuable research work has been done using the technique.

Many different tests are also available for testing rock specimens and these include determination of compressive or tensile strengths, modulus of elasticity, strengths on discontinuities and creep effects. Tables 4 and 5 of BS5930 (pages 71–75) give complete schedules of laboratory tests on soils and rocks with information as to where full details of the tests can be found.

11

Instrumentation

11.1 The purposes of instrumentation

Instrumentation is perhaps not generally regarded as a part of a normal site investigation but it is an investigation technique in the true sense of the word and a very important one at that. Our knowledge of soil behaviour and the way in which structures interact with the soil is by no means complete. The variability of soils and the difficulties associated with representative and undisturbed sampling have been stressed many times in this book and it should be obvious that if we can monitor the performance of actual structures in the field a great deal can be learnt.

It is true that samples can be tested in the laboratory and the results successfully applied in design but this does not necessarily reveal the full story. This is the reason that in recent years more and more structures have been instrumented to monitor their performance. It has been stated by Hanna (1973) that 'experience is the comparison of measured field performance against design assumptions'. This is essentially the 'observational method' which relies on the field measurement of actual movements, loads, stresses and pressures. The observational method can be used in two ways. First it can be used on one structure to give information for the design of future similar structures; an instrumented structure can in fact be regarded as a full scale *in situ* test. Secondly it can be used in conjunction with a thorough site investigation to monitor and if necessary modify the works as they proceed. This process involves producing a design based on all the information available and selecting certain quantities, such as settlement and pore water pressure, that can be observed during construction. The probable values of these quantities are then calculated for the most unfavourable set of circumstances. Actual conditions can then be compared with these unfavourable

262

conditions and the design modified where necessary. Instrumentation costs can be fairly high in relation to normal site-investigation costs but even so they will only represent a small proportion of total project costs and can lead to appreciable benefits.

Instrumentation does not have to be complex to be useful. It is worth remembering that one's own eyes are highly sophisticated instruments themselves and can be used directly to assess movements and indirectly to assess loads, by observing the deflection of a sheet pile wall for instance. The observant engineer can gain a great deal simply by carefully looking at what is happening during and after construction. The usefulness of observation can be extended by the precise measurement of levels at various stages of construction or by monitoring known lengths such as the distance between two bridge abutments. To go a stage further there are a variety of instruments which can be installed in and around the works to measure loads, pressures and movements and these will be considered in the subsequent sections of this chapter.

Instruments can be used to control the safe construction of embankments by monitoring horizontal movements, pore water pressures and settlements and these can warn the engineer of impending failure and enable precautions to be taken. They can also indicate when settlement is complete prior to surfacing a road. Research in the field has many advantages over research in the laboratory but full instrumentation is essential if the lessons learnt are to be applied to future works. Instruments can help in the evaluation of new materials, design techniques or construction plant. Some form of instrumentation may also be needed for contract measurement since if, for example, an embankment were to settle 200 mm into the natural ground more fill material would be needed.

Before looking at individual instruments and their application mention should be made of installation, operation and maintenance. Careful planning is obviously essential. The engineer must consider what quantities he wishes to measure and how he is to measure them. The method used for measurement must be such that it can be used for as long as is necessary throughout the construction process without being destroyed by the works themselves. The instruments must be installed carefully to the correct line and level and protected such that they operate efficiently. The programme of installation must be carried out sufficiently well in advance of the works so that it does not interfere with them and so that it is co-ordinated with any other geotechnical works such as the installation of sand drains. Some instruments need to be installed in boreholes and most of the investigation techniques described earlier in this book can be used to sink the boreholes. There must be adequately trained staff to read and maintain the instruments and to process and interpret the results. Finally, the instruments will often need additional protection from site traffic, weather and vandalism as the works proceed.

11.2 Load measurement

Many of the external loads on a structure can be calculated to some degree of accuracy but the way these loads distribute themselves throughout the structure to the foundations and their components is often difficult to determine. One example would be the load acting on an individual pile of a large group. It is also difficult to predict what loads are induced in structural elements by variable materials such as soils. Two examples in the research field where load measurement might be useful are an excavation strut and a ground anchor. Load measuring devices or dynamometers are relatively simple but consideration must be given to the applied load range, the environment in which they are used, their cost, their accuracy and the means by which they are to be read.

One of the simplest devices is the proving ring as shown in Fig. 11.1. This is usually a high-tensile steel ring which deforms elastically under load and they are available with capacities up to 250 tonnes. The deformation is measured using a dial gauge or a transducer and a calibration chart is used to convert this to load. The dial gauge shown in Fig. 11.1 operates on a mechanical rack and pinion principle which rotates the needle on the dial. They can measure to an accuracy of about 0.002 mm per division. A transducer, an electrical device, can be used as an alternative, the operating principle of which is shown in Fig. 11.2. An iron core moves within three coils. The inner coil is activated by an alternating current and this induces a voltage in the secondary coils, the magnitude of which depends on the position of the iron core. The voltage which is usually up to about 2 millivolts can be read using a digital voltmeter. The transducer has the advantage that a reading can be taken remotely from the proving ring and can be linked to data logging equipment.

An alternative to the proving ring is the force measuring block which can be used for loads up to 1000 tonnes. These operate on a similar principle to the proving ring namely the measurement of deformation of an elastic body. One version developed by the National Physical Laboratory consists of a steel cylinder machined from a solid bar to form four struts. A cell for measuring loads in ground anchors is also available and this utilizes the deformation of a steel disc.

Loads can also be measured indirectly in a number of different ways. If the properties of say a strut are known then its deformation can be used to calculate the load in it. The deformation must be measured accurately and a number of instruments utilizing simple dial gauges are available. Another method is to use the principle of photoelasticity. When a cylinder of optical glass is strained by the application of load, interference fringe patterns are visible in the glass when it is illuminated with polarized light. By counting the number of visible fringes the stress can be estimated.

There are also load cells which utilize strain gauges bonded to their surface. One example is shown in Fig. 11.3 but there are many others, some in the shape of thick

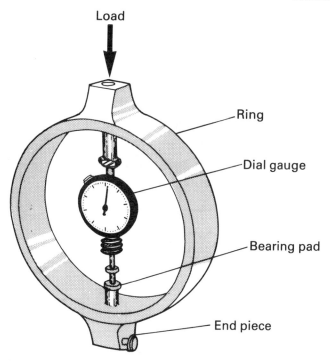

Load

Ring

Dial gauge

Bearing pad

End piece

As load is applied ring deforms and
dial gauge measures the deformation
which can be converted to load using a
calibration chart

Fig. 11.1 Proving ring.

discs. A strain gauge operates on the principle that the resistance of a zig-zag length of wire decreases when it is shortened. Thus the change in resistance indicates the amount of strain which can be used to calculate the stress and hence the load. One arrangement of strain gauges is shown in Fig. 11.3. Under axial load R_1 and R_2 compress whilst R_3 and R_4 extend. The changes in resistance are measured using a Wheatstone Bridge circuit as shown with the output varying depending on the load applied.

Another load cell uses the principle that the natural frequency of vibration of a stretched wire will vary depending on the tension in the wire. Any applied load will cause strain and this will alter the tension in the wire and therefore the natural frequency. The cell contains two electromagnets one of which is used to excite the wire whilst the other acts as a pick-up. The closer the wire is to the magnet the more current that will be generated and therefore the frequency of the changes in the current will correspond to the frequency of the wire. Yet another load cell involves the measurement of hydraulic pressures in a device similar to a hydraulic jack.

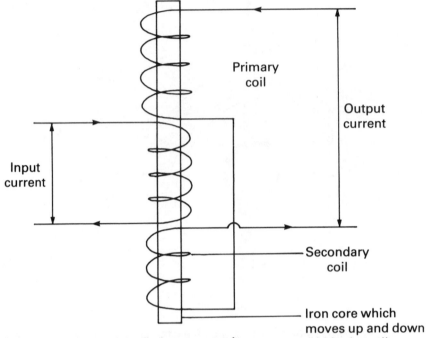

Fig. 11.2 The principle of the displacment transducer.

11.3 Earth pressure measurement

Pressures can exist in a soil mass due to the weight of overburden, water or external loads and it should be noted that a vertical load on a soil mass will generate both vertical and horizontal pressures. Pressures can also be locked in a soil mass due to its past history and pressures can be generated by compaction and left 'locked' into the soil. These pressures may act on structural surfaces such as the backs of retaining walls and so generate loads. It may be necessary, particularly in the research field, not only to know the magnitude of these pressures but also their distribution. This might apply to the retaining wall already mentioned or to the distribution of pressures beneath a raft foundation.

One problem with the measurement of earth pressures is that as soon as a cell or other instrument is introduced into a mass of soil the stress field in the vicinity of that cell will be altered by the cell itself and it will be this altered stress field that will be measured and not the naturally occurring one. It has been found that with a cell type instrument the errors can be minimized by making the cell as flat as possible with a stiff diaphragm and a stiff, thick outer guard ring. One example is shown in Fig. 11.4 where the pressure on

266

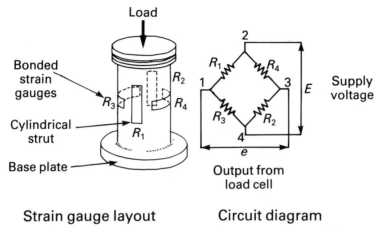

Load

Bonded strain gauges

R_2

R_4

R_3

Cylindrical strut

R_1

Base plate

R_1 R_4

R_3 R_2

2

1 3 E Supply voltage

4

e

Output from load cell

Strain gauge layout   Circuit diagram

Fig. 11.3   Load cell (after Hanna, 1973).

the flat plate deflects the diaphragm which alters the tension in the vibrating wire and hence its frequency. This effect was described in Section 11.2. An alternative instrument utilizes strain gauges on a diaphragm to detect changes in pressure in much the same way as a load cell.

Another commonly used earth pressure cell is a hydraulic one known as a Glötzl cell. In this case use is made of a thin, flat, oil-filled sensing pad which may be circular or rectangular. Since the pad is thin stress distortion is kept to a minimum. An increase in pressure on the pad causes an increase in pressure in the oil and this is measured mechanically as shown in Fig. 11.4. A small constant volume of oil is pumped through a pressure chamber. When its pressure equals the pressure in the pad a diaphragm deflects and allows oil to escape up the return line. Under steady state conditions the pumped pressure can be measured and will be equal to the pad pressure unless corrections have to be made for any difference in elevation between the pad and the pump. This unit is simple, reliable and relatively cheap.

In the Carlson stress meter a thin film of mercury under pressure causes a diaphragm to deflect, the strain in which is measured electrically. The Waterways Experimental Station cell (WES cell) is similar.

If the pressures that are to be measured are dynamic ones, say due to machine vibrations or the passage of a vehicle, cells with very quick response times must be used and this is not easy to achieve.

Since pressure in soil acts vertically and horizontally or in fact in any direction it can be resolved on any plane into stresses perpendicular to that plane and shear stresses along it. Gauges are available to measure these shear stresses. One type uses strain gauges on a deflecting diaphragm and another uses strain gauges bonded to thin webs

267

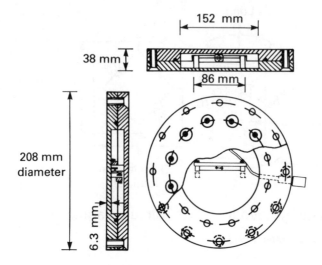

152 mm

38 mm

86 mm

208 mm
diameter

6.3 mm

Vibrating wire earth pressure cell (After Thomas and Ward)

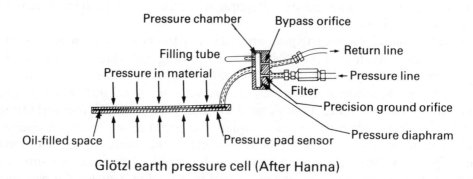

Pressure chamber   Bypass orifice

Filling tube   → Return line

Pressure in material   ← Pressure line

Filter

Precision ground orifice

Oil-filled space   Pressure pad sensor   Pressure diaphram

Glötzl earth pressure cell (After Hanna)

Fig. 11.4 Earth pressure cells.

which deflect in the direction of normal load and bend in the direction of shear. Earth pressures can also be deduced indirectly by measuring strut loads or the strains in a sheet pile for example.

When considering the measurement of earth pressure the instrument chosen should ideally be simple, durable, accurate, reliable, easily installed and calibrated, easily read, cheap and should cause the minimum of interference. No single type fulfills all these requirements and the engineer must choose one which most nearly fits his needs.

11.4   Pore water pressure measurement

The shear strength of soils was discussed in Section 10.3 and it was shown that the effective shear strength was related to effective cohesion, effective angle of shearing resistance and pore pressure by the equation:

$$\tau = c' + (\sigma - u) \tan \phi'$$

(see also Fig. 10.8). In this equation σ is the total normal stress acting on the shear surface. The effective stress σ' is equal to the total stress minus the pore water pressure

$$\sigma' = (\sigma - u)$$

In the effective stress condition c' tends to be small and thus the pore water pressure u has a highly significant effect on shear strength and is therefore important in problems involving shear failure such as shown in Fig. 10.7. Since the prediction of pore pressures and the way in which they change is difficult to predict it is often necessary to find a way of measuring them on site. The instrument employed to do this is known as a piezometer and there are a number of different types.

The slope shown in Fig. 10.7 will be safe providing the shear strength of the soil on the slip circle is sufficient to resist the weight of soil trying to cause failure. Now in the effective stress condition the shear strength is as defined in the equation above but we know that c' is small and therefore the shear strength is mainly controlled by the effective stress $(\sigma - u)$ thus the bigger the pore pressure u then the smaller is the effective stress and the lower the factor of safety against failure. A natural slope may be quite safe with a low water table but should the water table rise the factors of safety might fall below unity when a slip would occur. Thus it is extremely important to know the value of u if we are to know the true factor of safety. In the case of embankment construction the placing of layers of fill will cause the build up of pore water pressure in the subsoils and these pore pressures will dissipate with time. The more permeable the subsoils then the faster this will occur. Thus if we can measure the build up of pore water pressure we can stop placing fill when the factor of safety gets too low and re-start when the pore pressures have dissipated and the shear strength increased.

The basic principle of all piezometers is that the pore water pressure in the soil is transmitted through a porous element where it can be measured in a number of different ways. In considering the type of piezometer to use the engineer should consider such questions as accuracy, reliability, disturbing effects, response times, durability and the way in which it is to be read. The engineer must also consider just where it is necessary to measure the pore water pressures and how the results are to be used.

The simplest forms of piezometers were discussed in Section 6.12 and these included standpipes and simple tubes to measure pore water pressures at different levels. These are also the cheapest. However, it is impractical in the case of embankments or dams to keep placing fill around a mass of vertical plastic tubes and a means of obtaining the pore pressure remotely must be found. One way of doing this was developed by the Building Research Station and is shown in Fig. 11.5. The pore pressure is transmitted through the porous element at the bottom where it causes a deflection in a diaphragm. In the example shown the deflection is measured using the vibrating-wire principle described previously and such piezometers are sometimes termed acoustic piezometers. The deflection of the diaphragm can also be measured using strain gauges. This type of instrument does not therefore rely on a vertical tube and the wires and air line can be laid in trenches to a suitable reading point. The purpose of the air line is to maintain atmospheric pressure on the non-water side of the diaphragm. These electrical instruments are fairly expensive and cannot measure negative pore pressures. They require calibration at appropriate temperatures and can give misleading results if any gas is present.

In the air-pneumatic piezometer shown in Fig. 11.5 there is the same porous element but there is a thin flexible membrane-type valve instead of the diaphragm. Two air lines are connected to a chamber on the opposite side of the membrane. Air or nitrogen is forced down one air line and when its pressure equals the pore water pressure it forces open the membrane valve and flows up the return line to a flow indicator. The balance pressure can then be read off a Bourdon gauge. Like the acoustic piezometer this type is cheaper than the electric types, is simple, quick to respond and reliable but again will not record negative pore pressures. In the oil-pneumatic piezometer oil is used instead of air or nitrogen.

A hydraulic piezometer is simply a porous element with two tubes connected to it as shown in Fig. 11.5. This type, although cheap and simple, does have a number of problems although negative pore pressures or suctions can be measured. First the porous element must be chosen such as to prevent air entering it. This tends to occur when soils are not fully saturated as in compacted fill materials. The instrument measures pore pressures by measuring the head of water using mercury manometers; a manometer simply being a U-tube filled with mercury. The pore pressure goes to one side of the tube and a constant pressure from a header tank to the other. The imbalance in the mercury in the U-tube indicates the difference in pressure between the header tank and the pore pressure. It is important not to have air in the tubes and since it tends to find its way into the system it is important that de-aired water is circulated around the system before a measurement is taken. This is rather a laborious process but necessary if true pore pressures are to be measured. The system is rather prone to leaks and must be protected against freezing.

Acoustic depth measurement can be used to determine the water level in a standpipe. A transponder clamps to the standpipe and this measures the time for a sound signal to bounce off the water surface. Readings can be taken remotely to ± 1 mm and the system

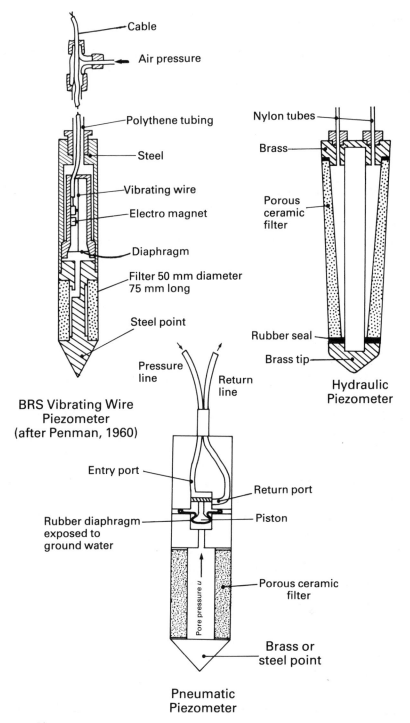

Cable

Air pressure

Polythene tubing

Steel

Vibrating wire

Electro magnet

Diaphragm

Filter 50 mm diameter
75 mm long

Steel point

**BRS Vibrating Wire
Piezometer
(after Penman, 1960)**

Nylon tubes

Brass

Porous
ceramic
filter

Rubber seal

Brass tip

**Hydraulic
Piezometer**

Pressure
line

Return
line

Entry port

Return port

Piston

Rubber diaphragm
exposed to
ground water

Pore pressure *u*

Porous ceramic
filter

Brass or
steel point

**Pneumatic
Piezometer**

Fig. 11.5 Piezometers.

requires no de-airing but obviously negative pore pressures cannot be measured.

The methods of installing piezometers were described in Section 6.12. They can also be pushed into the ground but there is a risk of smearing clay over the porous element which reduces its permeability and therefore its true response time. This can be overcome by driving the piezometer in with a retractable sleeve. In the case of the above remote reading types the tubes or wires can be laid in trenches to a gauge house. They must, however, be laid in a bed of sand and protected from construction traffic, excavators and so on. Hydraulic piezometers can also be used to measure the *in situ* permeability of the ground in which they are placed by carrying out *in situ* falling head or constant head permeability tests as described in Chapter 8. It must be remembered that piezometers can take some time to settle down to a true reading and it is important that they are installed sufficiently in advance of any earthworks for a true base reading to be obtained (see Hannah, 1973).

11.5 Measurement of movement

It is obviously important that no engineering structure moves any further than it can safely do nor should settlement or movement detract from its appearance and function. It may therefore be important to measure settlements, movements or deformations and there are many ways in which this can be done. Some have already been mentioned but there are others.

The simplest technique is to measure movements by precise surveying or levelling and there are many excellent instruments on the market. The instruments can be used in conjunction with carefully installed reference pins or settlement points to determine changes in elevation, position, length or offset from a datum line. These are the sort of measurements that can be easily incorporated into any construction project and a great deal can be learnt from them. Measurements can be made using a steel tape and corrected for sag, tension, temperature and ground slope or they can be established by triangulation using accurate theodolites. Modern electronic instruments for use in distance measurement include infra-red transmitters and lasers.

There are also photogrammetric methods which use precise cameras to take a series of photographs. Measurements can then be taken from the photographs and distances calculated. The system is not particularly accurate but has the advantage that each photograph contains a record of numerous potential movements. Photographs can also be taken over a period of time and compared. The development and expansion of cracks in structures can also be monitored and one instrument uses a tensioned invar wire with a plug-in read out unit.

Where it is necessary to maintain a constant datum from which to measure other settlements it is necessary to ensure that the datum itself does not settle and in this case a steel tube embedded into bedrock and protected by a casing can be used. This is known as a rock benchmark. If the casing is allowed to move with the ground and has a steel plate fixed to it at ground level the settlement of the ground overlying the bedrock can be measured. This can be done with a simple ruler measuring between plate and tube or with a dial gauge if more accuracy is required.

If it is necessary to measure several separate settlements within a soil mass there are various vertical tube settlement gauges available. One example where such a gauge might be used would be in a situation where an embankment was to be built on a layer of peat overlying a layer of clay resting on bedrock and where it was necessary to differentiate between the settlements of the peat, the clay and different layers within the embankment. All the gauges rely on a string of telescoping tubes to which a series of plates are attached. An electronic probe which detects the positions of the plates can be lowered down the tube as shown in Fig. 11.6. A similar system uses spider magnets which are lowered down a borehole and exploded or pneumatically released into the sides as is shown in the lower part of Fig. 11.6. If the tube is surrounded by backfill it must be of an equal stiffness to that of the surrounding ground for accurate results. The important thing is that the tubes telescope in on themselves as the ground compresses and are not restrained by the backfill.

Where it is inconvenient to have tubes extending through an embankment alternative systems must be used. One such system is shown in Fig. 11.7 which is able to give the full profile of settlement beneath an embankment. In this system a measuring torpedo is pulled through a PVC tube. The torpedo can either contain an overflow gauge or a sensitive strain-gauged pressure transducer. The overflow gauge simply relies on pouring water into one end of a roughly U-shaped plastic tube until it overflows at the other end which is the point where the settlement is to be measured. If the input end has a graduated vertical tube attached to it then the water level in it will be the same as the level of the overflow end. In the case of the pressure transducer this is mounted inside a torpedo which is pulled through the tube. The tube is filled with ethylene glycol and the transducer measures the fluid pressure. The higher the pressure the lower is the torpedo.

An automatic settlement plotter is available and this utilizes a loop of small-bore plastic tubing which can be up to 1200 m long. Prior to measurement the tube is filled with water but when measurements are to be made mercury is introduced at one end to form a mercury/water interface. The mercury is then pumped round the loop at a known rate and the settlement deduced from the hydraulic pressure. The higher the pressure the deeper the mercury/water interface. The pressure is plotted automatically with respect to time and if the rate of pumping is known the position of the mercury/water interface can be calculated; the elevation of the interface can be calculated from the hydraulic pressure.

Single-point remote settlement gauges can also be used. One type relies on the overflow principle described above whilst a rather more sophisticated version is shown

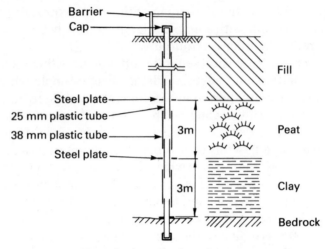

Electrical vertical settlement gauge

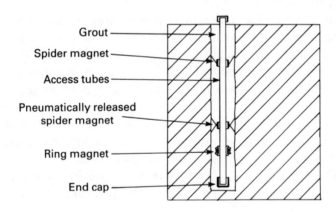

Alternative means of detecting vertical position

Fig. 11.6 Settlement gauges.

in Fig. 11.8. In the normal overflow gauge the reading tube must be at the same level as the measuring point and this can be restrictive if the measuring point is at some depth below ground level. To get over this problem a constant, measured air pressure is applied to the body of the cell, thus enabling the two mercury manometers to be positioned several metres above the measuring point.

Another means of achieving a remote reading is to use a mercury settlement gauge. In this method nitrogen is forced into a closed cell which contains mercury. The

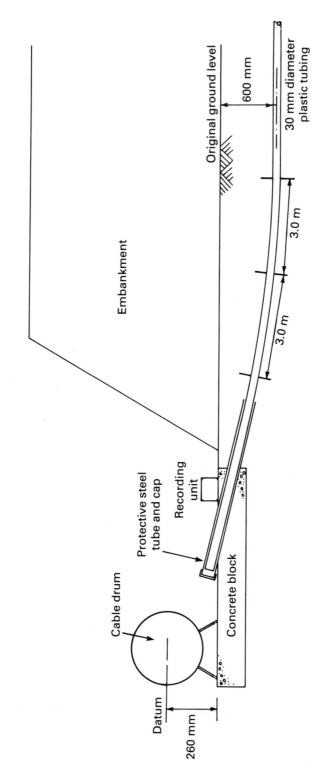

Fig. 11.7 Full profile settlement system.

pressure in the nitrogen is then slowly reduced until the mercury level drops to the bottom of the cell and breaks an electric circuit. The pressure in the nitrogen is then slowly reduced until the mercury flows back and closes the electric circuit. The nitrogen pressure then equals the pressure due to the head of mercury and thus the elevation of the cell can be calculated. The principle of this instrument is also shown in Fig. 11.8. A by-pass diaphragm can be used instead of the electrical circuit. Once the nitrogen pressure equals the mercury pressure a diaphragm opens and there can be no further increase in nitrogen pressure.

Another remote multi-point system uses floats in small water-filled chambers. The floats rise and fall with the water levels and cause movement in displacement transducers (see Fig. 11.2) thus the relative positions of each of the floats within their chambers can be determined.

Horizontal movements can be measured using telescoping tubes as in the vertical settlement gauge. Alternatively a tensioned wire device or extensometer can be used. In this case if the tension of an anchored wire is kept constant, relative movements between the wire and a fixed datum can be measured. This can be used to measure deformations in tunnels and can be used vertically or horizontally.

Horizontal movements can also be calculated if the inclination of a flexible tube is measured at fixed intervals down its length. The principle of these 'inclinometers' is shown in Fig. 11.9. A torpedo with sprung wheels runs down guide slots in the flexible tube and its inclination to the vertical measured at say 0.5 m intervals. Thus the deviation can be calculated as gauge length times the sine of the inclination and it can be determined in two mutually perpendicular directions by rotating the torpedo through 90° between two successive sets of readings. The inclination of the torpedo can be measured using a pendulum moving across a coil as shown in Fig. 11.9 or using a vibrating-wire strain-gauge transducer or more accurately using a pair of servo accelerometers whose electrical output depends on inclination. The backfill around the inclinometer tubing must have a stiffness equal to or higher than that of the surrounding ground for accurate results. The reason is that unless the backfill is stiff the ground might deform without moving the tube.

If it is necessary to simply determine the position of an active failure surface a small diameter plastic tube can be used. If shear were to occur a small torpedo lowered down the tube would hit the kink in the tube thus indicating the level of the shear surface but not the amount of movement.

11.6 Instrumentation in practice

In this, the final section of the chapter, three instrumented engineering works will be described in order to illustrate the practical application of the instruments described in the previous sections. In the first example shown in Fig. 11.10 a flexible steel oil-tank on

276

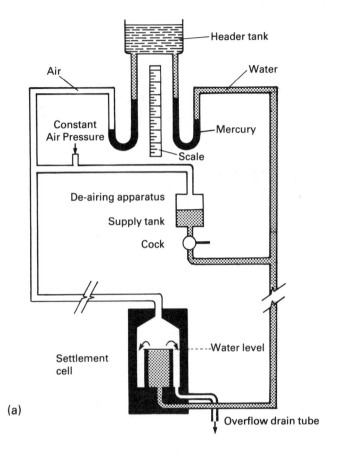

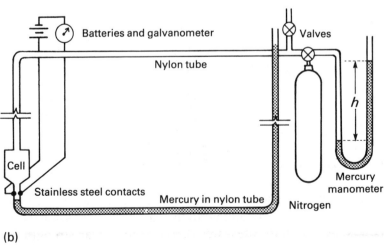

Fig. 11.8 Settlement gauges. (a) Hydraulic settlement gauge. (b) Mercury settlement gauge.

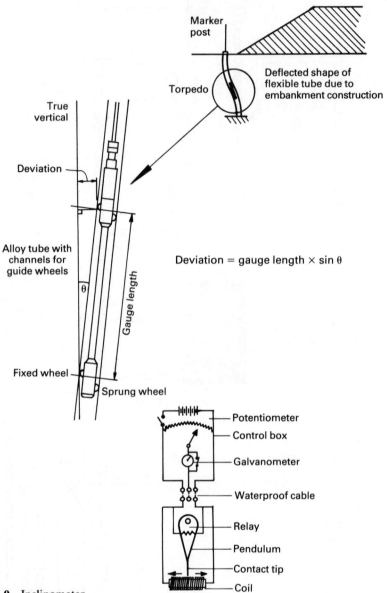

Fig. 11.9 Inclinometer.

soft ground has been instrumented as shown. During test loading as the tank is filled with water, pore pressures will build up in the clay thus decreasing its strength, hence the piezometers. As the pore pressures dissipate the shear strength of the clay will increase and settlement will occur, hence the settlement gauges. There may also be

278

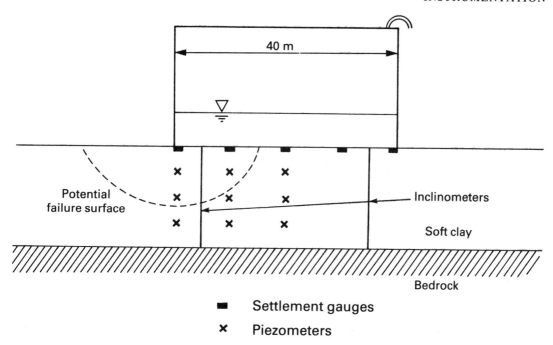

Fig. 11.10 Instrumented oil-tank installation.

some lateral movement of the clay radially outwards from the tank and hence the inclinometers. Thus with the results from the instruments and the results of laboratory tests, the rate of filling can be controlled such that the factor of safety against failure is maintained at an adequate level at all times. Similar instrumentation might be used for an embankment or a dam as it is constructed.

Figure 11.11 shows an instrumented retaining wall. From the readings on the instruments shown the movement of the wall can be checked as can the settlement of the backfill. The distribution of pressures on the back of the wall and beneath its base can also be assessed. The strain gauges in the concrete will give the tensile and compressive stresses in the wall. Information provided from such an installation would lead to a better understanding of the soil/structure interaction and not only would it ensure that the wall itself was safe but might also lead to improved methods of design, by making them safer or more economic or both. To realize how important earth pressures can be in design a number of calculations could be carried out to determine the variation in load on the wall. A saturated soil with no drainage would exert twice the force of that exerted by a dry soil.

Instrumentation suitable for an excavation is shown in Fig. 11.12. The settlement gauges might show whether or not there was any risk to adjacent structures. The strain

279

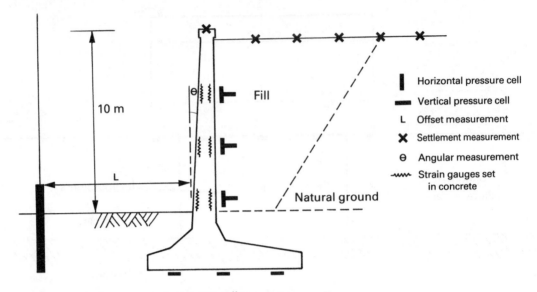

Fig. 11.11 Instrumented retaining wall.

gauges would show the stresses in the sheet piles and the load cells would show the forces in the struts. The piezometers would show the pore water pressures and whether or not there was any risk of piping. The instruments would thus indicate the overall safety of the excavation, the need for more struts or perhaps the need for groundwater lowering. These results might also lead to improved techniques in the future.

A summary of the application of instrumentation to specific geotechnical problems was produced by R. Jardine and Kent County Council in 1981 and this is shown in Table 11.1, which appears on pages 282 and 283. There are many different ways of automatically recording the output signals from instrumentation using chart recorders, paper tape, magnetic tape and so on and they can even be linked to warning lights should movements or pressures reach an unsafe level.

The way in which the results of instrumentation are to be used should be considered carefully. In some applications it is worth drawing up simple charts so that the results can be interpreted quickly. One example might be a graph relating pore pressure and height of fill to the factor of safety.

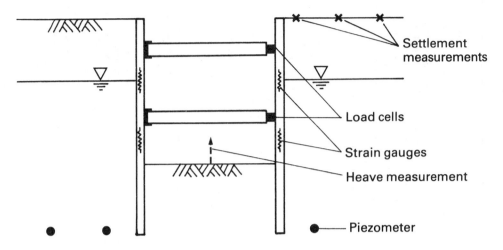

Fig. 11.12 Instrumented excavation.

Table 11.1 Application of instrumentation to geotechnical problems. (After Jardine, 1981).

Geotechnical problem	Reliability of predictions based on routine investigations	Monitoring gauge type	Accuracy of measurement	Problems in use	Comments
Vertical movements					
Long- and short-term settlement of structures and earth works on sands, stiff clays and soft rocks, also short term settlement of earth works on soft clays	Generally poor	(1) Survey targets (2) Hydraulic overflow gauges (3) Hydraulic profile gauges (4) Magnetic settlement devices	All around 1–2 mm	(1) Can be damaged on site (2) Require remote reading station, can be damaged by freezing (3) Can jam in use, expensive equipment (4) Must be connected up with flexible tubing to avoid jamming, with soft grout backfill	Relatively straight forward, can show patterns and rates of movements. Gives parameters for future designs, but can be difficult to use in predicting failure except in controlled situations such as pile tests
Long-term settlement of structures and earth works on soft clays	Generally good	As above	As above	As above	Can be difficult to judge when settlement will be over, but of use in evaluating stability of stage construction
Horizontal movements					
Long- and short-term behaviour of slopes, cuttings and embankments	Generally poor	(1) Survey points (2) Inclinometers	As above	Inclinometer equipment is expensive and often unreliable. Boreholes must be grouted to suit particular situation, liable to damage on site	Horizontal displacement data can be very useful in determining patterns of movement. Can be difficult to use in predicting failures except in controlled situations
Use in piles, retaining walls, etc.	Generally poor	(1) As above, also electronic levels and electrical/displacement transducers	Can be better than 0.1 mm	Requires special design for each case – can be time consuming and expensive	Of great use in soil/structure interaction problems as checks on design
Stresses/Loads					
Stresses within a mass of fill (e.g. a large embankment dam)	Good to fair within homogeneous fill, more difficult with zoning, layering etc.	(1) Diaphragm gauges	Fair to poor, vibrating wire more accurate and stable than other types. Depends on installation	To obtain the two-dimensional state of stress a rosette of five gauges is required	The state of stress varies a throughout the mass and it is very expensive to monitor more than a few particular points. Details of installation very important 'Closure' pressure gives a value of minor principal effective stress in homogeneous clay and a value nearer to intermediate principal effective stress in rolled fills. Of use in dam construction
		(2) Hydraulic fracture tests	Uncertain in layered fills	Easy to perform on hydraulic piezometers, inexpensive equipment	

Application	Accuracy within foundations	Instrument	Response/accuracy	Installation notes	Remarks
Stresses within a foundation (soft clay)	Good to fair within homogeneous foundations	(1) Thin push in diaphragm gauge (pneumatic transducer)	Good to very poor	Calibration can change massively during installation through peat or similar firm layer	Measures total horizontal normal stress only. Can be used to obtain at-rest earth pressure but calibration should be checked after use
Stresses within a foundation (soft clay)	Good to fair within homogeneous foundations	(2) Hydraulic fracture tests	Fair to good	As (2) above	'Closure' pressure gives minor principle effective stress in homogeneous clay
Stresses within a foundation (stiff clay)	Good to fair within homogeneous foundations	(1) Hydraulic fracture tests	?	Fracture may not be achieved and fissures may confuse results	Not certain which stress is being measured
Stesses within a fill or foundation – soft or stiff clay	Good to fair within homogeneous soils	Pressure meter (self boring or Menard type)	Good to fair	Pressure meter is cylindrical and only strictly applicable where horizontal stress is equal in all directions with no vertical shear stress	Various theories of interpretation can be used, operation is expensive and time consuming
Soil/structure contact pressures	Good to poor depending on particular situation	Diaphragm gauge	Fair if care is taken on installation, vibrating wire types are most reliable	Can be affected by temperature effects with concrete cooling etc.	Strictly only valid for 'flat' distributions of purely axial stress.

Measurement of Pore Water Pressures

Application	Accuracy	Instrument	Response/accuracy	Installation notes	Remarks
Establishing the ground water regime in a site investigation	Not applicable	Casagrande piezometer	Good	Must be installed carefully time for equalization depends on soil type and can be up to 2 months for some clays.	Inexpensive and reliable. Can be used for *in situ* permeability testing
Monitoring changes in pore water pressure due to construction, tides, weather etc. for sands or silts	Fair to poor	Casagrande piezometer	As above	As above	As above
As above for clays	Good to poor	(1) Pneumatic piezometer	Good (approx. 2kN m^{-2}) resolution — Rapid response	Must be installed carefully with correct grout and saturated tip — Can give major problems in gassy soils	Instrument cannot be de-aired – hence long-term problems in partially saturated or peaty clays. Cannot be used for permeability or hydraulic fracture tests
		(2) Electrical piezometer	Vibrating wire gauges very good, resistive gauges good to fair. Very rapid response	As above	As above, also problems with voltage loss in leads and calibration drift for resistive gauges
		(3) Hydraulic peizometer	Very good fairly rapid response (approx. 0.2 kN m^{-2} resolution)	Transducer read outs can give poor response times and equalization read-out stations must be heated in winter	Piezometers can be de-aired, and used for hydraulic fracture and permeability tests. Manometer units are robust, but special care is required for transducer read-outs

12

Other investigation methods and geophysics

12.1 Introduction

Pile load tests, plate bearing tests, *in situ* shear tests and field trials are all other investigation methods with the potential to provide information which would be difficult if not impossible to obtain in any other way. Whether or not they are used on any particular site will bring into play questions such as the amount and adequacy of information already acquired, finance available, the importance of additional information, how critical the design is and so on. The geotechnical engineer should therefore make his recommendations on the need for such tests in a rational manner.

The variability in the nature and structure of soils has been stressed many times throughout this book together with the importance of carrying out representative sampling and testing. Certain *in situ* tests were described in Chapter 8 and whilst some of these may well be better than sampling and laboratory testing they still suffer from scale effects. One way of ensuring that the ground is stressed in as realistic a way as possible is to carry out large-scale field tests or field trials since these will most nearly simulate the behaviour of the proposed works without the problems of representativeness or the effects of disturbance. The tests described above are approaching the scale of the works and if say a trial embankment were considered it should be clear that it would stress a considerable volume of soil complete with many of its variations in lithology and structure. These are described in Sections 12.2–12.5 and often tend to come after the main ground investigation. They are relatively expensive but there is no reason why they should not be an integral part of the main ground investigation where they can be justified.

Geophysical techniques as described in Sections 12.6–12.9 are investigation tools in their own right and their possible use should be carefully considered at any stage of the investigation. However, they are not foolproof and in some cases will produce no useful information whatsoever but in the right conditions, and the word right must be stressed, they can provide a great deal of useful information very cheaply and very quickly. The geophysical techniques described in this chapter were originally developed in the exploration for oil and minerals where it was usually the large scale, deep geology that was being investigated. In the civil engineering situation the materials of interest are generally at much shallower depths and tend to be more variable because of the effects of weathering, water tables, recent deposits and so on. This does not mean that geophysical techniques cannot be used but it does mean that they must be used with care and with consideration of their potential advantages and limitations.

Geophysical techniques essentially rely on different materials exhibiting different properties and can only cope with relatively simple sequences of strata. Many engineers are sceptical of the use of geophysics since they are aware of instances where geophysics has failed to provide the answers required of it. Some of these failures are due to the fact that the geological or site conditions were simply not recognized as being unsuitable for the use of geophysics but others are due to poor specification, use of the wrong techniques, inexperienced staff and poor interpretation. These two latter points are particularly important since considerable skill and experience are required to carry out, analyse and interpret the results of a geophysical survey and if the engineer does not possess that skill he should be prepared to bring in a specialist who does. As is the case with all site investigation techniques – in the wrong hands the techniques are useless but with the correct use they can produce great benefits in terms of safe, economic design. In fact geophysics can sometimes be used to test the geotechnical engineer's hypotheses regarding ground conditions. For instance he may assume certain strata are continuous between two boreholes and use geophysical methods to check that this is true and that the methods do not reveal any anomalies. An integrated approach using boring, *in situ* testing and geophysics can often pay dividends.

12.2 Pile load tests

Pile tests are all too often regarded as part of the construction process itself where one or two piles are selected for testing. This is desirable from the point of view of making sure the piles are sound but when a test pile fails there can often be high costs and delays in redesigning the pile system or lengthening the piles. On multi-million pound projects with large numbers of piles it makes much more sense to carry out pile load tests prior to construction, since at this stage action can be taken without disrupting the works and the works themselves can be more precisely designed. Pile tests during the investigation will give information on the best type of pile to use, installation problems, lengths, working loads and settlements.

The piles that are to be tested should be of a similar type to those proposed for the works themselves and should be installed to the depth determined by conventional design. Working loads and settlements can then be checked. Full records should be kept during the installation and testing of each pile and these should include details of the piles themselves, dates, reinforcement and concrete used, driving records, lengths, position, ground heave, constructional problems and test method. The driving record should contain tabulated entries of time, depth, number of blows for each 500 mm to start with and reducing to 100 mm and 25 mm as founding level is approached. The performance of the equipment used should also be described. It is also useful if the temporary compression is recorded with each hammer blow as the pile is near its set. This can be done by sticking a sheet of graph paper to the pile and erecting a smooth board across, and just in front of, the pile. By resting a pencil on the board so that it just touches the graph paper a small graph will be produced showing the permanent 'set' in millimetres per blow and the temporary deformation of the pile with each hammer blow.

It is good practice to study the behaviour of the pile after stopping driving for a few hours and then re-starting since this may well occur during construction and it is worth knowing what to expect. The validity of dynamic formulae used in predicting ultimate resistance should also be checked. Some materials will show evidence of softening after re-starting whereas others will tend to tighten up on the pile.

For bored piles the records should include a log of the strata penetrated, ingress of water, foundation level and any other relevant data.

The arrangement of the pile load test itself is shown in Fig. 12.1. The illustration shows the use of kentledge as a means of providing the dead load but a frame fastened to three or four screw piles could equally well be used providing the anchor piles are at a reasonable distance from the pile itself. The important things to record during the test are load, settlement (which includes elastic deformation of the pile itself) and time but the test itself can be performed in two ways. The most common method, known as the maintained load test, is to increase the load in fixed increments up to say one-and-a-half times the working load and to record settlement with respect to time after each increment. When the rate of settlement is less than say 0.25 mm h^{-1} the next increment can be added. The load should be recorded to an accuracy of $\pm 2\%$ and the settlement to the nearest 0.10 mm. If a hydraulic jack is used continuous slight pumping may be needed to maintain a constant load. Once the working load has been reached this should be maintained for a period of 12 h to observe the settlement and the test load might be maintained for 48 h. Once this period is complete the load can then be removed in the same increments and recovery noted. The pile could then be loaded to failure as described below. Alternatively the load can be removed after application of the working load to check that the soil is behaving elastically before progressing to the full test load and this method is to be preferred. It should be remembered that the

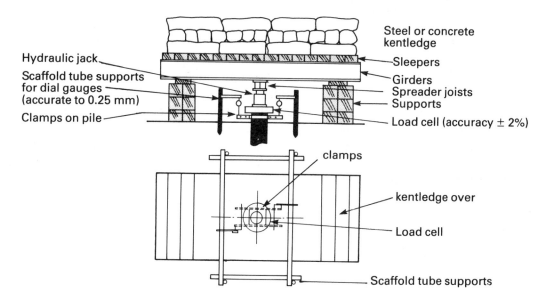

Hydraulic jack

Scaffold tube supports
for dial gauges
(accurate to 0.25 mm)

Clamps on pile

Steel or concrete
kentledge

Sleepers

Girders

Spreader joists

Supports

Load cell (accuracy ± 2%)

clamps

kentledge over

Load cell

Scaffold tube supports

Screw piles can be used as an alternative to kentledge and
settlement can be measured using displacement transducers,
optical instruments or stretched wire (after Tomlinson)

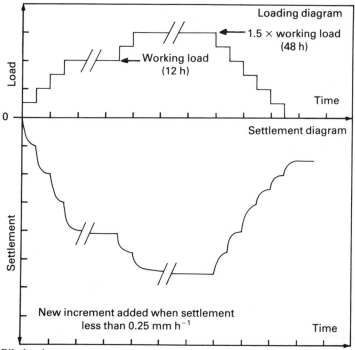

Loading diagram

Load

1.5 × working load
(48 h)

Working load
(12 h)

Time

0

Settlement diagram

Settlement

New increment added when settlement
less than 0.25 mm h^{-1}

Time

Fig. 12.1   Pile load test.

settlement of a group of piles may well be more than that of a single pile.

The other type of pile load test is the constant rate of penetration test where the pile is steadily jacked into the ground at a constant rate of downward movement of somewhere in the region of 0.1–0.2 mm per minute until failure occurs. Failure is defined either as the load at which the pile continues to penetrate with no further increase in load or the point where the load has produced a settlement of one-tenth of the pile diameter. This test is much quicker but does not give as much information as the previous one nor does it indicate how much elastic settlement has occurred. It can also require much more kentledge or anchorage.

As well as testing piles in compression they can also be jacked out of the ground in order to assess tensile loads and skin friction. This can also be applied to ground anchors in soil and rock. Further details of pile testing are given in *Code of Practice* BS2004: 1972 and CIRIA report P67.

12.3   Plate bearing tests

The main advantage of plate bearing tests is that there are no problems with soil disturbance since all that is involved is the measurement of settlement of a loaded plate. In addition a relatively large, and therefore representative, volume of soil is put under test. Plate bearing tests can come in all shapes and sizes from the simple jack up test under the back of a lorry as described in Section 5.3 to much larger tests involving kentledge or anchor piles. The principle, however, remains the same, that is of measuring settlement against load.

Load can either be added incrementally or a constant rate of penetration test can be carried out. Tests can even be carried out in conjunction with multi-point settlement gauges as described in Section 11.5 to indicate the amount of settlement of different layers. The tests can give extremely useful information on shear strength, settlement and modulus of a soil.

Plate bearing tests in boreholes or shafts present a problem of transmitting the load to the bottom of the borehole. This can be done with a steel column, jacks and kentledge or it can be done using an arrangement similar to that shown in Fig. 12.2. In this case it is the friction of a column of concrete that provides the reaction force. The procedure is to drill a borehole preferably 300 mm in diameter, clean out the bottom and lower down a steel plate of marginally smaller diameter. This plate has a steel rod or tube attached to it which extends to ground level. A doughnut shaped rubber pressure bag with a connecting pressure line is then placed over this rod to rest on the plate. A plastic debonding tube is placed over the central rod and the borehole backfilled with high-slump concrete. After a suitable curing period a datum beam can be set up and the pressure bag inflated using a hydraulic pump. By measuring the pressure the load on the plate can be calculated and of course the settlement is recorded. It is essential to check that there is no rise in the concrete backfilling since if there was it would negate the test.

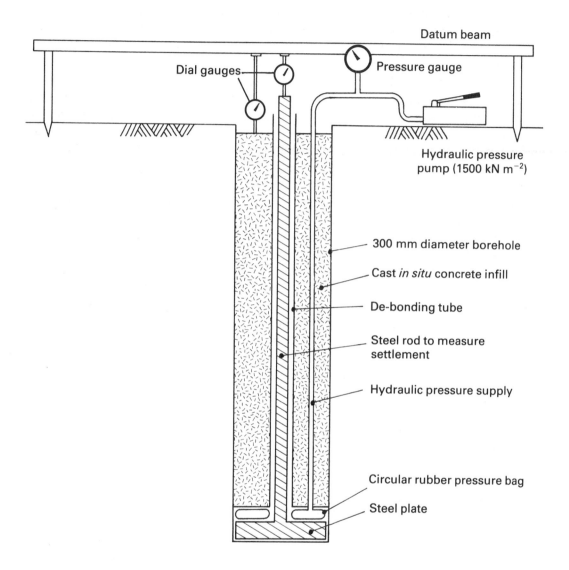

Datum beam

Dial gauges

Pressure gauge

Hydraulic pressure pump (1500 kN m^{-2})

300 mm diameter borehole

Cast *in situ* concrete infill

De-bonding tube

Steel rod to measure settlement

Hydraulic pressure supply

Circular rubber pressure bag

Steel plate

In order to determine Young's Modulus use formula shown in Figure 5.9 multiplied by depth factor (see Burland, 1969)

Fig. 12.2   Borehole plate-bearing test.

This test gives useful information on the load/deformation behaviour of deep foundations and in some cases it may be possible to take the load up to failure.

It should be remembered in all plate bearing tests that it is only the ground to a depth of about one-and-a-half plate diameters that is being stressed to any extent and care must be taken if the results are to be used to extrapolate for the behaviour of a large-scale foundation. If for instance a small-scale test were carried out on a stiff layer which was underlaid by a softer one, the test would bear no relation to the performance of a large-scale footing. To get over this sort of problem and to ensure that a representative amount of ground is stressed large-diameter plates can be used but of course the reaction forces required rise accordingly and they can become very expensive.

One simple but quite effective method involves loading a lorry-mounted metal waste skip which has a contact area of about 1.8 m by 1.8 m and is therefore stressing the ground to a depth of about 2.7 m. Settlement of the skip is measured by periodic levelling against a fixed bench mark. The method was developed for assessing settlement characteristics on refuse and waste disposal tips where settlement can be substantial and can carry on for a long time but it could equally well be used on other compressible materials. About 30 kN m^{-2} can be generated by filling the skip with sand but this could go up to 120 kN m^{-2} if steel were used. These loadings are relatively modest and are unlikely to indicate the failure load but the settlement/time graph obtained can be very useful. With this and with all plate loading tests the strata beneath the plate must be known if the results are to be interpreted sensibly.

Many different situations can be simulated by plate bearing tests and one in particular is a study of the effect of vibrations on foundations as might occur under a machine base. Most soils behave differently under static and dynamic loads and if it is a dynamic or vibratory situation that will arise in the works it may be advisable to study this effect by applying oscillating or cyclic loads to the plate. This can be done using hydraulic systems and recording the dynamic response of the soil. In some situations it is necessary to know what extent the soil beneath the footing will transmit vibrations and in this case recorders can be placed at various points radially outwards from the plate.

Plate bearing tests can also be carried out by jacking horizontally across a trench and although the results are not directly comparable to vertical ones strength and elasticity data can be obtained. For further discussion on plate bearing tests see BS5930 pages 59–63.

12.4 *In situ* shear tests

In order to measure the shear strength of soils or rocks directly in the field a cut block of soil or rock can be loaded horizontally as is shown in Fig. 12.3. This is very similar to the shear box test described in Section 10.3. The normal load has to be provided by ground anchors or kentledge but the horizontal reaction can be provided by jacking off the side

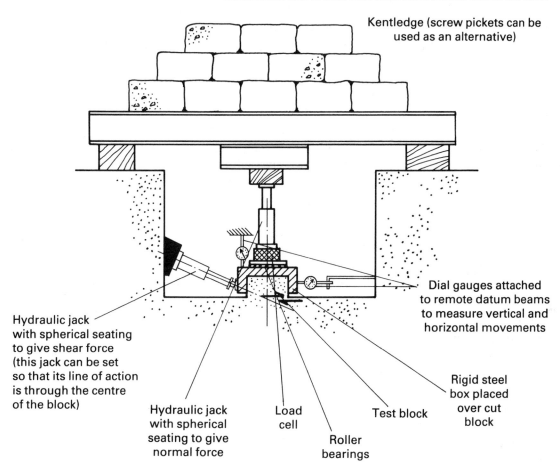

Fig. 12.3 *In situ* shear test.

of a trench. Once again it is important to measure deformation and a datum beam with its feet some distance from the block under test is needed. If the block is not loaded to failure and the shear deformations are not too great it is possible to measure shear strength at different normal loads and hence obtain a graph similar to that shown in Fig. 10.9. This does not give the failure envelope since the soil has not been loaded to failure but it does give values of c and ϕ; albeit that they are slightly conservative. Alternatively a number of separate tests can be carried out to failure at different normal loads in which case the true c and ϕ values can be determined.

If the soil is sheared slowly the test is essentially a drained one and the effective strength parameters c' and ϕ' will be obtained. One of the major advantages of this sort of test is that virtually undisturbed soil is being stressed providing the test block has

291

been cut carefully. The test block itself is normally about 1 m square and with many soils the chances are that this will be fairly representative of the soil mass as a whole but with jointed, fissured or bedded rocks this may not be true and care is needed to select an appropriate block. Even when a representative block is chosen the strength characteristics obtained will tend to be optimistic of the strength of the rock mass in its entirety unless shear takes place directly along a weak bedding plane. However, this effect will not be as marked as when a small sample of rock is tested in the laboratory. The amount of hand preparation necessary for a test such as has been discussed makes the procedure an expensive one but it does give valid results.

12.5 Field trials

A field trial is essentially a full-scale test where a part of the proposed works is built, instrumented and loaded. If necessary, loading can be taken up to failure. This might be done with say one column base out of twenty, a section of embankment, a length of tunnel, or a soakaway. With uniform ground conditions this procedure, although possibly expensive, can be extremely useful since all the problems of sample disturbance and representativeness disappear. However, the site of the trial must be chosen after careful examination of existing site investigation information because it is only by this means that the trial itself and its associated instrumentation can be planned.

As stated the chosen trial is normally a part of the proposed works and as such the first design and therefore that of the trial will be based on the normal ground investigation with modification to the design following at a later stage should the trial show it to be necessary. Instrumentation was covered in the previous chapter but it is worth repeating that the type and position of instruments must be chosen so as to give the information that is needed. Consideration should also be given to the time intervals at which the instruments are read. Information is normally required on movements, earth and pore water pressures and settlements. The instruments should also enable the form of failure to be defined if loading is taken to failure. In the case of slip circles the pore water pressures on the failure surface need to be known for detailed analysis. It is no use installing instruments which give irrelevant information and missing out those which truly show how the works are performing and how they are affecting the natural ground.

The precise construction method and timing must be recorded, for instance with a trial embankment the rate of construction must be known, as should the field density of the fill used. If the trial is not full scale then scale effects will have to be considered before the results are used. It is normal to try and choose a worst-case condition for the trial itself although there are times when this might not be easily recognizable. Before the results of the field trial are extended to cover similar works elsewhere a careful check is needed to ensure that the ground conditions are similar and that the extrapolation is valid. The use of a field trial should enable the preliminary design to be further sophisticated and hopefully made either safer or more economic. It should also give valuable information on the way the actual works will perform and help answer questions relating to the amount and time of settlement, ground stability, ground movements, rates of filling and so on. Where a field trial has been taken to failure it may be possible to use 'back analysis' in order to derive values of soil properties which can then be used in design. This process can also be used with natural phenomena such as landslides.

12.6 Resistivity surveys

For resistivity surveys to provide useful information they rely on different materials having different resistances to the flow of electric current. Rubber has a high resistance, iron has a low one, pure water is somewhere in between but salt water has a relatively low resistance. Just as these variations occur in the common materials described above there are variations from one soil type to another. However, one soil type will exhibit different resistivities depending on its degree of saturation and two totally different soils may possess virtually the same resistance. Thus there is room for ambiguity and as with any geophysical technique some accompanying borehole data is required if interpretation is to be made. There are however, many possible sequences of strata which simply cannot be interpreted to the necessary degree of accuracy by the use of geophysics and these should be recognized before time and money is wasted on a survey. On the other hand there are situations where geophysics can provide a great deal of useful information very quickly and very cheaply.

The Wenner resistivity survey technique is illustrated in the upper part of Fig. 12.4. Basically four copper-plated steel electrodes are driven into the ground at a suitable spacing. A direct, or more commonly a low-frequency alternating, current is then applied to the two outer electrodes and the potential difference between the inner two is measured on a voltmeter. From these results the apparent resistivity of the ground can be calculated in ohm metres from the equation $\rho_a = 2\pi d\, \Delta V/I$ where ρ_a is the apparent resistivity, d the electrode spacing in the Wenner configuration, ΔV the potential difference and I the current. The apparent resistivity reflects all the strata through which the current flows and depends on the resistivity of the materials themselves and their thicknesses. Figure 12.4 shows three alternative electrode arrangements but these require the use of different formulae to calculate apparent resistivity and are not as much used as the Wenner array.

Figure 12.5 shows the ranges of values that are likely to be obtained for different soils and rocks. A large part of the differences can be accounted for by differences in the quantity and salinity of the pore water and it can be seen that knowledge of a soil's resistivity does not enable an unambiguous decision to be made as to its type. It should

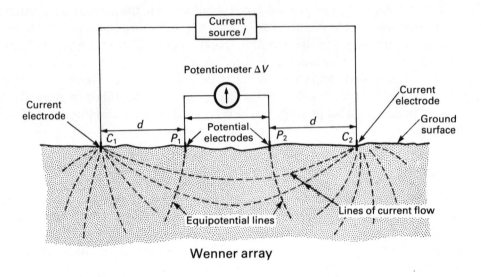

Wenner array

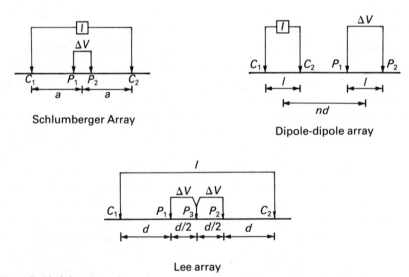

Schlumberger Array

Dipole-dipole array

Lee array

Fig. 12.4 Resistivity surveys.

be remembered that resistivity might vary from month to month due to changes in moisture content.

If a small number of near horizontal layers are to be investigated in depth the centre point of the Wenner array is kept constant and the electrode spacing d is increased thus

294

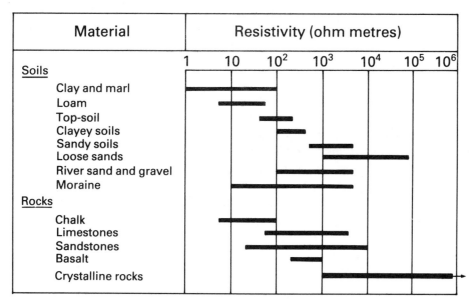

Fig. 12.5 Approximate ranges of resistivity of soils and rocks (after Abem, 1971).

forcing the current flow deeper and measurements are taken at each of these different spacings. This is known as vertical profiling or electrical sounding and a graph is obtained of depth or electrode spacing against apparent resistivity. The ground succession is then interpreted by comparing the curve with a great number of theoretical standard curves until a match is found. This is obviously open to ambiguity and depth to boundaries will only be to within ±20% and even then it is only boundaries where there is a reasonable difference in resistivity that will be revealed. The upper part of Fig. 12.6 shows three examples. In the first situation there is homogeneous ground to a considerable depth and the same resistivity will be obtained irrespective of electrode spacing. In the second situation there are two layers with the upper layer having a true resistivity of four times that of the lower layer. As can be seen the plot of apparent resistivity (dotted line) that will be obtained from a survey is not precise. The third illustration shows a three-layer case of low–high–low resistivity and again an indistinct curve is obtained which would have to be matched with the theoretical curves to arrive at any sort of interpretation and even then it would not be very accurate. The technique will not detect thin layers at depth and there is the problem of equivalence in that thick layers of low resistivity can give similar curves to thin layers of high resistivity. There are additional problems with dipping strata and natural electrical currents in the ground.

If the ground varies horizontally, say from side to side of a suspected fault, this could be investigated using a horizontal probing technique. In this case the whole array of electrodes is moved bodily from station to station along a straight line crossing the feature to be investigated and keeping the electrode spacing constant. In this case a graph similar to that shown in the lower part of Fig. 12.6 might be obtained. This shows material to the right of the fault (or other feature) having a resistivity five times that of the material on the right.

A recent development in geophysics which is similar to resistivity surveying is terrain conductivity measurement. This uses a hand-held 4 m-long boom which contains the equivalent of a Wenner electrode spread but uses transmitters and receivers instead of cables and electrodes. In this case the induced current flow is measured. The instrument can be used on a grid in much the same way as a resistivity survey or it can be carried over the ground in a search for anomalies.

It should be remembered with resistivity surveys that quite subtle measurements are being made and that high-voltage cables, gas mains and other metal pipes can render a survey useless. To sum up, the techniques can be used for simple geological situations where there is a good contrast in electrical resistivity between a small number of layers but requires some skill to interpret the results correctly.

12.7 Seismic surveys

Seismic techniques fall into two categories, seismic refraction and seismic reflection. The former is the one most commonly used in site investigation but both depend on there being a difference in the speed with which shock waves travel through different kinds of soil and rock. Some of the differences in these velocities are shown in Fig. 12.7 where it can be seen that waves travel faster through rock than they do through soil. Changes in velocity also occur if there are different degrees of weathering.

The basic refraction method is shown in Fig. 12.8 where a shock wave, from either a hammer blow, a dropped weight or a small explosive charge, is generated on the left of the diagram. This shock wave travels through the strata shown in three different ways to a series of geophones which measure the time taken for the wave to travel from the source to the point in question. The wave can either travel directly just below the surface to the geophones (route A–A) or it can be reflected back to the surface from the lower layer (route B–B) where it may or may not be detected by a geophone (in the case shown in would not be). On the third route (C–C) the wave travels down to the lower layer and then travels along just below the top of it. As it does so it is continually transmitting waves back to the surface where they can be picked up by the geophones. Now if the velocity in the lower layer is higher than that in the upper layer (which it has to be for the method to work) then it is possible for the wave travelling along route C–C to arrive at a geophone before the A–A wave. If the times of arrival of the waves are plotted relative to their position as shown in the upper part of Fig. 12.9 a graph of first arrivals (solid line) will show a distinct kink. From the position of this kink the depth to

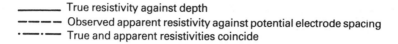

True resistivity against depth
Observed apparent resistivity against potential electrode spacing
True and apparent resistivities coincide

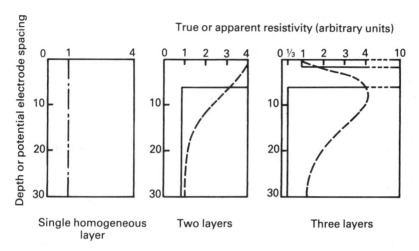

True or apparent resistivity (arbitrary units)

Single homogeneous layer

Two layers

Three layers

Vertical Profiling

True resistivity
Observed apparent resistivity

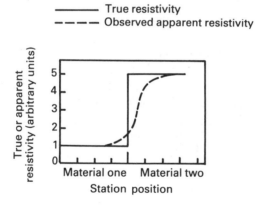

True or apparent resistivity (arbitrary units)

Material one   Material two
Station position

Horizontal Profiling

Fig. 12.6 Interpretation of resistivity surveys with variation of apparent resistivity with depth or horizontal position (after Griffiths and King, 1965).

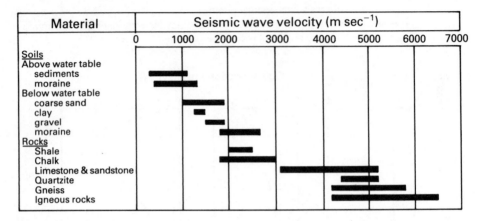

Fig. 12.7 Approximate ranges of seismic wave velocity of soils and rocks (after Abem).

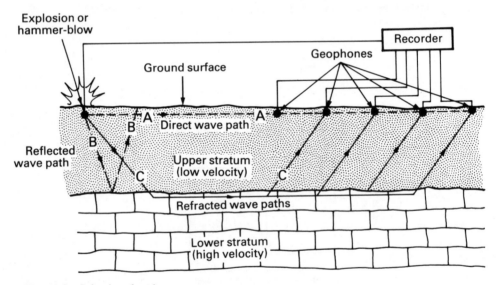

Fig. 12.8 Seismic refraction survey.

the lower stratum can be calculated using the equation shown. If the geophones are connected up to a chart recorder which has a series of pens oscillating in sympathy with the shock waves then a result similar to that shown in the lower part of Fig. 12.9 will be obtained. If the paper is run through at a known speed the times of arrivals can be calculated. An alternative is to display the oscillations on a cathode ray tube and photograph it.

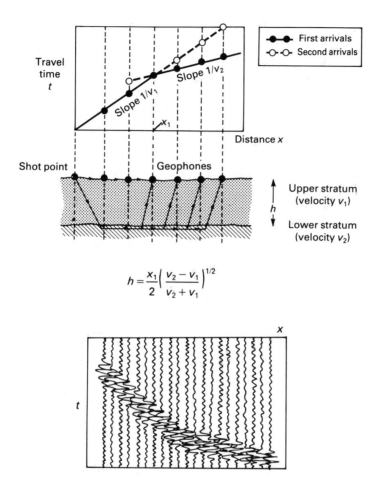

$$h = \frac{x_1}{2}\left(\frac{v_2 - v_1}{v_2 + v_1}\right)^{1/2}$$

Simplified recorder chart

Fig. 12.9 Interpretation of seismic refraction survey (after West and Dumbleton).

Since the wave forms can be weak there are instruments available which automatically add up the results of several hammer blows to give a clearer picture. This is known as signal enhancement. It is possible to extend this method to three layers providing each layer is reasonably thick and has a successively higher velocity but beyond this interpretation is very difficult. Remember that soil above and below the water table will have different velocities and a water table essentially introduces another layer into the problem.

Geophones are very sensitive instruments and any background noise due to traffic or machinery will effectively mask the results. Under ideal conditions the method will give strata changes accurate to about ±0.75 m and is most useful in detecting the thickness of overburden or the depth to bedrock. It is not much use for interpreting strata in the top 1.5–3.0 m.

Knowledge of seismic velocity in a soil or rock can give an indication of its modulus of elasticity and charts are available relating velocity to rippability, ease of tunnelling and so on. New techniques for seismic surveys are being developed which use vibrating energy sources.

For the exploration of sites under water the energy source can be the discharge of an electric spark under water which produces rapidly expanding bubbles and this is known as a sparker survey. Other energy sources known as boomers, which involve a magnetically repelled metal plate, and pingers are also used under water. It is not necessary to have several geophones since one geophone can be used at a series of different positions but this makes the survey rather time consuming. Once again borehole control data is necessary if the results are to be interpreted sensibly since a low velocity layer at depth will confuse the results. To sum up there are, as with all geophysical methods, many limitations to the successful use of the method but it is quick, cheap and informative in the right situation.

In the reflection method it is the timing of the B–B wave that is measured. The time of the first arrivals represent the time taken for the wave to travel down to the higher velocity layer and bounce back. Thus the depth to the layer can be calculated but this is about all that can be sensibly interpreted from the results. There are a number of other less-used techniques available and the reader is advised to read Griffiths and King, 1965.

12.8   Borehole logging

The geophysical techniques so far described have been concerned with detecting changes in strata across a site and must be used in conjunction with boreholes. However, there are a whole range of techniques which can be used down a single borehole in order to reveal additional information on the strata present.

One technique is shown in Fig. 12.10 which is a sonic probe containing a transmitter and a receiver. Various measurements are taken of the velocity of sound through the rock surrounding the borehole. Variations in velocity may indicate changes in strata and a knowledge of the velocity of sound waves can indicate certain rock qualities.

Devices similar to the sonic probe can measure changes in resistivity, gravity, temperature and natural radioactivity. The absorption of radioactive rays from an artificial source can give an indication of density, porosity and moisture content. Multiparameter probes are available which incorporate some or all of the above techniques.

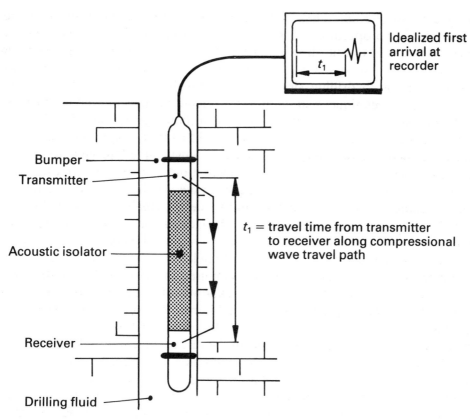

Fig. 12.10 Borehole velocity logging device.

Measurements need not only be taken in a single borehole but the transmitter can be inserted in one borehole and the receiver in another thus giving a possible indication of rock properties between boreholes. This technique is known as crosshole shooting. It is also possible to use the transmitter down the hole and the receiver at ground level. An unexpected change might indicate a cavity or other anomaly. Correlation of strata between boreholes can also be assisted using these techniques.

It can sometimes be useful to use the cores taken from boreholes to measure their geophysical properties in order that these results can be used in other geophysical surveys. Television cameras can also be lowered down boreholes to inspect the strata. This and other techniques were briefly described in Section 7.10.

12.9 Other geophysical techniques

There are a number of other less-used geophysical techniques which can sometimes provide useful information. These essentially involve the detection of anomalies in various geophysical properties. It is perhaps easiest to appreciate these techniques by reference to Fig. 12.11. The drawing shows the variation in signal received as an antenna is traversed across a buried electric cable. Such a survey is obviously recommended prior to drilling since boring through a high voltage cable can be disastrous. Similar techniques can be used for telephone lines but metal pipes can be detected more easily if a signal is attached to them. Plotting the lines of sewers, plastic pipes, earthenware pipes and so on can be difficult if not impossible unless a transmitting torpedo is inserted into the pipe and slowly pulled through it.

If extremely accurate instruments are used variations or anomalies may be detected in natural properties if measurements are taken on a grid basis. A gravimeter can be used in association with precision levelling to detect small changes in the earth's gravitational field and these may indicate changes in rock type. This method has sometimes been able to detect cavities, shafts and buried objects.

Alternatively changes in the earth's magnetic field can be measured using a sensitive magnetometer and this too has sometimes been used to detect shafts, cavities and ore bodies. A recent development on similar lines known as fluxgate gradiometry measures the vertical gradient of the earth's magnetic field; in other words its rate of change with depth. This has been used to detect mineshafts. Another form of electro-magnetic surveying involves comparing the intensity of the vertical magnetic field with that in the horizontal direction at a number of positions and then looking for anomalies.

Changes in the electrical self potential of the ground may indicate differences in geochemical activity, cables or mineworkings. Changes can also be detected in natural radioactivity or in the response to an artificial source of radioactivity. Even a ground-probing radar has been developed which essentially gives a subsurface profile of the back scatter from electro-magnetic transmissions. This technique can sometimes reveal cavities, voids, cables or approximate geological profiles. It is sometimes known as electro-magnetic subsurface profiling. In the marine environment echo sounding and side-scan sonar are frequently employed to assess the underwater geology, the latter giving a topographic type map of the seabed.

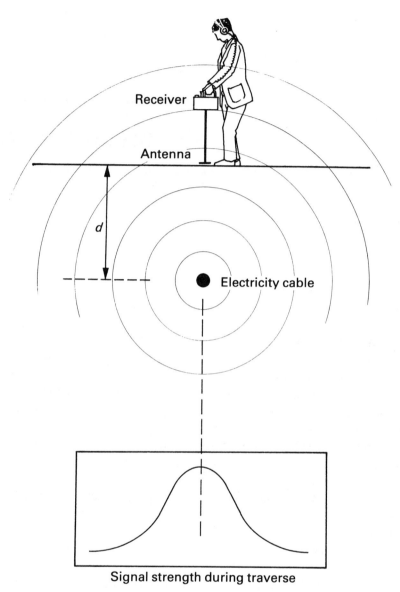

Receiver

Antenna

d

Electricity cable

Signal strength during traverse

Fig. 12.11 Detection of underground services.

13

Site investigation reports

13.1 Introduction

The importance of the engineering report dealing with a site investigation cannot be overemphasized. It is often the only record of what may have been a long, complex and expensive investigation and as such it must contain all the relevant information that has been gained. It must contain this information in a clear, concise fashion and it may also give an interpretation of the results obtained together with recommendations for the design and construction of the works themselves.

The interpretation of the ground conditions and the test results followed by the formulation of the recommendations may be done by the organization that carried out the fieldwork or it may be done by an independent consulting engineer who may also have carried out the preliminary desk study and planned the field work. Site investigation is a specialist field of civil engineering and it should be carried out by experienced specialists.

The site investigation process requires continual decision making. Decisions must be made at the start in order to define the objectives of the investigation and how these objectives are to be achieved. At the field-work stage decisions are made as to what equipment to use, where to use it and how best to use it. The engineer must decide what samples he requires, how he is to test them and how he is to interpret the results. Suitable methods of analysis should be chosen and finally decisions made as to recommendations which will lead to a feasible, safe and economic design. The site investigation report represents the crystallization of all these decisions and clearly it must be well presented.

The site investigation itself will have been planned to provide answers for the design engineers and as it progressed it should have been reviewed to ensure that it was in fact producing the information necessary to give these answers. It is, therefore, essential that the site investigation report contains results which satisfy the initial objectives. If for any reason it cannot, perhaps due to financial restrictions, then it should say so and recommendations should be made for additional work if this is necessary. Although the report may be regarded as an end product it is strictly speaking only the end product of one stage of the investigation. In Chapter 3 the investigation process was discussed and it was stressed that in its broadest sense site investigation covered activities up to and even beyond the actual construction of the works.

The report on the main stage of the investigation can in some ways be regarded as a document for discussion. Prior to the investigation the design engineer will not have known the ground conditions and hence may only have had a few alternative preliminary designs available for the geotechnical engineer. Once the investigation had started it is to be hoped that discussions took place between the geotechnical engineer and the design engineer with a view to rejecting the unsuitable alternatives and further investigating the feasible ones. However, by the end of the main investigation it may still not have been possible to finalize a design and the geotechnical engineer will be forced to produce a report which to some extent will have to discuss the works in general terms. For this reason the report must, as far as possible, contain all the information necessary to formulate the final design even though this may not have been discussed in detail. This is what is meant by the investigation being on-going.

Once the design engineer has the report he will further sophisticate his design in the light of the information the report contains and this in turn may enable the geotechnical engineer to refine his recommendations. These recommendations may be that a full-scale trail is carried out or that the works are instrumented and so the investigation goes on. One other important feature that should not be overlooked is the monitoring of the works themselves. This is perhaps the most fruitful area to look to for extending our engineering knowledge. Were the ground conditions as predicted? Were the excavations completed without problem? Did the structure settle the amount predicted and how long did it take? The answers to questions such as these are vitally important if the engineer is to improve his knowledge and understanding of the way soils behave. It will also enable a better report to be produced the next time similar conditions are encountered.

Experience is the cornerstone of good engineering and every engineer learns something new from every job he tackles. However, the question the engineer should ask is whether or not he is gaining as much as he might do. Careful observation and extra monitoring will produce definite benefits when compared with what is obtained from a casual glance.

Before dealing with the site investigation report in more detail it is worth reflecting on the image that the report produces. To most readers the report will be the only tangible result of the investigation and as such the whole investigation will be judged on the appearance and contents of this report. No matter how carefully and accurately the investigation has been carried out there will be doubt in the reader's mind if he finds errors, even simple typing errors, in the report so it is well worth ensuring that a high quality document is produced.

13.2 Technical report writing

There are many excellent texts covering the use of the English language and the writing of technical reports. A number of these texts are listed in the bibliography. Any author is treading on dangerous ground when his work contains statements of how it should be done. Nevertheless it is worth briefly mentioning some of the key points in good report writing even though the reader may be able to find areas in the text where these recommendations have apparently, though not deliberately, been ignored. Good communication is a skill that must be learned and practised.

13.2.1 Clear thinking

The author of any report must be able to define the objectives of the report and understand exactly what it is he is reporting. He must consider his readers and be able to assemble his data, present it in an orderly fashion and reach justifiable conclusions.

13.2.2 Accuracy

The report must obviously be accurate in terms of results obtained and technical facts. It is equally important that it is accurate in its presentation. Every error observed by the reader will cast doubt on the validity of the report and the investigation itself.

13.2.3 Clarity

Anyone can confuse or mislead another with the written word; the skill comes in presenting information in such a way that it is easily assimilated by the reader. Simplicity is the keynote and it is also worth remembering that a simple illustration can often say much more than a whole page of text. Wooliness and verbosity are to be avoided at all costs. Technical jargon should only be used if the author is certain it will be understandable to his readers. The author must always clearly differentiate between fact and opinion, in other words does he *know* something to be true or is he surmising it to be so.

13.2.4 Completeness

Any technical report must contain all relevant information that has been gained, but the author must ensure that no irrelevant information is allowed to cloud the basic objectives of the report.

13.2.5 Logic

Information should be presented in a logical manner and in a logical order. Logic is the science of reasoning and is vital to understanding.

13.2.6 Ambiguity

The author should be careful that his statements are not ambiguous and that the reader will grasp his true meaning. If he is certain of his facts he should say so and should only use words like 'perhaps' or 'may' when there is a genuine element of doubt.

13.2.7 Justification

Where interpretations are made these should be justified either by reasoned argument or by means of calculations in as simple a way as possible.

13.2.8 Consistency

There should always be consistency not only in the arguments used but also in the presentation.

13.2.9 Grammar

Language is essential to civilization and grammar represents the ground rules of language. Good, grammatically correct English is a pleasure to read and is the essence of good communication.

The normal sequence of producing a report is to collect all the data and write a draft which is edited and rewritten where necessary. The author should then make a critical evaluation of his work to ensure that he has satisfied his basic objectives in a simple, clear, precise and logical manner. If time permits it is often worthwhile putting the report aside for a week or two before this stage. Once this stage has been reached the author should finally be prepared further to polish his work, to make it more readable and interesting and to improve its presentation. Figure 13.1 is a flow chart illustrating the various steps in the publication of a site investigation report.

13.3 Report format

The actual format of any site investigation report is a matter of individual taste and it will vary from engineer to engineer. It will also vary depending on the nature of the investigation. However, it should always follow the principles laid out above and should be set out in a logical sequence. A suggested general-purpose format is given below. It must be stressed that this is in no way intended to be definitive but it should serve as a simple guide. Consideration should be given throughout the report to the use of illustrations which can often get over complex concepts in a very simple manner.

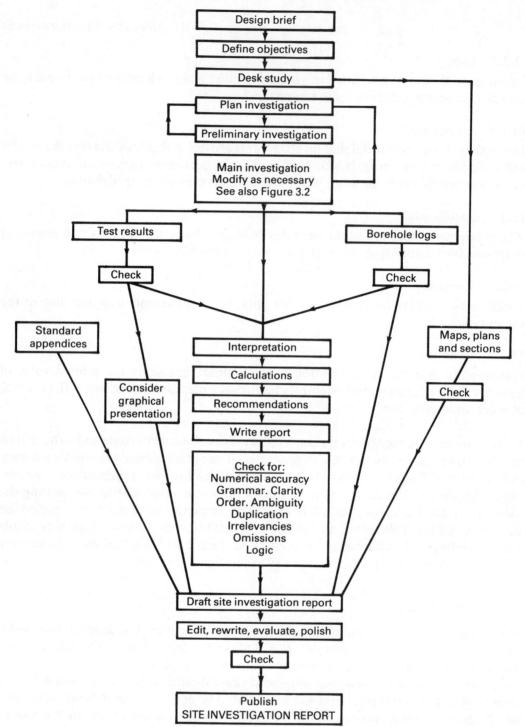

Fig. 13.1 Steps in the preparation of a site investigation report.

13.3.1 Title

This should be kept brief and to the point.

13.3.2 Contents

The contents should be listed in order to facilitate easy reference.

13.3.3 Abstract/Summary

It has been shown that many recipients of a report will only read the summary and it is, therefore, vitally important that it succinctly crystallizes the main features of the investigation and hopefully encourages further reading.

13.3.4 Introduction

This section can be used to describe briefly the proposed works and their location with reference to a suitable plan. A brief statement should also be given of the type of investigation that has been carried out, the design brief, the objectives of the investigation in relation to the design brief, who it was carried out for and when.

13.3.5 Description of the site

In this section land usage, topography and geology of the site should be described with reference to geological and Ordnance Survey maps, not only current editions but also to old editions if these show previous land usage. The main soil and rock types shown on the maps, their structure and their origins should be briefly described so that a comparison can be made between what is shown on the maps and what is found in the ground. A plan showing the site and its geology can be included in an appendix. Reference should also be made to past, present or future surface or underground mineral workings and any important features such as springs, drainage patterns, land forms and so on.

13.3.6 The investigation

A full account should be given of the exact methods that have been adopted and the equipment that has been used. Details of boreholes, trial pits and probings should be given together with their range of depths and a brief description given of such things as *in situ* testing and instrumentation where appropriate. Any particular difficulties should also be noted. If the investigation has included the examination of old records, aerial photographs and past reports this too should be mentioned. Plans should be given defining the exact position of each borehole.

13.3.7 Results of the investigation

Details of the ground conditions that the investigation has revealed can now be described with reference to the borehole logs which will form an appendix to the report.

General descriptions should be given of the soils and rocks encountered and their distribution. In this respect simplified soil profiles can be helpful. Notes should be made of the distribution of groundwater and the readings of piezometers. Any unusual features, anomalies and so on should be described and comments given on features observed when walking over the site such as drainage patterns and man made features. Details of any special features revealed by the aerial photographs can be included in this section and it is worth remembering that illustrations such as sketches, photographs and plans can often make complex topics much clearer. Interpretation as to the distribution of strata between boreholes may be included in this section and reference made to geological cross sections. Comments could also be given on the structural geology and groundwater regimes.

13.3.8   Results of *in situ* and laboratory testing

It is not intended that this section should include all test results since these are best included as an appendix but it should include a discussion on the types of tests that have been carried out, either *in situ* or in the laboratory, and summaries of the properties of each of the main soil types. An indication should be given, for each test and each soil type, of the range of test results and perhaps an indication of typical or design values. Again any peculiarities or anomalies should be commented on and justification given for accepting or rejecting particular test results. The graphical presentation of results can help a great deal in respect of such things as variation in properties with depth or correlation of one soil property with another and this can all be linked in with the soil profiles described in the previous section. If tests have been carried out to a particular standard it will be sufficient to say so but where they have not the test procedure should be described.

13.3.9   Appendices

Although these will occur at the end of the report they should be mentioned here since the recommendations sections that follow will refer to them. The major appendix will be the borehole logs and their explanatory key. These were discussed in Chapters 6 and 7. The second major appendix may be the test results and use can be made in this section of summary sheets although some engineers prefer to see the actual test results themselves. However, summary sheets with results presented in depth order can easily be read alongside the borehole logs. Detailed results and test curves may be required for compaction testing, effective stress testing, sieve analysis, consolidation tests and the like. There may also be records of groundwater levels with respect to time.

Other appendices might contain specialist reports on say mining, geophysical surveying or mineralogical studies. Appendices might also be used to illustrate standard details or methods of construction. One standard appendix that can usefully be inserted in most soil reports is a set of explanatory notes for the non-expert. This can give brief details of standard site investigation procedures and notes on the nature and purpose of the various field and laboratory tests. It can also include a warning as to the limitations of an investigation in which only a minute percentage of the total ground affected by any engineering project has been examined and tested.

13.3.10 Recommendations

Soil mechanics and site investigation are by no means precise sciences and no site investigation can ever be said to be complete. There are problems in that only a very small percentage of the ground is sampled and an even smaller percentage tested. There is also the natural variability of the ground, sampling disturbance and the empirical nature of many of the methods of testing and analysis. Add to these problems the uncertainty about exactly what will happen during construction and it will be appreciated that more than a little art rather than science comes into the picture.

The geotechnical engineer leans heavily on case histories and personal experience and for this there can be no substitute. The above is not intended to paint a gloomy picture; merely to place site investigation in its true light. It is no use expecting a soil report to give bearing capacities or settlements accurate to three significant figures. However, predictions can be, and indeed are, made with only a small element of risk and providing judgement is added to assess what risk can be taken in what circumstances these predictions are valid. There have been failures in the past and there will doubtless be failures in the future but the important thing is to learn from them and to thereby improve site investigation procedures and methods of analysis. Site investigation in its broadest sense should be regarded not only as a design tool but also as an insurance policy; an insurance against the unknown, as much of which as possible should be revealed by the geotechnical engineer.

The final part of any report may or may not be the analysis, conclusions and recommendations. If recommendations are not produced the report is known as a factual report. For the investigation to be of any use recommendations must be produced but there is a growing tendency for them to be written as a separate document to the previously described factual or descriptive report. This tendency arises since the client might appoint a consulting engineer to do the desk study and plan the investigation. He might let a contract for the site investigation field work and ask for a descriptive report only. The conclusions and recommendations would then be produced by the consulting engineer who would be able to liaise with the client throughout the design phase. By whatever means the recommendations are produced they must give the design engineer the information he needs in order to produce a feasible, safe and economic design. The information necessary will vary depending on the type of works that are to be undertaken.

Described in the following sections are the types of recommendations that should be made in relation to particular features. Jobs might incorporate some or all of these features.

It is beyond the scope of this book to describe how the calculations and analyses are carried out and how the recommendations are arrived at. This is a function not only of the investigation but also of soil mechanics theory and practice plus considerable experience and is covered in numerous texts, some of which are listed in the bibliography. The five sections that follow do, however, serve as something of a checklist for the engineer writing the recommendations and they also give an indication of the sort of information that the design engineer can expect from a competently executed investigation and report.

The data on which any analysis or recommendation is based should always be defined and the author must make it clear what is fact and what is opinion. He must always be prepared to justify any opinions he may have.

13.4 Recommendations for earthworks (see Fig. 13.2)

Earthworks in civil engineering comprise the excavation or placement of soils and rocks usually to produce cuttings or embankments although a general raising or lowering of ground level might also be carried out. The British Standard *Code of Practice* BS6031:1981 covers the whole subject of earthworks.

The engineer concerned with the placing of soil and rock to increase ground level or to produce embankments will wish to know first of all whether or not the natural ground is capable of safely supporting the imposed load. He will need to know how much the ground will settle and how long it will take and whether or not his side slopes will have an adequate factor of safety against both long and short-term slope stability failure or if they should incorporate berms. He will need to know whether restrictions need be placed on the rate of filling in order that pore pressures built up will dissipate fast enough in the subsoils to allow the shear strength to increase. In this respect the type of instrumentation and monitoring that might be necessary needs to be known. If there is a stability problem the design engineer will wish to know if the properties of the subsoils can be improved, if drainage would help or if it is necessary to use lightweight fill, alternatively if there is a settlement problem would surcharging help?

The design engineer will also wish to know something about the sort of material he can use to build the embankment and whether or not it can be obtained from cuttings elsewhere on the job. He will need to know its density and compaction characteristics, how it should be compacted, the upper limit of moisture content that should be attached to its use, its compacted CBR, its susceptibility to frost heave, and the amount it will itself settle when incorporated in the embankment. Before the embankment is built it will be necessary to know whether or not topsoil, peat or other soft materials should be removed and if so the amount, whether or not subsoil drainage need be incorporated, whether or not benching is necessary on side-long ground or whether any other pre-construction stabilizing works are necessary. These then are the sort of questions the

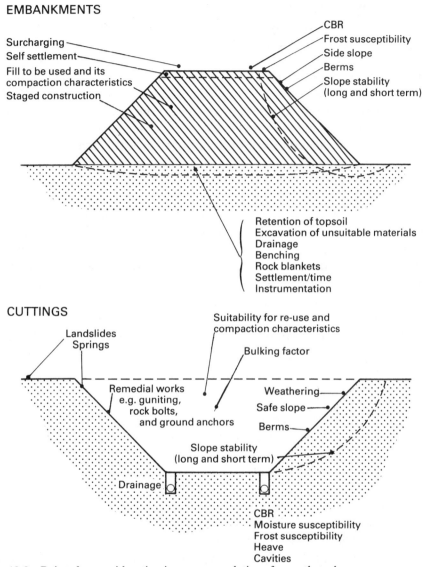

Fig. 13.2 Points for consideration in recommendations for earthworks.

design engineer will be asking and the geotechnical engineer should, therefore, offer recommendations in his report to answer them. Obviously not all embankments will encounter all the above problems but the points described in this and subsequent sections should always be considered first and only dismissed if irrelevant.

Turning now to cuttings and the removal of material there are a number of factors in common. The first thing is whether or not material removed can be used satisfactorily

313

elsewhere in embankments or as an aggregate. However, the design engineer will also need to know how easily the material can be removed, how much it will bulk on excavation, how best to excavate it, whether or not rock breaking plant will be required, whether or not material will have to be excavated below the water table and how best to deal with any flows of groundwater. If some material is not suitable for re-use and must be carted away to tip it is important to know exactly how much is involved since this will greatly affect the contract price. In fact the questions asked by the design engineer are not only related to producing a feasible, safe and economic design but also to the production of an accurate bill of quantities since this leads to more accurate tendering and greatly reduces the risk of claims by contractors.

The safe side slopes and their factors of safety in both the long and short term must be considered together with the need for long-term monitoring. This may involve estimation of rates of weathering or assessment of the need for guniting or rock bolting with a balance being achieved between optimum side slope, minimum remedial works and minimum maintenance. The necessity for drainage, berms and the possible occurrence of springs must also be discussed. The base of the cutting might be the formation to a new road and California Bearing Ratio, frost susceptibility and moisture susceptibility must all be taken into account, as must possible heave or the existence of mine workings. If the cutting is to be made into sidelong ground or at the foot of a slope the possibility of this precipitating a landslide must be considered. Obviously not all these factors will occur on every cutting but they might.

13.5 Recommendations for structures (see Fig. 13.3)

Obviously structures cover a range from a small dwelling to a large factory or a suspension bridge and for the geotechnical engineer to give the best recommendations he must have as much information as possible on exactly what the design engineer has in mind. At the preliminary stages this may not be very much but a dialogue should develop whereby the design engineer discusses his project and the geotechnical engineer discusses the ground conditions. This should lead to a further sophistication in the design enabling the geotechnical engineer to offer more detailed recommendations and so it goes on. The British Standard *Code of Practice* CP2004 on the design of foundations covers most of the points that need to be considered and there are several good text books on foundation design.

For simple spread foundations recommendations are necessary on safe bearing capacities at various depths together with estimates of associated total and differential settlements and the times for these settlements to occur. The ease of excavation, possible problems of water ingress and the possible use of caissons should be discussed as should the possibility of attack by soil or groundwater sulphates, acids or chlorides. If the footing is to be subject to horizontal loads a knowledge of the base friction is

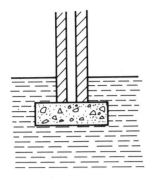

Spread foundations
Ease of excavation, ingress of water
Sulphates/acids/saline conditions
Base friction
Bearing capacity/depth relationship
Settlement/time both total and differential
Benefits of ground treatment
Shrinkage/heave
Frost susceptibility
Old mine workings, need for grouting
Effects of vegetation
Use of buoyant foundations and flotation effects
Alternative use of deep basements and rafts
Effects of vibrations and eccentric loads

Piled foundations
Safe loads/depths/settlements
Differential settlements
Effects of earthworks and lateral loads
Negative skin friction
Choice of type and length of piles
Installation problems
Required set for driven piles
Sulphates/acids/saline conditions
Effects of past, present and future mining
Effects of vibrations
Effects of earthquakes
Effects of piles on surroundings
Effects of eccentric loading
Group effects

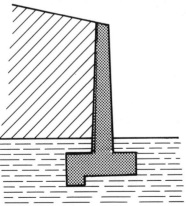

Retaining walls
Active and passive earth pressures
Base friction
Overall stability
Drainage
Presence or generation of landslides
Sulphates/acids/saline conditions
Bearing capacity/depth relationship
Total and differential settlements
Construction sequence and problems
Effect of surcharging
Need for piling or ground treatment
Need for ground anchors and their design

Fig. 13.3 Points for consideration in recommendations for structures.

315

needed. If the footing is to be submerged or is buoyant then flotation effects must be considered for different ground water levels. If the footings are to support machinery the effects of vibration on the subsoils should be assessed (see British Standard CP2012). Alternative types of foundations such as rafts or deep basements can be discussed as can the benefits that might be accrued from some form of ground treatment such as vibro-flotation, grouting or dynamic consolidation. Past, present and future vegetation may have an effect on the foundations as might old tipped material, mineworkings, shafts, adits and wells. If the foundation design is extremely critical or highly sensitive to ground movements it may be necessary to install monitoring systems and recommendations should be given on these where applicable. All recommendations should take into account not only the works themselves but also what effect the works will have on neighbouring structures and vice versa. Figure 13.4 illustrates, in the form of a flow diagram the steps that might be followed in the design of a shallow spread foundation. Other design processes would follow a similar sequence.

If piled foundations appear to offer the most economic solution to the problems then their lengths and safe working loads should be discussed as should founding levels, sets, group effects and settlement. Some advice should be given as to the most appropriate type to use in the particular situation together with possible installation problems. Estimates should be made of any negative skin friction, the effects of adjacent earthworks, differential settlements and lateral pressures. Aggressive ground conditions must be taken into account and also the effects of salt water. The effect of the noise, vibration and soil displacement of piles on their surroundings should also be considered. Foundations might also have to be designed for a given earthquake intensity and be such as to resist the effects of permafrost.

Retaining walls are a particular form of structure that might involve spread footings or piles and are covered by British Standard Code of Practice CP2002. Additional information over and above that required for spread or piled foundations will be needed by the design engineer. For instance he will need to know the active and passive pressures acting on the wall, its resistance to sliding and the overall factor of safety against a slip circle type failure. He will need to know whether to use a spread foundation or a piled one and whether ground anchors would lead to a more economic design. He may also require guidance on the relative merits of sheet piles, diaphragm walls or contiguous bored pile walls as appropriate to the particular site. Landslides can have a very dramatic effect on retaining walls and some have been built with a singular lack of success in preventing movement.

13.6 Recommendations for highways, excavations and drainage works (see Fig. 13.5)

Recommendations for highways can encompass the results of a wide range of investigations, from simple trial pits for a minor improvement to boreholes, studies of

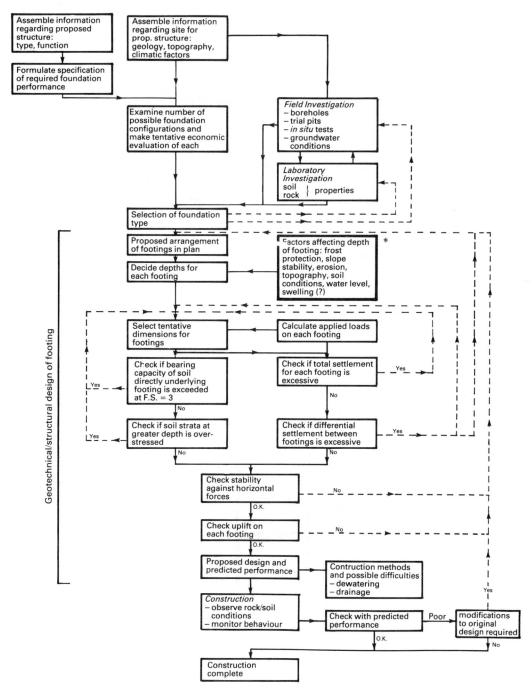

* These factors frequently control foundation design

Fig. 13.4 Flow diagram for design of shallow foundations (after *Foundation Engineering Manual* (1978) Canadian Geotechnical Society).

317

Highways

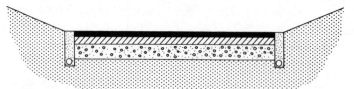

Specification of materials
Traffic loading
CBR of sub-grade
Sub-base type and thickness

Mineworkings
Excavation of unsuitable material
Frost susceptibility
Soil stabilization

Drainage

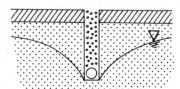

Ground water regime
Drain capacity
Effects of silting up
Road levels
Use of soakaways
Springs, marshes, bogs etc.

Artesian conditions
Erosion effects
Leachate control
Aquifer contamination/exploitation
Settlements induced by groundwater
   lowering

Excavations

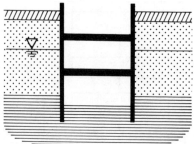

Support required and its design
Ease of excavation
Groundwater flow and its control
Rock levels
Piping
Heave
Tunnelling (including roof and side support)
Dewatering

Sheet piling
Diaphragm walling
Contiguous bored piles
Ground anchors
Induced movements
Grouting
Safety
Design of caissons and coffer dams

Fig. 13.5 Points for consideration in recommendations for highways, drainage works and excavations.

318

aerial photography and regional geological mapping for route location in undeveloped country. This latter study can be a real challenge to the geotechnical engineer since he will have very little hard data or borehole information at his disposal. Nevertheless he must seek to find a route which will be feasible, as economical as possible and one that avoids serious geotechnical problems. He may also be concerned with sources of material with which to build the highway.

Highway construction obviously involves embankments and structures which were discussed in the earlier sections but it also involves the pavement design itself. The soil report must therefore give advice on the bearing qualities of the sub-grade and its design California Bearing Ratio. This is not an easy figure to derive since consideration must be given not only to the test results obtained but also to whether or not the sample was at an equilibrium moisture content, whether or not the sub-grade will be adversely affected by wet weather and trafficking and whether or not it will be affected by frost action.

Having established a California Bearing Ratio for design, consideration should then be given to the number of axles and their loadings which the road must carry and what thickness of what materials are needed to accommodate these. It may be advisable to consider improvement of the sub-grade by drainage works or soil stabilization or it may even be necessary to remove and replace it with something better if it is of very low strength.

Excavations are a part of virtually every civil engineering contract undertaken but they are features which are often given too little consideration especially in view of the number of deaths unstable excavations have caused. Safety then must be of prime importance to the geotechnical engineer and he must produce recommendations which will lead to a stable excavation; BS6031 gives some useful information on the stability of excavations. He must also consider the best method of excavation, how easy it will be to dig, where rockhead occurs, whether or not boiling or heave will be a problem, what groundwater control will be needed and what type of support will be required. He should also consider whether or not the excavation will lead to settlement of any adjacent structures. There are several means of supporting excavated faces including sheet piling, diaphragm walling, and contiguous bored piling. Each of these methods has its own particular advantages and disadvantages and these may need to be discussed.

Tunnels are a special form of excavation. The factors mentioned above have to be considered although perhaps in a different way. The most appropriate tunnelling method is of critical importance together with the way in which the tunnel is to be lined both permanently and temporarily. The precise rock types, their structures, zones of weakness, faults and so on can all have a substantial effect on the works and to reveal this information deep boreholes are required especially when a tunnel is to pass through a mountain. Ingress of water, overbreak, use of compressed air, grouting and rock bolting should all be considered with a view to producing the safest and most economical design possible.

Water is commonly a major problem in many engineering works and good drainage is of paramount importance. Consideration should be given to the treatment of springs, marshes and bogs, to the effect of water on the subsoils and the works, to the pressures and quantities of water likely to be encountered and how best to deal with them either permanently or temporarily. River banks and levees may be required and their stability should be assessed. If drainage is to be by way of soakaways then tests may be needed to assess their potential performance.

13.7 Recommendations for dams (see Fig. 13.6)

The cost of civil engineering works associated with dams is often higher than with other projects. A dam can involve earthworks, structures, tunnels, roads, spillways and in fact often encompasses the whole range of civil engineering work and as such the site investigation work required is extensive. It is not only the dam site itself that must be fully assessed but also the catchment area, the sides of the reservoirs and the lines of tunnels, roads and spillways. The work is demanding since there is so much at stake not the least being the lives of people who will be living downstream of the dam once it is complete.

Dams are usually placed in valleys and there have been catastrophes in the past where deep buried channels filled with soft materials were not fully recognized. There was also a major disaster at Vaiont when a whole section of the valley side slid into the waters of the dam causing a huge displacement of water.

The stability of the dam and its surroundings is obviously of prime importance. Its foundation must be fully assessed together with permeability and seepage beneath and around it, the need for cut-offs and the stability of abutments. Spillways should be assessed for stability and the effects of scour. Tunnels, turbine houses and other underground works require consideration as does the nature of the bed of the reservoir and of the catchment area. Rock structure is extremely important and the presence of faults or other planes of weakness can have a profound effect on the design and its stability. The effects of earthquakes may have to be considered. An assessment will be needed as to how fast the reservoir will silt up and where construction materials can be obtained from and how they will perform. The problems involved are wide ranging in the extreme and every phase of the site investigation, whether it be geological mapping, boreholes, geophysics or whatever, must be carried out with great care.

13.8 Miscellaneous recommendations

The preceding sections have described many of the problems that must be considered

320

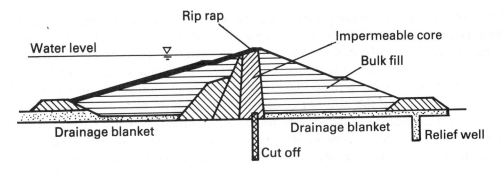

As for embankments but with special attention to foundation stability, faults, buried channels, jointing and fissuring

Consider reservoir characteristics; subsoils, silting up, retention of water
Seepage; through, under and around the dam
Ancilliary works; tunnels, foundations for turbine houses, construction of spillways, stilling basins etc.

Catchment area; nature and run-off characteristics
Stability of reservoir banks
Earthquakes; stability of dam and associated works
Construction materials; source, quality, properties, behaviour, pore pressure dissipation, permeability

Access roads; see Figure 13.3

Fig. 13.6 Points for consideration in recommendations for dams.

by the geotechnical engineer involved with site investigation work and the type of recommendations that are needed to satisfy the design engineer but there are many more. The investigation may have been carried out to evaluate the potential of an aquifer and recommendations may be needed based on the borehole information and on pumping tests. Docks, railways and sewage works encompass a variety of problems. Tips and made ground can be encountered in any previously developed area as can shafts, wells, mineworkings and backfilled quarries. All these demand special consideration. The works themselves should not be viewed in isolation but the effect they will have on their surroundings and the effect their surroundings will have on them should be considered; considerations such as amounts of vertical and horizontal movements and settlements due to ground water lowering or increased loading.

The geotechnical engineer will often be involved in assessing the cause of failures, either natural or induced by man and a great deal can be learnt from them. Landslides are a common failure. Of course these can occur without the intervention of man, but whatever the cause a thorough investigation is required to assess the type of slide, the location of the failure plane, the immediate and long-term factors of safety and the form that the most effective remedial works should take. Embankments too can fail, as can any structure or retaining wall and invariably the subsoils and groundwater conditions must be investigated if the cause or causes are to be determined.

Before concluding these sections on recommendations it is worth stressing the need for sound engineering judgement. The geotechnical engineer must forever be on his guard for the unexpected. He should consider the facts, do his calculations and make his judgement and he should be prepared to back this up with calculations, reasoned argument, past experience and reference to previous case histories and research work.

13.9 Checking reports

The importance of the site investigation report has been stressed already and it should be clear that close checking is vital prior to publication. Checks can take a number of forms, for example checks on numerical accuracy or grammatical accuracy, but it is well worth someone reading the report who has not been closely connected with the investigation. He or she will be able to view the report through the eyes of a typical recipient and hopefully spot areas lacking in clarity. These are often not seen by the authors who may have been too close to the job and perhaps taken certain facts for granted. It must be remembered that in many cases the report may finally be read by someone who is not a specialist in geotechnical engineering and as such it must be written in a manner understandable to the non-specialist. Any specialist must always be able to justify his opinions and to do this he may have to refer to calculations, references or to a reasoned argument. Whichever it is it should be done clearly and without risk of misinterpretation.

To return to the question of checking it is a good idea to do this with a definite policy in mind and some suggestions are given below. The checker should first make sure that everything is in a logical order and that there are no unnecessary duplications of information or irrelevancies. He should check that nothing of importance has been omitted and that no unnecessary technical jargon has been used. The use of long words often detracts from a report, for example why use 'terminate' when 'end' will do or 'accordingly' when 'so' will do or 'furthermore' when 'then' will do; the list is a long one. The report should be in good English and grammatically correct. Systematic checks are needed that all data, particularly data involving figures, is presented correctly and that there are no mathematical errors in the presentation nor in the numbering of figures or references. The conclusions should be checked to ensure that they are based on sound arguments and there should be no ambiguity in meaning. However, above all else the report must be readable and should be a credit not only to the authors but to the whole investigation team.

322

14

Safety

14.1 Introduction

Ground investigation can often be a heavy, arduous and dirty job and accidents, even tragedies, do occur. The object of this chapter is to outline personal responsibilities and methods of work which, it is hoped, will help reduce the incidence of accidents in the industry. Too often the attitude of mind is one of apathy, an attitude which the Robens Committee in 1974 identified as being one of the major causes of accidents in industry. This attitude of mind costs industry money in lost production, sick pay, compensation claims, medical care and damage to expensive equipment. What cannot be measured in terms of money is the pain and suffering of the injured persons, or the grief of a family over the loss of one of its members who dies in an industrial accident.

Humanitarian reasons demand that everyone takes a close look at their own work situation and their own attitude towards safe working. In the first instance all people at work must accept their personal responsibility for the safety of themselves and others who may be affected by the work activity. Legislation cannot be effective in making places of work and work processes safe; the complete co-operation and participation of all concerned is required irrespective of the type of work that is carried out.

14.2 Personal responsibilities

The Health and Safety at Work Act 1974 defines the responsibilities of both management and operatives. Legal sanctions can be applied where a person does not accept his responsibility and does not fulfil his legal obligations. Where an injury does occur or a dangerous situation exists, an investigation by the Health and Safety

Executive can reveal the person responsible who could then be prosecuted and penalties applied. The penalties are a £400 maximum fine or a £400 fine and 2 years imprisonment.

The responsibilities of a manager are:

(1) To ensure so far as is reasonably practicable, the health, safety and welfare at work of all employees.
(2) To provide and maintain plant and systems of work that are safe and without risk to health.
(3) To make arrangements for ensuring safety and no risk to health in the use, handling, storage and transport of articles and substances.
(4) To provide information, instruction, training and supervision to ensure the health and safety of all employees at work.
(5) To maintain any place of work under their control in a safe condition and without risks to health, and to provide safe access and egress.
(6) To provide and maintain a working environment that is safe, without risks to health and with adequate welfare facilities.
(7) To provide a written statement of general safety policy and the arrangements made to carry out that policy.
(8) To conduct his work to ensure that persons not in his employment are not exposed to risk to health or safety from the work.

The responsibilities of all employees at work are:

(1) To take care of the health and safety of themselves and of others, including the general public, who may be affected either by their acts or by their omissions at work.
(2) To co-operate with their employers so that the employers' duties and requirements under any of the relevant statutory provisions can be carried out and complied with.
(3) Not to interfere with or misuse anything provided in the interest of safety, health or welfare.
(4) To use protective equipment when it is provided and when the law requires its use.

14.3 The law relating to site investigation in the UK

The Health and Safety at Work Act 1974 is the main piece of legislation covering all places of work but it is couched in general terms. The intention is that all previous legislation, e.g. The Factories Act 1967 will be replaced by Codes of Practice or new detailed legislation in the future. Until this comes about all the old legislation remains in force as Relevant Statutory Provisions, the main ones applying to site investigation work are:

The Construction (General Provisions) Regulations 1961
The Construction (Lifting Operations) Regulations 1961
The Construction (Working Places) Regulations 1966
The Construction (Health and Safety) Regulations 1966
The Protection of Eyes Regulations 1975
The Factories Act 1961

The Construction (Lifting Operations) Regulations 1961 impose requirements as to the construction, use and examination of lifting appliances, lifting gear and lifting tackle used in the construction industry. A drilling rig comes within the scope of these regulations and in simple terms must be:

(1) Properly made and strong enough for the work it is to do.
(2) Kept in good order.
(3) Properly inspected once per week and a record of these inspections kept on Form 91 (Part I).
(4) Thoroughly examined before first use and the examination repeated every 14 months. A record of the 14-monthly examinations must be kept on Form 91 (Part II).

Wire ropes, chains and loose lifting gear must not be used unless:

(1) They have been tested and examined. A certificate of test must be obtained for each item (Form 87 for ropes, Form 97 for chain and loose gear).
(2) They are marked with the safe working load and identity mark.
(3) They are examined every 6 months. A record of examination to be kept on Form 91 (Part II).

The Construction (Health and Welfare) Regulations lay down standards for the health and welfare of operatives and the standards of first aid equipment and treatment.

Other legislation might also affect site investigation work, for example, the Asbestos Regulations, Abrasive Wheels Regulations, Highly Flammable Liquids and Liquid Petroleum Gases etc. There are also special regulations to be observed when dealing with work over water, in excavations, with explosives, with radioactive materials, in large diameter boreholes and on motorways. Certain abstracts of the legislation must be posted on sites and displayed in cabins or caravans.

The Protection of Eyes Regulations 1975 are of such importance that some explanation is required. The number of accidents to unprotected eyes is very high and the horrific injuries resulting from these accidents make it imperative that all operatives become aware of their responsibility to use eye protection. The law is definite. The employer must provide eye protection of the standard prescribed in the regulations for all employees employed in the processes named in the schedules to the regulation. The eye protection must be suitable for the process and for the person who is at work in the process. Eye protection must be properly maintained and enough stocks available to replace any which are lost or damaged. The employee must use the eye protection, take care of it and report to his employer any defects, loss or damage. In any work process where there is risk to the eyes, whether it is dust, flying particles or harmful liquids, the operative must use eye protection. Some of the processes which might be applicable to site investigation work are listed below:

(1)　Shot blasting.
(2)　Use of high pressure water jets.
(3)　Use of hammers, chisels, punches etc.
(4)　Use of power saws or abrasive wheels.
(5)　Use of corrosive substances.
(6)　Use of compressed air.
(7)　Welding.

14.4　Site planning

Site investigations often take place on private land, the access having been negotiated with the owners. It is important that his land be damaged as little as possible. Consideration must be given to preventing damage to crops, trees and fences. Livestock must be protected and prevented from straying and equipment and boreholes must be fenced off as necessary. Records should be kept of initial site conditions and damage caused by drilling operations. Where necessary photographic evidence should be obtained.

Indiscriminate movement of vehicles causes a high proportion of land damage. Movement of vehicles should be planned to avoid unnecessary travel across any land which could be damaged by the vehicles. The nearest most suitable access for an ambulance or fire appliance should also be determined. Safe routes onto sites should be planned taking due regard of existing land conditions and the availability of parking for vehicles, site cabins or caravans. Where livestock may be affected gates and fence breaks should be secured after entry to prevent straying. Cabins and caravans should be sited on firm ground, preferably clear of the rig working area, yet easily accessible to prevent the need to use vehicles for travel between the rig and cabins.

The position of all services (electricity, gas, water, GPO lines, sewers, oil lines etc.)

should be determined from drawings supplied by the appropriate authority and/or use made of effective detection equipment. Any doubts or problems should be resolved on site by consultation with the appropriate authority. The position of overhead lines should be noted and provision made to avoid them.

At least one member of each drilling crew should be trained in first aid. First aid equipment should be regularly checked and replenished as necessary. Instructions on accident procedures should be posted in site cabins and any injury to personnel recorded. Appropriate fire extinguishers must also be available on site and personnel should be trained in their use. All drilling crews should have a list of emergency telephone numbers.

Where drilling operations take place on roads or where they affect road traffic, signs and cones must be placed in accordance with Chapter 8 of the Traffic Signs manual and the Highway Authority must be consulted. The signed zone should cover all areas where vehicles are parked or equipment stored. Precautions must be taken to protect members of the public from hazards created by the work operation and there must be no risk to them. Warning notices, barriers and footpath diversions should be provided where necessary. Where rigs are left on site overnight, they must be left in a safe condition and secure from children and vandals who might be attracted to them. Excavations and boreholes may require fencing and lighting if left open overnight.

An untidy site is an unsafe site and an inefficient one. Equipment and tools should be laid out in a neat orderly manner and the free passage of men and materials planned.

14.5 Site hazards

A summary of some potential site hazards is shown in Fig 14.1. First of all the manufacturer's recommended procedure for rig erection should be followed at all times. Where site conditions do not allow the procedure to be followed a safe system of erection should be laid down in conjunction with the supervisor. Overhead obstructions should be noted before erecting the rig and work should not start on any borehole until the positions of all services have been determined. The drilling rig should be checked that it is in a safe, stable working condition and that the correct equipment, shackles and slings are available and in good condition. Before putting the rig into operation, a pre-operational check should be made to ensure that the rig is level, that all bolts, pins and locking devices are correct and secure and that the controls, brakes, clutch and engine stops are functioning correctly. Unnecessary equipment should be cleared away.

The position of any electricity cables should already have been determined but where doubt exists as to their position they should be uncovered by hand excavation. There should always be adequate clearance from any overhead lines, preferably 10 m, and the rig should not be moved in the upright position beneath them. Should any doubt exist the Electricity Authority should be consulted. If contact should be made with a power

327

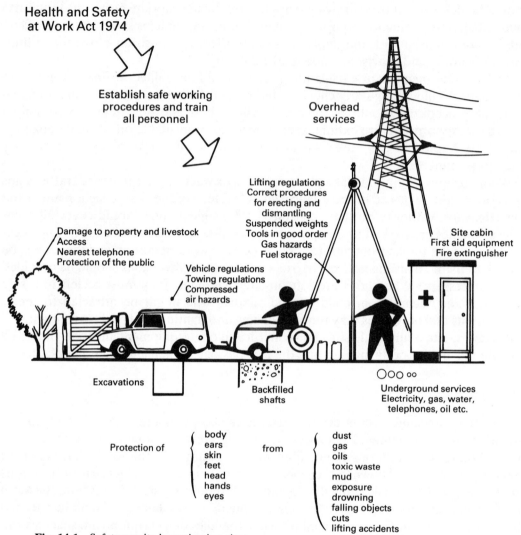

Health and Safety
at Work Act 1974

Establish safe working
procedures and train
all personnel

Overhead
services

Lifting regulations
Correct procedures
for erecting and
dismantling
Suspended weights
Tools in good order
Gas hazards
Fuel storage

Damage to property and livestock
Access
Nearest telephone
Protection of the public

Vehicle regulations
Towing regulations
Compressed
air hazards

Site cabin
First aid equipment
Fire extinguisher

Excavations

Backfilled
shafts

Underground services
Electricity, gas, water,
telephones, oil etc.

Protection of { body ears skin feet head hands eyes } from { dust gas oils toxic waste mud exposure drowning falling objects cuts lifting accidents }

Fig. 14.1   Safety on site investigation sites.

line the equipment in contact with it should not be touched and no attempt made to rescue anyone who is still in contact with it. It may be possible to push or drag a person clear of contact by using a long, dry, wooden pole or a dry fibre rope but no chances should be taken and expert assistance should be obtained if there is any doubt.

The position of gas mains should also be determined and excavated by hand if doubt exists as to the exact position. High pressure gas mains will explode violently if breached. If a gas main is fractured or pierced the rig engine must be stopped and the

328

area cleared of personnel upwind of the breach. All smoking and naked lights should be stopped and no attempt should be made to move equipment or backfill the hole. The public should be kept away. If necessary traffic should be prevented from entering a gaseous area and the Gas Board, Police and Fire Service contacted.

Underground oil pipes could be overlooked if care is not taken in planning the site operations. They do exist and carry large quantities of petroleum liquids at high pressure. The location of underground pipes must be ascertained and rig crews notified of the location. In emergency the Police and Fire Service should be called after ensuring the risks of ignition are minimized. GPO lines, water services and sewers do not have the same hazard potential as Electricity, Gas and Oil services. Nevertheless, the inconvenience to the public and the high cost of repairs make it essential that the same care is given to their location and safe-keeping.

The manual handling of heavy equipment is an essential part of drilling operations. The correct methods of lifting should be known and used by the rig crews. Back injuries are created by using wrong lifting methods and lifting excessive weights. When the weight to be handled is likely to injure a person, assistance must be obtained. Where two or more people are to lift, one person must take charge and give directions to co-ordinate effort and action. When lifting weights the feet should be approximately the width of the hips apart with one foot slightly in front of the other. The back should be straight with the legs bent so as to reach down to the load. The load must be firmly gripped by the hands. Looking down at the load at the moment of lift should be avoided as this encourages the back to bend. The arms should be kept as close to the body as possible and the lift made smoothly with no jerking or snatching actions. When lifting from the ground position the back muscles should not be used to pull the load up but rather the knees bent and the thigh muscles used to rise with the load. Wherever possible, mechanical means of lifting heavy weights should be used.

Exposure of the hands to oils, pitch, tar, degreasing agents and dusts can induce various types of skin disease. The use of gloves, barrier creams and frequent washing with soap and water will reduce dermatitis hazards. Degreasing agents are available which present no hazard and they should be used at all times. Dirty and greasy overalls and workclothes can also create skin diseases and skin contact with oils, tars and greases must be kept to a minimum.

Foreign bodies in eyes present a hazard which must not be ignored. The law requires that suitable eye protection must be provided by employers and the law requires that the person for whom it is provided shall use that eye protection at all times that the eyes are at risk. Inhaling dust from boreholes can be dangerous as comparatively small amounts of dust from some materials can produce incurable chest diseases, for example silicosis and asbestosis. Where personnel are exposed to dust blown up from boreholes dust masks should be worn.

Escaping gases from boreholes can affect rig crews and a dust mask will not give any protection. All rig personnel should be able to recognize the general symptoms of gassing and know the subsequent first aid action to take. When drilling where there is a possibility of striking a coal seam or old mine workings where gas might be present, there must be no smoking or naked lights within 15 m of any open borehole both during drilling operations and any period when a borehole is left open.

Mud presents various problems during drilling operations apart from bogging down vehicles and rigs. Footing becomes insecure, driving a vehicle with muddy footwear creates a hazard, climbing on the rig with muddy boots requires more care, rigs become unstable through the legs sinking into mud and mud carried on to roads by site vehicles presents a road hazard. Where excessive water is used, the area round the borehole can become a sea of mud and precautions must be taken to eliminate this hazard. Drainage channels should be made to direct excess water away from the drilling area and the rig should be stabilized on broad timbers to prevent the legs sinking. Vehicle wheels must be cleaned of excessive mud before going on to public roads. Care must be taken with manual handling of weights when footing is insecure.

Accidents involving tow bars being dropped on feet do occur and care is needed when coupling/uncoupling them. Safety footwear should be worn and feet kept clear at all times. The towing pin must be of an approved design with a safety clip or split pin being used. The towing eye and draw bolt should be examined for fatigue fractures. The vehicle being towed must have serviceable wheels, tyres and brakes and a trailer plate must be fitted and be in working order. It is a good idea to use a safety chain between vehicle and rig since rigs have been known to part company from the towing vehicle. All vehicles and trailers should be kept in good mechanical and roadworthy condition and any tools and equipment carried must be securely stowed. Where possible an observer should be stationed to assist when reversing vehicles and no person should ride on any trailed vehicle.

Fuel for engines must be carried in appropriate jerry cans of metal construction with secure spout caps. The cans must be clearly identified and marked as to their content and flammability. Buckets of the open type should not be used to fuel machines and spillage must always be avoided. Smoking and naked lights should be prohibited whilst fuelling machines and in areas where fuel is stored.

When misused, compressed air is dangerous and the introduction of compressed air into any body orifice can kill. When using compressed air to clean down the rig, eye protection should be worn by all personnel in the vicinity. Overalls and clothing must not be dusted down with compressed air and it should be treated with great respect at all times.

All lifting appliances, wire ropes and winching equipment are subject to regulations (see Construction (Lifting Operations) Regulations). Wire ropes and winches are subject to great stresses and often to mis-use and frequent examination and maintenance is required. A wire-rope dressing should be applied to the rope, not oil or grease. The rope should be replaced if badly kinked or if in any ten diameters the total visible broken wires exceed 5% of the total. Knots should not be tied in wire ropes or chains, instead bulldog clips should be used in the recommended manner. Winches and all equipment should be operated correctly and hands kept clear of ropes feeding on to the winch drum. Loose fitting workclothes with trailing ends which may get caught in rotating machinery should not be worn. When changing a wire rope a replacement of the same type and specification as fitted by the manufacturer should always be used. The machinery and equipment involved in site investigation work is potentially dangerous and care and commonsense is needed to avoid losing a finger. The driller should have a clear view of the whole operation and if the work is noisy suitable signals should be agreed between all the men involved.

Where there is a risk of ground giving way, all personnel must wear safety harnesses secured to ground anchors to prevent falls into hidden shafts and holes. If a vehicle is used as a temporary measure to secure a lifeline, that vehicle must be immobilized to prevent its being driven whilst a man is attached to it. Ignition keys must be removed and kept by a responsible person who will ascertain that before the vehicle is moved all lifeline attachments have been removed. The investigation of old filled-in mineshafts by drilling down the centre of the shaft presents safety hazards to both drilling equipment and crews. To overcome the hazards, each operation must be pre-planned and a safe system of work laid down to suit the individual investigation.

Where a known shaft is to be investigated not only must all normal precautions be observed but additional precautions need to be taken. Ground anchors should be installed near to the mineshaft and personnel must wear safety harnesses with the lifeline attached to the ground anchors at all times they are over the mineshaft top. To avoid the use of long lifelines a steel wire rope spanning the mineshaft and secured at each end by a ground anchor would allow personnel relatively free movement on a short lifeline clipped on to the wire rope. One person should be appointed to stay off the mineshaft top at all times and be in a safe position to observe the work and obtain assistance should any emergency arise. A means of testing for gas should be available on site and the crew should know how to test for gas from the borehole. No smoking or naked lights should be allowed within 15 m of the borehole and fire extinguishers should be available in close proximity to the rig.

A steel girder frame of suitable size and adequate strength with regard to the weight to be carried and the width of the mineshaft should be assembled either at the side of the shaft and winched into position or assembled across the shaft. Platforms using sleepers should be laid across the framework to form a platform wide enough to hold the drilling rig and leave sufficient room for the operators to work. The drilling rig should be winched or man-handled into position on the platform and secured to the steel framework or secured by steel wire guys to ground anchors. Sleepers can be removed to allow the drill to work but these should be kept to a minimum and gaps created by

331

removal of sleepers should be covered to prevent the falls of personnel.

In isolated, high, cold areas the weather can change dramatically in minutes. It is possible to wander away from a rig in bright sunshine, wearing only light clothing and suddenly be enveloped in dense, icy moorland fog. Exposure in these extreme conditions in inappropriate clothing can be hazardous. Foul-weather clothing should be kept within reach in isolated areas. In desert areas problems of exhaustion and dehydration can occur.

No-one should stand beneath a suspended weight. Peering down a borehole with the drill tool suspended above you could be disastrous should the wire break or the brakes fail. Trial pits and excavations over 1.2 m in depth where collapse of the sides is likely must be securely timbered to prevent collapse. Safe access and egress must be provided and consideration given to ventilation and the build up of heavy gases. If personnel could fall into water where there is a risk of drowning, rescue equipment must be provided and fencing erected to prevent falls. Certain Board of Trade Regulations also apply to work over or adjacent to water. Where working platforms are required they must be erected in accordance with regulations. Where platforms have to support the rig and equipment, due regard must be paid to the extra loading caused by such operations as casing withdrawal. There is a Code of Practice, CP2011, relating to safety precautions in the construction of large diameter boreholes for piling and other purposes.

Waste disposal on land-fill sites is usually strictly controlled but in the past indiscriminate disposal of caustic and toxic waste took place on both public and private tips. Where the materials have surfaced over a period of time they can be recognized and steps taken to neutralize them. With a drilling operation, the hazard remains hidden until the borehole gives the material or gas an outlet to the surface, bringing with it a hazard to the crew. Drilling rig crews should be warned that the drill may bring harmful materials to the surface. Extra care should be taken when drilling on landfill sites. Eye protection, dust masks and gloves should be used by the crew in this operation.

The likely hazards are acid, alkali, asbestos dust, poison, gas and tar. Washing facilities with a plentiful supply of water are essential to this type of work. Hands must be thoroughly washed before smoking, eating or using the toilet. Where sickness, headache or faintness affects any member of the drilling crew, the site must be evacuated and assistance obtained. If any burning sensation on the skin occurs, it should be washed thoroughly with copious amounts of water. Chemical analysis of the material should be obtained before the work resumes and a safe system of work devised and followed.

When dismantling and removing the rig from site the manufacturer's recommended method should be adopted. All equipment should be cleaned and checked for defects. All debris should be removed from site and excavations and boreholes reinstated correctly. Any fence or hedge breaks should be made good, all gates closed and as much damage as possible rectified.

14.6 Protective equipment

Drilling personnel should be provided with all necessary protective clothing and this must be used where the work situation demands it. On work which extends on to roads, high visibility clothing should be worn. Helmets and safety footwear should be worn at all times in the vicinity of the drilling rig. Safety helmets, gloves, dust masks, safety harnesses, eye protection and ear muffs are designed and issued to protect personnel from hazards to health. The law provides for legal sanctions against personnel who do not use equipment provided for their safety. Personnel have a legal duty to use safety equipment, to take good care of it and to report any defect or loss.

Tools are provided for all work situations. They require good care and maintenance to remain in a safe condition. Tools should not be improvised and any damaged tools should be discarded or properly repaired.

Rig crews are prone to minor cuts and abrasions which could be infected by Tetanus spores in the soil they handle. It is therefore recommended that rig personnel be innoculated against Tetanus.

14.7 Miscellaneous

In any work activity where men and machines are involved considerable care has to be taken to ensure the safety of the men. Physical contact between man and machine in an accident situation invariably results in severe injury to the man. It is, therefore, important that safe procedures and safe systems of work are followed where machines are at work. The manufacturers of drilling rigs realize the dangers of a mishandled machine and have produced safe procedures for rig personnel to follow. These recommended procedures must be followed at all times. Where site conditions make it impossible to follow recommended procedures, full consultation between supervisors and engineers must take place to ensure that any alternative procedure agreed upon is a safe one.

Every operative in a drilling rig crew must be fully trained in all operations and be able to work as part of a team. To mould operatives into a team which can work efficiently and safely, requires training. This should be a continuous process so that co-operation and effort towards safe working is sustained at a high level at all times. Training should not be confined to drilling rig work procedures, but should include items such as first aid, fire fighting and other safety subjects.

The object of this chapter is to motivate personnel to think about the safety of themselves and others at work. If staff involved in site investigation look for the hazards on their sites and question the effectiveness of the methods used to correct those hazards then the chapter will have served its purpose. There is no substitute for sound common sense and recognition of potential hazards. Remember that all accidents must be recorded and that the Health and Safety Executive have a right to investigate any they choose.

Appendix A

Specification and bill of quantities for ground investigations

This appendix provides a simple general-purpose specification and a typical bill of quantities. It is not intended to be definitive. Obviously the requirements of individual investigations will vary widely and it is up to the geotechnical engineer to decide exactly what work is needed. He may wish to expand the specification, modify it, add items to the bill of quantities or delete them. In all cases the engineer should consider the exact form of the contract and its conditions, indemnities, what instructions for tendering he should provide, what information he needs to give to the contractor and what information he expects from the contractor. Provisions for access, checking of surfaces, indemnities and damages demand special attention. The specification is essentially that produced by the Association of Ground Investigation Specialists which was based on the Department of the Environment Model Contract Document published in 1976. The bill of quantities is also based on this source. The Institute of Civil Engineers, the Association of Consulting Engineers and the Federation of Civil Engineering Contractors are, at the time of writing, drafting a 'Conditions of Contract for Ground Engineering'.

The ground investigation must not be confused with the whole site investigation. As has been illustrated in the text of this book there are many ways in which information for design purposes can be gained and ground investigation is only one of them, albeit an extremely important one.

There is a growing trend for a specialist geotechnical engineer to carry out all the preliminary investigations, to liaise with the design engineers and to decide what information is needed and how best to obtain it. He may then produce the tender documents for the exact work he requires and also supervise its execution. The tender will probably only ask for a factual report and it will be the independent geotechnical engineer who provides the interpretation and produces the recommendations. He is then in a position to liaise further with the design engineers, to request additional work as necessary and generally to see the whole scheme through to the final design and even to the finished works or beyond. There is much to be said for operating in this manner since it is essential for the geotechnical aspects of any design scheme to form an integral part of the whole design process and not to be viewed in isolation.

THE SPECIFICATION

A.1 General

A.1.1 Definitions

These definitions are for the purpose of this ground investigation contract only.

The expression 'soil' shall include any material not classified hereunder as rock or made ground.

The expression 'rock' shall mean hard strata found in ledges or masses in its original position which in normal excavation would have to be loosened by blasting or pneumatic tools or if by hand, by wedges and sledge hammers; or strata which in drilling require the use of diamond or tungsten carbide bits; or boulders exceeding 0.3 m in thickness measured parallel to the axis of boring.

The expression 'made ground' shall mean any deposit or construction which has been formed by man as distinct from geological agencies.

The term 'exploratory hole' shall mean any kind of hole made to explore ground conditions.

'Site' means the working areas at, and the access routes to, all the exploratory holes, and any area provided by the Employer as a compound for offices, etc.

'Engineer' shall mean the appointed representative of the Employer.

A.1.2 Notice of entry and access

The Engineer shall arrange with the occupiers, in agreement with the Contractor, the details of the access routes to be used. Only the agreed access routes to and between exploratory holes shall be used.

A.1.3 Making good

All walls, fences, hedges, etc., breached or otherwise disturbed during the progress of the Works shall be immediately repaired with stockproof barriers irrespective of whether stock is occupying the land or not; and in the case of gates, an equivalent replacement shall be used.

A.1.4 Making good working areas

The Contractor shall confine his operations to the minimum area of ground required for the Works and shall strip topsoil for each exploratory hole and set it aside for re-use. When work has been completed at each exploratory hole position, the Contractor shall re-spread the topsoil and leave the site in a clean and tidy condition. He shall make good damage in the vicinity of the hole to the satisfaction of the Engineer.

A.1.5 Payment for making good

Where the exploratory hole positions and access routes have not been specified prior to tender, the reinstatement of these areas will be paid for on a prime cost basis and provision for this made in the Bill of Quantities.

Where exploratory hole positions and access routes have been specified prior to tender, a separate item is provided in the Bill of Quantities for the Contractor to price.

A.1.6 Compensation for unavoidable damage

Any claims for compensation by owners or occupiers for damage to crops, ground surface, hedges or fences which are deemed to be unavoidable shall be referred to the Engineer.

A.1.7 Written instructions to site staff

The Contractor shall give written instructions to his site staff on all relevant aspects in the Specification such as sampling frequency, ground water records and the procedure required for dealing with obstructions.

A.1.8 Ground elevation

The ground elevation referred to Ordnance Datum of each hole shall normally be provided by the Engineer. Where the Contractor is required to carry out this service a separate item in the Bill of Quantities is included.

A.1.9 Standards and Codes of Practice

The British Standards and Codes of Practice quoted in the specification and Appendices shall be those current at the time of invitation to tender.

A.1.10 Methods of exploration

The Engineer may require exploration to be carried out by all or any of the following methods:

Percussion boring with shell, auger or clay cutter, with or without sampling and in either cased or uncased holes.
Hand auger borings with or without sampling.

Probing in soft soils with small diameter rods and a probe head of approximately 25 mm diameter.

Rotary drilling through soil or rock either from the bottom of a percussion boring or from original ground level and either with or without core recovery.

The excavation of inspection pits.

The excavation of trial pits.

Penetration vane tests.

In situ testing and static and dynamic probing in soils as specified separately.

A.1.11   Mine workings

When boring in regions known to contain mine workings, shafts or other similar works the Contractor shall consult the Engineer on any special requirements. Should any coal, voids, disturbed ground, faulting, loss of drilling water or any other evidence suggesting mining be found during exploration, the Contractor shall inform the Engineer immediately and await his further instructions.

A.1.12   Inspection pits and precautions for services

The Contractor shall start all exploratory holes located within the boundaries of public highways and elsewhere if the presence of underground services or field drains is expected by means of a hand-excavated inspection pit not less than 1.2 m deep.

Hand-operated power tools may be used to assist excavation where hard strata such as road pavements cannot be broken without the use of such tools. Boring shall not begin until the presence or otherwise of all services has been established. The positions, depths and dimensions of all services encountered shall be measured and recorded in the Daily Report, and strata recorded as set out in clause 2.5.

A.1.13   Backfilling exploratory holes

The Contractor shall backfill and compact all exploratory holes in such a manner that no subsequent depression is formed at the ground surface due to settlement of the backfill.

Where special infilling to exploratory holes is required, the Contractor shall consult and agree with the Engineer a procedure for such infilling.

A.2   Borings

A.2.1   Diameter of boring

The mimimum diameter of borings or internal diameter of casing shall be 150 mm. Where borings are of such depth that the advancement of a casing becomes impracticable or where obstructions are likely to be met, such as boulders in glacial till requiring the procedures outlined in A.2.6, then the Contractor shall bore at or provide casings of sufficient diameter, up to a maximum of 250 mm, to complete the work. Should any boring prove abortive because of the Contractor's failure to begin operations with a sufficiently large diameter boring for the scheduled depth, for reasons other than obstructions, then the Contractor shall be liable for any necessary enlargement at his own expense.

A.2.2 Use of clay cutters

Clay cutters shall be of a pattern approved by the Engineer, and the combined weight of a clay cutter and any sinker bar shall not exceed 150 kg in the case of 150 mm diameter borings and 180 kg in the case of 200 mm borings. In cases where the use of clay cutters is considered likely to cause critical disturbance, other approved methods such as the use of a hand-operated auger or penetration boring with a piston sampler shall be employed. Separate payment shall be made for this work at rates to be agreed.

A.2.3 Use of shells (or bailers)

In ground where even the careful withdrawal of close fitting shells causes ingress of the soil into the borehole, the Contractor shall not only maintain a head of water as specified in A.2.4, but shall also use a shell of diameter at least 25 mm less than that of the borehole casing.

A.2.4 Addition of water to borings

The Contractor shall not advance the boring by adding water except in the case of dry granular soils and stiff clays. For conditions in cohesive soils where the addition of water is permitted the Contractor shall use the absolute minimum amount of water necessary for advancing the bore. Where boring reveals soft alluvial soils or where sub-artesian groundwater loosens granular soils the Contractor must at all times add and maintain a head of water to at least ground level during all operations to counteract the disturbance caused by the removal of overburden.

A.2.5 Daily reports

The various types of soil, the variations in consistency, the sequence and the depths to changes in strata shall be recorded as boring proceeds, to be compiled as a Daily Report with information as set out in A.9.2.

A.2.6 Obstructions

In borings where hard strata are encountered, through which the auger, shell or clay cutter cannot penetrate, which may or may not be bedrock, the Contractor shall use chiselling techniques for a limited time, in an attempt to penetrate the obstruction, or break it up sufficiently for fragments to be recovered and identified.

Should the obstruction be penetrated in this limited period, and further percussion boring be required at a greater depth, the Contractor shall break out the obstruction sufficiently to enable boring, *in-situ* testing and sampling to proceed.

Should the obstruction not be penetrated the Contractor shall consult and agree with the Engineer the use of the following methods:

(1) Further use of chiselling techniques.
(2) The abandonment of the boring and commencement of a further borehole nearby, both boreholes to be paid for at the billed rates.
(3) The use of rotary drilling or other methods.

A.3 Rotary drilling

A.3.1 Types of drilling

Rotary drilling may be required starting from ground level, or to extend soft ground boring which cannot penetrate further, or to prove obstructions in soft ground borings prior to breaking them out.

A.3.2 Types of bit and equipment

Drilling, both with and without core recovery, may be required in all materials and not only in continuous solid rock strata. The Contractor shall bring to site well-maintained equipment suitable for the required work and to achieve the best possible core recovery.

A.3.3 Rock core recovery

Rotary core drilling shall be carried out in such a manner that the maximum amount of core of the specified diameter is recovered, and the type and state of the drill bit, feed rates and management of the drill shall be such as to achieve this.

A.3.4 Drill runs

Drill runs shall not exceed 3 m in length and the core barrel shall be removed from the drill hole as often as may be required in order to get the best possible core recovery. When any recovery is less than 80% for a full length drill run then the next drill run shall be reduced to 1 m.

A.3.5 Drilling fluids

The drilling fluid shall normally be clean water or air. Where appropriate and with the approval of the Engineer drilling muds or additives may be used.

A.3.6 Removal of cores

Core barrels shall be held horizontally whilst cores are extruded, which shall be by applying a constant pressure without vibration and in a manner to prevent disturbance of cores. The cores shall be extruded into rigid plastic receiving channels of approximately the same diameter as the cores. The channel and core together shall then be wrapped in transparent polythene sheeting and secured with adhesive tape before being placed in the core box. The core shall be properly re-wrapped after logging. It shall be rigidly and securely contained by its box, with rigid spacers indicating any missing lengths and filling any unused spaces.

A.3.7 Core boxes, packing arrangement, labelling and storing

Core boxes shall be soundly constructed of timber or other approved material, fitted with stout carrying handles, fastenings and hinged lids and shall be to the approval of the Engineer. The total weight of cores and box shall together not exceed 60 kg. Cores shall be placed in the box with the shallowest core to the top left hand corner, and for every compartment the shallower core shall be to the left, the top being considered adjacent to the hinged section. The outside of the core box shall be clearly marked to show the drill hole reference number and the depths below the surface of the cores. Inside the box the depths of each drill run shall be clearly marked. Core boxes at the end of each day's work shall be stored secure from interference and protected from the weather. Core boxes shall remain the property of the Contractor.

A.3.8 Daily reports

Information as set out in A.9.3 shall be recorded as drilling proceeds, to be compiled as Daily Reports.

A.3.9 Examination of cores

The cores shall be examined and logged by a geotechnical engineer. Where the cores are of a type which could deteriorate with time or be damaged by transportation, logging shall be carried out on site. In cases where the presence of this geotechnical engineer would not otherwise be required on site, a separate item for payment is included in the Bill of Quantities.

A.3.10 Retention or disposal of cores

All cores shall be kept for 1 month after submission of the approved report and will be discarded after that time unless otherwise instructed by the Engineer.

A.4   Observation and trial pits

A.4.1   Exploratory pits for examination of subsoil

The depths, number and location of exploratory pits shall be generally as shown on the Drawings and Schedules.

The Contractor shall excavate observation pits by hand or machine in such a manner to enable personnel to enter safely to permit *in situ* examination of the subsoil, soil sampling and testing as required.

Trial pits shall generally be constructed by machine to enable a visual examination to be made from ground level.

A.4.2   Groundwater

The Contractor shall keep exploratory pits free of water by pumping or other means to permit continuous work. A small pump, nominal 50 mm size, shall be provided at no extra cost for this work. Should a larger pump be required, then additional payment will apply at agreed rates.

A.4.3   Topsoil

Topsoil over the area to be excavated shall be removed and stockpiled separately before any subsoil is excavated. This topsoil shall be re-spread over the area after backfilling of the exploratory pit.

A.4.4   Turfing

Where ordered by the Engineer, turves shall be removed from the areas of the pit, the spoil heap and the machine, and shall be relaid on completion.

A.4.5   Support to pit sides

The Contractor shall supply, fix and remove on completion sufficient support to the sides of the observation pits to protect anyone entering and working in the hole. The materials used for this support and the installation shall be to the approval of the Engineer.

A.4.6   Backfilling

Exploratory pits shall be backfilled as soon as practicable once the work in the pit is completed, unless otherwise directed by the Engineer. They shall be filled and the backfilling compacted, any surplus being heaped proud over the pit site in such a manner that no subsequent depression is formed.

If pits are to remain open beyond the day of excavation the Contractor must provide adequate barriers and/or lighting to ensure the safety of the public and others.

The cost of providing this protection is included as a separate provisional item in the rates.

A.5 Sampling

A.5.1 Best accepted practice for sampling

The preparations for and methods of taking samples, together with their size, preservation and handling shall be in accordance with the Civil Engineering Code of Practice BS5930 'Site Investigations'.

A.5.2 Protection against freezing

All samples shall be protected at all times from temperatures below 5 °C.

A.5.3 Sampling frequency

The Contractor shall take samples as follows.

At each change in soil type or change in consistency a small disturbed sample shall be taken. Immediately following this an 'undisturbed' sample shall be taken in cohesive soils, a 'bulk disturbed' sample in granular soils, or a field test carried out as appropriate. Further small disturbed samples shall be taken at intervals in the same stratum midway between successive 'undisturbed' or bulk samples.

In addition to the above the maximum distance between 'undisturbed' or bulk samples measured centre to centre shall not exceed 1 m for the first 5 m below ground level, formation or foundation level whichever is the more appropriate, and thereafter at intervals of 1.5 m as required.

The Engineer may require samples in excess of the above to be taken.

A.5.4 Small disturbed samples

Small disturbed samples shall not be less than 0.7 kg. They shall be placed immediately in airtight containers, which they should sensibly fill.

A.5.5 Preparations for sampling

Before taking an 'undisturbed' sample the bottom of the boring shall be carefully cleared of loose materials and where a casing is being used the sample shall be taken from below the bottom of this casing.

A.5.6 Core samples in cohesive soils

'Undisturbed' core samples in cohesive soils shall be taken using open-drive sampling equipment, and the sample tube shall have a minimum length of 450 mm where percussion boring methods are used. The cutting shoes shall be clean and without burred edges. The number of blows, weight of drop hammer, height of drop and length driven and recovered may, if required, be recorded. Following a break in the work, such as over-night stoppage, boring shall be advanced by 0.75 m before further core sampling. The ends of the samples shall be carefully coated with layers of low melting point microcrystalline wax to give a thickness of at least 9 mm, to provide an effective seal against changes of moisture content. Any unfilled space in the sample tube shall be filled with a suitable packing to minimize disturbance in transit.

A.5.7 Abortive sampling

Where an attempt to take an 'undisturbed' sample is aborted because of non-recovery, the boring shall be cleaned out for the full depth to which the sampling tube has been driven and the recovered soil saved as a disturbed sample. A fresh attempt shall then be made from the level of the base of the aborted attempt, and the Contractor may use a core catcher between the cutting shoe and sampling tube; alternatively, an additional sample tube may be coupled.

Where full recovery is not achieved the actual length of sample in the sampling tube shall be recorded and the reason for only partial recovery shall be noted.

Payment for samples driven but not recovered in whole or in part shall be at rates to be agreed with the Engineer.

A.5.8 Bulk disturbed samples

Bulk disturbed samples of either cohesive or non-cohesive soils shall be approximately 25 kg. They shall be representative of the zone from which they have been taken and the following sampling procedure shall be adopted. For non-cohesive material all the recovered soil sample shall be retained: any water present should be carefully decanted in a manner ensuring retention of fines. Bulk samples of cohesive material shall consist of the least disturbed material available whether from a boring or trail pit.

A.5.9 Groundwater samples

Samples of groundwater shall be taken from each boring in which water is found. Where more than one groundwater table is found, each one shall be sampled separately. Where water has been previously added for boring purposes, the boring shall be baled out before sampling until only uncontaminated groundwater is present in the boring. The sample shall be not less than 0.5 litres. The container shall be thoroughly rinsed with the groundwater before sampling.

A.5.10 Recording positions of samples

The depths from which all samples are taken shall be recorded. For 'undisturbed' samples the level at the top of the sample and the length of sample obtained shall be given, together with the depth of casing and the level of groundwater. For 'bulk disturbed' samples the limits of the sampled zone shall be recorded. Water samples shall be related to the depth of the relevant water strike or the short term rest level.

A.5.11 Packing of samples

The Contractor shall be responsible for the packing of all samples and their transport to his laboratory.

A.5.12 Retention and disposal of samples

All samples shall be kept for a period of 1 month after submission of the approved report and will be discarded after that time unless otherwise instructed by the Engineer.

A.5.13 Special sampling

(a) Special samples

The Engineer may require the use of special sampling techniques in borings. Where special samples are required a separate item has been provided in the Bill of Quantities and this should be priced by the Contractor in accordance with the more detailed clauses below.

(b) Piston samples

The Engineer may require continuous piston sampling or piston samples in a boring to be taken in sensitive soils. Equipment shall be of a pattern approved by the Engineer and all the Contractor's arrangements shall be such as to ensure the least possible disturbance to samples.

(c) Block samples

The Engineer may require block samples to be taken in the trial pits or in specially excavated pits. These must be cut by hand as far as possible with the minimum disturbance to the block of soil or rock to be removed. No water shall be allowed to come into contact with the sample and it should be protected from wind and direct rays of the sun. Orientation and location must be clearly marked before removal and it should then be coated and packed in accordance with the procedure in BS5930.

A.6 Groundwater observations

A.6.1 Groundwater measurement records

Groundwater when encountered shall be measured and recorded in the following manner.

When water is first encountered the depth from ground level to the point of entry shall be recorded together with the casing depth and boring operations suspended for not more than 20 min to allow the free static water level to develop, which shall also be recorded together with the time taken for this rise in water level to occur. If at the end of the period of 20 min the water level is still rising, this shall be recorded together with the depth to water below ground level. Boring shall then be continued. Time spent in this manner shall be measured for payment under the relevant standing time item for the rig.

An exception to the above is where groundwater occurs as a slow seepage into the boring. In this case the point of entry of the seepage shall be recorded, and boring continued.

The same procedure shall be followed when further water entries are observed.

Water levels shall be recorded at the beginning and end of each shift.

On each occasion when groundwater is recorded the depth of the boring, and the length of casing inserted in the boring, and the time shall also be recorded.

A.6.2 Installation of standpipes

Standpipes shall be installed in borings as instructed by the Engineer for recording the highest groundwater level encountered and changes in this level.

A.6.3

Standpipes shall consist of steel or UPVC tubing of diameter of at least 12 mm. Slots or holes shall be formed in the lower 1.5 m of pipe, or a porous element provided. The lower end shall be plugged to avoid entry of soil during installation and the total length of each standpipe shall be recorded.

A.6.4

The boring shall normally be backfilled with clean gravel or coarse sand to within 1 m of ground level, and thereafter with impervious material to prevent the entry of surface water.

A.6.5

Adequate arrangements shall be made by the Contractor to protect the top of the standpipe.

A.6.6

The groundwater level shall be recorded immediately before and after installation of the standpipe and the sounding device shall also be used to confirm the total length of the standpipe installation. Readings of water levels should be made daily during the period of the site works with an approved sounding instrument to be provided by the Contractor. Where more frequent or subsequent measurements are required by the Engineer, provision for payment is included in the Bill of Quantities.

A.6.7   Installation of piezometers

When measurements of head of water are required in a particular stratum piezometers may be installed. Piezometers differ from standpipes in that their active tips are sealed within a particular stratum. Piezometers may be of the Casagrande single tube, hydraulic or pneumatic twin tube, or electrical transducer types, or other types as required by the Engineer. Piezometer readings shall normally be made daily by the Contractor during the period of the site works and with instruments approved by the Engineer. Separate items are provided in the Bill of Quantities for the supply, installation and monitoring of piezometers.

A.7   *In situ* testing

A.7.1   Trained personnel

All *in situ* testing is to be carried out by personnel who have been trained, and are experienced in the use of the equipment, the test methods and the recording of results. The penetration resistance test will generally be carried out by rig operators, but other *in situ* tests shall be performed by Engineers or Technical Assistants.

A.7.2   Standard penetration resistance test

The penetration resistance may be measured using the test equipment and procedure as described in BS1377, test no. 19. The drive hammer shall be of the type incorporating an automatic trip mechanism to ensure free fall. The number of blows required to penetrate six successive increments of 75 mm shall be recorded.

The maximum intervals between tests measured centre to centre shall be 1 m for the first 5 m below formation level and thereafter 1.5 m intervals.

When tests are performed in soils containing gravel the driving shoe of the split barrel sampler may be replaced by a solid 60° cone, or the split barrel sampler with solid cone may be replaced by an identically dimensioned solid test rod.

If required by the Engineer, these tests shall be extended to record blow counts greater than 50, provided that the total blow count does not exceed 75, including the seating drive. The test may also be terminated after 50 blows, if for 75 mm penetration or less the blow count exceeds 20.

Where a solid cone is used or where no soil is recovered in the split sampler a disturbed sample shall be obtained from the position of the test.

In granular soils below the ground water level, a head of water to at least groundwater level must be maintained not only during the test, but also during the shelling work before and after the test. The actual water level in the boring shall be noted on the Daily Report.

Great care shall be taken to ensure that the test is carried out below the level of the borehole casing, and that the hole is fully cleaned to the level of the base of the casing.

A.7.3 Calibration of measuring instruments

Where load displacement or other measuring equipment is used or where the nature of the equipment is such that calibration is required from time to time, then the Contractor shall have such instruments calibrated at intervals consistent with their usage. Copies of the calibration charts shall be available for inspection by the Engineer.

A.7.4 Vane shear testing

The Engineer may require *in situ* vane tests in soft or sensitive cohesive soils either in borings or using penetration equipment. Separate items are provided in the Bill of Quantities for mobilization, setting up at location and for the type of test.

The equipment and method of test shall be in accordance with BS1377. An apparatus in which the torque is applied through a worm and pinion mechanism shall be used.

Where vane tests are being performed close to another exploratory hole the distance between holes shall be not less than 1.5 m measured from the perimeters of the holes.

For tests in borings a small disturbed sample representative of the ground from where the test was performed shall be obtained.

Where the tests are carried out in boreholes a head of water shall be maintained at all times to at least groundwater level.

A.7.5 Dutch cone penetration test

The testing procedure shall generally be in accordance with the static cone penetration test as recommended in the *Report of the Sub-Committee on the Penetration Test for use in Europe* (ISSMFE, 1977).

Mechanical cone penetrometers shall be of the Dutch mantle cone or Dutch friction sleeve types (reference types M1 and M2 in the above-mentioned report); electric cone penetrometers shall be of the Fugro-type or Delft Soil Mechanics Laboratory type or other similar approved type.

Cone end resistance and local side friction resistance shall be measured at intervals of not more than 0.20 m when using a mechanical cone penetrometer, and continuously when using an electric cone penetrometer. The rate of penetration shall be approximately 20 mm per second.

The cone shall have an area of 1000 mm^2 and an apex angle of 60°. The reaction equipment provided shall have a minimum thrust capacity of 100 kN and the cone penetrometer shall be capable of testing to depths up to 20 m in suitable ground conditions. When using an electric cone penetrometer, cones of differing sensitivity to suit varying ground conditions may be employed.

The cone penetrometer equipment shall be erected to within 2° of the vertical. If required, deviation from the vertical could be monitored when using electric cone penetrometers. Bent probing rods shall not be used. Rods shall not be left in the ground overnight.

A cone penetrometer test shall not be performed within 25 borehole diameters of an existing borehole.

When in use the static cone penetrometer shall be under the direct supervision of an experienced technical assistant from the contractor's staff who is fully conversant with its use.

The cone penetration test results should be reported in graphical format using the following scales:

Depth	10 mm to 1 m
Cone end resistance	10 mm to 2 MN m^{-2}
Local side friction	10 mm to 0.05 MN m^{-2}

Variations can be allowed provided that for both axes the same factor is used. When using an electric cone penetrometer the friction ratio shall be plotted alongside the graphs of cone end resistance and local side friction. The following additional information shall be presented on the graphs:

(a) Job name and location
(b) Contractor's name
(c) Penetration test reference number
(d) Date of test
(e) Type of penetrometer
(f) Type of cone

A.8   Laboratory testing

A.8.1   Schedule of tests

A programme of testing shall be agreed between the Engineer and the Contractor.

A.8.2   British Standards BS1377 and BS5930

All storing, preparation and testing of samples shall generally be in accordance with the British Standards Specifications BS1377 and BS5930.

A.8.3   Information to be submitted

The information to be submitted by the Contractor for each test shall be in accordance with BS1377.

A.9   Reports

A.9.1
The Contractor shall prepare Daily Reports for each exploratory hole which shall be submitted if required to the Engineer after completion of the exploratory holes to which they refer. The Daily Reports shall contain the following information where relevant.

A.9.2
Information for boring Daily Report:

a.   Job name and location.
b.   Contractor's name.
c.   Exploratory hole reference number.
d.   Dates of boring referred to the depth at the end of each working day or shift.
e.   Plant in use.
f.   Diameters and depths of all casings used.
g.   Depth of each change in stratum.
h.   Records of ground water.
j.   Preliminary description of each stratum.
k.   The depths at which samples were taken or the limits between which bulk samples were obtained.
l.   The depths of all *in situ* tests.
m.   Any addition of water to the boring.
n.   Details of time spent in overcoming obstructions.
o.   Details of services or drains located.
p.   Details of instruments installed and backfilling.

A.9.3
Information for rotary drilling Daily Reports:

a.   Job name and location.
b.   Contractor's name.
c.   Exploratory hole reference number.
d.   Dates of drilling referred to the depth at the end of each working day or shift.
e.   Plant in use.
f.   Diameters and depths of all casings used.
g.   Depth of each change in stratum.
h.   Records of ground water.
j.   Brief description of each stratum.

k. The depths of all *in situ* tests.
l. Orientation of the drill-hole given as an angle to the horizontal.
m. Method of penetration and flushing system.
n. Type of core barrel and bit used.
o. Depth of and finish of each core run.
p. Core diameters and depths to changes in core diameter.
q. Comments on flush returns.
r. Total core recovery for each core run with information as to possible location of core losses.
s. Details of instruments installed and backfilling.

A.9.4

Information for Observation and Trial Pit Reports:

a. Job name and location.
b. Contractor's name.
c. Exploratory hole reference number.
d. Dates of excavation referred to the depth at the end of each working day or shift.
e. Plant in use.
f. Depth of each change of stratum.
g. Records of groundwater and notes on the quantity of water pumped from the hole.
h. Brief description of each stratum, together with sketches of the strata encountered.
i. The depths at which samples were taken or the limits between which bulk samples were obtained.
k. The depths of all *in situ* tests.
l. Details of time spent in overcoming obstructions.
m. Details of services or drains located.
n. The dimensions of the trial pit in plan.
o. Remarks on the stability of the sides of the hole and notes of the support used.

A.9.5   Records of exploratory holes

Exploratory hole records to be submitted in the final report shall include all the information set out in the following clauses, such information having been modified as necessary in the light of laboratory testing and the further examination of samples. Where appropriate, *in situ* test results shall be given in the exploratory hole records or otherwise presented in tabular or graphical form.

A.9.6

Information for boring Records:

a. All the information set out in A.9.2.
b. Ground level referred to Ordnance Datum.
c. Elevation of each stratum referred to Ordnance Datum.
d. Symbolic legend of strata in accordance with BS5930 drawn to a suitable scale.
e. Engineering description of each stratum in accordance with BS5930.
f. Records of groundwater observations.
g. Any other comments.

A.9.7

Information for rotary drilling Records:

a. All the information set out in A.9.3.
b. Ground level referred to Ordnance Datum.
c. Elevation of each stratum referred to Ordnance Datum.
d. Symbolic legend of strata in accordance with BS5930 drawn to a suitable scale.
e. A systematic description of the strata by a geotechnical engineer which shall include: weathered state, strength, structure, colour, grain size, texture, alteration state, cemented state, mineral type and rock name as each one is appropriate.
f. Rock Quality Designation (RQD).
g. Geotechnical engineer's assessment of the core recovery.
h. Azimuth of the drill hole.
j. Any other comments.

A.9.8

Information for observation and trial pit Records:

a. All the information set out in A.9.4.
b. Ground level referred to Ordnance Datum.
c. Elevation of each stratum referred to Ordnance Datum.
d. Symbolic legend of strata in accordance with BS5930 drawn to a suitable scale.
e. Engineering description of each stratum in accordance with BS5930.
f. Records of groundwater observations.
g. Any other comments.

A.9.9 Site plan

The Engineer will provide a suitable plan for the plotting of the exploratory holes.

THE BILL OF QUANTITIES

When using any bill of quantities reference should also be made to the conditions of contract, the specification, a schedule of exploratory holes and any appendices as appropriate. The rates are intended to include all necessary labour, materials, plant, temporary works, other obligations, overheads and profits.

As stated previously the requirements of different investigations vary widely and the content of individual bills of quantities will also vary. Several items may be left out on some contracts but on others the engineer may decide to insert special items to cover such things as geophysics, piston sampling, special *in situ* testing and so on. Whether or not any special items are included it is a good idea to allow for a lump sum for special testing and for contingencies since it is not usually known at the tender stage exactly what will be encountered.

Some tenders include an item for the provision of a report which is deemed to cover all necessary interpretation and recommendations. Some ask for a purely factual report with interpretation being done by an independent geotechnical engineer and others have bill items for engineer and technician time spent on the report. However, all contracts should demand a factual report containing records of all exploratory holes, *in situ* test records, laboratory test results and plans.

A bill of quantities is shown on the following three pages.

Item	Description	Unit
1	Allow for the establishment on site of all plant, equipment and services.	Item
2	Allow for supplying .... copies of the full report	Item
3	Allow for backfilling and making good at the positions of all exploratory holes, access routes and site compounds.	Item
4	Allow for determining the ground elevation relative to Ordnance Datum at the positions of all exploratory holes	Item

Borings

5	Bring shell and auger plant to the site of each hole, erect, dismantle and move from one hole to the next a distance not exceeding 100 m.	No
6	Extra over item 5 for distance exceeding 100 m but not exceeding 500 m etc.	No
7	Extra over item 5 for erecting and dismantling over water not exceeding 3 m deep	No
8	Bore with shell and auger from ground level to not exceeding 10 m.	Lin m
9	Ditto but between 10 m and 20 m below ground level etc.	Lin m
10	Break out naturally hard strata and man-made obstructions.	Rig/hour
11	Standing time for shell and auger plant and crew.	Rig/hour
12	Bore with hand auger from ground level to not exceeding 5 m etc.	Lin m

Sampling

13	Obtain undisturbed core samples of 100 mm in diameter.	No
14	Obtain small disturbed samples.	No
15	Obtain bulk disturbed samples.	No
16	Obtain ground water samples.	No

Rotary drilling

17	Bring rotary drilling plant to the site of each hole, erect, dismantle and move from one hole to the next a distance not exceeding 100 m.	No
18	Extra over item 17 for moving a distance exceeding 100 m but not exceeding 500 m etc.	No
19	Rotary drill to produce rock cores of not less than 54 mm diameter from ground level to not exceeding 10 m depth. Price to include for packaging, transport and storage of cores.	Lin m
20	Ditto but between 10 m and 20 m below ground level etc.	Lin m
21	Standing time for rotary drill and crew.	Rig/hour

354

Item	Description	Unit

Probing

| 22 | Bring probing equipment to the site of each probe hole and probe from ground level to not exceeding 10 m etc. | Lin m |

Piezometers

23	Supply porous element for piezometers.	No
24	Supply and install piezometers in accordance with the specification.	Lin m
25	Supply and install protective cover to piezometer in accordance with the specification.	No
26	Take readings of water levels in piezometers.	No

Inspection pits and trial pits

27	Excavate inspection pit by hand from ground level to not exceeding 1.5 m, the plan area to be not less than 1 m^2.	Lin m
28	Extra over item 27 for breaking out obstruction including road construction	Lin m
29	Erect and dismantle approved temporary support to sides of inspection pit from ground level to not exceeding 1.5 m.	Lin m

In situ *soil testing*

| 30 | Perform vane shear tests in borings or with penetration vane equipment from ground level to not exceeding 10 m. | No |
| 31 | Perform Standard Penetration Test. | No |

Laboratory soil testing

32	Moisture content determination.	No
33	Liquid limit, plastic limit and plasticity index.	No
34	Specific gravity determination.	No
35	Particle size distribution.	No
36	Particle size distribution for fine grained soils.	No
37	Organic matter content determination.	No
38	Sulphate content of soil or water determination.	No
39	pH value determination.	No
40	Dry density/moisture content relation using 2.5 kg rammer.	No
41	Dry density/moisture content relation using 4.5 kg rammer.	No

Item	Description	Unit
42	California Bearing Ratio in laboratory.	No
43	Unconfined compression test on 38 mm diameter samples.	No
44	Compressive strength determination in undrained triaxial compression on 38 mm diameter samples (set of three tests).	No
45	Compressive strength determination in undrained triaxial compression on 102 mm diameter samples, multi-stage testing.	No
46	Consolidated undrained triaxial compression test with pore water pressure and volume change measurements on 38 mm diameter samples. Consolidation and compression stage together not exceeding four days (set of three tests)	No
47	Consolidated drained triaxial compression test with volume change measurements on 38 mm diameter samples. Consolidation and compression stage together not exceeding four days (set of three tests).	No
48	Drained shear-box test for residual shear stength determination not exceeding seven days (set of three tests).	No
49	Determination of the one-dimensional consolidation properties	No
50	Allow for any special testing as required by the Engineer.	Provisional sum

Appendix B

List of useful addresses

Sources of information

Admiralty Chart Establishment, Hydrographic Department, Ministry of Defence, Taunton, Somerset.

Ministry of Agriculture, Government Buildings, Tolcarre Drive, Pinner, Middlesex.

Chief Inspector of Ancient Monuments, Department of the Environment, Fortress House, 23 Savile Row, London W1X 2AA.

British Standards Institution, 2 Park Street, London W1A 2BS.

Department of the Environment, 2 Marsham Street, London SW1P 3EB.

Institute of Geological Sciences, 5 Princes Gate, South Kensington, London.

Land Utilization Survey, King's College, Strand, London WC2.

Meteorological Office, Bracknell, Berks.

Mining Record Office, Health and Safety Executive, Thames House North, Millbank, London SW1P 4QJ.

National Coal Board, Hobart House, Grosvenor Place, London SW1.

Ordnance Survey, Romsey Road, Maybush, Southampton.

Ordnance Survey, Air Photographs Officer, Department of the Environment, Whitehall, London SW1 3BL.

Public Records Office, Chancery Lane, London WC2.

Soil Survey of Great Britain, Rothamsted Experimental Station, Harpenden, Herts.

Water Data Unit, Department of the Environment, Reading Bridge House, Reading.

Drilling rigs and equipment

Boyles Bros., Bowes Street, South Gosforth, Newcastle-upon-Tyne NE3 1TH.

Castle Drilling Rigs (1978) Ltd., Dernstall House, 32/34 The Strait, Lincoln LN2 1JD.

Christensen Diamond Products Ltd., Govett Avenue, Shepperton, Middlesex TW17 8AH.

Compair Construction and Mining Ltd., Cambourne, Cornwall TR14 8DS.

Conrad Stork, Waarderweg 80-2031 BP Haarlem, PO Box 1551-2033 BP Haarlem, Holland.

Craelius Co. Ltd., Long March, Daventry, Northants NN11 4DX.

Duke and Ockenden Ltd., River Road, Littlehampton, Sussex.

English Drilling Equipment Co. Ltd., Lindley Moor Road, Huddersfield, West Yorkshire.

Halifax Tool Co. Ltd., Southowram, Halifax, West Yorkshire HX3 9TW.

Hands England Ltd., Flint Road, Letchworth, Herts SG6 1HH.

Hydraulic Drilling Equipment Ltd., Imperial Buildings, Horley, Sussex.

Longyear UK Ltd., Holbrook Green, Holbrook, Sheffield S19 5FE.

Pilcon Engineering Ltd, Stephenson Road, Houndmills, Basingstoke, Hants.

Stewart Ross & Co. Ltd., St. Albans Road, Sandridge, Herts.

J.K. Smit & Sons Ltd., Mochdre, Colwyn Bay, North Wales LL28 5HE.

Tower Drilling Equipment Ltd., Storforth Lane Industrial Estate, Hasland, Chesterfield.

L.M. Van Moppes & Sons Ltd., Tuffley Crescent, Gloucester GL1 5NG.

In situ testing equipment and instrumentation

Cambridge Insitu, Little Eversden, Cambridge CB3 7HE (Camkometer)

Electrolocation Ltd., 129 South Liberty Lane, Bristol BS3 2SZ (Cable location equipment).

Fugro Ltd., Breakspear Road, Ruislip, Middlesex (Electric cone penetrometer).

Geotechnical Instruments, Geotechnical House, Hatton, Warwickshire (Instrumentation).

Linden Alimak AB, S-93103 Skelleftea, Sweden (Pore pressure probe).

Menard Techniques Ltd., 20 High Street, Woking, Surrey G21 1BW (Pressuremeters).

Soil Instruments Ltd., Bell Lane, Uckfield, East Sussex TN22 1QL (Instrumentation).

Laboratory testing equipment

Cartographic Engineering, Landford Manor, Salisbury (Stereoscopes).

C.F. Casella & Co. Ltd., Regent House, Brittania Walk, London N1 7ND (Stereoscopes).

Engineering Laboratory Equipment Ltd., Eastman Way, Hemel Hempstead, Herts HP2 7HB.

Leonard Farnell & Co. Ltd., Station Road, North Mymms, Hatfield, Herts AL9 7SR.

Wykeham Farrance Engineering Ltd., Weston Road Trading Estate, Slough SL1 4HW.

Bibliography

General

Bolton, M. (1979) *A Guide to Soil Mechanics* Macmillan, London.
BSI (1981) *Code of Practice for Site Investigations* British Standards Institution BS5930:1981.
Canadian Geotechnical Society (1978) *Foundation Engineering Manual.*
Capper, P.L. and Cassie. W.F. (1976) *The Mechanics of Engineering Soils* 6th edn, Chapman and Hall, London.
Hoek, E. and Bray, J. (1974) *Rock Slope Engineering* Institution of Mining and Metallurgy, London.
Lambe, T.W. and Whitman, R.V. (1979) *Soil Mechanics* Wiley, New York.
Jaeger, J.C. (1972) *Rock Mechanics and Engineering* Cambridge University Press, UK.
Jaeger, J.C. and Cook, N.G.W. (1979) *Fundamentals of Rock Mechanics* 3rd edn, Chapman and Hall, London 1979.
Rowe, P.W. (1972) The Relevance of Soil Fabric to Site Investigation Practice. *Geotechnique* **22** (No. 2).
Science and Engineering Research Council, (1981) *Long-Term Research and Development Requirements in Civil Engineering,* London.
Scott, C.R. (1980) *An Introduction to Soil Mechanics and Foundations* Applied Science Publishers, Barking, UK.
Scott, R.F. (1963) *Elements of Soil Mechanics* Addison Wesley, London.
Smith, G.N. (1978) *Elements of Soil Mechanics for Civil and Mining Engineers* 4th edn, Granada, St. Albans, UK.
Stagg, K.G. and Zienkiewicz, O.C. (1968) *Rock Mechanics in Engineering Practice* Wiley, New York.
Terzhagi, K. and Peck, R.B. (1968) *Soil Mechanics in Engineering Practice* Wiley, New York.
Tomlinson, M.J. (1980) *Foundation Design and Construction* Pitman, London.
Winterkorn, H.F. and Fang, H. (1975) *Foundation Engineering Handbook* Van Nostrand Reinhold, New York.

Chapter 1

Bell, F.G. (1975) *Site Investigation in Areas of Mining Subsidence* Newnes-Butterworths, London.

Cripps, J.C. and Woodman, J.P. (1980) Discussion: Design Parameters in Geotechnical Engineering *Proceedings of the 7th European Conference on Soil Mechanics* Brighton, **4**, 98.

Glossop, R. (1968) The Rise of Geotechnology and its Influence on Engineering Practice. *Geotechnique* **18**, (no. 2).

Gordon, J.E. (1979) *The New Science of Strong Materials or why you don't fall through the floor.* Penguin Books, Harmondsworth, UK.

Gordon, J.E. (1979) *Structures or why things don't fall down.* Penguin Books, Harmondsworth, UK.

Chapter 2

Attewell, P.B. and Farmer, I.W. (1976) *Principles of Engineering Geology* Chapman and Hall, London.

Bates, D.E. and Kirkaldy, J.F. (1979) *Field Geology in Colour* Blandford Press, Poole, UK.

Blyth, F.G.H. and DeFreitas, M.H. (1974) *A Geology for Engineers.* Edward Arnold, London.

Flint, R.F. (1971) *Glacial and Pleistocene Geology* Wiley and Sons, Chichester, UK.

Himus, G.W. and Sweeting, G.S. (1968) *The Elements of Field Geology* University Tutorial Press, London.

Holmes, A. (1965) *Principles of Physical Geology* Nelson, London.

Institution of Civil Engineers (1976) *Manual of Applied Geology for Engineers,* London.

Institute of Geological Sciences *British Regional Geology* (A series of volumes covering 18 regions in the British Isles – see Fig. 2.11), London.

Leggett, R.F. (1962) *Geology and Engineering* McGraw Hill, London.

Maclean, A.C. and Gribble, C.D. (1979) *Geology for Civil Engineers* George Allen and Unwin, London.

Midland Geotechnical Society (1975) *The Engineering Behaviour of Industrial and Urban Fill* University of Birmingham, UK.

Midland Geotechnical Society (1975) *The Engineering Behaviour of Glacial Soils* University of Birmingham, UK.

Rayner, D.H. (1967) *The Stratigraphy of the British Isles* Cambridge University Press, UK.

Chapter 3

Allum, J.A.E. (1966) *Photogeology and Regional Mapping* Pergamon Press, Oxford.

Coates, D.R. (1981) *Geomorphology and Engineering* Allen and Unwin, London.

Dumbleton, M.J. (1973) *Available Information for Route Planning and Site Investigation.* Report LR591, Transport and Road Research Laboratory.

Dumbleton, M.J. and West, G. (1970) *Air Photograph Interpretation for Road Engineers in Britain* Report LR369, Transport and Road Research Laboratory.

Dumbleton, M.J. and West, G. (1974) *Guidance on Planning, Directing and Reporting Site Investigations* Report LR625, Transport and Road Research Laboratory.

Dumbleton, M.J. and West, G. (1976) *Preliminary Sources of Information for Site Investigations in Britain* Report LR403, Transport and Road Research Laboratory.

Geological Society Engineering Group Working Party (1972) The Preparation of Maps and Plans in Terms of Engineering Geology. *Quarterly Journal of Engineering Geology* **5**, (No. 4).

Heath, W. (1981) *Inexpensive Aerial Photography for Highway Engineering and Traffic Studies* Report SR632, Transport and Road Research Laboratory.
West, G. and Dumbleton, M.J. (1975) *An Assessment of Geophysics in Site Investigation for Roads in Great Britain* Report SR680, Transport and Road Research Laboratory.

Chapter 6

BSI (1975) *Methods of Testing Soils for Civil Engineering Purposes* British Standards Institution BS1377:1975.
Cedergren, H.R. (1977) *Seepage, Drainage and Flow Nets* Wiley, New York·
Hvorslev, M.J. (1949) *Subsurface Exploration and Sampling of Soils for Civil Engineering Purposes* Waterways Experimental Station, Mississippi.

Chapter 7

BSI (1974) *Rotary Core Drilling Equipment* British Standards Institution BS4019:1974.
Cumming, J.D. (1956) *Diamond Drill Handbook* J.K. Smit and Sons, Colwyn Bay, UK.
Geological Society Engineering Group (1970) The Logging of Rock Cores for Engineering Purposes. *Quarterly Journal of Engineering Geology* 3, (no. 1).
McGregor, K. (1967) *The Drilling of Rock* Maclaren and Sons, London.

Chapter 8

Baguelin, F., Jezequel, J.F. and Shields, D.H. (1978) *The Pressuremeter and Foundation Engineering* Transtech Publications.
Gibson, R.E. and Anderson, W.F. (1961) In situ measurement of soil properties with the pressuremeter. *Civil Engineering and Public Works Review, London.*
Hvorslev, M.J. (1951) *Time Lag and Soil Permeability in Groundwater Observations* Bulletin 36, US Waterways Experimental Station, Vicksburg.
ISSMFE (1977) *Recommended Standards for Penetration Testing in Europe.*
Sanglerat, G. (1972) *The Penetrometer and Soil Exploration* Elsevier, London.
Schmertmann, J.H. (1969) *Dutch Friction Cone Penetration Exploration of Research Area at Field 5, Elgin Air Force Base, Florida.* US Army Waterways Experiment Station Contract Report S-69-4.
Schmertmann, J.H. (1975) Measurement of In situ Shear Strength. *Proc. conf. on in situ measurement of soil properties* American Society of Civil Engineers, North Carolina State University 2, pp. 57–138.
Searle, I.W. (1979) The Interpretation of the Begemann friction jacket cone results to give soil type and design parameter. *Design Parameters in Geotechnical Engineering* 2, pp. 265–270 (Proceedings of the 7th European Conference on Soil Mechanics, Brighton).
Wroth, C.P. and Hughes, J.M.O. (1973) An instrument for the in situ measurement of the properties of soft clays. *Proceedings of the 8th International Conference on Soil Mechanics and Foundation Engineering, Moscow* 1.2, pp. 487–494.

Chapter 10

Ackroyd, T.N.W. (1957) *Laboratory Testing in Soil Engineering.* Soil Mechanics Ltd.

362

Bell, F.G. (1980)*Engineering Properties of Soils and Rocks* Newnes-Butterworths.

Bishop, A.W. and Henkel, D.J. (1962) *The Measurement of Soil Properties in the Triaxial Test* Edward Arnold, London.

Head, K.H. (1980) *Manual of Soil Laboratory Testing* Pentech Press.

Lambe, T.W. (1951) *Soil Testing for Engineers* John Wiley and Sons, Chichester, UK.

Vickers, B. (1978) *Laboratory Work in Civil Engineering Soil Mechanics* Granada, St. Albans, UK.

Chapter 11

Hanna, T.H. (1973) *Foundation Instrumentation* Trans Tech Publications.

Jardine, R.J. (1981) *Instrumentation.* Lecture Notes from County Surveyors Society Short Course in Site Investigation, Guildford.

Peck, R.B. (1968) Advantages and Limitations of the Observational Method in Applied Soil Mechanics. *Geotechnique* **19**, (no. 2).

Chapter 12

Burland, J.B. (1969) Reply to Discussion. *Proceedings of the Conference on In situ Investigations in Soils and Rocks* BGS.

Dunning, F.W. (1970) *Geophysical Exploration* HM Stationery Office, London.

Griffiths, D.H. and King, R.F. (1965) *Applied Geophysics for Engineers and Geologists* Pergamon Press, Oxford.

Stewart, M. and Beavan, P.J. (1980) *Seismic Refraction Surveys for Highway Engineering Purposes* Report LR950, Transport and Road Research Laboratory.

Weltman, A.J. (1980) *Pile Load Testing Procedure* CIRIA report, p. 67.

Chapter 13

Barrass, R. (1978) *Scientists Must Write* Chapman and Hall, London.

BSI *Earthworks* British Standards Institution BS6031.

BSI *Earth Retaining Structures* British Standards Institution CP2002 (under revision).

BSI *Foundations* British Standards Institution CP2004.

BSI *Foundations for Machinery* British Standards Institution CP2012.

Bureau of Reclamation (1960) *Design of Small Dams* US Department of the Interior.

Cooper, B.M. (1964) *Writing Technical Reports,* Penguin Books, Harmondsworth, UK.

Dumbleton, M.J. and West, G. (1976) *A Guide to Site Investigation Procedure for Tunnels* Report LR 740. Transport and Road Research Laboratory.

Fowler, H.W. (1965) *A Dictionary of Modern English Usage* Clarendon Press, Oxford.

Geological Society Engineering Group (1981) *Sand, Gravel and Crushed Rock Aggregates for Construction Purposes* Report Draft.

Gowers, E. (1962) *The Complete Plain Words* Penguin Books, Harmondsworth, UK.

Partridge, E.H. (1965)*Usage and Abusage: A Guide to Good English* Hamish Hamilton, London.

Roget, P.M. (1982) *Thesaurus of English Words and Phrases* Penguin Books, Harmondsworth, UK.

Thomas, H.H. (1976) *Engineering of Large Dams* Wiley, New York.

Turner, B.T. (1978) *Effective Technical Writing and Speaking* Business Books, London.

Index

364